Rethinking the City

Interdisciplinary in approach, this book employs the key concepts of fragmentation and reconfiguration to consider the ways in which human experience and artistic practice can engage with and respond to the disintegration that characterises modern cities. Asking how we might unsettle and decrypt the homogeneous images of cities created by processes linked to capitalism and globalisation, it invites us to consider the possibility of reimagining and rethinking the urban spaces we inhabit.

An exploration of the complex relationship between aesthetics, the arts and the city, *Rethinking the City: Reconfiguration and Fragmentation* will appeal to scholars across various disciplines, including philosophy, urban sociology and geography, anthropology, political theory and visual and media studies.

Maria Filomena Molder is Professor Emeritus at NOVA University Lisbon and a researcher at IFILNOVA. Her philosophical interests converge towards aesthetical issues concerning poetry and art. Reading Dante, Kant, Goethe, Baudelaire, Nietzsche, Wittgenstein, Benjamin, Pessoa, Broch or Colli, she has acquired the conviction that art and poetry are forms of knowledge of a generative kind: they allow us to see the very conditions under which reality is perceived by granting us a presentation of it. Ever since the beginning of her research, she has sought to demonstrate the fertility allowed by aesthetical issues towards the understanding of what philosophy can be.

Nélio Conceição (PhD, NOVA University Lisbon, 2013) is a researcher at IFILNOVA (NOVA Institute of Philosophy). His research focuses on aesthetics and the philosophy of art, with recent work addressing topics within the philosophy of photography, film-philosophy and the philosophy of the city. He has co-edited the volumes *Aesthetics and Values: Contemporary Perspectives* (Mimesis International, 2021), *Conceptual Figures of Fragmentation and Reconfiguration* (IFILNOVA, 2021) and *Planos de pormenor: leituras críticas sobre a experiência da cidade* (Húmus, 2023). He is the author of *A realidade em exercício: a fotografia, da fenomenologia a Walter Benjamin* (Edições do Saguão, 2023).

Nuno Fonseca (PhD, NOVA University Lisbon, 2012) is currently a researcher at the NOVA Institute of Philosophy (IFILNOVA) and coordinates the "Aesthetics and Philosophy of Art" research group at CultureLab. He investigates various topics in Aesthetics and Philosophy of Art, both in the context of the arts and of everyday urban life. He has taught philosophy courses at NOVA FCSH, and, since 2021, he co-teaches the course "Urban Aesthetics: Philosophy, Art and the City". He has co-edited several books and authored chapters and articles on the city and urban experience, such as *Planos de Pormenor* (2023) and *A cidade nas práticas artísticas* (2023).

Routledge Studies in Urban Sociology

This series presents the latest research in urban sociology, welcoming both theoretical and empirical studies that focus on issues including urban conflict, politics and protest, social exclusion and social inclusion, urban regeneration and social class, and the ways in which these affect the social, economic, political, and cultural landscape of urban areas.

Titles in this series

The Making of Place and People in the Danish Metropolis
A Sociohistory of Copenhagen North West
Christian Sandbjerg Hansen

Deindustrialization and Casinos
A Winning Hand?
Alissa Mazar

Urban Regeneration and Neoliberalism
The New Liverpool Home
Clare Kinsella

Entrepreneurial Governance in the Neoliberal Era
Local Government and the Automotive Industry
Oliver Cowart

Urban Preppers and the Pandemic in New York City
Class, Resilience and Sheltering in Place
Anna Maria Bounds

Rethinking the City
Reconfiguration and Fragmentation
Edited by Maria Filomena Molder, Nélio Conceição and Nuno Fonseca

For more information about this series, please visit: www.routledge.com/sociology/series/RSUS

Rethinking the City
Reconfiguration and Fragmentation

Edited by Maria Filomena Molder,
Nélio Conceição and Nuno Fonseca

LONDON AND NEW YORK

First published 2025
by Routledge
4 Park Square, Milton Park, Abingdon, Oxon OX14 4RN

and by Routledge
605 Third Avenue, New York, NY 10158

Routledge is an imprint of the Taylor & Francis Group, an informa business

© 2025 selection and editorial matter, Maria Filomena Molder, Nélio Conceição and Nuno Fonseca; individual chapters, the contributors

The right of Maria Filomena Molder, Nélio Conceição and Nuno Fonseca to be identified as the authors of the editorial material, and of the authors for their individual chapters, has been asserted in accordance with sections 77 and 78 of the Copyright, Designs and Patents Act 1988.

All rights reserved. No part of this book may be reprinted or reproduced or utilised in any form or by any electronic, mechanical, or other means, now known or hereafter invented, including photocopying and recording, or in any information storage or retrieval system, without permission in writing from the publishers.

Trademark notice: Product or corporate names may be trademarks or registered trademarks, and are used only for identification and explanation without intent to infringe.

British Library Cataloguing-in-Publication Data
A catalogue record for this book is available from the British Library

Library of Congress Cataloging-in-Publication Data
Names: Molder, Maria Filomena, editor. | Conceição, Nélio, editor. | Fonseca, Nuno, editor.
Title: Rethinking the city : reconfiguration and fragmentation / edited by Maria Filomena, Nélio Conceição and Nuno Fonseca.
Description: Abingdon, Oxon ; New York, NY : Routledge, 2025. | Includes bibliographical references and index.
Identifiers: LCCN 2024035984 (print) | LCCN 2024035985 (ebook) | ISBN 9781032590974 (hardback) | ISBN 9781032590998 (paperback) | ISBN 9781003452928 (ebook)
Subjects: LCSH: Cities and towns. | Sociology, Urban. | Art and cities.
Classification: LCC HT151 .R428 2025 (print) | LCC HT151 (ebook) | DDC 307.76—dc23/eng/20241026
LC record available at https://lccn.loc.gov/2024035984
LC ebook record available at https://lccn.loc.gov/2024035985

ISBN: 978-1-032-59097-4 (hbk)
ISBN: 978-1-032-59099-8 (pbk)
ISBN: 978-1-003-45292-8 (ebk)

DOI: 10.4324/9781003452928

Typeset in Sabon
by Apex CoVantage, LLC

Contents

Contributors biographies viii
List of figures xii
Acknowledgements xiv

1 Introduction: the ongoing reconfiguration of the city 1
 MARIA FILOMENA MOLDER, NÉLIO CONCEIÇÃO
 AND NUNO FONSECA

PART I
Fragmentation and reconfiguration: urban and
historical tensions 13

2 Cities of memory and ruins of the present: reflections
 in wartime 15
 FABRIZIO DESIDERI

3 My schizoid city 26
 DAVID KISHIK

4 Lisbon's phantom limb syndrome: lineaments
 of spectral ethnography 38
 ANDREA PAVONI

5 The ambivalences of intimacy and aesthetic and political
 reconfigurations of the common world 60
 NÉLIO CONCEIÇÃO

PART II
City, place and the political — 77

6 From the *domus* to the *urbs*: the place of life — 79
ANDREW BENJAMIN

7 Navigating Marx's collective *praxis* and Kierkegaard's individual *practice* in the swarming-dream city of capitalism — 100
BARTHOLOMEW RYAN

8 Contemporary identity politics and the city: more than fragmentation — 117
IRANDINA AFONSO

PART III
Urban experience, aesthetic concepts — 133

9 Towards a political ecology of urban ambiances — 135
JEAN-PAUL THIBAUD

10 Urban life scenes in Georg Simmel: passages between house and city — 150
ADRIANA VERÍSSIMO SERRÃO

11 The art of dwelling as tacit *philia* — 167
TIAGO MESQUITA CARVALHO

PART IV
Cities, fragments and the arts — 183

12 Odysseus impounded: lost sailors, lost times, lost loves — 185
GRAEME GILLOCH

13 Drifting through Lisbon in a home movie archive — 199
INÊS SAPETA DIAS

14 The periphery is not where the city ends but where it begins to unfurl: contributions to an architecture of the metropolis from Renaudie and Gailhoustet to Druot, Lacaton and Vassal 219
JOÃO GONÇALVES PAUPÉRIO

15 On some fragments of *Trás-os-Montes*, a film by António Reis and Margarida Cordeiro 234
MARIA FILOMENA MOLDER

Index 249

Contributors biographies

Adriana Veríssimo Serrão is Associate Professor Emeritus at the Faculty of Letters of the University of Lisbon. She holds a master's degree in Kantian aesthetics and a PhD in Ludwig Feuerbach's anthropology. Her main research areas are philosophical anthropology, aesthetics, philosophy of nature and philosophy of landscape. She is the coordinator of several books on philosophy of landscape. Some of her prominent authored books are *A Humanidade da Razão. Ludwig Feuerbach e o projecto de uma antropologia integral*; *Pensar a Sensibilidade: Baumgarten – Kant – Feuerbach*; *Filosofia da Paisagem. Estudos*. She has translated works by Kant, Ludwig Feuerbach and Georg Simmel.

Andrea Pavoni is Assistant Research Professor at DINAMIA'CET, University Institute of Lisbon, Portugal. His research explores the relation between materiality, normativity and aesthetics in the urban context. He is a fellow at the Westminster Law and Theory Lab, co-editor of the Law and the Senses Series (University of Westminster Press) and an associate editor at the journal Lo Squaderno, Explorations in Space and Society. He is the author of *Controlling Urban Events. Law, Ethics and the Material* (Routledge 2018) and, with Simone Tulumello, of *Urban Violence. Imaginary, Security, Atmosphere* (Lexington 2023).

Andrew Benjamin is currently Honorary Professor in the School of Communication and Cultural Studies in the Faculty of Arts at the University of Melbourne.

Bartholomew Ryan (PhD, Aarhus University) is a philosopher, musician and researcher at IFILNOVA, NOVA University Lisbon. He is the coordinator of the research group 'Forms of Life and Practices of Philosophy' at IFILNOVA. Amongst his various publications interpenetrating philosophy and literature, he is the author of *Fernando Pessoa: Critical Lives* (Reaktion Books, 2024) and *Kierkegaard's Indirect Politics: Interludes With Lukács, Schmitt, Benjamin and Adorno* (Brill, 2014), and is the co-editor of *Fernando Pessoa and Philosophy: Countless Lives Inhabit Us* (Rowman & Littlefield, 2021). In music, he leads the international band *The Loafing*

Heroes and released a solo album called *Jabuti* (under the name *Loafing Hero*) in 2022.

David Kishik lives in New York and teaches philosophy at Emerson College. He is the author of *To Imagine a Form of Life*, a series of five books that include *The Manhattan Project* and *Self Study*.

Fabrizio Desideri (1953) lives in Florence and is Professor Emeritus of Aesthetics at the University of Florence (Italy). He is Editor in Chief of the peer-reviewed online journal *Aisthesis. Pratiche, linguaggi e saperi dell'estetico* and co-editor of the journal *Atque*. He is a member of the scientific board of many philosophical journals. His research is mainly focused on aesthetics and meta-aesthetics, philosophy of mind, theory of consciousness and history of aesthetics. His last books include *Origine dell'estetico. Dalle emozioni al giudizio* (Carocci, 2018); *Walter Benjamin e la percezione dell'arte* (Morcelliana, 2018); *Oggetti attivi* (Mimesis, 2021) and *L'ascolto della coscienza* (Inschibboleth, 2023).

Graeme Gilloch is Professor of Sociology at Lancaster University. He is the author of three monographs exploring Critical Theory – *Myth and Metropolis: Walter Benjamin and the City* (1996); *Walter Benjamin: Critical Constellations* (2002) and *Siegfried Kracauer: Our Companion in Misfortune* (2015). He is the co-author of *The Cinema of Nuri Bilge Ceylan* (with Bulent Diken and Craig Hammond [2018]) and has co-edited four collections, most recently *Siegfried Kracauer: Selected Writings on Propaganda and Political Communication* (with Jaeho Kang and John Abromeit [2022]). He has published numerous articles and essays on cinematic, visual and literary representations of cityscapes; memory, haunting and ghosts; and contemporary neo-noir fiction.

Inês Sapeta Dias is a programmer at Cinemateca Portuguesa. She finished her PhD in 2018 with a thesis on cinema programming. Since 2004, she has been organising cinema programmes and book editions, mostly at Arquivo Municipal de Lisboa – Videoteca, where she was responsible for launching projects such as TRAÇA (moth) – a home movie showcase, "Imaginaries Topographies" or What Is the Archive? In 2008, she finished the film *Winter's Portrait of a Burnt Landscape* (16mm, 40'), and she is now co-directing a TV series of 13 episodes titled *Atlas of an Amateur Cinema*. Since 2019, she has been teaching at the independent art school Ar.Co.

Irandina Afonso is a PhD candidate in the Doctoral Programme in Philosophy of the Faculty of Arts and Humanities of the University of Porto, Portugal. She holds a PhD scholarship (ref. UI/BD/150998/2021; DOI: 10.54499/UI/BD/150998/2021) from the FCT – Portuguese National Fund for Science, Research and Technology at the Research Group Philosophy & Public Space of the Institute of Philosophy (UIDB/00502/2020). She is a member of the PaPSIN – Philosophy and Public Space International Network and the Red Internacional de Investigación Filosofía y Ciudad. Her research interests include identity politics, philosophy of the city and public space, non-binary gender studies, contemporary subjectivity and social and political thought.

Jean-Paul Thibaud, sociologist, is an honorary CNRS senior researcher at Cresson – Research Center on Sonic Space and the Urban Environment, UMR Ambiances Architectures Urbanités. His field of research covers the theory of urban ambiences, ordinary perception in urban environment, sensory culture and ethnography of public places, anthropology of sounds, qualitative in situ methodology and sensitivities to lifeworlds. He has directed the CRESSON research lab and has founded the International Ambiances Network. Jean-Paul Thibaud has published numerous papers on urban ambiances and has co-edited several books in this field of research: https://cv.archives-ouvertes.fr/jean-paul-thibaud.

João Gonçalves Paupério (1992) is a master in architecture from the University of Porto (FAUP). As an architect, he has co-founded atelier local (2019), an architectural practice based in Valongo (PT), which he directs together with Maria Rebelo. As a researcher, he is currently a PhD candidate at the Center for Studies in Architecture and Urbanism (CEAU-FAUP) in Porto, where he undertakes his research with a grant (2020.08189.BD) from the Portuguese Foundation for Science and Technology (FCT). His research is being advised by Joaquim Moreno, Virgílio Borges Pereira and Sébastien Marot.

Maria Filomena Molder is Professor Emeritus at NOVA University Lisbon and a researcher at IFILNOVA. Her philosophical interests converge towards aesthetical issues concerning poetry and art. Reading Dante, Kant, Goethe, Baudelaire, Nietzsche, Wittgenstein, Benjamin, Pessoa, Broch or Colli, she has acquired the conviction that art and poetry are forms of knowledge of a generative kind: they allow us to see the very conditions under which reality is perceived by granting us a presentation of it. Ever since the beginning of her research, she has sought to demonstrate the fertility allowed by aesthetical issues towards the understanding of what philosophy can be.

Nélio Conceição (PhD, NOVA University Lisbon, 2013) is a researcher at IFILNOVA (NOVA Institute of Philosophy). His research focuses on aesthetics and the philosophy of art, with recent work addressing topics within the philosophy of photography, film-philosophy, and the philosophy of the city. He has co-edited the volumes *Aesthetics and Values: Contemporary Perspectives* (Mimesis International, 2021), *Conceptual Figures of Fragmentation and Reconfiguration* (IFILNOVA, 2021), and *Planos de pormenor: leituras críticas sobre a experiência da cidade* (Húmus, 2023).

He is the author of *A realidade em exercício: a fotografia, da fenomenologia a Walter Benjamin* (Edições do Saguão, 2023).

Nuno Fonseca (PhD, NOVA University Lisbon, 2012) is currently a researcher at the NOVA Institute of Philosophy (IFILNOVA) and coordinates the "Aesthetics and Philosophy of Art" research group at CultureLab. He investigates various topics in Aesthetics and Philosophy of Art in the context of both the arts and everyday urban life. He has taught philosophy courses at NOVA FCSH, and, since 2021, he co-teaches the course Urban Aesthetics: Philosophy, Art and the City. He has co-edited several books and authored chapters and articles on the city and urban experience, such as *Planos de Pormenor* (2023) and *A cidade nas práticas artísticas* (2023).

Tiago Mesquita Carvalho is a researcher in the Philosophy and Public Space Research Group at the Instituto de Filosofia in FL-UP with a project concerning responsibility and catastrophes. He has a master's degree in both environmental sciences (IST-UTL) and environmental philosophy and aesthetics (FL-UL). He obtained a PhD in FC-UL with a dissertation on how the good life demands the use of things, crossing virtues, ethics and philosophy of technology. He was part of the FCT project "Landscape Philosophy and Architecture" led by Professor Adriana Veríssimo Serrão. In 2017, he also translated Jan Gehl's classic oeuvre *Life Between Buildings*.

Figures

4.1	Map of Lisbon highlighting the Marvila and Beato Riverfront	39
4.2	Picture of the Hub Criativo do Beato taken from Avenida Infante Dom Henrique	50
4.3	Picture of the Marialva tower taken from the railway overpass	52
5.1	Carla Filipe, *Corpo-mente I (Vísceras) You are Sexual, Remember A ambiguidade da experiência da cidade A ideia sobre comunidade Corpo-mente lll O impulso sobre a comunidade* 2015–16, Indian ink on paper (6 elements)	61
5.2	Carla Filipe, Drawing *School*, pen, decal, marker, collage on cardboard	63
5.3	Installation view, "Carla Filipe: In my own language I am independente", Fundação de Serralves – Museu de Arte Contemporânea, Porto, Portugal, from 23 March 2023 to 24 September 2023	64
6.1	Details from *Tomb of the Statili (Sepulcrum Statiliorum)*, Museo Nazionale Romano, Rome	84
6.2	*Romulus und Remus bauen die Mauern von Rom*, Unknown (circa 1501–1625), Herzog August Bibliothek Wolfenbüttel: D 4 Geom. 2° (1–91)	85
6.3	Frontispiece of Marc-Antoine Laugier's *Essai sur l'architecture* (2nd ed. 1755)	91
13.1	Map of Lisbon with spots for the spaces found in the home movie archive	204
13.2	Two shots of the same detail of Marquês de Pombal statue filmed in different decades	205
13.3	Frames of similar camera movements found in different home movies	206
13.4	Frames of the same space filmed in different decades	207

13.5	Shots of people rowing at Campo Grande Garden's lake, from two different home movie collections	208
13.6	Frames taken from home movie collections and *Lisboa, Crónica Anedótica*	209
13.7	Frames taken from home movie collections and *Lisboa, Crónica Anedótica*	209
13.8	Views over Monsanto taken from home movies and *Lisboa, Crónica Anedótica*	210
13.9	Frames with different views of and from Monsanto	211
13.10	Map of the routes identified in the home movie archive	213

Acknowledgements

The editors would like to thank the authors for their contributions to this book, for their patience with the editorial requirements and for their commitment to the various stages of the book's preparation.

We are grateful to Paula Carvalho, Bruno C. Duarte, Alexandra Dias Fortes and Susana Ventura, who helped us to organise the International Conference "Thinking the City through Fragmentation and Reconfiguration: Aesthetic and Conceptual Challenges" (Lisbon, 1–3 June 2022), which provided the initial impetus for the preparation of this book.

We are also grateful to the School of Social Sciences and Humanities, NOVA University Lisbon (NOVA FCSH) and the NOVA Institute of Philosophy (IFILNOVA) for their institutional and academic support. Special thanks go to Catarina Barros, Cláudia Marques and João Mourão for administrative support. Thanks are also due to Carolyn Benson for the linguistic revision of several chapters and for her flexibility and reliability in managing deadlines and requests and to the editorial staff at Routledge who accompanied us in the preparation of the book at different stages: Neil Jordan, Helen Pritt, Kriti Rana, Gemma Rogers and Alice Salt. Particular thanks are due to Graeme Gilloch for his enthusiasm and editorial input.

This book has been published with the support of the FCT – Fundação para a Ciência e a Tecnologia, under IFILNOVA's project UIDP/00183/2020, the project "Fragmentation and Reconfiguration: Experiencing the City between Art and Philosophy" – PTCD/FER-FIL/32042/2017, Norma Transitória – DL 57/2016/CP1453/CT0040 (https://doi.org/10.54499/DL57/2016/CP1453/CT0040) and Norma Transitória – DL 57/2016/CP1453/CT0098 (https://doi.org/10.54499/DL57/2016/CP1453/CT0098). Finally, we would like to thank our many colleagues in the project team who, in different ways and directly or indirectly, contributed to the organisation of events and to the discussions that took place at them, thus helping to materialise and strengthen the scholarly dimension of years of work, the importance and timeliness of which we hope is reflected in this volume.

1 Introduction

The ongoing reconfiguration of the city

Maria Filomena Molder, Nélio Conceição and Nuno Fonseca

Context

The complex relationships between aesthetics, the arts and the city have taken on new and manifold forms in the last 150 years. The development of modern metropolises and the emergence of new technologies have both generated and necessitated new modalities and tools for learning about, studying and reinventing the urban experience. Cities continue to prompt fundamental aesthetic and existential questions concerning how we feel, perceive and inhabit the spatial and temporal structures that condition the human experience, as well as our relationship with nature and the non-urban in general.

True, Western philosophy emerged out of an intimate relationship with the *polis*, but it has never been easy to make the terms of the multiple historical and conceptual interactions between philosophy and the city explicit. Urban phenomena present particular challenges for, and are illuminated in distinctive ways by, philosophical questioning and conceptual analysis. Our critical understanding of metropolitan complexes – their histories, conditions, trajectories, and futures – lend themselves to and reward aesthetic, social, ethical and political interrogation. Some of these challenges and interrogations inspired a research project that ran from 2018 to 2022, titled "Fragmentation and Reconfiguration: Experiencing the City Between Art and Philosophy". This book is one of the most important (and chronologically, the last) of a series of outcomes of this research project.[1]

The concepts of reconfiguration and fragmentation provide a guiding thread for the contributions to this volume and the ways in which they develop the rapport between philosophical thought and the city. These two terms are associated and resonate with other conceptual couplings, such as construction and destruction, fragment and whole, the singularity of the particular and the theoretical tendency to search for a comprehensive synthesis. The main goal of this book is to explore the creative and dialectical tensions between reconfiguration and fragmentation, which provide fertile ground for critical reflection – a space for both thought and practice, for praxis. In this sense, it seeks to explore the different ways in which human experiences and artistic practices engage with and respond to the fragmentation that characterises modern cities. The book aims to disturb and disrupt the hegemonic and homogenous images of contemporary cities that have been created by processes associated with capitalism and globalisation, (re)presentations that time and again obscure other forms of living and indeed deny the very possibility of reimagining and rethinking the spaces we inhabit.

The concept of fragmentation does not necessarily presuppose nostalgia for a lost unity. Rather, as part and parcel of the very processes of modernity itself,[2] fragmentation provides the essential materials – shards, tesserae, scraps, minutiae, moments, instances, glimpses, details, vignettes, cases and case studies – that provide critical, albeit provisional, access to an understanding of our present time. The epistemological and historical model opened up by Benjamin's unfinished work on the Parisian arcades is particularly relevant in this context.[3] At the same time, the concept of reconfiguration presupposes the very possibility of rethinking, reconstructing and reimagining urban spaces, which is of the utmost importance not only for a philosophical consideration of the city but also for the artistic practices that have been inspired by it and that seek to express it.

Against this background, our goal in this book is to present the reader with a philosophical collective work that takes a necessarily interdisciplinary approach, intersecting philosophy with sociology, history, political science, literary and cultural studies, visual art and media and gender studies. Our pair of key concepts – reconfiguration and fragmentation – both ensures a degree of originality and provides a basis for drawing strong connections between fundamental topics in philosophy and aesthetics and contributions from other fields and case studies.[4]

Thinking about the reconfiguration and fragmentation of cities becomes all the more pertinent the more we consider the global and local processes that deeply affect our cities, forcing them to reinvent and reconstruct themselves. We need only consider the ecological crisis or the constant threats to democracy that are reflected in the use of urban space, the recent pandemics and wars that have not only destroyed cities but have forced us to think about what to do with and amidst their ruins.

This combined philosophical and conceptual basis, steeped in critique, alterity and emancipatory struggles and an interest in the manifold guises of modern cities, gives the book a relevance that is not limited to a specific historical period or sociological context. Indeed, like the ceaseless tension between reconfiguration and fragmentation, the continuing interplay between past and present runs through the book like a disquieting force that goes to the heart of the crisis of our historical present and the way in which this crisis expresses itself and constitutes our urban lives.

Structure and content

The book is divided into four parts, each of which comprises chapters that share certain perspectives, viewpoints, and thematic or methodological affinities (but that also intersect with and evoke themes, approaches, authors and cities dealt with in other parts of the volume). Their arrangement and sequence also helps to illuminate structural elements of the book.

The first part, "Fragmentation and reconfiguration: urban and historical tensions", attempts to respond to the challenges posed by the conceptual pair that inspired the research project and its overall philosophical approach to the city: the irrevocable tension between the centrifugal and centripetal forces of fragmentation and reconfiguration, which are undeniably determined by the historical nature of urbanisation processes and the dynamic character of the urban social drama – both collective and individual. This is where the past summons the present and where ruins, as both a historical and an aesthetic category, raise the question of cultural memory and collective identity. But it is also where the challenges of coexistence, the constant negotiation between the private and the public, the tensions between citizenship, desire and intimacy are played out against the horizon of common values and the "distribution of the sensible".[5] Recent events such as the wars in Eastern Europe and the Middle East, but also the Covid-19 pandemic, have indelibly marked our time and the daily lives and dynamics of cities, particularly those most directly affected by them. It would have been unthinkable to write a book about the fragmentation and reconfiguration of cities without taking into account these unavoidable events.

The first chapter begins with a reflection on the ruins of the present in times of war. Fabrizio Desideri evokes images of destroyed cities, disfigured by war, as revealing the symbolic power of ruins in a philosophy of history inspired by Benjamin: history as an endless *Trauerspiel*. Ruins carry this ambiguous tension with the past, taking us back to images of glorious cities in times of peace while at the same time revealing their wreckage. Invoking the aesthetic thought of the Sicilian Rosario Assunto, the chapter also refers to the distinction between two types of ideal cities, one under the sign of the mythological figures of Amphion and Orpheus, based on a sense of measure with a centred experience expressing cyclical time, the other under the sign of Prometheus, linked to the logic of excess and endless accumulation, where intentional time, guided by the idea of progress, destroys the relationship between places and memory. This last type represents present-day cities, which are governed by a functionalist logic and the anarchic accumulation of capital and commodities. The third part of the chapter focuses on the theme of cities of memory as constitutive parts of the construction of identity. This image of the city under the filter of memory reflects the relationship between historical depth and experience, which contains within itself a prophecy of the future, which, from a Benjaminian perspective on history, is not without its ruins and therefore the imminence of catastrophe, but also the prospect of redemption. The chapter leaves us with a fundamental question: how can the cities of memory, in their fragmented character, including the sense of ruin, contain a critical force towards the present?

David Kishik offers a meditation on his "schizoid city", New York, before, during and after the pandemic – a city that, according to the author, is indifferent to a world from which it has withdrawn, its inhabitants not only divided from one another but also split within themselves. This division is fuelled not by anger but by a hunger for love, even if they still fear its consequences. This meditation is carried out in the "self-study" style that Kishik has been developing in recent work and is seen through the lens of the psychoanalytic theory of object relations, originally advocated by Donald Winnicott, Harry Guntrip, Ronald Fairbairn and R. D. Laing. In his attempt to cultivate a conversation between psychology and philosophy on contemporary urban life, however, Kishik also evokes the literary references of Paul Auster, Franz Kafka, Fernando Pessoa and Olivia Laing.

In the following chapter, Andrea Pavoni, also inspired by Walter Benjamin's dialectical images, focuses on the eastern part of the city of Lisbon, more specifically on the Marvila and Beato neighbourhoods on the banks of the Tagus, considered by current magazines and tourist marketing to be some of the trendiest areas of the city but where the past is reflected like a spectre in the ruins of the present. Pavoni offers what he calls a spectral ethnography of this area of Lisbon, identifying, in a kind of X-ray of an unrealised plan for a bridge over the River Tagus, the outlines of an amputated, phantom limb in the Marvila and Beato area. The catastrophe (the virtual amputation) and the ruins (allegorical fragments of a past to come) are mainly the result of the 2008 financial crisis and the expectations created by the Promethean logic of progress. Pavoni updates Benjamin's philosophy of history with the notion of "future ruins", borrowed from the artist Robert Smithson, which serves here to expose the submerged contradictions of future trajectories that already exist, albeit invisibly, in the emptied landscapes of the present. The chapter then attempts to account for these spectral realities and the spatial and temporal fragmentation of the city they express.

In the last chapter of this first part, Nélio Conceição revisits the "modern discovery of intimacy" and analyses the challenges it poses for a philosophical understanding of the city, especially at the aesthetic and political levels. These challenges are particularly problematic in the context of the fragmentation of the modern urban experience, which in this chapter is read in the light of Hannah Arendt's notion of the "common world", developed in *The Human Condition*. To address art's capacity to engage with difficult issues in a direct and fruitful way, this chapter finds inspiration in the work of the Portuguese artist Carla Filipe and the way in which she combines intimacy with an aesthetic and political reconfiguration of the common world. Precisely because modernity has involved the progressive transformation of private space into a space of intimacy, Conceição delves into various processes of individualisation, self-absorption and withdrawal from a perspective that intersects the sociological and historical contributions of Richard Sennett and Simmel's and Benjamin's analyses of ambivalent experiences in modern metropolises while also focusing on art's capacity to problematise our "urban intimacy" and its call for a reconfiguration of the common world.

Whereas the chapters in the first part in many ways evoke and discuss political aspects associated with urban issues and tensions, those of the second part, "City, place and the political", focus on these political aspects more directly – whether they are located in the tension between the individual and the collective or in relations of power, whether in the form of insidious forces of exclusion or as impetuses for the emancipation of communities and identities. It is thus important for these reflections that these tensions, struggles and conflicts are situated in concrete urban circumstances, in places that harbour and re-signify the relationships, dynamics and lives of those who inhabit them and negotiate their place of belonging, be they Seneca's Rome, Kierkegaard's Copenhagen, Marx's London or Lefebvre's Paris.

This is clearly evident in Andrew Benjamin's chapter, which argues that the development of biopolitics requires thinking about the situated nature of human beings and therefore of citizens. Tracing the movement from the *domus* (house) – where place is defined in relation to the individual – to the *urbs* (city) – where the subject, the citizen, must be redefined in relation to others – the chapter is concerned with the city as a locus of experience, where "differentials of power" – a term that underscores that differences are never pure but "inevitably constructed in terms of diminished or augmented access to the benefits inherent in the organisation of human life" – are inscribed in the memories and foundational images of cities. Andrew Benjamin then analyses two origin myths represented in two images, one of the founding of Lavinium, the legendary city built by Aeneas, then a refugee of the Trojan War, and another of the founding of Rome, in which Romulus and Remus build the walls of the city. The author stresses that the myths of the origin of the *urbs* entail modes of exclusion, "differentials of power" – in the ancient city, the exclusion of slaves; in the contemporary city, the exclusion of refugees – which must be overcome through a critical redefinition of hospitality, a vindication of the "right to the city", and a reconfiguration of the contemporary *urbs*.

In the following chapter, Karl Marx – a forefather of what Henri Lefebvre and David Harvey would later champion as a revolutionary attitude towards exclusionary, bourgeois and capitalist metropolises – is one of the two contemporary "disruptive dialecticians" (the other being Søren Kierkegaard) who are brought to the fore in a philosophical and social critique of the modern city. Bartholomew Ryan evokes these well-known 19th-century philosophers to explore their pioneering and revolutionary, if not subversive, attempts to infuse philosophical thinking into praxis in the modern city, putting particular emphasis on the tension between the collective and the individual. In his famous "The Seducer's Diary", Kierkegaard identifies himself as "Johannes", a subversive "single individual" who Ryan envisages as a sort of *flâneur* who sought to disturb the "pillars of the bourgeoisie" and denounce "the crowd-man" (not to be confused with the character from Edgar Allan Poe's short story "The Man of the Crowd" but rather *Mængden*, a symbol of the collective and a word that Kierkegaard takes to mean "untruth"). On the other hand, Marx shows us that the isolated and alienated proletarian can emancipate himself only in the collective, a collective in which he is aware of his position in the class struggle and the revolutionary impetus. The revolution (and its triumph) is possible only in the streets of the modern metropolis, where clandestine meetings, pamphlet distribution and the formation of something like an urban guerrilla movement can take shape.

The last chapter of this second part also deals with the urban political tensions between the individual and the collective, social fragmentation and reconfiguration but from the perspective of what is known as identity politics. Irandina Afonso starts from the recognition that contemporary cities are places of opportunity and freedom but also of oppression, violence, domination and conflict and are therefore conducive to the production of inequality, insecurity, isolation, exclusion and social injustice. A number of contemporary factors, trends and processes – including ecological challenges, successive economic crises and imbalances, globalisation, migratory flows, increasing and widespread urbanisation and the weakening of democracies and of the welfare state – have all exacerbated social tensions; urban violence; vulnerability; injustice and discrimination based on race, gender, country of origin, religion, age, physical and mental disability; sexual preference and the like. Despite the existing debate on the effectiveness of contemporary identity politics, which risks reinforcing fragmentation and depoliticisation (Fukuyama), Afonso argues, in a subtly optimistic tone, that the former may actually contribute to a positive transformation of urban coexistence, social and political change and even the overcoming of aspects of social fragmentation. Read through this lens, contemporary identity politics has the potential to promote a theoretical and practical reassessment of social categories, political concepts, epistemological perceptions and even metaphysical assumptions, fostering the development of new solidarities and social and existential emancipation.

The third part, "Urban experience, aesthetic concepts", brings together chapters that focus more on the aesthetic and anthropological dimension of the urban experience, taking into account the ecological perspective that has emerged in recent studies on sensibilities towards the environment and also the material and technological frameworks that underlie everyday life and cultural dynamics in contemporary cities.

A pervasive aestheticisation of urban life has slowly been transforming our constant and multifarious transactions with the environment (natural and built) and with other citizens, challenging the traditional frameworks of the "distribution of the sensible" and thereby claiming a new kind of rapport between aesthetics and politics – one that Jean-Paul Thibaud suggests is a sort of "political ecology of urban ambiances". In this chapter, the French sociologist takes up the notion of "ambiance" (akin to the concept of *atmosphere* promoted by the new German phenomenology and in particular by the aesthetic thinking of Gernot Böhme) insofar as it allows us to understand our multisensory relationships, both passive and active, with urban spaces, forging the notion of an *ambient sensitivity*, that is, a diffuse and permeable sensitivity to everyday life. The challenge here is to understand the processes of aestheticisation at work in cities and also the reconfiguration of citizens' attention spans by digital technologies and new media and new sensitivities to climate change and the ecological crisis, all of which affects our existential security and emotional stability. According to Thibaud, this new "ambient sensitivity" intensifies our awareness and shared attunement with other life forms and life worlds in general. Rather than feeling detached and separate from other humans and non-humans, we should resonate and be in tune with all that surrounds us, allowing ourselves to be affected by a mixture of strangeness and enchantment, an openness to the otherness and uniqueness of every living creature, and an exhilarating enthusiasm for exploration, discovery and wonder in response to the world around us.

A certain kind of aesthetic porosity, no longer of the body in relation to the environment through an ecological sensibility but now between interior and exterior, private and public, house and city, is what we find in the next chapter, where Adriana Veríssimo Serrão takes up Georg Simmel's famous analyses of the social, aesthetic and anthropological transformations of experience in modern metropolises at the dawn of the 20th century. Simmel's influential and now classic studies – which were not only sociological but, as the author insists, authentically philosophical – on urban culture, the modern experience of shock and social fragmentation, changes in the sensibility of citizens, their *blasé* character and the acquisition of new cultural tastes and interests allow us to understand two trends emphasised by Serrão: on the one hand, a growing preponderance of the culture of objects in everyday urban life over an intellectual or spiritual culture (which Simmel sees as a sign of the tragic evolution of modern culture) and the consequent appearance of new aesthetic categories related to the organisation of space, furniture, design and decorative styles; on the other hand, an ambivalent relationship between domestic space, the haven of the citizen who protects herself from the enervation of public life and the frenetic rhythms of the city, and the atrium or lobby, where she prepares herself, where she cultivates her taste and her capacity for expression (through clothing, adornment, manners), to return to the public sphere and see her singular subjectivity transformed into an inevitable idiosyncratic intersubjectivity. Serrão illustrates this characteristic of *homo urbanus* as an intermediate being between two worlds through the metaphors of the *bridge* and the *door*.

Tiago Mesquita Carvalho focuses on dwelling as a relational art that connects places and communities and involves collective processes that call for tacit knowledge and the hermeneutic task of interpreting the built environment, which may escape or even resist technocratic models for planning and conceiving urban spaces. He argues that the technical and professional knowledge that has taken hold of architecture and urban planning – governed as it is by a logic of geometrisation, the functional optimisation of artefacts and the maximisation of exchange value to the detriment of use value – has intensified social fragmentation, preventing an authentic appropriation of space by citizens and members of local communities and perhaps even constituting an obstacle to the emergence of communities. The author advocates a revaluation of the techniques or art of dwelling through a reappraisal by means of an existential and hermeneutic philosophy of technology and of situated, contextual, sustainable and intersubjective forms of knowledge. These have the potential to foster a reconfiguration of the urban experience, a renewal of "life between buildings" (to invoke Jan Gehl's proposal) that can serve as the upholstery of a thriving and vibrant community sustained by a "tacit *philia*".

Finally, the fourth part of this book, "Cities, fragments and the arts", comprises chapters that analyse tensions, issues and urban phenomena by appealing to or critically questioning artistic practices that – as was the hallmark of the project that paved the way for this book – have always contributed to problematising, reappraising and reconfiguring the modern and contemporary urban experience. The authors of these chapters are in dialogue with literature (more specifically neo-noir fiction, which was originally an urban genre but which in this particular case evokes the novel and the epic), with architecture (a hybrid art that generates habitable space, structuring the landscape and the boundaries of the city) and with cinema (auteur cinema and auteur-less cinema, or what we often call home movies, both of which reconfigure the imaginary of the city through its apparent absence and through unconscious or improvised camera movements).

Graeme Gilloch revisits the novel *The Lost Sailors* (*Les marins perdus*) by the Marseillais writer Jean-Claude Izzo, in a style that is inspired by its novelistic undulations but also by concepts and motifs taken from the writings of Walter Benjamin. As Gilloch explains, the French writer shows us Marseille through the eyes of a sailor – "a modern-day Odysseus" who returns to the city 20 years later, more lost on land than at sea and trying, in a way, to reconfigure not only his memories but also his past, his lost loves, through a rambling perambulation in which he collects fragments of experiences, feelings and affections, regrets, revelations and elusive moments of loss and reencounter. Gilloch also reflects on how the writer vividly and expressively captures the multisensory aesthetic experiences that are possible only in Izzo's hometown (its flavours, smells, sounds, sunlight fluctuations, ambiences and atmospheres), along with Marseille's character as a port city, a pole of attraction or refuge for immigrants, passengers, exiles, orphans, wanderers and other outcasts. According to Gilloch, Izzo's writing evokes a feeling of nostalgia and longing which finds its ancient referent in the epic figure of Ulysses, torn between the desire to venture somewhere else and the desire to return home.

There is a floating movement, a psychogeographic drift, in the exercise that Inês Sapeta Dias proposes in the following chapter. This is an exercise in montage, based on scattered materials from an archive of home movies that capture aspects of the city of Lisbon from different points of view and at different times. In this archive, the author identifies repeated places and, on this basis, arranges lines of images, creating a journey through the (image of the) city, a kind of atlas – not without parallels to Aby Warburg's *Atlas Mnemosyne* – which aims to map the urban space and bring out, by means of montage, the recurrences, absences and radical differences and to organise, through associations and continuities, the impressions recorded by the anonymous authors of the images, loaded with affective and emotional connections to the places and moments captured by the camera. With this exercise in reconfiguration from fragments, Sapeta Dias aims to test the aesthetic and conceptual affinities between the *atlas* and the *psychogeographic map* (a notion derived from Guy Debord's theory of the *drift*) and the multiple ways of inhabiting the city through its representations and reframed perceptions.

João Gonçalves Paupério casts a critical and inquisitive eye over the outskirts of Paris, an area known as "la zone" at the time of Haussmann's great urban renovation, when it became a place for the forsaken rejects of the bourgeois city and subsequently inscribed in the urban imaginary as the threshold between the urban and the rural, where the city begins or ends, depending on the centripetal or centrifugal perspective of the movements that colonised it. The title says it all: "[t]he periphery is not where the city ends, but where it begins to unfurl". Focusing on the work of two teams of architects from the 1970s and 1980s (Renaudie & Gailhoustet) and the first decade of the 21st century (Druot, Lacaton & Vassal), Paupério reveals these peripheral areas as places of ideological conflict and artistic creativity, interpreting these architects' responses to challenges linked to social housing as ways of showcasing architecture's ability to subvert and politically reconfigure the city through the emerging and fracturing urban potential found in the margins of the metropolis.

In the last chapter, Maria Filomena Molder offers an offscreen reflection on the city through a film by Portuguese directors António Reis and Margarida Cordeiro, *Trás-os-Montes* (1976) – a film in which there is no city, in which the modern city is absent insofar as it does not appear onscreen, and in which the city is nonetheless the reason for the disappearance, the desolation, and the desertification and abandonment of the countryside and of rural space. This reflection is based on several sequences or "fragments". The film itself is also a sumptuous collection of fragments. The reflection is carried out as a new montage, although it does not pretend to be a substitute for the original because it is not an artistic operation but rather a conceptual montage inspired by Benjamin and Goethe, one that dispenses with purely deductive and inductive operations because it speaks for itself, is *index sui*, simply following the inner logic of the images and characters. The film depicts the consequences of the rural exodus and emigration, accelerated by the centripetal – or centrifugal, depending on the perspective – movement of the Industrial Revolution and the unbridled urbanisation that has drained the countryside, local cultures, and our intimate relationship with nature. In Portuguese, the word for "offscreen" (*fora de campo*), like the French *hors-champ*, means "outside the field", and here, in this film, it is the city that is outside the field. From the outset, the city defines itself as standing outside of or against the countryside, against nature.

Although it has its origins in the city, philosophy has often been characterised by an anti-urban feeling born out of a critical view of the city, a temptation to flee to the margins of the city or to the countryside, although the philosopher soon realises that he/she must return to the city, which is, after all, his/her natural home. This is why it is increasingly important to articulate a philosophy of the city, a philosophy in the city and with(in) the city. But then again, rethinking the city philosophically does not fail to evoke, today and ever more, its relationship with the countryside, with nature, so often one of conflict, so often marked by the absorption and exhaustion of resources – a splintered relationship but one that calls out to be mended, re-stitched and reconfigured.

Acknowledgements

This work was supported by the FCT – Fundação para a Ciência e a Tecnologia, under the project UIDP/00183/2020, the project PTCD/FER-FIL/32042/2017, Norma Transitória – DL 57/2016/CP1453/CT0040 (https://doi.org/10.54499/DL57/2016/CP1453/CT0040) and Norma Transitória – DL 57/2016/CP1453/CT0098 (https://doi.org/10.54499/DL57/2016/CP1453/CT0098).

Notes

1 It stems from work carried out at the last event held by the project, the international conference "Thinking the City through Fragmentation and Reconfiguration: Aesthetic and Conceptual Challenges" (Lisbon, 1–3 June 2022). It is also worth mentioning the three collective books published previously under the auspices of the project: Conceição et al., *Conceptual Figures of Fragmentation and Reconfiguration*; Conceição and Fonseca, *Planos de pormenor*; Fonseca et al., *A cidade nas práticas artísticas*.
2 Frisby, *Fragments of Modernity*.
3 Benjamin, *The Arcades Project*.
4 The book builds on the research project's distinctive philosophical background: the tense relation between fragmentation and reconfiguration, as explored in Goethe's morphological thinking and in authors that have an affinity with it (e.g., Simmel, Benjamin, Kracauer, Nietzsche, Wittgenstein, Foucault, Deleuze, Joyce, Proust and Pessoa). It sheds light on the extent to which artistic practices absorb and respond to the fragmentation of diverse human experiences in modern cities by exploring the creative tensions between fragmentation and reconfiguration, which open up space for both critical reflection and artistic "room for play" (or *Spielraum*, as Benjamin puts it) as a site of critique and contestation.
5 Rancière, *The Distribution of the Sensible*.

Bibliography

Benjamin, Walter, *The Arcades Project*, translated by Howard Eiland and Kevin McLaughlin, Cambridge, MA: Harvard University Press, 2002.
Conceição, Nélio, Gianfranco Ferraro, Nuno Fonseca, Alexandra Dias Fortes and Maria Filomena Molder, eds., *Conceptual Figures of Fragmentation and Reconfiguration*, Lisbon: IFILNOVA, 2021.

Conceição, Nélio and Nuno Fonseca, eds., *Planos de pormenor: leituras críticas sobre a experiência da cidade*, V. N. Famalicão: Editora Húmus/IFILNOVA, 2023.

Fonseca, Nuno, Humberto Brito, João Oliveira Duarte, Susana Ventura and Susana Viegas, eds., *A cidade nas práticas artísticas*, Lisbon: IFILNOVA, 2023.

Frisby, David, *Fragments of Modernity: Theories of Modernity in the Work of Simmel, Kracauer and Benjamin*, Oxon, UK: Routledge, 2013.

Rancière, Jacques, *The Politics of Aesthetics. The Distribution of the Sensible*, edited and translated with an introduction by Gabriel Rockhill, London: Continuum International Publishing Group, 2004.

Part I

Fragmentation and reconfiguration

Urban and historical tensions

2 Cities of memory and ruins of the present

Reflections in wartime

Fabrizio Desideri

Ruinae

The ruin of the present: the present as *ruina*. The Latin verb *ruere* from which the noun *ruina* derives means "to rush" (to hurry): to make haste but also to break, to shatter, to collapse and to disrupt. The terminus was connected by linguists to the root of the Greek *rôo-mai* ("I move quickly") which is the same as *rèô* (to flow) but also to the Sanskrit *rauti* (past participle *ruta*), which in the Vedas has the sense of breaking (*ruta* indicates precisely being broken). In Latin, *ruere* has often been associated with a movement of time that is more than a slow flow, rather assuming the meaning of a looming advancing, the act of precipitating suddenly and in the instant itself with inexorable abruptness: a break in the ordinary and natural course of events.

To move into a reflection on cities, on what they have become and can always become, stemming from this sense of ruin sounds certainly less problematic, today[1], than it would have been just about some years ago. To consider the ruin as a summary and expressive figure of the current historical time, of the *Jetztzeit*, seems like a task, an *Aufgabe*, dictated by the blood-soaked signature of our times. As a task, this consideration implies a radical revision or extension of the interpretative paradigm by which we think of the image of ruins. What is called into question here is the interpretation of ruin as a significantly autonomous form, both in aesthetic and metaphysical terms, which Georg Simmel entrusts to a short, very dense essay of 1907, dryly titled *Die Ruine* (later inserted, in 1911, in the volume *Philosophische Kultur*).

Let us briefly recall the Simmelian theses to highlight the specificity of our reflections. In the ruin – as Simmel states – something happens that is the reverse of what happens in a work of art. While in the latter, the spirit celebrates its victory over nature imprinting its own autonomous legality on it, in the ruin (of a temple or of any other building) the opposite happens: the balance, the equation between spirit and nature shifts in favour of the latter. The process of decay producing the ruin thus becomes the expression of a "kosmische Tragik":[2] nature takes revenge for the violence to which it was subjected by spirit. Those elements that in the architectural building were

DOI: 10.4324/9781003452928-3

composed in the unity of a form, by virtue of a natural decadence as the effect of an anarchic agency of nature, are separated, revealing an original enmity. The stone is thus freed, little by little, from the yoke burdening it to return to the autonomous legality of one's own forces. What at first glance could appear as "ein sinnloser Zufall [a meaningless chance]"[3] soon takes on "a new meaning": that of revealing to the intuition how the "spiritual *Gestaltung*" is no longer rooted in the human-too-human "conformity to purposes" set by reason but in a depth where the intertwining of "unconscious natural forces" finds a common root. Thus, the ruin, in its acquired significance, reveals the human soul itself as a "Kampfplatz":[4] an unpacifiable battlefield between opposite poles and divergent impulses. A passage, the latter, which in Simmel's reflection is a prelude to a final image, where the aesthetic value of the ruin joins the metaphysical one: the image of an extreme "Friedlichkeit" (pacificity), of a profound peace that touches the sacred: the image of ruin as the seat of a life that has taken leave of itself, present form of a "past life", "extreme strengthening and fulfillment of the present form of the past [*der Gegenwartsform der Vergangenheit*]".[5]

Curiously, considering that in the same year Simmel published the volume on *Die Probleme der Geschichtsphilosophie*, in the writing on the ruin the term history never appears. Ruin as an effect of intentional destruction, "*through* freedom" (to quote Kant of § 43 of the *Kritik der Urteilskraftt*),[6] does not have for Simmel that significance which ruin as an effect of nature possesses. Nevertheless, the conceptual grid that articulates the phenomenology of the aesthetic–metaphysical sense of ruin is drawn entirely from the historical–anthropological arsenal of war: from original enmity to the "battlefield" up to extreme peace, the one in which the image of ruin delivers the present to the past while attesting to its persistence. With respect to this image, it is now a question of considering the ruin as a direct figure of the present, an expression of the broken circle that tightens today between time and concept.

The ruin as an allegorical icon of history is, moreover, the subject of fundamental considerations in a section of the second part of Walter Benjamin's book *Origin of the German Trauerspiel*. Dissonant toward his own time, not assignable to any school or philosophical current and at the same time expression of another *Stimmung* of thinking compared to the one that could be sensed by reading Heidegger's *Sein und Zeit*, Benjamin's book establishes an essential relationship with the theme of ruin as the most suitable for capturing the *katastrophè* of historical time in an image. Almost as if precisely this image and its allegorical power subjected the concept of the "now" to an essential twist, offering a sort of problematic bridge between the system of revelation developed in Rosenzweig's *Stern der Erlösung* and the revolutionary caesura contained in Lukács's *Geschichte und Klassenbewußtsein*. With the ruin, through its figure, "history enters the scene".[7] It does so, inscribed on the veiled face of nature: "written . . . in the sign-script of transience".[8] The same notion of decadence at the center of the Simmelian essay would still seem to dominate here. Yet this is a wrong impression. What emerges inscribed in the ruin is a new character: neither pure anarchy of nature nor historical weaving of events but *Natur-Geschichte*, History-Nature as *Trauerspiel*, mourning staging, a dramatic play of passions sucked into a whirling fury annihilating them. The decay, "the incessant decline",[9] therefore, concerns this figure of history that unfolds in a space of worldly immanence, in the scene of the *saeculum* that is condensed in the political perimeter of the Court. A figure of history, hence, which, having left behind the eschatological tension between *civitas dei* and *civitas hominis*, no longer even bears the character of a confrontation between two ages of the spirit (as could have been the case for Renaissance). It rather takes on the meaning of the catastrophic consummation of the relationship between the Christian era and the ruins of Antiquity. The ruins of the ancient temple, its remains which in the Renaissance figuration were still background to the place of Christ's birth, undergo a radical transformation in the scriptural and scenic space of the Baroque *Trauerspiel*. This is no longer the sign of a new beginning in time, but the expression of an inconsolable precipitate of time, effect or residue of the catastrophic reversal of temporal rhythm into space. The ruin/allegory thus corresponds to the *Naturgeschichte* as an effigy of the present in a continuous transition between the effectiveness of historical images and the task of deciphering their meaning. An effigy that sounds like a challenge for thought as it returns to the present with the recurrence of war scenarios that we were under the illusion of having consigned to the past of European history.

Recalling the harshness with which actuality presents us daily ruins of cities and scenarios of destruction could also have the effect of a rhetorical artifice that exempts us from thinking the ruin in its meaningful pregnancy. A step to avoid this risk might be to consider the historical meaning of the ruin not in a naturalistic direction but in an ethical one. Therefore, it is a matter of no longer thinking of ruin as a sinking of nature into the chaos that precedes all order but rather as a consequence of evil misuse of our freedom that constitutes a secession from a "good life".

Already in this interpretative direction, in this revealing the ruin produced by the human operating as an expression of a literally infernal time, it becomes an apocalyptic allegory, a splinter that the *katastrophikón*[10] of time, the rushing of history into heaps of rubble, paradoxically expels from itself, like a fragment of the "star of redemption", an occasion or chance for a thought that has enough *vis imaginativa* to grasp it. Thus, in this grab, the inverse movement of the allegorical meaning of ruin can be grasped as an apocalypse of historical happening as a *Trauerspiel*. In this inversion, the thought lifts its gaze upwards to consider the celestial vault as the background of each construction. In this reversal of interpretative direction, the ruin not only attests to the fact that the modern and ultramodern facies of war, from Guernica to Mariupol, have elected cities as a space for conflict and an object of destruction (in that absence of reasons perfectly clarified by

18 *Rethinking the City*

Sebald in his *On the Natural History of Destruction*) but also testifies to the idea that resists these destructive forces whose implicit telos essentially seems to be that of razing to the ground.

We can thus assert for the ruins of cities, that the present gives us back as its true image, what Karl Borinski in a passage quoted by Benjamin from his *Die Antike in Poetik und Kunsttheorie* observes about the architectural remains of the Ancient:

> The broken pediment, the ruined columns shall bear witness to the miraculous fact that the holy edifice has withstood even the most elemental forces of destruction – lightning and earthquake.[11]

The miracle, as shall be merely observed, becomes even more eloquent when the forces of destruction are those released from war machines. Yet with a warning that sounds like a correction to the conclusion of Borinski's passage. Precisely because, ultimately, at the origin of the destruction of war, there is human reason in its freedom (and it would be a mistake, here, to dissolve the idea of freedom *in a blind obeying to impulses*), ruin as a result of intentional acting no longer concerns the last legacy of the Ancient and even less can it take the form of "a picturesque field of rubble".[12] As the "picturesque" disappears, however, the field of rubble remains and the ruin, as a new theatrical space of a senseless human action, speaks again to assume a significance perhaps not understood by Simmel in its autonomous value but certainly by Benjamin, both in the book on *Trauerspiel* and – with a sense of historical urgency – in the theses "On the Concept of History".

The city of Prometheus

This new talking to us from the ruins, this actuality of their meaning, as well as expressing the foolish viciousness at their origin, may also overturn itself by antiphrasis in testimony of an "indestructible life" that is opposed to every spirit of decadence. It tends to do so with two different accents, certainly destined to intertwine, to recall each other and sometimes to merge into a single voice: the heroic accent of the idea at the origin of European cities and the elegiac one of memory that in the life of their inhabitants preserves their image. In both cases, a dialectical image of the city is revealed. The medium of this revelation are the ruins in their plurality, no longer the single ruin. When it is not a matter of considering the effect of a natural decay anymore, and the focus shifts onto the human *operari* who aims to destroy a city, the ruin loses its unity of image by virtue of which – as Simmel observes – it maintains an aesthetic value passing into metaphysical meaning. In the war-*theatrum* that re-proposes history as an endless drama, ruins are a multiple, ghostly appearance of a hyper-object that annihilates the very existence of a city, demolishing the unmistakable profile its palaces, its houses, its churches draw by rising upwards. Having reached the zero-degree of its existence, the devastation and rubble that make its look unrecognizable (think of certain Ukrainian cities devastated by the current war or of Berlin filmed by Rossellini in *Germania anno zero* or the other German cities razed to the ground of which Sebald speaks),[13] the allegory of the ruin can be reversed in a rethinking of the idea that informs the life of a city starting from its origin.

A thought that does not surrender to the existing, nor resign itself to the ruins of the present as if they were a destiny, can dare at this point to rethink the poetics of the European city in the complexity of tensions and conflicting elements that constitute the matrix of its idea and, along with it, that one aspect that no fury of war can destroy. It is a merit of the Italian philosopher of Sicilian birth Rosario Assunto to have thought of the plurality of poetics that concur in defining the European city in its historical configuration, emphasizing, in this regard, a radical opposition between the shape of the medieval and Renaissance-city on the one hand and that of the modern city on the other. The starting point of Assunto's considerations in several of his essays collected in a volume titled *La città di Anfione e la città di Prometeo* is, however, the thought of a "city of ideas or logos",[14] even before that of an ideal city: a city that finds the reason for its existence in beauty and the rhythm of its buildings and internal articulations in measure. A Platonic and Neoplatonic city, therefore, a city of logos as town of the vertical man, dotted with statues that invite to contemplation, a city whose life is marked by the arts that not only imitate nature but correct it rooting back to principles. Cities as works of art,[15] lastly, where the space of the temple and the profane space harmonize one with each other in respecting the places. The Renaissance neo-Neoplatonism of Ficino, Alberti, and Filarete has an active memory of this city. We find pictorial representation of it in the painting *La Città ideale* in Urbino, theoretical advances in Alberti's *De re aedificatoria* and also historical examples in cities such as Enea Silvio Piccolomini's Pienza. As Assunto underlines, the Platonic and Neoplatonic inspiration of Renaissance poetics is declined in different directions: from that inspired by Alberti's Platonism of proportions and symmetries to that inspired by the Neoplatonic metaphysics of light by Filarete. As Assunto further observes, the ideal dimension of the city's Renaissance poetics does not neglect the concreteness of urban life in its various articulations to which different ways of building correspond always in relation to different *loci*. Alberti's conception is exemplary in this regard, first in the concern to make different eras and different conceptions of the organization of space interact; aiming precisely to gather into one the Renaissance principle of perspective as an artifice and invention of a "heroic" ratio with the respect and care for places, preserved in the curved interweaving of streets and alleys that wind around the space of the central square. The beauty of the city, therefore, as the unity of a manifold diversity of perspectives that manage to compose themselves in a shape. Aesthetics and politics, finally, as converging aspects of a single idea of the city that makes up the exploratory industriousness of the Renaissance-man and the contemplative verticality of the medieval one. Some historic cities still bear witness to this idea of the city, this ideal city, but it comes forward as the presence of a past that is now ineffective and as object of reckless consumption. For Assunto, the conflict between this idea of the city and the form of modern city is irreconcilable. In the modern and contemporary city, the aesthetics of proportion and measure and the composition by difference have been replaced by the principle of accumulation and homogenization, by a time without quality that empties the differences of places from the inside in view of an expansion without order and measure. A critical point of separation between the two cities occurs, for Assunto, precisely in the Baroque age, with the opposition between the philosophy of Leibniz, who thinks of the city as a monad and therefore as *diversitas unitate compensata*, and that of Bacon, who celebrates omnipotence of knowledge, configuring it as a technique that subdues nature to the point of dominating and reinventing it. The monad-city, still bearing memories of that Renaissance "measure", is opposed by the city-artifice, which ultimately seeks to destroy nature, foreshadowing in the New Atlantis "a totally urbanized, mechanized world where nothing is natural".[16] Albeit the Baconian conception is still a minority in its time, it is however destined to become the main vector of modern culture since the mid-1700s, expression of a rationalizing and functionalist urbanism. The entire modern movement in architecture is, thus, brought back by Assunto to the knowledge/power that designs the city ex novo, as a technical–functional organization of social life, subjugation–domination or circumscription of nature within well-defined limits, completely in antithesis with that balance between grace and nature that informs the Leibnizian city. On the one hand, in conclusion, there is the primacy of function, on the other, that of representation.

If the dominator of the modern metropolis or megalopolis is the functionalist poetics or antipoetics, the opposition with the Platonic inspiration of the Renaissance and Leibnizian city is brought back by Assunto to the classical bed of the myth, in terms of an opposition between the city of Amphion/Orpheus, where the stones of the buildings are harmoniously arranged by music, and the city of Prometheus, where the theft of fire gives rise to a technique that forgets the Muses, is expression of a ratio separated from nature and mutilated in its will to power. Inevitably, for Assunto, the Promethean city triumphs in modern times, as demonstrates the spirit of European reconstruction after the Second World War, marked by an anxiety to start from scratch, oblivious to what happened, driven by the will to adapt the new image of city to the dominant and pervasive "technologization of the world".

The sense of the opposition outlined by Assunto between the city of Prometheus and that of Amphion/Orpheus overlooks an essential element: the intimate connection between the war and the origins of the *polis*. Recalling this connection shall dispel the suspicion that our reading of Assunto remains a mere digression unrelated to our starting point: the ruin as an intrinsically actual figure of the present in *tempore belli*. Despite the unavoidable intertwining of the two forms-ideas of cities, it is certainly the Promethean one that prevails, along with its own time that – as we have seen – is that of "automatic repetition", of a systematic emptying of the physiognomy of places aimed to make room for the functionality of artifice as a priori neutralization of every event, eager to trivializing, or re-functionalizing the "freedom of the unexpected", the catastrophic break of chance. This certainly does not happen for the Platonic city, for the idea of a city founded and governed by the measure giving shape to the ideal and historical cities of the Renaissance. Suffice it, here, to recall the beginning of the *Laws*, the last Platonic work, where Kleinias the Cretan remembers how war is the end of the constitution of his city for a reason connected to human nature itself: "what most humans call peace he held to be only a name; in fact, for every-one there always exists by nature an undeclared war among all cities".[17] Guarding the laws of the polis must hinge on that, holding that *polemos* concerns the intimate constitution of each of us, to the point that "the first and best of all victories, [is] the victory of oneself over oneself; and being defeated by oneself is the most shameful and at the same time the worst of all defeats".[18] On this basis, the same unit of the Polis is conceived as a single thing, built in the form of a circle, perched "on the highest ground – for the sake of both defense and cleanliness",[19] to appear as a single bastion even if its defense cannot only be entrusted to walls and fortifications, which may turn into ruins at any time.

The same concern to defend the city from the destruction of war dominates Alberti's considerations in Book V of *De re aedificatoria*, with the difference from Plato that here it is the architect's design work being decisive. On this basis, Alberti shows extreme attention to differentiate the construction of the fortress from the city in relation to the form of government (whether it is a king or a tyrant), however aiming to ensure that "a fortress is not made only to parry the assaults, but also to repel the assailants";[20] and in any case, however you want to consider it, "the highest point of the walls or the key of the city, the fortress must be threatening, hard, wild; it must be resistant to sieges and impregnable".[21]

With these remarks, we can go back to the starting point to argue that the ruins produced by war are an internal possibility in the constitution of the image of a city, even in the very heart of Europe or in any case at its borders: in the historical *theatrum* that directly involves it. Paradoxically, the fact that the ruins of war belong to history as a *Trauerspiel*, to the point that the space of its drama has moved from the baroque court to the cities, is considered almost a parenthesis precisely in the conception that Assunto considers as Promethean. A conception which can still be considered as one of the two conceptions of technology opposing each other in Benjamin's essay on the work of art (and in particular in its third version), namely technology as a domination–exploitation of nature versus technology as an expression of a synergistic relationship with it, based on measure and balance. What we shall account for here, thus, is the technology which finds its almost natural outcome in war; and war in this perspective is neutralized in its character of historical caesura in the formation of the city and the States: war, in other words, as an opportunity for profit. What, on the other hand, is never the case for the actors it implies in the armed and destructive conflict. We could thus conclude this second part of our reflection, advancing the thesis according to which the ruins of the present, which forcefully give us back the images of cities devastated by war, reveal the hiatus or dramatic fracture that binds the even different ideas of cities up to the interpenetration of them in a single historically effective image. The empty space of this fracture, sometimes covered by the forgetfulness of a thought without memory, is so suddenly occupied by the ruins as a hyper-object charged with a new-yet-ancient significance. As a wound in the current *imageability* of a city, to borrow the expression used by Kevin Lynch in a very important book,[22] that of the ruin is more than an image. As an effect of war devastation, ruins, in fact, involve individual and collective destinies, public events and private tragedies that intertwine and overlap in the human life and in the very image of a city.

Cities of memories

As Aldo Rossi recalls in his influential book, *The architecture of the city*, it is the horizontal cross-section of archaeologists what offers us a "primordial and eternal fabric of life", like an "immutable pattern"[23] of that irreducible plurality of forms of life, destinies and identities that unite in the stratified image of a city. Together with the sections of the archaeologists, we are reminded of this – Rossi observes – also by the images of European cities after the bombings of the last world war:

> [D]isemboweled houses where, amid the rubble, fragments of familiar places remained standing, with their colors of faded wallpaper, laundry hanging suspended in the air, . . . the untidy intimacy of places.[24]

In the ruins and disembowelments of the bombed cities, it is the intimacy of an individual and family life that is exposed shamelessly; to be disfigured are the homes of childhood as well as childhood itself: an image of "the interrupted destiny of the individual, of his often sad and difficult participation in the destiny of the collective".[25]

What is called into question by the ruins of the war is the same intimate bond that connects, in memory, the identity of each one to the architectural image of the house and to the permanent possibility of its destruction. In the first part (called "Cellar" and followed by "Vestibule" and "Dining Hall") of *Einbahnstraße*'s aphorism titled "No. 113", Benjamin shows himself to be perfectly aware of this connection between ruins and self-memory:

> We have long forgotten the ritual by which the house of our life was erected. But when it is under assault and enemy bombs are already taking their toll, what enervated, perverse antiquities do they not lay

bare in the foundations. What things were interred and sacrificed amid magic incantations, what horrible cabinet of curiosities lies there below, where the deepest shafts are reserved for what is most commonplace.[26]

The motif of a Self-Identity as the construction of that house, of which one's life consists, is here closely bound with the metaphor of war, with what its destruction brings to light: the rituals and sacrifices that marked the time of construction, the once-removed secrets resurfacing, the hidden abysses in what up until then seemed pure and insignificant everyday life. Shedding light with the force of a last-day-flash are the two enigmatic verses (perhaps by Benjamin himself) placed in epigraph to the entire aphorism:

The hours that hold the figure and the form
  Have run their course within the house of dream.[27]

What is true for the house is true for the entire city made up of buildings, streets, places, and forms of life. The gash of houses reduced to ruins while shamelessly displaying broken destinies reveals fragments of that city of memory that is intertwined, individually and collectively, with the historical image in it growing by layers overlapping in apparent disorder. As Aldo Rossi recalls, in this regard, that dark side, that *logos adelos* (unmanifest) that links the foundation of a city to the myth and the ritual dimension cannot be overlooked. Perhaps, it is precisely this dimension, connected to the time–space of the origin that only the ruins of the present seem to reveal, the one that found shelter – surviving in the most unexpected forms – in that dream-house and, therefore, in that city of memory that always trespasses into the oneiric domain, defining an inalienable part of our identity.

In a Proustian dialectic between voluntary and involuntary memory, the city of memory, in its composition of remembrances, dreams, hopes and regrets, both individual and collective, interpenetrates with the historical one to form a single image that carries within itself, in its own same origin, the possibility of ruin both in its effectiveness and in the allegorical power that informs each frame. Thus, in the *theatrum* of a *Trauerspiel* that still shows the melancholic *facies* of history, the city reveals the idea at its origin borders on that of destruction; and this reaffirms the eternity of its ruins. Consequently, our city of memory is always – to cite a Bruce Springsteen's song – our "city of ruins". With a final thought: in light of the last day that always concerns our "here and now", the images layered in the multilevel city existence flow like a fleeting and transitory spectacle; what remains are the rubble of which each building is made up.

The research that Benjamin dedicates to the Berlin of his childhood is effective evidence of this interpenetration of the city of memory with the image that a city historically offers of itself. The exploration of the city, from the lodges to the *Tiergarten*, from the grandparents' house to the *Kaiserpanorama*, renews the child's amazed gaze in writing. To reveal itself even before

24   Rethinking the City

the historic city in the fusion of different epochs marked by its monuments is the city inhabited by mythical powers: the less suitable places become, in the eyes of both the child and the reader, experiences of the threshold, passages to a world populated by gods, demons and witches, as happens with the table under which the child hid from the eyes of adults. Hiding from adults thus assumes the sense of preparing oneself for passages and experiences reserved for the future. As Benjamin himself notes, the images of his metropolitan childhood "perhaps are capable, at their core, of preforming later historical experience".[28] As happens in one of the most famous passages of *Berlin Childhood around 1900*, the one dedicated to the "Victory Column". The "sphere of Grace that encircled the radiant Vittoria overhead"[29] (erected in memory of the battle of Sedan) was contrasted below by an ambulatory in which the child had never dared to enter, fearing to find the grim and terrible images seen in a luxury edition of Dante's *Inferno*:

> To me, the heroes whose exploits glimmered in the portico were, secretly, quite as infamous as the multitudes forced to do penance while being, lashed by whirlwinds, encased in bloody tree stumps, or sealed in blocks of ice. Accordingly, this portico was itself the Inferno.[30]

Thus, in the eyes of Benjamin as a child, an experience of the future war is prefigured. An experience that would have been spared Benjamin: that of hell which constitutes the *other part* of any victory, the same hell of which Sebald writes in *On the Natural History of Destruction*.

Notes

1 "Today" refers to the context of war in Ukraine and Gaza.
2 Simmel, *Philosophische Kultur*, 138.
3 Ibid., 139.
4 Ibid., 143.
5 Ibid., 145 – author's translation.
6 Kant, *Kritik der Urteilskraftt*, § 43.
7 Benjamin, *Origin*, 180.
8 Ibid.
9 Ibid.
10 For the concept of *katastrophikón*, see Desideri, *Walter Benjamin e la percezione*, 124–126. The notion of *katastrophikón* referred to Benjamin is here developed in counterpoint with that of *ekstatikón* defined by Heidegger in *Sein und Zeit*.
11 Borinski, *Die Antike in Poetik*, 193–194, cited in Benjamin, *Origin*, 180.
12 Ibid.
13 See Sebald, *Natural History of Destruction*, 10–70.
14 Assunto, *La città di Anfione*, 61–72 and passim.
15 Ibid., 91–98.
16 Ibid., 132 – author's translation.
17 Plato, *Laws*, 626a [4].
18 Ibid., 626e [5].
19 Ibid., 778c [166].

20 Alberti, *L'Architettura*, 348 [Book V, Chap. III].
21 Ibid., 350 [Book V, Chap. IV].
22 See Lynch, *The Image of the City*.
23 Rossi, *The Architecture of the City*, 22.
24 Ibid.
25 Ibid.
26 Benjamin, *One-Way Street*, 46.
27 Ibid.
28 Benjamin, *Berlin Childhood*, 38.
29 Ibid., 47.
30 Ibid.

Bibliography

Alberti, Leon Battista, *L'Architettura* [*De re aedificatoria*], testo latino a cura di Giovanni Orlandi, Introduzione di Paolo Portoghesi, Milano: Edizioni Il Polifilo, 1966.
Assunto, Rosario, *La città di Anfione e la città di Prometeo. Idea e poetiche della città*, Milano: Jaca Book, 1984.
Benjamin, Walter, *One-Way Street and Other Writings*, translated by Edmund Jephcott and Kingsley Shorter, introduction by Susan Sontag, London: NLB, 1979.
Benjamin, Walter, "On the Concept of History", in *Selected Writings*, Vol. 4, edited by Howard Eiland and Michael W. Jennings, translated by Edmund Jephcott, 389–397, Cambridge, MA: Harvard University Press, 2003.
Benjamin, Walter, *Berlin Childhood around 1900*, translated by Howard Eiland, Cambridge, MA: The Belknap Press of Harvard University Press, 2006.
Benjamin, Walter, *Origin of the German Trauerspiel*, translated by Howard Eiland, Cambridge, MA: Harvard University Press, 2019.
Borinski, Karl, *Die Antike in Poetik und Kunsttheorie von Ausgang des klassischen Altertums bis auf Goethe und Wilhelm von Humboldt, Vol. 1: Mittelalter, Renaissance, Barock*, Leipzig: Dieterich'sche Verlagsbuchhandkung, 1924.
Desideri, Fabrizio, *Walter Benjamin e la percezione dell'arte. Estetica, storia, teologia*, Brescia: Morcelliana, 2018.
Heidegger, Martin, *Sein und Zeit*, Halle: Max Niemeyer, 1927.
Kant, Immanuel, *Kritik der Urteilskraft*, Frankfurt a. M.: Suhrkamp, 2011.
Lukács, Georg, *Geschichte und Klassenbewußtsein*, Berlin: Malik, 1923.
Lynch, Kevin. *The Image of the City*, Cambridge, MA: MIT Press, 1960.
Plato, *Laws*, translated with notes and an interpretive essay by Thomas L. Pangle, Chicago: The University of Chicago Press, 1988.
Rosenzweig, Franz, *Der Stern der Erlösung*, Frankfurt a. M.: Kauffmann, 1921.
Rossi, Aldo, *The Architecture of the City*, introduction by Peter Eisenman, translated by Diane Ghirardo and Joan Ockman, revised for the American edition by Aldo Rossi and Peter Eisenman, Cambridge MA: MIT Press, 1984.
Sebald, Winfried Georg, *On the Natural History of Destruction*, translated by Anthea Bell, New York: Random House, 2003.
Simmel, Georg, *Die Probleme der Geschichtsphilosophie: Eine erkenntnistheoretische Studie*, München: Duncker & Humboldt, 1905.
Simmel, Georg, *Philosophische Kultur. Gesammelte Essais*, Leipzig: Klinkhardt Verlag, 1911.

3 My schizoid city

David Kishik

During the height of the pandemic I used to bike every morning to a small park by the East River to work on what turned out to be a little book called *Self Study*.[1] Whenever I lifted my eyes from the laptop screen, while sipping hot coffee from my thermos, I could see the Manhattan and Brooklyn Bridges stretching right in front of me, under which the Upper New York Bay and the Statue of Liberty set my horizon. But whenever I turned my gaze to the right, to the skyscrapers downtown, I began to reflect back on a larger book of mine, titled *The Manhattan Project*.[2]

This lecture that turned into a paper is an attempt to put these two books in dialogue with one another: to connect my psychoanalytic research on the schizoid position with my urban research on New York, capital of the twentieth century. It begins as a primer on the schizoid position, which might seem irrelevant to the attempt of this collection to rethink the city. But as it progresses, I hope to show the deep implications of this psychogeography, which Freud already toyed with in *Civilization and Its Discontents*.[3]

Freud claims that even the psyche of an infant continues to live in that of the adult. But a city, he shows, functions very differently from a brain. As old parts of a city like Rome are destroyed and new ones rise up, the urban landscape must betray its past. If a city were indeed like a mind, he reasons, then all the different structures that ever occupied this or that block would appear superimposed one on top of the other, just as I can recall the morning of 2020 by the East River and then, without even blinking, the morning of 2022 I spoke at a conference in Lisbon about all of these questions.[4]

The schizoid position may be a personal psychopathology that I both suffer and benefit from. Yet during the pandemic I began to think about it as a widespread social norm. My argument is that the city before, during, and after the pandemic, but especially the city to come, the one in which we are going to live in the future, is what I call a *schizoid city*. This is true about New York, which might be the schizoid capital of the world. But the implications of what follows might ring true in many other places. I therefore wish to consider my schizoid city as a paradigm for something much bigger than itself.

To begin, let us compare *The Phenomenology of Spirit* and *The Devil Wears Prada*, a movie that beautifully illustrates Hegel's conception of

DOI: 10.4324/9781003452928-4

self-consciousness.⁵ The film tells the story of a young wannabe, arriving at the big city with a very specific notion of who she is – a serious journalist. But then she gets a job as an assistant to a fashion editor, the eponymous devil. It is not a coincidence that in *The Arcades Project* Benjamin, following Leopardi, refers to fashion as Madame Death.⁶ In the beginning of the movie, the protagonist indeed sees the fashion world she fell into as pure negativity, as a nihilistic death drive. So she strongly resists her fate, because this is definitely not what she came to be when she moved to this metropolitan hellscape.

But as the movie progresses, the protagonist basically sells her soul to the devil or her boss, to corporate or capitalist America, to the Sisyphean pursuit of new trends, to fashion or death, and becomes an integral part of it. Which seems to be the sad end of the movie, but it's not. Because by the end, the viewer realizes the true moral of this modern tale: that rarely do people come to the city to become what they wanted to be in the first place. We *want* the city to change us; this is what it is *supposed* to do. I personally fault myself for coming to New York, 25 years ago, knowing exactly what I wanted to be, and who I wanted to be with. I wanted to be a philosopher, and I wanted to live with my partner. Both are actually still the case today.

So I am a bad example for the point I am trying to make, which is that we often come to a city not exactly knowing what we want to become, and then we become something we didn't even imagine possible. That is why the movie ends with the protagonist embracing a new identity and becoming her true new self. And this is a perfect Hegelian happy ending if there ever was one. It is what he calls self-consciousness. In the beginning, *myself* is just an *empty I*. It is essentially nothing. I can only become myself, I can only become a subject, I can only become a true *I*, by relating to the thing that is not *I*, to an *other*, who is a negation of myself. I achieve self-consciousness by relating to a consciousness that is not my own.

As a consequence, I am split, I am divided, I am fragmented. I am myself, and I am not myself. "I am twofold within myself", Hegel confessed in a personal letter.⁷ And if this is the case, then the self is always divided in the sense that it is schizoid, since *skhizein* in Greek means *split* or *fragmented*. But we need to better understand why are we divided within ourselves, why are we divided from each other, and why does the experience of the city feel to us so fragmented? Why do I so often feel split from the city in which I live, a city which I love, or hate, or am indifferent toward? And finally, why is the city usually divided from the country or the world that surrounds it?

Here is a quote from *The Divided Self* by R. D. Laing. It describes a schizoid man which Laing calls a shut-up self, which in other places is called shut-in:

> this shut-up self, being isolated, is unable to be enriched by outer experience, and so the whole inner world comes to be more and more impoverished, until the individual may come to feel he is merely a vacuum. The sense of being able to do anything and the feeling of possessing

everything then exist side by side with a feeling of impotence and emptiness. The individual who may at one time have felt predominantly "outside" the life going on *there*, which he affects to despise as petty and commonplace compared to the richness he has *here*, inside himself, now longs to get *inside* life again, and get life *inside* himself, so dreadful is his inner deadness.[8]

An evocative way of thinking about the schizoid position is to imagine a life that doesn't seem to be alive. Sure, at first you get this feeling of a rich inner existence, and a sense that the outside world, or the city outdoors, is poor or even evil. As a result, you tend to separate yourself from this malicious or impoverished surrounding. But if real life is my ability to relate to the thing that is not *I* – for a subject to relate to an object – then sooner or later I am going to feel impoverished within myself, stuck in my closed room. So I decide to venture out. This attempt to come in and out of my relationship to what is *not* me, this in-and-out program, is at the core of the schizoid position. It is basically an aversion to life or a will to nothingness. In this sense, the schizoid ideal is not dissimilar to what Nietzsche calls the ascetic ideal.

If we open the DSM or another professional–psychological list of symptoms that are associated with schizoid individuals, we find the following: introverted, self-sufficient, withdrawn, unemotional, impersonal, indifferent, and ultimately deeply lonely. It wouldn't be a big leap for any reader to personally relate to one or more of these descriptors or relate them to someone you know. But this is not an attempt to pathologize anyone. I treat here the schizoid position as a philosophical position that propels us to rethink city life in the twenty-first century, without passing final judgment about its positive or negative effects.

Consider two iconic modern authors who were associated with the schizoid position. The first one is Kafka. Think about the protagonists in his three unfinished novels and compare them to characters in Shakespeare's plays. Kafka's characters don't seem to have much of a family. They don't really have any substantial relationships. It is not easy to imagine them loving someone or being loved by anyone in a sustainable way. Are they even human? Laing claims that the people both in Shakespeare's and in Kafka's literary universes live inside some kind of a prison, but at least in Shakespeare's prison they find some good company.

In Kafka, there is always an object to which the protagonists want to relate: the law, the castle, America. But this relationship always fails them. It remains deeply frustrating. In Lacan's lingo, we could say that Kafka writes about subjects who relate to objects that are always already lost, so we know deep in our bones that no relationship is ever going to be achieved in those novels. Like mice, a schizoid character ventures out to get some cheese but then retreats back in because of some perceived danger. Kafka once said that he is a cage in search of a bird.[9] This is such a poignant description of the schizoid position.

Or consider "The Burrow", Kafka's short story about an unidentified animal that just digs deeper and deeper holes, tunnels, and underground rooms, trying to avoid a confrontation with some kind of unknown creature.[10] We never know what menace or danger lies outside that leads the animal to dig these deeper and deeper holes. But by the end, we realize that, most probably, there is no clear and distinct danger. The architecture we behold is not an escape route but a grave, which the animal is obviously digging for itself. This is a wonderful illustration of what Klein calls a schizoid-paranoid position.[11]

Compare Kafka to Pessoa, who once wrote a tourist guide about Lisbon, the city where he was born, where he did virtually all his work, and where he died. The most striking thing about this short text by this extraordinary writer is how dreary and uninspired it is. We want to say that Kafka lived in Prague, and Pessoa lived in Lisbon, but this is not quite right. Existentially speaking, they both lived inside themselves. As Zenith's biography makes abundantly clear, everything for Pessoa was essentially a dream.[12] Pessoa wanted to create a nation within his own literature. He was totally self-sufficient or, that, at least, was his highest aspiration. All his different internal objects, all his different heteronyms, can only converse with each other. Though various heteronyms interacted with Lisbon in various ways, it can be argued that Pessoa the man was shut-in to the point everything outside himself, outside his literature, was either redundant or unimportant, including Lisbon.

Rather than Deleuze and Guattari's schizoanalyis, the great philosophers of the schizoid condition are Fairbairn and Guntrip. These two mid-twentieth-century British therapists, associated with the school of object relations theory, are well known within professional psychoanalytic circles, but they are rarely read or referred to in the wider theory world. Their starting point is the presupposition (inspired perhaps by Hegel) that the meaning of life is relations with others.[13] If so, then the schizoid person who withdraws inward, who is shut in, suffers from the worst possible psychological predicament.

"According to my way of thinking", Fairbairn writes,

> everybody without exception must be regarded as schizoid . . . The fundamental schizoid phenomenon is the presence of splits in the ego; and it would take a bold man to claim that his ego has so perfectly integrated as to be incapable of revealing any evidence of splitting at the deepest levels.[14]

From this perspective, we are all, to some extent, divided. We all exist on a schizoid spectrum, even if this term is rarely used or even known, even among people familiar with psychoanalytic theory. Again, to be extra clear, the schizoid condition is treated here not only as a personal affliction but also as a social configuration, which we must make sense of within an urban context and far beyond.

How does one become the schizoid person that one is? The answer, for Fairbairn, has something to do with what he calls the moral defense. Imagine this scenario: a little girl with a broken arm arrives at the hospital with her father. Her abusive dad was the one who broke her arm, but what will the girl say to a doctor or a nurse who comes to examine her? She will rarely say, "Daddy did it". She will probably say something along the lines of, "I did it myself", or "I tripped and fell" or even, "I deserved it". Why would she say that? Why can't she face the truth?

Fairbairn explains this situation by saying that "it is better to be a sinner in a world ruled by God than to live in a world ruled by the Devil".[15] This is basically Augustine's point: we see that there is evil in the world, but why? And why are we having trouble to declare that God is the culprit? So we will say instead that we, humans, are the original sinners. We are responsible for the evils of this world. Because we want to keep believing in the goodness of God or Dad. It is very difficult to live in a world where we recognize that the metaphoric or the actual father is, like every human, both good *and* bad. So we tend to create these idealized splits, and we imagine this perfect father and perfect God, and then we turn ourselves into little devils.

However, the opposite move can often be as tempting. According to the moral defense, I think that the world or the city is good, and that I am the one who is not good, so I must split and separate myself from the world or the city, or else they will be contaminated by my evil ways. But the inverse fantasy can also make perverse sense. We hear people say all the time that they hate the city, or that they hate the world, or that they hate other people. In such cases, we separate ourselves from the surrounding to keep our supposed purity, goodness, or perfection. This is what I call the immoral defense: instead of idealizing the other, I idealize myself as a marker of the good.

But, of course, evil resides in the very gaze that sees evil all around itself.[16] If all I see around me is evil, if I go out into the city and all that I smell is stench, then maybe I smell just as bad? This is how we need to think about the infamous line from Sartre that hell is other people. Hell is not really other people, and the city is not hell (just as the city is not heaven). Hell is the life of the person who *thinks* that hell is other people. If you think that other people are hell, or that the city is hell, then *this thought* is true hell. But of course, it is in your head, for the most part. The critical stance is not simply in the world; it is not an objective judgment of some miserable state of affairs. Critics must be implicated in their own critique.

Both the moral and immoral defenses lead to the same end result: I build a wall between me and the world or me and the city. Either the city (or other people) aggress me, or I aggress the city (or other people). It could even merely be a microaggression, but I still feel the need to build a thick protection that encases me and thus divides me from you. I can build a wall to separate me from you, or you from me, because I think that either I am going to defile you, or you are going to defile me. This is the schizoid logic in a nutshell (both literally and idiomatically).

The mantra in object relations theory is that we seek persons not pleasures. It is a direct jab at Freud, who assumes that we are driven by the pleasure principle. He thinks that a subject has an innate drive that can be released by interacting with this or that object that fits the bill. This object will enable the subject to get some release from the tension that was built inside and hence to get some satisfaction. But what is an object, for an object relations theorist? An object is another person that a subject relates to, that a human has emotions toward, that is *cathected*. And what are pleasures from this perspective? Pleasures are signposts on the way to relate to other people. Pleasure for pleasure's sake can easily be a marker of a difficulty in forming said relations.

If I have some pleasurable experience with you, I seek first and foremost you and not the pleasure. The pleasure (or pain) is still very important but mainly as a guide that will allow me to navigate the landscape of my interpersonal relations. I don't just use you as an object to satisfy my pleasure that I may have had even before I was born and certainly before we met. This is the main difference between a drive theory and a relational theory, between Freud and Fairbairn. Both Klein and Lacan still hold on to this fantasy that Freud calls a drive. Object relations theory doesn't consider the drive a necessary hypothesis. Instead, it asks us to operate according to the reality principle, to situate ourselves by understanding our place among other people. And *other people* is what *reality* means from this perspective of object relations theory.

Guntrip argues that schizoid problems represent a flight from life while Oedipal problems represent a struggle to live. A schizoid person just wants to stay born. There's no death drive at play. You just want to stay alive in the full sense of the word, because your tendency (I wouldn't call it a drive) is to withdraw, to go back and retreat, regress back into the womb, where everything is indistinguishable, unseparated, not yet fragmented. In the beginning of life there is no division into subject and object, good and bad, nature and nurture, self and other. So the most difficult and most important task of every schizoid person is to stay in the world, and to stay engaged with the city in all its unidealized multitudes.

From this perspective, the Oedipal complex is good for the schizoid, who prefers to sleep with Mommy and kill Daddy than to feel *nothing*, which is what an indifferent schizoid ultimately feels. At least I am in the world. Conflict is therefore a thing to seek out rather than avoid. "When you cannot get what you want from the person you need", Guntrip writes, "instead of getting angry you may simply go on getting more and more hungry".[17] Anger leads to aggression that leads to depression. Hunger leads to a schizoid position where one is constantly searching for the other person.

Love made hungry is therefore another powerful way of thinking about the schizoid position. It is a kind of social malnutrition or even self-starvation. As a consequence, we cannot tell a schizoid, like the Beatles, that "all you need is love". This is akin to telling an anorexic person, "all you need is food". Yes, I know that I need love, just as I know that I need food, but there is something that doesn't allow me to really seek it out, digest it, and get nourished by it.

Indifference is a hallmark of the schizoid position, which is not too far from what Simmel calls urban *blasé*.[18] Guntrip says that

> retreat into indifference is the true opposite of love, which is felt to be too dangerous to express. Want no one, make no demands, abolish all external relationships, and be aloof, cold, without any feeling, do not be moved by anything.[19]

The Stoics are from this perspective textbook schizoids. Love may destroy: this is also the logic of the pandemic. Biologically, if I hug grandma, I may kill her, I may destroy her. But maybe she is the one infected, so she will destroy me. But this is a psychological issue even more than just a biological one.

There is always a looming danger behind sharing love and intimately relating to one another. If we are afraid that such love may destroy, from either direction (I will devour her or she will devour me), then we are going to retreat into a false schizoid security. As an urban society, we then tend to slowly but surely fragment. When everybody is alienated from everybody else, pleasure is simply not going to cut it. The name of the game is not really *Sex and the City* but *Love in the City*. I used to see the cities I'm most familiar with as a reservoir of infinite carnal temptations. These days they tend to narrow down to the handful of real relations I still nurture in each.

What follows is a quote from Auster's *New York Trilogy*. It is a description of a late-twentieth-century *flâneur*:

> New York was an inexhaustible space, a labyrinth of endless steps, and no matter how far he walked, no matter how well he came to know its neighborhoods and streets, it always left him with the feeling of being lost. Lost, not only in the city, but within himself as well. Each time he took a walk he felt as though he were leaving himself behind, and by giving himself up to the movement of the streets, by reducing himself to a seeing eye, he was able to escape the obligation to think, and this, more than anything else, brought him a measure of peace, a salutary emptiness within.[20]

Over the years I grew suspicious of the beloved figure of the *flâneur*. We like to fetishize this nineteenth-century Parisian character. We are enchanted by him (but why not her?). The *flâneur* is like the secret prince of the modern city, if you ask Benjamin. But as I reread the by-now canonical descriptions of the *flâneur*, I began to see a disturbed, isolated, or simply sad individual. Is he really moving through the city streets, or is he more similar to a hamster on a wheel? Who does he relate to? The man of the crowd in Poe is not feeling comfortable in his own company. This is why he seeks out the crowd. How does one become as empty as a *flâneur*? Though he has "the keys to the streets", the urban gate remains for him forever impassable.[21]

In Auster, Quinn, the character that is described in the beginning of the book as a *flâneur*, turns by the story's end to a homeless man. In so doing, the nineteenth-century Parisian *flâneur* metamorphosed into New York's homeless person, both as the quintessence or the paradigm of the modern city and as a figuration of the schizoid position. I like to imagine a time travel machine with which I land in nineteenth-century Paris. Upon landing, I would immediately look for a *flâneur* and just stop him, in an attempt to figure out who he is and how did he get there. Will he be willing to just sit down, have coffee, and talk to me? Will he invite me over to his dreary and lonely room? Will I invite him to mine? Could we find a way to relate to each other? My suspicion is that the *flâneur* rarely had relationships with anybody, and this is what I find most disturbing.

I conceptualize the homeless as an exhausted *flâneur*.[22] To be homeless is to bring to a standstill the constant movement of the urban stroll. The homeless person usually sits or lays down. Because what is there to really see or do in a city, in this capital of capital, if one is homeless? So I wasn't at all surprised to find the following quote in a first responder's guide to abnormal psychology, which is a manual that police officers and ambulance workers consult in preparation for their interaction with homeless people in New York and other cities. Here is the description:

> Law enforcement personnel will be familiar with the homeless individual who wanders the streets alone, never speaking to anyone, neither involved with nor interested in any close relationships. It is likely that many of the homeless could be diagnosed as schizoid personalities who experience no pleasure in interpersonal relationships, avoid closeness with anyone, and engage exclusively in solitary activities. If officers were to engage such a person in conversation, they would find a very cold, detached, and indifferent individual who would display little emotion and would be unlikely to respond to any praise or criticism that might be offered.[23]

You can tell a schizoid person that she's amazing or that she's horrible. But within her entrenched state of indifference she wouldn't really care about either positive or negative feedback. It wouldn't change her position. There is this chicken and egg problem when it comes to mental health and social class. Those who suffer from deep psychopathological problems, but they also lack a good support system (economic, social, familial, communal), might very well end up in the streets. If you do have a good enough support system, you may be flown over the Atlantic to give a talk in a conference and then be asked to publish it in an essay collection.

We can think of the homeless person as an economic refugee, instead of a political one. Homelessness is a paradigm case of modern urban life, because it distills this basic sense of abandonment, which is also the origin of the schizoid position. What is it to feel abandoned by the metropolis, by the mother city? Is the city *good enough*, as Winnicott would call it, toward its inhabitants? How can the city release or drop us with little prior warning and zero grief?

For Winnicott, the good-enough caregiver holds the infant, creating what he calls a holding environment.[24] But does the city hold us from falling into pieces and fragmenting? Do we live in a mother city or a city of orphans? Don't we all need to hold each other, even as adults, lest we fall? By holding I simply mean being with each other, loving and caring for each other. Just *being*, rather than *doing*. But can capital care, or feel, or even love? And if not, can modernity produce anything other than husks of desubjectified subjects, devoid of their own inner true selves?

Let us turn to a famous line from Jacobs's *The Death and Life of Great American Cities*, where she speaks about how city sidewalks "bring together people who do not know each other in an intimate, private social fashion and in most cases do not care to know each other in that fashion".[25] The urban others, beside the very few who you know personally, are neither friends nor enemies; they are strangers. You don't love them, or hate them, but just kind of indifferent toward 99 percent of the people in your city. So what is a city? Could it ultimately be a conglomeration of indifferent strangers?

In *The Lonely City*, Olivia Laing depicts the urban space as this vast and pervasive stretch of loneliness.[26] There are, supposedly, eight million lonely individuals in New York. But what is the source of this sense of isolation? The book does not really explain the lonely condition as much as describes it, albeit beautifully. I found it strange, though, that she never mentions R. D. Laing, who, as we have already seen, gave us one of the best causal explanation for how people turn into lonely individuals: precisely because they are entangled in the schizoid logic, because they cope with a sense of abandonment by pretending not to need anybody but themselves.[27] We should not take for granted the fact that we are lonely, fragmented from each other, from the city, while the city, in turn, is divided from the rest of the world. We owe it to ourselves, and each other, to figure out, with the help of psychoanalysis and adjacent discursive fields, why do we fall into this lonely predicament.

And we need to learn how to think about our own city not just as a cluster of strangers that we can network with or use to get ahead, or get something done, or get some desire fulfilled. Can the city simply stand for the very few people we have meaningful relationships with and strong emotions toward, those we truly love, but maybe also those we really hate? Think of all the actual family and friends and lovers that you have, maybe even those you no longer have, because they are dead, or because they broke up with you, or you with them, but they still exist, like ghosts walking in the nightly streets. *The Manhattan Project* opens with a discussion of NY, by which I did not only mean the initials of New York but also the initials of the person I came to this city to live with. For me, at least, this city has always been conflated with this singular person that I am still intimately related to.

To understand the fragmented city even better, we must go back to *The Divided City*, the title of Nicole Loraux's intricate history of civil war in

Ancient Greece. The word for civil war in Greek is *stasis*. It seems misleading to think about *stasis* in modern English, where it denotes inactivity or immobility. How can *stasis* also stand for strife, a movement of people at each other's throats within the constellation of a civil war? Loraux's answer is that

> the city is a mixture as long as citizens of all kinds mix with one another. Only the stirring ensures the success of the process: harmony is not static . . . If there is no agitation, there is division.[28]

The reference here is to an anecdote about Heraclitus, who attended a conference of sorts in Athens, where everybody was talking about the idea of civil harmony. After those in attendance gave their opinions, they finally asked Heraclitus what he thought about civil harmony. But he just remained silent. Instead of speaking, he made a little performance: he took a cup, added water, barley, and some other ingredients, took a spoon, and stirred it. He showed the potion to everybody and basically said, *behold, this is civil harmony*.

We need mixture. *Stasis* is civil war because we are stuck in our positions. We don't interact with each other, we don't exchange germs or ideas, we don't express hate and love in close physical and spiritual proximity. This is a schizoid standstill, and this is what leads to the divided city, where we are all shut in within ourselves, unable to even agitate each other, let alone care about one another. So this is why stasis makes perfect sense as a word for civil war even today, because civil war is not really about being at each other's throats but about having each other at arm's length. Stasis therefore reminds me of how we were during the pandemic. But how closer to each other are we today, as we still cherish our work from home, as we remain unmixed, or unstirred, and unmoved, by others.

Instead of fragmentation, I would like to save the last word to the idea of reconfiguration. In the *Arcades Project*, Benjamin laments that "we have grown very poor in threshold experiences".[29] This is even more true today, almost a century later: what happens when our home turns into our office, but also into our private theater and our private restaurant? When do we experience this threshold between the intimate and the communal? We leave nothing behind: neither war nor work, neither private pain nor public shame, neither the sacred nor the profane, neither our nature nor our culture. Modern life's porosity precludes the introduction of clear boundaries.

Many big modern cities still feature majestic yet strange arches, like the Arc de Triomphe in Paris, Brandenburg Gate in Berlin, Rua Augusta in Lisbon, and the Washington Square Arch in New York. But why did the city's elders find the urge to build replicas of triumphal arches from Ancient Rome, under which the army passed as it returned from yet another colonial conquest? The Roman soldiers had to walk under such an arch. By doing so, they passed through a threshold that separated war from peace, soldier from citizen, someone who can kill a person with impunity from someone who needs to pay their taxes. The arches also symbolized protection from any bad spirits and even pandemics: the path was believed to be too narrow for such ills to pass through, along with the men who marched through the gate.

Which leads me to propose a public art project or a piece of performance art. When these lines were written, in 2022, we still lived in some twilight zone, since we didn't quite know where we stand. Was this still a pandemic time, when we had to be separated from each other, or was this already the day after, a new state of peace? Were we finally able to come back to be with each other? If only we could have had a procession in New York and other cities, in which the citizens passed under their gates to symbolize the end of the "War on Covid", where they could experience the threshold and leave the pandemic behind, creating a moment that separates between these two monumental events.

At the top of the Washington Square Arch there is a quote from George Washington himself, with which I would like to leave you: "The event is in the hand of God".[30] The Heideggerian *Ereignis*, the event, is not in the hand of any single human being, not even the man who liberated New York from tyranny, where he was later sworn as the first US sovereign, in what was then the new nation's temporary capital. Only a God can save our cities. As for our states, it is about time to admit that they are all lost causes.

Notes

1 Kishik, *Self Study*.
2 Kishik, *The Manhattan Project*.
3 Freud, *Civilization and its Discontents*, 44.
4 Kishik, *The Manhattan Project*, 217.
5 Hegel, *Phenomenology of Spirit*, 104–119. Frankel, *The Devil Wears Prada*.
6 Benjamin, *The Arcades Project*, 62.
7 Hegel, quoted in Kishik, *Self Study*, 24.
8 Laing, *The Divided Self*, 75.
9 Kafka, *The Blue Octavo Notebooks*, 22.
10 Kafka, "The Burrow".
11 Klein, "Notes on Some Schizoid Mechanisms".
12 Zenith, *Pessoa*, 669–671.
13 Guntrip, *Schizoid Phenomena*, 19–20.
14 Fairbairn, *Psychoanalytic Studies*, 7–8.
15 Ibid., 67.
16 Žižek, quoted in Kishik, *Self Study*, 23.
17 Guntrip, *Schizoid Phenomena*, 24.
18 Simmel, "The Metropolis and Mental Life".
19 Guntrip, *Schizoid Phenomena*, 27.
20 Auster, *The New York Trilogy*, 4.
21 Benjamin, *The Arcades Project*, 437–438 [M 11,1].
22 Kishik, *The Manhattan Project*, 184.
23 Dorfman and Walker, *First Responder's Guide*, 112.
24 Winnicott, *The Child, the Family*, 52.
25 Jacobs, *The Death and Life*, 55.
26 Laing, *The Lonely City*.
27 Laing, *The Divided Self*.

28 Loraux, *The Divided City*, 109–110.
29 Benjamin, *The Arcades Project*, 494 [O 2a, 1].
30 Washington, quoted in Kishik, *The Manhattan Project*, 236.

Bibliography

Auster, Paul, *The New York Trilogy*, New York: Penguin, 1990.
Benjamin, Walter, *The Arcades Project*, translated by Howard Eiland and Kevin McLaughlin, Cambridge, MA: The Belknap Press of Harvard University Press, 1999.
Dorfman, William and Walker, Lenore, *First Responder's Guide to Abnormal Psychology: Applications for Police Firefighters and Rescue Personnel*, New York: Springer, 2007.
Fairbairn, William Ronald D., *Psychoanalytic Studies of the Personality*, London: Routledge, 1952.
Frankel, David, *The Devil Wears Prada*, Los Angeles: 20th Century Fox, 2006.
Freud, Sigmund, *Civilization and Its Discontents*, translated by James Strachey, New York: W. W. Norton & Company, 2005.
Guntrip, Harry, *Schizoid Phenomena, Object-Relations and the Self*, London: Routledge, 1992.
Hegel, Georg W. F., *Phenomenology of Spirit*, translated by A. V. Miller and with an analysis of the text and foreword by J. N. Findlay, Oxford: Oxford University Press, 1977.
Jacobs, Jane, *The Death and Life of Great American Cities*, New York: Vintage, 1992.
Kafka, Franz, "The Burrow", in *The Complete Stories*, edited by Nahum N. Glatzer, 325–359, New York: Schocken Books, 1946.
Kafka, Franz, *The Blue Octavo Notebooks*, edited by Max Brod and translated by Ernst Kaiser and Eithne Wilkins, Cambridge, MA: Exact Change, 1991.
Kishik, David, *The Manhattan Project: A Theory of a City*, Stanford, CA: Stanford University Press, 2015.
Kishik, David, *Self Study: Notes on the Schizoid Condition*, Berlin: ICI Berlin Press, 2023.
Klein, Melanie, "Notes on Some Schizoid Mechanisms", *International Journal of Psycho-Analysis* 27 (1946): 99–110.
Laing, Olivia, *The Lonely City: Adventures in the Art of Being Alone*, New York: Picador, 2016.
Laing, Ronald D., *The Divided Self: An Existential Study in Sanity and Madness*, London: Penguin, 2010.
Loraux, Nicole, *The Divided City: On Memory and Forgetting in Ancient Athens*, translated by Corinne Pache and Jeff Fort, New York: Zone Books, 2002.
Simmel, Georg, "The Metropolis and Mental Life", in *The Blackwell City Reader*, edited by Gary Bridge and Sophie Watson, 103–110, Malden – Oxford: Blackwell, 2010.
Winnicott, Donald, *The Child, the Family, and the Outside World*, London: Penguin, 1964.
Zenith, Richard, *Pessoa: A Biography*, New York: Liveright, 2021.

4 Lisbon's phantom limb syndrome

Lineaments of spectral ethnography

Andrea Pavoni

*Pelo Tejo vai-se para o Mundo.
Para além do Tejo há a America.*[1]

Introduction

The contemporary urban condition is, increasingly, one of fragmentation. Under the exhilarating, ever-accelerated machination of capital desire, cities enter less and less fathomable circuits of financial speculation whose complexity and scale exceed the experience of the inhabitants and the agency of the actors involved. As a result, urban spaces are stretched and bent, folded and hollowed out in many ways. Some may be deterritorialised to an extent that their fate becomes dependent on financial–economic conditions that have no longer any embedding with their socio-material properties. Others may be slowed down to the point that time, there, seems to have frozen. While these dynamics compose and recompose planetary urbanisation at an unintelligible rhythm, the normative image of the smart, creative, green, liveable, cool ... city adds cosmetic layers on the urban, making physically distant neighbourhoods overlap and physically adjacent neighbourhoods drift apart. How to account for this condition? How to make sense of the experience of fragmentation that ensues? Most importantly, how to do so by "remain[ing] focused on the fragmentary", as Walter Benjamin was able to, that is, by meeting urban fragments on their own terms rather than explaining them (away) via structural determinism and dialectical elucidation?[2] This is the challenge this chapter takes up, looking at the riverfront of Marvila and Beato, two boroughs on the east side of Lisbon, Portugal. In the last decade, the Marvila and Beato Riverfront [MBR], a tiny stretch of land, sitting between the river Tagus and the railway line, has been drifting away, socio-economically, financially and aesthetically, from the wider part of their boroughs, sitting west of the railway. It all began with the railway, the country's first, a wound in the urban fabric around which unactualised futures, abandoned pasts and alternative presents have been tangled up. The text seeks to attend to these stratifications by exploring their historical development and attuning to their spectral materiality.

DOI: 10.4324/9781003452928-5

Figure 4.1 Map of Lisbon highlighting the Marvila and Beato Riverfront.
Source: Author.

Trauma

In his unorthodox Freudian-Marxist blend, Benjamin showed us how to refrain from exercising the explanatory determinism of rigid Marxism while keeping in sight its critique of political economy. He did so by treating ideological representations not as a mimetic reflection of socio-economical structures but as their distorted expression, which often comes to be phantasmagorically materialised in the urban fabric.[3] His theoretical and methodological toolbox is an invaluable resource to explore the political aesthetics of social imaginaries as they materialise on the urban surface in allegorical forms, as dreams do. Interpreting these dreams requires a peculiar art of noticing, researching and writing – hence Benjamin's experimentation with *flânerie*, hashish, surrealism, montage and so on. In his recent work on Iquitos, Peru, Japhy Wilson provided a compelling example of what this may entail, proposing a surrealist methodology of researching and writing aimed at deconstructing the paranoiac imaginaries that feed contemporary urbanisation by disentangling them from the materiality of the built environment.[4] I have particularly been attracted by Wilson's JG Ballard-inspired suggestion that "the interpretation of external reality through the prism of psychotic breakdown might provide a more appropriate approach to our current predicament than those of state and academic sense-making".[5] This effort resonates with works on urban trauma that have come out in the last decade, mostly engaging with the consequences of shocking events – for example, wars, disasters, attacks – by exploring their embedding in the urban.[6] As Jay Emery summarises, "a focus on urban trauma enables a theorisation of the embodied and affective impacts, as well as the politics entangled with them".[7] I believe such an approach is particularly promising. Moving beyond the causal explanation and self-evident observation, it allows to attend to those spaces and times "that didn't quite fit with what was happening around them. Spaces ever so slightly out of joint, where the anomalous, the marginal, while clearly visible, remained so slightly undetectable".[8]

Spectrality

The urban trauma I am interested in exploring here, in fact, does not result from specific events, let alone violent or catastrophic ones, but rather emerges as a slow and protracted "wearing out" of the urban fabric.[9] In the MBR, this has been the result of the schizophrenic juxtapositions of desire and nostalgia, development and decline, hope and resignation, that the place has undergone since 19th-century industrialisation all the way to 21st-century start-up urbanism. To explore this complexity, I mobilise a specific neuropathic pain that takes the form of a delusional, psycho-physiological hallucination, the phantom limb syndrome, investigating its spectral entrenchment in the atmosphere and built environment of the MBR. Justin Armstrong defines "spectral ethnography" as a methodology aimed to explore abandoned spaces – he refers, for instance, to Hall's "un-spaces", Augé's non-places – by attending to the felt absence of the past presences that can be experienced in them and the material-embodied relations through which they are embedded onto the urban fabric.[10] I believe its scope can be expanded. What essentialising notions such as Augé's fail to grasp, in fact, is "the constitutive role of non-sites in all sites" of capitalist modernity, that is, the fact that under the spatial logic of global capitalism, non-places proliferate *within* the composition of each place.[11] It is not simply abandoned spaces that lend for a spectral ethnography: every urban space is already haunted by the force of what is not there, no longer or not yet: every urban experience is, to some extent, ghostly.[12] Hence, this text is based on a spectral ethnography I conducted on the MBR, mixing archival research and psychogeographical perambulations, with the purpose of attending to the embodied materiality of the imaginaries that are there frictionally juxtaposed. I am aware that the relation between the MBR and such historically protracted and complex dynamics can only be partially accounted for, let alone in a book chapter. This is not a problem, however, if we get rid of the totalising aspiration, explanatory conventions and conventional structure of the academia. In introducing his intoxicating exploration of shamanism, Michael Taussig observes that to "release . . . the enormous energy of history" that lies entrapped within the linear narration of historicism – what Benjamin did by diffracting such a linearity through the principle of montage – "special modes of presentation" are needed, modes that go "against the magic of academic rituals of explanation . . . with their alchemical promise of yielding system from chaos".[13] Inspired by this suggestion, I organised the following text as a fragmentary exposition in which theoretical reflection, archive material and psychogeographical account are juxtaposed in a series of self-sustaining section, via a non-linear montage, as an attempt to adhere more closely to the sense of fragmentation and hallucinatory juxtaposition I have been researching and experiencing in the MBR.

Mirante

In *Rua de Marvila*, in the homonymous neighbourhood, a short alleyway next to a car service takes to a quirky tower, rising from a jumble of wires, hanging clothes and corrugated roofs. Built in the 17th century by the Marquis of Marialva, its romantic balcony testifies for the refashioning it underwent in the 19th century while the tags and the cemented entrance for its last, turbulent decades. The tower, or lookout [*mirante*], hangs perilously on a cliff just over the railway, inaugurated in 1856, Portugal's first, an early achievement by the engineer and politician António Maria de Fontes Pereira de Melo. Fontes, who was said to be obsessed with railways,[14] was given the newly formed Portuguese ministry of *Public Work, Commerce and Industry* one year after the 1851 military insurrection that brought about the so-called *Regeneração*, a period of relative political stability characterised by a marked ideology of progress that championed economic development and infrastructural modernisation, with the aim to bring what was perceived as a hitherto poor and backward country at the level of the *civilised* ones. The period is known as *Fontismo*, after Fontes, who would eventually serve as Prime Minister (1871–1887). Under his guide, Portugal pursued its own way to modernisation through a mix of infrastructural development and spectacular display, with railways and bridges playing a prominent role. On 28 October 1856, it is said that the king Dom Pedro V observed the train's inaugural journey from the Marialva tower. From there, across the unbuilt landscape, the train was visible almost to infinity, as if it were progress' vanishing point.[15] Other accounts situate the king inside the train. Whatever the location of his *body natural*, it is likely the young Pedro was enjoying himself. Perfectly embodying the spirit of Fontismo, in his earlier formative travels across the continent, rather than museums, monuments or ancient ruins, he had toured "a Europe of iron bridges as monuments of sophisticated engineering, one of industrial technology and exhibitions".[16]

Industrialisation

Stretching between Parque das Nações to the north and the train station of Santa Apolonia to the south, the MBR is separated from the rest of Marvila and Beato by the railway track. West of the railway lies the valley of Chelas, once a rural landscape of *quintas* (estates), palaces and convents, where Lisbon's aristocracy came to rest. After the liberal revolution (1820) had led to the dismantlement of much of their properties, the 19th century-capitalist expansion retuned the area to the rhythm of industrialisation. The logistical advantage of its position, between the railway and the river, meant that the MBR was soon crowded with factories and deposits of tobacco, sugar, soap, wine, phosphorus, rubber, flour and weapons. The atmosphere was filled with their smells, the soil with their toxic pollutants. A vast population of workers came to inhabit the land west of the railway, often living in *bairros de lata* (informal settlements), a dense communal living around which a strong sense of sociality emerged while the negative reputation the area still suffers as of today from the outside began to materialise.[17]

Material progress

At the time of Fontismo, a lively debate in the country opposed those who insisted that Portugal's way to modernity required "material progress" to be complemented by "moral progress", that is, political and social advancement; and those who believed, like Fontes, that Portugal had more important "material" necessities that needed to be addressed first with urgency and efficacy.[18] In a climate heavily influenced by positivistic science and an optimist teleology of progress, Fontismo assumed the contours of a socio-technical imaginary through which the relation between politics and the betterment of social life would be framed in industrial and infrastructural terms.[19] While a similar process could be observed at the time around Europe and beyond, in a peripheral and socio-economically backward South European country like Portugal, this familiar imaginary did assume a further delusional connotation, linking modernisation with the quest to *bridge the gap* with the European elite Portugal deeply felt belonging to, given its past imperial greatness.[20]

Phantasmagoria

"Every epoch dreams the one that follows it", said Jules Michelet, a quote Benjamin was particularly fond of.[21] An epoch's dreams are often permeated by mythical elements, utopian images that idealistically promise to overcome (class) conflict and contradiction. While, as Ernst Bloch taught him, the utopian impulse these images contain should not be hastily dismissed as mere ideology, for Benjamin, according to Buck-Morss, "it was upon the transforming mediation of matter that the hope of utopia ultimately depended: technology's capacity to create the not-yet-known".[22] Benjamin believed that the technological advancement of the 19th century, insofar as foregrounding the "functional" aspect of technology over what he dismissively termed the aestheticising, "ornamental style" of architecture, held the capacity to unfold the potential of technology itself, providing the necessary *mediation* that collective dreams required to materialise. Hence his penchant for engineers: "It was the engineers who, together with workers, gave shape to the 'new' nature of industrial forms: railroads, machines, and bridges".[23] Yet, all too often, engineering feats ended up being themselves monumentalised as aesthetic expressions of progress, seeking to conceal the latter's failure to actually encompass the wider society. As the hybris of progress materialised in grand infrastructures, a series of contradictions ensued, between functionality and spectacle, pragmatism and exhibitionism, eventually turning technological advancement into mere phantasmagoria.

Exposição

In 1865, Porto hosted the first International Exhibition to be held outside of England and France. A replica of the Crystal Palace – built in London for the 1851 International Exhibition – provided a material statement to the country's ambition, "validating its position among the first-order nations as regards social progress", as a commentator put it then.[24] 133 years later, a few kilometres north of the MBR, in Parque das Nações, Lisbon hosted Portugal's second international exhibition. It was a chance for the city to regain the international visibility it once had as capital of an ultramarine empire and to crawl out of the consequences of the dramatic economic crisis of the 1980s. With a host of scintillating new buildings, parks, artworks and a novel riverfront, the 1998 Expo turned what had become a landscape of industrial corpses into a shiny heterotopia of colonial *saudade* where everything, from architecture to toponymy, was conjured to celebrate the glorious age of discoveries – while glossing over its violent unfolding. The *Vasco da Gama* bridge, Lisbon's second – after the iconic *25 de Abril*, inaugurated in 1966 – and by then Europe's longest, was inaugurated for the occasion. This remarkable regeneration project symbolised a renewed urban condition for the city, embodying the promise that it would spill over the surroundings.[25]

De-industrialisation

The economic crises that followed the end of the dictatorship kick-started a dramatic process of de-industrialisation which led to the closure of the majority of factories, turning the MBR into a polluted post-industrial wasteland, socially and logistically separated from the rest of the city: a nostalgic fragment of an era that was no longer. On the west side of the railway, the slow relocation of informal housing inhabitants into social housing projects would later create high-density bubbles of mono-class residents. These building complexes, whose design in many cases involved famous architects, were carried out with often uncoordinated planning strategies and remained vastly isolated, separated by an oversized road network that fragmented the valley into vast tracts of dilapidated land lacking pedestrian infrastructures and decent public transports. In 1964 and 1992, two strategic plans sought to tackle the main urban questions of the Chelas valley – its internal fragmentation, the separation from the rest of the city, the question of housing –, for the most part failing to do so.[26]

Saudade

Eduardo Lourenço relates the proverbial Portuguese *saudade* (nostalgia) to the remarkable and relatively short-lived imperial greatness the small country achieved in the 16th century and to the long decline that followed since. *Saudade*, accordingly, would be an affective orientation towards a future which is predicated upon the obsessive attempt to reproduce a past whose conditions are long gone, according to the assumption that "if once there was greatness, then there must be forever".[27] The consequence, argues Lourenço, is that the Portuguese consciousness oscillates between a complex of inferiority for the present situation and a complex of superiority for the glorious past, a mismatch between the *central* position Portugal believes it deserves to occupy in the world and the reality of its century-long peripherality. This suggestive interpretation is consistent with the climate of Fontismo, in which "the willingness and effort to appropriate the paths of modernity contrasted with the impoverished country where a discourse of 'behindness' and 'backwardness' embedded the national mind and the national printed public sphere".[28] The contradiction, that Lourenço believes Portugal began to become aware of particularly at this time, was concealed beneath the spectacle of engineering works at home and colonial imperialism abroad, as emphatically captured by the photography of Karl Emil Biel.[29] Often, the collective is "not even aware that it is dreaming", writes Susan Buck-Morss, paraphrasing Benjamin, "with the inevitable result that symbol turns into fetish, and technology, the means for realizing human dreams, is mistaken for their actualization".[30] Fontismo, in fact, perverted the 19th-century desire for emancipation into an imperialistic dream of self-affirmation. As a result, it not only left Portugal extremely rural, poor and with one of the highest illiteracy rates in Western Europe. In its attempt to catch up with the European "elite", Fontismo did also overstretch the country beyond its actual capacities, until reliance on private initiative and foreign debt backfired, triggering a dramatic economic crisis that led to bankruptcy in 1892. At that time, by severing its dream vision of expanding its African colonies, the British Empire's *Ultimatum* had already awakened Portugal to the unpracticality of its colonial ambitions and the reality of its imperial subalternity.[31]

Bridges

In 1876, Miguel Carlos Correia Pais drew the first official plan for a bridge over the Tagus. A visionary character, Pais also proposed various suspended viaducts connecting the hills of a city he wanted to turn into a cosmopolitan capital.³² His bridge was to take off just over a Carmelite Convent, the *Convento das Grilas*, in the MBR, about a kilometre south of the tower of Marialva. For the engineering capabilities of the time, bridging the two sides of the wide estuary of the river facing Lisbon was an anachronistic quest. Yet the feat inspired many writers, engineers, and politicians belonging to a rising bourgeoisie that wanted to raise Lisbon's international profile to the level of other European capitals.³³ When in 1897 the convent gave way to the Manutenção Militar, a factory for the supply of bread and biscuits for the army, the chief engineer Joaquim Renato Batista argued that this would have allowed Portugal to "stand shoulder to shoulder with the 'civilised populations'".³⁴ A similar, implicit desire of recognition can be seen in the visionary writings of those – like the engineer Melo de Matos, the symbolist writer Fialho de Almeida, or the journalist Reinaldo Ferreira – that, lamenting the backward Lisbon of the early 20th century, fantasised on a future Lisbon that, via grandiose monuments and futuristic infrastructure, would finally become a world-class city.³⁵ Almeida, the most quixotic of the lot, went as far as suggesting that the historical neighbourhoods of Mouraria and Alfama be demolished and rebuilt from scratch, as he saw them far too degraded, dangerous, and unhygienic for an imperial capital. Among these at-times delirious suggestions, prominent role was played by the dream of a bridge over the Tagus, an infrastructure that would have been able to link "the two Lisbon of the future".³⁶

Fado

"Desperately waiting for the effect of the Expo" – in a 2001 article thus titled, the *Pátio do Israel*, the area immediately surrounding the Marialva tower, is described as a "miserable and forgotten place" whose houses often lack running water, the terrain is in danger of sliding, and the common bathrooms – mostly absent private ones – are full of rats.³⁷ As the rapid-transit highways built to connect the city centre with the Expo bypassed it, the MBR further receded into an invisibility only sporadically interrupted by blips of media-inflated moral panic regarding episodes of crime and violence. While a few kilometres north, temporarily resuscitated, stood the Capital of the Empire, here lay its repressed doppelganger, the Capital of Nothing, as the name of a critical artistic intervention that took place in the very same year went.³⁸ As one of the participants to the intervention wrote,

> In the mental geography of Lisboetas (the people of Lisbon) it [Marvila] functions somewhat as a hole, a fracture of the city, a collection of wasteland, farms, convents, industrial buildings, decaying neighborhoods, council housing, railways . . . a place where nothing happens.³⁹

While the effects of the Expo were missing, its affects lingered over the area in the form of an ambivalent atmosphere, hovering between hopeful expectation

46 *Rethinking the City*

and bitter resignation.[40] The same ambivalence accompanied the grand plan for a third bridge over the Tagus that was disclosed in 2007. It was to take off on the very same spot in which Pais had imagined it 131 years earlier, just over the Manutenção Militar, which had by then become an empty, disused factory. The 15-kilometre bridge was meant to connect the MBR with the municipality of Barreiro, on the other side of the Tagus, and Lisbon with the Trans-European high-speed network. In 2012, however, as the consequences of the 2008 financial crisis began to hit Portugal, the hypothetical bridge was drastically amputated, its stump visible only in the preparatory drawings, its absence spectrally jolting on the surroundings for the year to come. Under the effect of yet another psycho-deflation, the MBR seemed to drift further away from the rest of the city, as if immersed in the sad atmosphere of an *urban fado*, under the spell of a *saudade* for the febrile social and communal life of the industrial past, in the midst of the present alienation, and before a seemingly bleak future.[41]

Phantom

After an amputation, the brain may fail to register the loss, remaining faithful to the original image of the body. This may cause the perception of a limb to persist as a ghost. Phantom limbs are no mere psychic hallucinations. They are hardwired into the neurological architecture of the brain – they may move, hurt, become paralysed – they are real. "A phantom is a portion of body image which is lost or dissociated from its natural, embodying home (the body)" and now "longs for a new home".[42] During this quest, the phantom may slip away, letting all sorts of troubling distortions and deformations emerge. Learning to live with a phantom is no easy feat. The grief must be processed against the false evidence of the senses and the normative force of the "normal" body, for instance, by "convincing" the phantom to find a "new home" in a prosthesis.[43] Phantom limbs are imaginary projections, appendages of dreams that strive to become self-fulfilling prophecies, prolonging bodies beyond their physical reality, promising unrealistic metamorphoses. Cities often experience phantom limb syndrome. Stubbornly believing in the healing force of progress, they mask their wounds beneath cosmetic surgery, prosthetic monuments, or inflated rhetorics of denial. Contrary to the optimistic fanfare of "urban" regeneration, however, "repair does not reduce the process of fracturing; it increases it, allowing meanings to proliferate beyond control".[44] It is an endless process that makes the linear temporality of progress explode into an uncontainable proliferation, and the urban fabric fragments under the weight of its contradictions. If for Benjamin the collective wish-images could *innervate* the collective imaginary and therefore hold the potential to prompt revolutionary action,[45] then the phantom limb syndrome stands for a "false", potentially toxic nerve stimulation, one that tends to turn the wish into fetish, the image into phantasmagoria, the emancipatory striving into a self-inflicting, delusional loop.

Pond

A short walk through the corrugate roofs of the *Pátio do Israel* leads to an empty brownfield, the former site of the National Soap Society [*Sociedade Nacional de Sabões*]. Founded in 1919, by the 1970s the SNS was one of the largest companies of the country. By the 1990s, it shut down. With a view to turn it into a real estate opportunity, the factory was demolished, its land bought and sold in the span of few years in a vortex of accelerated valorisation, until the plan for the third bridge brought everything to a halt: the site was where the bridge was to pass through.[46] Behind it, the pink building of the Industrial School Afonso Domingues rises among the rubble. Inside, most of the furniture has been vandalised or stolen. People occasionally use it to hang out and sleep. While the inside is slowly rotting away, the façade looks uncannily fresh. Renovation works had been carried out in 2010, only few months before it was closed to make space for the hypothetical path of the unbuilt bridge. It never reopened since.[47] "If we only pay attention to the roll-out of contemporary spatial products as exemplars of urban neoliberalism", argues AbdouMaliq Simone, "we might miss opportunities to see something else taking place, vulnerable and provisional though it may be".[48] This is the gist of *The Pond*, an artistic project developed by Pedro Queirós, Daniela Rodrigues and Inês Abreu, who set out to survey and explore the "afterlife of destruction", that is, the entropic decomposition and recomposition unfolding in this polluted site, where different forms of organic and inorganic life overlap, intersect and thrive.[49]

Rubble

I walk behind the school. I see a washing machine, a TV set, burnt tyres, a crack pipe, broken glass, dirty fabric, a lighter, another lighter, various weeds I don't recognise, a cat, the weary eyes of a man who looks from afar. Dogs are barking from behind a fence. A few clothes are hanging from a drying rack inside the building. Economic, financial and sociopolitical processes have precipitated on this site, violently so, opening up a curious spatio-temporal interval in the process. While former pupils lament its decay,[50] others, less concerned with its past glory, exploit the opportunities it offers. The post-industrial debris of this area unavoidably fascinate the ruinophilic gaze. This is a trap. To avoid the mere aestheticisation of the ruin, Ann Stoler proposes to focus on ruination instead, that is, the planetary process of destruction that keeps eroding the socio-material fabric of the urban, turning it into more or less invisible rubble.[51] Following this suggestion, Gaston Gordillo proposes to use the concept of rubble. While the ruin is always at risk of being fetishised, becoming a frozen symbol of a totalising narrative – for instance heritage, or urban blight –, the rubble provides a "lens through which to examine space negatively: by way of the places that were negated to create the geographies of the present".[52] Here, around the tower, the ghostly infrastructure of the unbuilt bridge can be felt, as an invisible rubble that keeps affecting the site, *in absentia*, a phantom limb that remains unacknowledged by the worn-out urban psyche.

Ecosystem

In 2013, introducing the Lisbon Creative Economy Book, the by-then Deputy Mayor for Economy and Innovation Graça Fonseca, who then went to become the country's Minister of Culture, after defining Lisbon as a creative, tolerant, innovative and safe city, stated its ambition to become "a key agent of the creative economy in Portugal, in Europe and throughout the world".[53] Since then, Lisbon has begun an aggressive strategy to refashion itself as a start-up and tech-oriented city, seeking to attract foreign capital, investors and expats while tweaking the legal infrastructure accordingly.[54] Contemporary start-up urbanism has given a renewed centrality to the urban environments "as privileged sites for technology-intensive interactive economies", especially revolving around the notion of "ecosystem", that is, breeding grounds in which start-up communities and other relevant organisations can meet, network, create and thrive.[55] Thanks to its logistical advantages – low rent, vast disused spaces, attractive riverfront and post-industrial aesthetics[56] – the MBR has become the perfect ecosystem of Lisbon's start-up strategy, centred around the *Hub Criativo do Beato* (HCB). The creative hub is the synecdoche of the creative city, the place in which Fordism and post-Fordism meet: a factory of creativity. As a content manager at StartUp Lisboa put it, the hub will be a catalysis of "positive social contamination" that will be "able to turn the Bermuda Triangle of inner-city Lisbon' – i.e. Beato and Marvila – into a new 'Brooklyn'".[57] These are the three main objectives the HCB is supposed to address: attract the "creative minds" flocking yearly for the Web Summit, the world's largest tech-conference that Lisbon is hosting since 2016; rebrand Lisbon "as a tech-oriented hotbed for entrepreneurs, digital nomads and global capital"; and propel the regeneration of Marvila and Beato.[58]

Air

From the tower, an overpass crosses the railway and leads, through weeds, waste, and debris, to a flight of stairs. It is the gateway to Rua do Capitão Leitão, the epicentre of a "cutting edge art scene", as real estate developers like to imagine it.[59] A couple of craft breweries and a few high-end art galleries signal we have entered the MBR. Close by is leafy *David Leandro da Silva* square, where the former headquarters of two wine companies – José Domingos Barreiros (founded 1896) and Abel Pereira da Fonseca (founded

1907) – face each other. Their flamboyant architecture is a reminder of their past success, when the logistical advantage of the river and the railway made the MBR a wine distribution hub.[60] In his *Peregrinações em Lisboa* (1938–1939), Norberto de Araújo recounts how David Leandro da Silva square smelled of "wine and oak".[61] In 2016, three independent breweries created the Lisbon Beer District, a concept aimed to re-signify the area and promote "urban revitalisation". By then, the area began to "smell of beer".[62] Two of those breweries have closed or relocated since. Today, according to real estate developers, "creativity" and a "new way of living" are in the air.[63] Among the key requirements for developing an "entrepreneurial ecosystem", writes Luísa Carvalho, is the capacity to attract real estate opportunities.[64] The MBR did comply. In 2019, the area had one of the lowest prices per square metre in Lisbon. By then, a 17 million investment turned a whole block, including the Barreiros building, into a luxury development prospect: Marvilla Collection promises a "future life, lived freely, in one of the safest cities in Europe. Lived on your own terms, surrounded by all the conveniences of new-age city life".[65] The building hosts the Marvila Art District, a series of ateliers artists enjoy for free until the redevelopment works do start.[66] Next door is the *Prata Riverside Village*, a residential complex designed by Renzo Piano. In the surroundings, luxury real estate projects are mushrooming.[67]

Unicorns

The HCB is located on the former premises of the Manutenção Militar, in the same spot where the first and the last of the unbuilt bridges over the Tagus took off. To reach it, it only takes a short walk from the Afonso Domingues School, descending a narrow street, passing by a luxurious palace. *It's only a myth until you make it true*: thus read a big poster on one of its walls, facing the ruins of a collapsed house. Born as a start-up incubator, the HCB has been upgraded by the new mayor, Carlos Moedas, into a Unicorn Factory. In the business sector, a unicorn is a private start-up company that is valued over US$1 billion. As the council website states, *Lisboa Unicorn Capital* is the new brand of the city, it aims to "establish Lisbon as a global hub for entrepreneurship, innovation and technology, working with the community to ensure Lisbon's success as the capital of innovation".[68] "More ambition is needed", Moedas claimed, asking rhetorically: "why Lisbon cannot be the European capital of Innovation?"[69] After all, their century-long colonial adventure has provided Portuguese people with an inherent curiosity and a capacity to improvise creatively, thereby making them perfectly equipped for the task.[70] Here is Moedas, again, as he upgrades Fontismo to the new challenge:

> We have to get the country growing, we have to have the courage, the audacity to get the country growing. And the only way to make our country grow is to invest in technology, science, innovation and to

50 *Rethinking the City*

make sure that those who have ideas today can actually have their own companies and make them grow.[71]

Bloomberg recently announced that the three best places in the world for digital nomads are Dubai, Miami, and Lisbon.[72] With respect to Lisbon, the price to buy a one-bedroom apartment in the city centre is 32% lower in Dubai and 21% higher in Miami while the average salary is, respectively, 341% and 291% higher.

Emblem

Diagnosing a phantom limb syndrome requires excavating the urban psyche, looking for the "memory-traces" of the invented pasts and abandoned futures which lie dormant within its tissues: a task for archaeologists, psychanalysts or soothsayers.[73] Benjamin, who was a bit of them all, discovered that certain images worked well for this purpose. He referred to them as *dialectical*, that is, images that are able to produce constellations in which the past flashes into the present, and the linear progress of history is shown as a frozen bundle of

Figure 4.2 Picture of the Hub Criativo do Beato taken from Avenida Infante Dom Henrique.

Source: Author.

contradictions.⁷⁴ Images, that is, in which the spatio-temporal stratification that constitutes the urban are made explicit. Benjamin developed this concept perverting Hegelian dialectics via allegorical thinking. Etymologically deriving from *allo* (other) and *agoreuo* (to say), the allegory is what "speaks of something else", circumventing the object's explicit meaning and exhuming its latent one – that which lies entrapped within the temporal strata of the collective unconscious – by reinserting it into a novel configuration in which its emblematic character [from *en* (in) and *ballo* (to throw, to put) – that is, to insert, to embed] is exhibited.⁷⁵ In the hand of the "allegorist", then, the object is disentangled from its mythical–ideological aura and foregrounded as *emblematic* of a given imaginary, as for instance was the case of the Parisian arcades he allegorically saw as ruins that signalled the inconsistency of the materialised positivity of 19th-century's positivism, as if they embodied, we would say following Gordillo's suggestion, the latter's invisible rubble.⁷⁶

Bundle

The tower of Marialva appears as one of such emblematic bundles. Around it, uncannily entangled, the conflicting imaginaries haunting Portugal's consciousness flicker: the memories of the glorious past, the resignation of present backwardness and the hopes for a future redemption.⁷⁷ It stands as an urban fossil: the decadent structure, the romantic aesthetics, the tags, the precarious position on a cliff over the railway, the sealed entrance to prevent further ransacking, the adjoining debris. Enigmatically isolated from the surroundings, it emblematically embodies the nostalgic conundrum nested within the Portuguese psyche that Lourenço diagnosed: the central position Portugal believes it deserves to occupy in the world and the bitter reality of its century-long, shaky subalternity.⁷⁸ In 2018, at a Lisbon City Council meeting, two deputies submitted a proposal for carrying out renovation works on the tower.⁷⁹ The proposal was voted and accepted. The deputies belonged to the very minoritarian Popular Monarchic Party [PPM] that presents itself as follows:

> For us, being monarchic means building a unified national project, protected and promoted by a monarch whose main function will be to unite the Portuguese and remind them that together we make up a great nation that has nine centuries of History and had a tremendous impact on Universal History.⁸⁰

No renovation works have begun since.

Build-up

Walking among the warehouses and cranes of the MBR can be a deceiving experience. The capital's dreamy images, reproduced in real estate billboards and magazines, assume a spectral consistency among these streets, signalling their existence through their felt absence. A few people can still be seen in

Figure 4.3 Picture of the Marialva tower taken from the railway overpass.
Source: Author.

what are often presented as the "trendiest" and most "creative" neighbourhoods of the city. Real estate websites boast "countless shops, services and leisure facilities", and yet the site is still for the most part empty. There are no markets, bakeries, cash machines, and notwithstanding the place is being sold as "perfectly connected" to the rest of the city, public transports are barely there.[81] The local "vibe", it seems, for the time being remains confined to glossy magazines, a few clubs and extemporaneous events while property prices skyrocket well beyond any gentrification prospect. Many bars and restaurants did open, and close, before the MBR actually began to be consistently populated. The place seems entrapped in an endless build-up which never quite kicks in, between a gone past and a yet-to-be future, as if ephemerality and transiency were being purposefully engineered to keep the place suspended, indefinitely under construction, while it quietly transitions from post-industrial decadence to luxury status, without having to deal with much community in between.[82]

Ruin

The urban, increasingly, is being turned into the rubble of a planetary construction site. The ensuing spectral fragmentation may indeed be what urban experience has become under planetary urbanisation, where everything seems to be permanently under construction *and* ruination at the same time.[83] I walk down south from the HCB, in about 600 metres I am before the Arroz Estúdios, another art space and venue where a Faustian pact between artists and developers has granted the former the place for free until redevelopment works begin. Recently, the UK street artist Kid Acne made a mural on the wall outside. It reads, in English, *You Had To Be There*. As the artist puts it, "For me, the phrase represents those good nights out, fun times and special moments that can only ever really be understood by the people who were there at the time".[84] While the MBR now reclaims an unprecedented cultural, financial and economic centrality, an uncanny *urban fado* seems to be still reverberating, paradoxically, through its atmosphere. *Saudade* is not gone. Only, its orientation has been reversed. It is a nostalgia for the futures that could have been, that have already gone, whose rubble is slowly rotting among the tissues of the present, imparting that eerie sense of inevitability – that sense of having always arrived *too late* – that the contemporary urban experience is unable to shake off.[85]

Acknowledgements

Andrea Pavoni's research is funded by FCT/MCTES [CEECINST/00066/2018/CP1496/CT0001] and [PTDC/GES-URB/1053/2021, https://doi.org/10.54499/PTDC/GES-URB/1053/2021].

Notes

1 "The Tejo Leads to the World/Beyond the Tejo there is America" – Pessoa, "O Guardador de Rebanhos", 149.
2 Buck-Morss, *The Dialectics of Seeing*, 160.
3 Benjamin, *The Arcades Project*, 392 [K 2,5].
4 See Wilson, "The Rotting City"; "Apocalypse and Utopia"; "Apocalyptic Urban Surrealism".
5 Wilson, "Apocalyptic Urban Surrealism", 719. For exploration of modern urbanisation in psychotraumatological fashion, see, for instance, Koolhaas, *Delirious New York*; Carter, *Repressed Spaces*; Vidler, *Architectural Uncanny*.
6 For example, Lahoud et al., *Post Traumatic Urbanism*; Till, "Wounded Cities".
7 Emery, "Urban Trauma", 653.
8 Simone, *The Surrounds*, 3.
9 Rachel Pain has particularly insisted on the need to also research the more subtle, non-eventful, chronic, long-term effect of urban trauma, see, for example, Pain, "Chronic Urban Trauma"; Emery, "Urban Trauma".
10 Armstrong, "Spectral Ethnography"; Emery, "Urban Trauma".
11 Osborne, *Anywhere*, 144; Mackay, *When the Site*; Pavoni, "Mapping the Plot".
12 Cf. Vanolo and Pavoni, "Ghosts [Crowds]"; " Ghosts [Phantasmagorias]".

54 Rethinking the City

13 Taussig, *Shamanism*, xiv.
14 Oliveira Martins, *Portugal Contemporâneo*, Vol. II.
15 José Sousa, an old Marvila-resident born in 1945, recounts how, still in his youth, "the train could be seen almost to infinity, as all the land was cleared". See www.youtube.com/watch?v=I9PM_lDhtbA
16 Vicente, "The Quest for Progress", 40.
17 Esteves, *A Criminalidade*.
18 Justino, "Fontismo: ideologia e política económica".
19 Jasanoff defines socio-technical imaginaries as "collectively held, institutionally stabilized, and publicly performed visions of desirable futures, animated by shared understandings of forms of social life and social order attainable through, and supportive of, advances in science and technology". Jasanoff, "Future Imperfect", 4.
20 Vicente, "The Quest for Progress".
21 Quoted in Buck-Morss, *The Dialectic of Seeing*, 114.
22 Buck-Morss, *The Dialectic of Seeing*, 115; Bloch, *The Principle of Hope*.
23 Buck-Morss, *The Dialectic of Seeing*, 126; Benjamin, *The Arcades Project*, 156 [F 3, 5]; 391 [K 1a,7].
24 Ribeiro de Sá, quoted in Rodrigues, *A participação portuguesa*, 16 (my translation).
25 In fact, the Expo-led regeneration resulted in further urban fragmentation and social segregation: Parque das Nações rapidly became a monocultural upper-class neighbourhood, its separation from the rest of the area emphasised by the barrier provided by the railway track. See Gonçalves and Thomas, "Waterfront Tourism", 342.
26 Tulumello, *Fear, Space and Urban Planning*.
27 Lourenço, *O Labirinto da Saudade*. See also Santos, "Between Prospero and Caliban".
28 Vicente, "The Quest for Progress", 39.
29 Pereira, "Herald of Progress". Buck-Morss, *The Dialectics of Seeing*, 120. For Benjamin, Buck-Morss argues, "technology was inherently progressive, promising socialist forms of living and culture; but so long as its development was appropriated for the purposes of capitalism and the state, it produced only reified dream images of that promise, a phantasmagoria" (Ibid., 143).
30 Ibid., 119.
31 The Ultimatum was a British memorandum that demanded the withdrawal of Portuguese troops from the territories of today's Malawi and Zimbabwe, *de facto* denying Portugal its wish to connect the territories of Angola and Mozambique.
32 Murtinho and Pais, "De Lisboa à Outra Banda"; Miranda, "As pontes do Tejo"; Barata, "Das colinas de Lisboa".
33 Fragoso Almeida, "Frente ribeirinha", 29.
34 Quoted in José, *A fundação e a organização*, 62.
35 Matos, "Lisboa do Ano 2000"; Almeida, "Lisboa Monumental"; Ferreira, "Reportagens Proféticas".
36 Almeida, "Lisboa Monumental". Matos did also envisage a tunnel under the Tagus, see "Lisboa do Ano 2000".
37 Neves, "Desesperadamente à espera".
38 See Caeiro, *Lisboa capital do nada*.
39 Campos, "A metáfora do nada".
40 Cf. Anderson and Holden, "Affective Urbanism".
41 "Fado" is a Portuguese music genre. The word means fate or destiny. On the notion of "urban fado", see Nunes and Sequeira, "O Fado de Marvila". For similar explorations of post-industrial nostalgia, see, for instance, Mah, *Industrial Ruination*.

42 Sacks, *Hallucinations*, ch. 15.
43 Ibid.
44 Deliss "Kader Attia", n.p. A brilliant artistic and political use of the notion of phantom limb is Kader Attia's exhibition: "Reflecting Memory".
45 Benjamin, "Surrealism".
46 Between 2001 and 2004, with a view to transform the area into a real estate opportunity, the company Lismarvila had bought the land for 26.2 million and demolished the factory buildings. In 2006, 60% of the land was sold for 56.2 million, thanks to an alteration of the Plano Director Municipal that had permitted the urbanisation of the area.
47 For example, Miranda, "Edifícios Abandonados".
48 Simone, "The Uninhabitable?", 151
49 https://theponds.info/THE-PONDS; Gordillo, *Rubble*.
50 See, for example, the Facebook page set up by the school former pupils, "Antigos alunos da Escola Industrial Afonso Domingues", www.facebook.com/groups/347677555295465/?locale=pt_BR
51 Stoler, "Imperial Debris".
52 Gordillo, *Rubble*, 11. See also Lee, *Spectral Spaces*.
53 Lisbon Creative Economy Book, 7.
54 Besides the absolute centrality played by tourism in Portuguese economy, initiatives such as the Golden Visa, Digital Nomad Visa, the tax exemption on cryptocurrency exchange, and convenient foreign retirement schemes are a testament of this intention, besides more structural measures such as the Novo Regime do Arrendamento Urbano [New Urban Lease Regime (Law 6/2006 and Law 31/2012)].
55 See, for example, Rossi and Di Bella, "Start-up Urbanism", 1000.
56 See Malta and Bourgard, "Marvila".
57 Interviewed by Scalzotto, "Smart-up Urbanism", 9. StartUp Lisboa is the private company that supervises the HCB project on behalf of the Câmara Municipal de Lisboa.
58 Scalzotto, "Smart-up Urbanism", 11.
59 See: https://mirabilisapartments.com/lisbon/marvilla-collection#:~:text=About%20the%20areaMarvila,crowds%20and%20vibrant%20life%2Dstyle.
60 See Pavoni, "Under Construction".
61 Araújo, *Peregrinações em Lisboa*, Vol. XV.
62 Branco and Rodrigues, "Marvila: o Lisbon Beer District".
63 "Creativity is in the air" can be read in the Marvilla Collection's website, see https://mirabilisapartments.com/lisbon/marvilla-collection; "Breath a new way of life", reads a billboard in the Prata Riverside Village.
64 How this might chime with some of her "smart city strategy" recommendation, such as "a city for everybody", remains enigmatic. See Carvalho, "Entrepreneurial Ecosystems".
65 From the Marvilla Collection brochure, page 9.
66 https://madmarvila.pt/.
67 For example, Alba, Atelier etc.
68 www.startuplisboa.com/blog/lisboa-unicorn-capital.
69 Naves, "Lisboa vai mesmo" (my translation). In December 2023, Lisbon has been named the European Capital of Innovation by the European Commission.
70 This is what some of Joel Göransson Scalzotto's interviewees have been keen to stress, see Scalzotto, "Smart-up Urbanism".
71 Lusa, "Fábrica de Unicórnios" (my translation).
72 Shepherd, "Lisbon, Miami and Dubai".
73 Smithson, "A Tour".
74 Benjamin, *The Arcades Project*, 462 [N 2a,3], 464 [N 4,1].
75 Pinotti, *Costellazioni*, 3.

76
> Just as there are places in the stones of the Miocene or Eocene Age that bear the impression of huge monsters out of these geological epochs, so today the Passages lie in the great cities like caves containing fossils of an ur-animal presumed extinct: The consumers from the preimperial epoch of capitalism, the last dinosaurs of Europe.
>
> Benjamin, *The Arcades Project*, 541 [R 2,3]

On Benjamin's use of the notion of fossil and ruin, see also Buck-Morss, *The Dialectics of Seeing*, 160–165.

77 See Pavoni, "Under Construction".
78 See Lourenço, *O Labirinto da Saudade*.
79 www.am-lisboa.pt/302000/1/009538,000419/index.htm.
80 www.am-lisboa.pt/505100/1/index.htm (my translation).
81 Recently, a small upmarket grocery and a cash machine appeared in the Prata Riverside Village.
82 When an existing community had to be dealt with, in fact, violent methods have been deployed, for instance when attempting to illegally evict the occupants of the Santos Lima building, a case whose resonance reached *the Guardian* (30 October 2018).
83 "aqui tudo parece que é ainda construção, mas já é ruína" ["here everything looks under construction but is already in ruins", as Caetano Veloso sang in his 1991 song *Fora da Ordem*, a paraphrase of a famous passage of Claude Lévi-Strauss' *Tristes Tropiques*.
84 Kid Acne, quoted in Montana Colors, "You Had to be There".
85 Cf. Fisher, *Ghosts of My Life*. In September 2023, the Arroz Estúdios announced that they have been given notice to leave.

Bibliography

Almeida, Fialho de, "Lisboa Monumental", in *Passado Lisboa Presente Lisboa Futuro*, edited by Manuel Graça Dias, 79–124, Lisbon: Parceria A. M Pereira, 2001 [1906].
Anderson, Ben and Adam Holden, "Affective Urbanism and the Event of Hope", *Space and Culture* 11 (2008): 142–159.
Araújo, Norberto de, *Peregrinações em Lisboa*, Vol. XV, Lisboa: Vega, 1993 [1938–39].
Armstrong, Justin, "On the Possibility of Spectral Ethnography", *Cultural Studies? Critical Methodologies* 10, no. 3 (2010): 243–250.
Barata, Ana C., "Das colinas de Lisboa: as 'avenidas aéreas' nunca construídas", *Cadernos do Arquivo Municipal* 9 (2018): 125–136.
Benjamin, Walter, "Chapter 12: Surrealism: The Last Snapshot of the European Intelligentsia", in *One-Way Street and Other Writings*, London: New Left Books, 1979 [1935–36].
Benjamin, Walter, *The Arcades Project*, translated by Howard Eiland and Kevin McLaughlin, Cambridge, MA: Harvard University Press, 2002 [1982].
Branco, Miguel and Luís Filipe Rodrigues, "Marvila: o Lisbon Beer District", *Timeout*, February 5, 2019. www.timeout.pt/lisboa/pt/coisas-para-fazer/marvila-e-o-novo-lisbon-beer-district
Buck-Morss, Susan, *The Dialectics of Seeing: Walter Benjamin and the Arcades Project*, Cambridge, MA: MIT Press, 1989.
Caeiro Mário, ed. *Lisboa capital do nada – Marvila, 2001 – criar, debater, intervir no espaço público*, Lisboa: Edições Almedina, 2007.
Campos, Luís, "A metáfora do nada"/"The Nothing Metaphor", in *Lisboa capital do nada – Marvila, 2001 – criar, debater, intervir no espaço público*, edited by Mário Caeiro, 464–469, Lisboa: Edições Almedina, 2007.

Carter, Paul, *Repressed Spaces: The Poetics of Agoraphobia*, London: Reaktion Books, 2002.
Carvalho, Luísa C., "Entrepreneurial Ecosystems: Lisbon as a Smart Start-up City", in *E-Planning and Collaboration: Concepts, Methodologies, Tools, and Applications*, 1120–1138, Hershey, PA: IGI Global, 2018.
Deliss, Clementine, "Kader Attia: The Phantom Limb in Art", in *Kader Attia: Reflecting Memory* [Exhibition Catalogue], Gli Ori, 2015.
Emery, Jay. "Urban Trauma in the ruins of industrial culture: Miners' Welfares of the Nottinghamshire coalfield, UK", *Social & Cultural Geography* 23, no. 5 (2022): 639–659.
Esteves Alina, *A Criminalidade na Cidade de Lisboa: Uma Geografia da Insegurança*, Lisboa: Colibri, 1999.
Ferreira, Reinaldo, "Reportagens Proféticas", in *Passado Lisboa Presente Lisboa Futuro*, edited by Manuel Graça Dias, 79–124, Lisboa: Parceria A. M. Pereira, 2001 [1906].
Fisher, Mark, *Ghosts of My Life: Writings on Depression, Hauntology and Lost Futures*, Winchester, UK: Zero Books, 2014.
Folgado, Deolinda and Jorge Custódio, *Caminho do Oriente. Guia do Património Industrial*, Lisboa: Livros Horizonte, 1999.
Fragoso Almeida, Rita, "Frente ribeirinha. O futuro em altura", in *A Lisboa que teria sido*, edited by António Miranda and Raquel Henriques da Silva, 28–41, Lisboa: EGEAC/Museu de Lisboa, 2017.
Gonçalves, Ana and Thomas Huw, "Waterfront Tourism and Public Art in Cardiff Bay and Lisbon's Park of Nations", *Journal of Policy Research in Tourism, Leisure and Events* 4, no. 3 (2012): 327–352.
Gordillo, Gaston R., *Rubble: The Afterlife of Destruction*, Durham: Duke University Press, 2014.
Jasanoff, Sheila, "Future Imperfect: Science, Technology, and the Imaginations of Modernity", in *Dreamscapes of Modernity Sociotechnical Imaginaries and the Fabrication of Power*, edited by Sheila Jasanoff and Sang-Hyun Kim, 1–33, Chicago: University of Chicago Press, 2015.
José, Inês F. V. *A fundação e a organização da Manutenção Militar de Lisboa (1886–1914)*, MA thesis, NOVA FCSH, 2017.
Justino, David, "Fontismo: ideologia e política económica", Paper Presented at the XXXI Encontro da Associação Portuguesa de História Económica e Social, Coimbra, November 18–19, 2011.
Koolhaas, Rem, *Delirious New York: A Retroactive Manifesto for Manhattan*, New York: The Monacelli Press, 1994.
Lahoud, Adrian, Charles Rice and Anthony Burke, *Post-Traumatic Urbanism*, London: John Wiley, 2010.
Lee, Christina, *Spectral Spaces and Hauntings: The Affects of Absence*, Abingdon: Routledge, 2017.
Lourenço, Eduardo, *O Labirinto da Saudade. Psicanálise Mítica do Destino Português*, Amadora: D. Quixote, 1978.
Lusa, "Fábrica de Unicórnios de Lisboa arranca com investimento de 8 milhões de euros", *Público*, October 28, 2022. www.publico.pt/2022/10/28/local/noticia/fabrica-unicornios-lisboa-arranca-investimento-8-milhoes-euros-2025682
Mackay, Robin, ed., *When Site Lost the Plot*, Falmouth: Urbanomic, 2015.
Mah, Alice, *Industrial Ruination, Community, and Place: Landscapes and Legacies of Urban Decline*, Toronto: University of Toronto Press, 2012.
Malta, João Carlos Malta and Joana Bourgard, "Marvila. A indústria foi-se, os criativos estão a chegar. Basta para", *Sapo*, February 29, 2016. http://rr.sapo.pt/noticia/47830/marvila_a_industria_foi_se_os_criativos_estao_a_chegar_basta_para_agarrar_o_futuro
Matos, Melo de, "Lisboa do Ano 2000", in *Passado Lisboa Presente Lisboa Futuro*, edited by Manuel Graça Dias, 41–78, Lisboa: Parceria A. M. Pereira, 2001 [1906].

Miranda, Antònio, "As pontes do Tejo em Lisboa e outras travessias", in *a Lisboa que teria sido* [Exhibition Catalogue], 140–151, Lisbon: Museu de Lisboa, 2017.

Miranda, Marta Gonçalves, "Edifícios Abandonados: a escola em Marvila que fechou por causa do TGV", *NiT*, September 3, 2016. www.nit.pt/fora-de-casa/na-cidade/09-03-2016-edificios-abandonados-a-escola-em-marvila-que-fechou-por-causa-do-tgv

Montana Colors, "'You Had to be There' – Kid Acne Produces a Slogan Mural Converted to an NFT by Arroz Estúdios", *Montana Colors*, November 18, 2021. www.montanacolors.com/en/noticias/kid-acne-nft-arroz-estudio/

Murtinho, Vitor and Teresa Pais, "De Lisboa à Outra Banda: a miragem da ponte", *Associação Portuguesa de Construção Metálica e Mista* 56 (2019). www.cmm.pt/site/index.php?module=store&target=publicStore&id_category=56&id=279

Naves, Patrícia, "Lisboa vai mesmo ter uma Fábrica de Unicórnios, captadora de startups", *Jornal de Negócios*, October 27, 2022. www.jornaldenegocios.pt/empresas/tecnologias/detalhe/lisboa-vai-mesmo-ter-uma-fabrica-de-unicornios-captadora-de-startups

Neves, Francisco, "Desesperadamente à espera do efeito Expo", *Público*, March 17, 2001. www.publico.pt/2001/03/17/jornal/desesperadamente-a-espera-do-efeito-expo-155687

Nunes, João P. S. and Ágata D. Sequeira, "O Fado de Marvila. Notas sobre a origem citadina e o destino metropolitano de uma antiga zona industrial de Lisboa", *Forum Sociológico* 21 (2011): 33–41.

Oliveira Martins, Joaquim, *Portugal Contemporâneo*, Vol. II, Lisboa: Guimarães Editores, 2018 [1895].

Osborne, Peter, *Anywhere or Not at All: The Philosophy of Contemporary Art*, London: Verso, 2013.

Pain, Rachel, "Chronic Urban Trauma: The Slow Violence of Housing Dispossession", *Urban Studies* 56, no. 2 (2019): 385–400.

Pavoni, Andrea, "Mapping the Plot. Towards an Archaeological Ethnography of the Future", in *Future Ruins: Lisbon*, edited by Jaspar Joseph Lester, Andrea Pavoni, Susanne Prinz and Julie Westerman, London: Trigger Point, 2020.

Pavoni Andrea, "Under Construction: Searching for Future Ruins on the Eastern Riverfront of Lisbon", *Mediapolis: A Journal of Cities and Culture* 7, no. 4 (2022). www.mediapolisjournal.com/2022/11/under-construction/

Pereira, Hugo Silveira, "Herald of Progress: Karl Emil Biel's Photographs of the Technical Modernisation of Portugal", *Photographies* 15, no. 1 (2022): 101–123.

Pessoa, Fernando. "O Guardador de Rebanhos", *Athena*, 4 (1925): 145–156.

Pinotti, Andrea, *Costellazioni. Le parole di Walter Benjamin*, Torino: Einaudi, 2018.

Rodrigues, Maria G. R., "A participação portuguesa nas exposições universais na perspectiva do Design de Equipamento", MA diss., University of Lisbon, 2014.

Rossi, Ugo and Arturo Di Bella, "Start-up Urbanism: New York, Rio de Janeiro and the Global Urbanization of Technology-Based Economies", *Environment and Planning A* 49, no. 5 (2017): 999–1018.

Sacks, Oliver, *Hallucinations*, New York: Alfred A. Knopf, 2012.

Santos, Boaventura de Sousa, "Between Prospero and Caliban: Colonialism, Postcolonialism, and Inter-Identity", *Luso-Brazilian Review* 39, no. 2 (2002): 9–43.

Scalzotto, Joel Göransson, "Smart-Up Urbanism: Critical Reflections on a Hub, Urban Regeneration & Smart Cultural Imaginaries in Lisbon", in *Position Paper*, Lisboa: ROCK (Regeneration and Optimization of Cultural Heritage in Creative and Knowledge Cities). Instituto de Ciências Sociais da Universidade de Lisboa, 2020.

Shepherd, Damian, "Lisbon, Miami and Dubai Ranked Best Places to Work for High Earners", *Bloomberg*, April 27, 2022. www.bloomberg.com/news/articles/2022-04-26/lisbon-tops-hybrid-working-ranks-for-globetrotting-executives?fbclid=IwAR2lg6MrQJbd8TcHtkndTUisNDo17o3BMCW2lYNObBf7zNo2Uj7O_62M9DY

Simone, AbdouMaliq, "The Uninhabitable? In between Collapsed yet still Rigid Distinctions", *Cultural Politics* 12, no. 2 (2016): 135–154.
Simone, AbdouMaliq, *The Surrounds: Urban Life within and Beyond Capture*, Durham: Duke University Press, 2022.
Singleton, Benedict, "The Long Con", in *When Site Lost the Plot*, edited by Robin Mackay, 105–120, Falmouth: Urbanomic, 2015.
Smithson, Robert, "A Tour of the Monuments of Passaic, New Jersey", in *Robert Smithson: The Collected Writings*, edited by Jack Flam, 68–75, Berkeley: University of California Press, 1996.
Stoler, Ann L., "Imperial Debris: Reflections on Ruins and Ruination", *Cultural Anthropology* 23, no. 2 (2008): 191–219.
Taussig, Michael, *Shamanism, Colonialism, and the Wild Man: A Study in Terror and Healing*, Chicago: University of Chicago Press, 1991.
Till, Karen E., "Wounded Cities: Memory-Work and a Place-Based Ethics of Care", *Political Geography* 31 (2012): 3–14.
Tulumello, Simone, *Fear, Space and Urban Planning. A Critical Perspective from Southern Europe*, Switzerland: Springer, 2017.
Vanolo, Alberto and Andrea Pavoni, eds. "Ghosts [Crowds]", *Lo Squaderno. Explorations in Space and Society* 62 (2022).
Vanolo, Alberto and Andrea Pavoni, eds. "Ghosts [Phantasmagorias]", *Lo Squaderno. Explorations in Space and Society* 64 (2023).
Vicente, Filipa, "The Quest for Progress between Porto and Europe: Photography, International Exhibitions, and Railways (1850–1900)", in *Exposições internacionais entre o jardim e a paisagem urbana. Do Palácio de Cristal do Porto (1865) à exposição de Paris (1937), [Exhibition Catalogue]*, 35–63, Porto: Fundação de Serralves, 2018.
Vidler, Anthony, *The Architectural Uncanny. Essays in the Modern Unhomely*, Cambridge, MA: MIT Press, 1992.
Wilson, Japhy, "Apocalypse and Utopia in the Salvagepunk Metropolis", *City* 27, no. 1–2 (2023a): 39–55.
Wilson, Japhy, "Apocalyptic Urban Surrealism in the City at the End of the World", *Urban Studies* 60, no. 4 (2023b): 718–733.
Wilson, Japhy, "The Rotting City: Surrealist Arts of Noticing the Urban Anthropocene", *Space and Culture* (2023c) [online first]: 1–12.

5 The ambivalences of intimacy and aesthetic and political reconfigurations of the common world

Nélio Conceição

Introduction

The aim of this chapter is to delve into the theme of intimacy and to analyse its relevance to a philosophical understanding of the city, particularly at an aesthetic and political level. There are certainly many ways of thinking about this issue, not least because the very notion of intimacy is polysemic and, as we will see throughout this chapter, allows for countless approaches. The focus will be on the irresolvable tensions, and thus the constitutive ambivalences, that it sets forth, both at the theoretical level and in artistic practice. To circumscribe fundamental concepts and to show art's capacity to touch on difficult issues in a direct and fruitful way, I will begin by focusing on the work of the Portuguese artist Carla Filipe, in which the tension between intimacy and the aesthetic and political reconfiguration of the common world is fully operative. The rest of the chapter will be guided by Hannah Arendt's thinking, with the goal of stressing the relevance of such notions as "common world", "plurality" and "space of appearance", as well as her analysis of the "modern discovery of intimacy" and its consequences for the political and the social sphere. By intersecting these analyses with the sociological and historical contributions of Richard Sennett, by returning to seminal *topoi* of Georg Simmel and Walter Benjamin and by placing particular emphasis on the issue of withdrawal and the way in which contemporary art problematises it, what follows aims to rethink the city from the point of view of intimacy, combining the reflexive capacity of artistic practices with aesthetic and political reflection.

Carla Filipe: art between intimacy and plurality

One of the rooms of the exhibition *In My Own Language I Am Independente* (sic) by Portuguese artist Carla Filipe, held at the Serralves Museum, Porto, in 2023, featured a series of six pieces which, both individually and because of the affinities between them, serve as an excellent prompt for rethinking the city and its aesthetic and political challenges.

DOI: 10.4324/9781003452928-6

The ambivalences of intimacy 61

Figure 5.1 Carla Filipe,
Corpo-mente I (Vísceras)
You are Sexual, Remember
A ambiguidade da experiência da cidade
A ideia sobre comunidade
Corpo-mente III
O impulso sobre a comunidade
2015–16, Indian ink on paper (6 elements).
Source: © Carla Filipe, photo credits Nélio Conceição. Reprinted with permission.

In the exhibition, this group was located in a room with other works that are paradigmatic of Carla Filipe's mode of working, which is highly attentive to communication mechanisms and the political context of Portugal in recent decades. Bringing together materials from newspapers, posters and leaflets – exhibited through processes of reconfiguration, fragmentation and repetition, as part of a humorous and ironic take on our surroundings that features the types of graphics often found in street murals – the works in this room bring to the fore two aspects that point in different but intersecting directions: on the one hand, to the tension between drawing and the written word; on the other, to the tension between the individual and the collective. These two aspects are particularly effective in this series of six pieces.

The exhibition as a whole is part of a strange language in which Portuguese and English are mixed in a transgression of linguistic and translation rules. They thus spring from a singular place, at once spontaneous, crude and germinal and seem to seek to connect with the plurality of the public and political dimension by exploring both a universe of popular and familiar references and aspects that are rescued from oblivion and brought into a shared imaginary: historical and political events, doctors' waiting rooms, anonymous and more or less famous women and men, Portuguese Railway Company (CP) plant pot competitions, autobiographical references. In an interview, referring to her work "Família" ("Family"), which delves into and transfigures these autobiographical and familiar references, Carla Filipa explains:

> This me is a plural me. And I know how to separate what really remains in my intimacy from what, even though it is intimate, I am interested in presenting and working with. In reality, this me that I present is also the other; it's also public, plural.[1]

This presentation can be seen as a way of addressing a plurality, a community.

As two of the pieces from the series of six tell us very pointedly, however, this "community" cannot be given from the outset, or else it may simply become impossible or artificial.[2] Unfolding the potential of a community demands the coexistence of a self with others. Art that has political goals can easily become artificial or difficult to grasp as art if it does not stem from this in-between realm: between intimacy and plurality, between self and other.

The writing that retains certain colloquial traits is also a way of circumscribing the guiding problems of the artist's works; it reveals a thought process, a way of operating or a dialogue with oneself in which language becomes a pivotal moment.[3] Language is not merely a way of communicating ideas but above all an exercise in thought, a way of approaching and distancing oneself from themes that are repeated, an exercise to which both the urban, irreverent graphics and the work on the human figure contribute. In the six pieces, at least explicitly, only female figures and voices are featured. The writing evokes an intimate knowledge while at the same time asserting itself publicly and confidently. But there is also a certain withdrawal: although four of the six pieces represent female figures, only one features a face. In one, the focus is on the viscera, the face positioned out of frame; in another, the face is obscured by the woman's hair; in another still, the figure has her back turned to the viewer, revealing her scratches. The absence of a face suggests a certain anonymity – which is also a way of delving into the in-between of self and other.

The ambivalences of intimacy 63

Figure 5.2 Carla Filipe, Drawing *School*, pen, decal, marker, collage on cardboard.
Source: © Carla Filipe, photo credits André Cepeda. Coleção Ana Marim e Jorge Gaspar. Reprinted with permission.

This group can be interpreted as consisting of two triptychs, each following a kind of magnetic pole that gives them consistency and at the same time creates fruitful dialectical polarities: the first triptych gravitates around intimacy and the body (visceral, sexual, and pulsional); the second gravitates around the sharing of a common space, touching upon the aforementioned ambiguities regarding community, and in particular regarding the experience of the city – the latter implies a relationship with the stranger/foreigner but also with the strangeness that characterises us as city dwellers, immersed as we are in faces whose mysteriousness constitutes both an attraction and a threat.[4]

The viscera of *Corpo-mente I (Vísceras)* [*Body-Mind I (viscera)*] are exposed with the intervention of external hands, as if the very interior of the body were being violated but at the same time freed. After all, these viscera belong to the body but seem also to be alien to it – an intimate strangeness that contaminates the other five pieces, uniting with the mysteriousness of the others with whom we live. As a whole, this is a universe that combines restlessness, intimacy and a desire for community and belonging, a desire that implies an awareness of its difficulty. The gestures typical of this universe are repeated in many moments of Carla Filipe's work, particularly those that

Figure 5.3 Installation view, "Carla Filipe: In my own language I am independente", Fundação de Serralves – Museu de Arte Contemporânea, Porto, Portugal, from 23 March 2023 to 24 September 2023.

Source: Photos: © André Cepeda. Reprinted with permission.

deal more directly with political issues, such as the work "Amanhã não há arte" ("Tomorrow there is no art"), placed at the centre of the room in the Serralves exhibition and speaking to the iconography of the Portuguese revolutionary period following 25 April 1974.

The rupture that the artist effects in the iconography of this period goes hand in hand with a political rupture, given that "today the sense of community is diluted. The exhibition ('Tomorrow there is no art') represents this dilution".[5] This is also a gesture – a warning? – aimed at the community of artists.

What this collection of works also reveals and prompts us to think about, in its reconfiguration of the modern and urban experience, is the constant tension between intimacy and the street, which it achieves through an archaeology of the present that feeds on this tension rather than trying to resolve it in a direct or scholarly way: humour, sarcasm and a taste for paradoxes are allies when it comes to scrutinising the interstices and irresolutions of human experience. Both exposed intimacy and the archaeology of the present summon up a plurality, and the city, understood as a paradigmatic community in which citizens – in both body and mind – live the polarity between public space and private space, is the setting where the multiple consequences of this plurality become more visible and where the poles clash and often intersect to the point of becoming indiscernible. To better understand, from a philosophical point of view, what is at stake here, the following sections will focus on i) how to conceive of the plurality of political and aesthetic perspectives in a context in which the very notion of community has become problematic; ii) how reflection on the city leads to a questioning of the philosophical and historical roots of the intimacy of modern individuals, in which the question of withdrawal appears as a polysemic gesture replete with ambiguities and iii) how, in the end, we can return to art to better circumscribe the intersection of the intimate and the political.

What follows, then, is not an attempt to construct a critical discourse or a conceptual armour around Carla Filipe's work but rather a deepening of some of the problems it raises. Largely guided by Hannah Arendt's thinking, this deepening is a reflection on the reconfiguration of the common world, with the aim of understanding why intimacy and a certain attraction to self-absorption provide infinite material for contemporary artistic practices and aesthetic reflections that find in the city not only an object of study but also a privileged stage on which to perform our own duality and the duality of our relationships with others.

Hannah Arendt: common world, plurality and space of appearance

Although Hannah Arendt's thinking does not deal directly with the city, and in particular with the modern city, it offers a twofold path to this "object" of study. On the one hand, her observations on the Greek *polis* are highly relevant to the development of her political thought, although her focus is above all on citizens, on the political plane on which humans meet through action and speech and share a common world, and not so much on the structure and materiality of the *polis*, which are ultimately a corollary of the former. On the other hand, both her analysis of the historical mutations that have led to a growing preponderance of social spaces in which the public and the private are indiscernible and the very question of the "modern discovery of intimacy"[6] seem to cut straight to the heart of a philosophical consideration of the city, one that traces the formation of urban life throughout modernity, in a political and aesthetic sense. Let us take a closer look at some of these connections.

In *The Human Condition*, Arendt recognises in the *polis* a fundamental correlation between freedom, action and speech.[7] In the *polis*, the public side of political life was clearly opposed to the sphere of private life, the family and the fulfilment of basic needs. Without transposing this model directly to other contexts (since, e.g., the Roman *civitas* and *res publica* raise other questions and imply other ways of understanding the public and the private realm and the question of property itself), Arendt characterises political life as the reality of what can be seen and heard by all. To share a common world, which both unites and separates those who inhabit it, is in this sense to share an interest in the same object, which presupposes plurality and a variety of perspectives.

> If action as beginning corresponds to the fact of birth, if it is the actualization of the human condition of natality, then speech corresponds to the fact of distinctness and is the actualization of the human condition of plurality, that is, of living as a distinct and unique being among equals.[8]

The correlation between action (natality) and speech (plurality) shows that the notion of "actualisation" has many consequences in Arendt's political thinking and that the fulfilment of human life implies the seminal assumption of the coexistence of men, *inter homines esse* ("to be among men"). This conception of the common world implies, on the other hand, a space of appearance, a potentiality that exists whenever a community is formed based on the correlation between action and speech, on the capacity of speech to reveal realities, on the capacity of action "to establish relations and create new realities".[9] In Arendt's view, power as *dynamis* or *potentia* should not be confused with strength or force; it is what sustains the space of appearance, thus being prior to the formal constitution of the public realm and the forms of government themselves.

At this point, it is important to make a small detour: while the walls and structure of city-states and their legislation were aimed above all at maintaining the possibility of an appearance in which citizens could relate to each other, the materiality of contemporary cities and their modes of socialisation often seem to call into question their potential character as a political community. We can even speak of processes of internal collapse, related both to the voracity of capitalism and the commodification of dwelling and to the social exclusion that easily deprives citizens of their voice and visibility. This difficulty becomes all the more clear when we consider the constitutive heterogeneity of contemporary cities. The space of appearance is always threatened by the very sharing of space, by processes of exclusion or separation between incommensurable elements (which, in the end, can invalidate the power of the common). On the other hand, if one broadly understands the city as a "body politic", one can easily see that, in purely statistical terms, the larger its population, "the more likely it will be the social, rather than the political that constitutes the public realm".[10] This was in fact one of the fundamental reasons why the Greeks were "quite aware of the fact that the *polis*, with its emphasis on action and speech, could survive only if the number of citizens remained restricted".[11] In any case, the emphasis on plurality guarantees, within the framework of the space of appearance, that heterogeneity will have a voice and visibility.

The irresolvable tensions of intimacy

According to Arendt, there are three events which, without being revolutionary in the sense that, for example, the French Revolution was, determined the character of the modern era:

> [T]he discovery of America and the ensuing exploration of the whole earth; the Reformation, which by expropriating ecclesiastical and monastic possessions started the twofold process of individual expropriation and the accumulation of social wealth; the invention of the telescope and the development of a new science that considers the nature of the earth from the viewpoint of the universe.[12]

The first and third events in particular are at the root of a form of alienation that resulted from the distancing, fostered by science, of the human being from the earth, which opened us to an infinite universe and to the possibility of observing the earth from the outside.[13] According to Arendt, this process presupposes alienation not from the *ego*, as Marx thought, but from the world.[14] Historically, it arose in the transition to a society based primarily on poor workers who were excluded from the protection of the family and property and their progressive integration into a new social class. This phenomenon, as is well known, coincided with the rise of industrialisation and large-scale urbanisation. It was accompanied by a decline in the public realm, a profound transformation of the private realm, as traditionally lived and conceived and the formation, in social terms, of a "lonely mass".[15]

It is certainly no coincidence that one of the fundamental features of the mental life of the metropolitan individual is that of loneliness.[16] Or rather loneliness, and thus isolation and fragmentation are counterpoints to the greater individual freedom and autonomy of city dwellers, freed from the ties of smaller communities. Whereas Simmel presents these aspects in accordance with the contradictions of the flow of life in modern cities, Arendt emphasises the growing importance of the various forms of alienation and the ambivalences of intimacy. The latter are inscribed in urban materiality, marked from the outset by the walls of the private home and by a turning inwards that grants the interior and its objects the capacity to reveal individuality. One can also add that this entails a certain reactive character; that is, just as the Simmelian *blasé* character reacts to the overstimulation of the nervous system, so the inwardness of modern subjectivity is, for Arendt, a reaction to the demands of the social world. One of the consequences of this reaction is the contagious charm of intimacy, which, considered irrelevant in the public realm, is nonetheless observable in the French, who have channelled their energies into *petit bonheur*:

> Since the decay of their once great and glorious public realm, the French have become masters in the art of being happy among "small things", within the space of their own four walls, between chest and bed, table and chair, dog and cat and flowerpot, extending to these things a care and tenderness which, in a world where rapid industrialization constantly kills off the things of yesterday to produce today's objects, may even appear to be the world's last, purely humane corner.[17]

There is a strong connection between this description and Walter Benjamin's understanding of the bourgeois interior in Convolut I, "The Interior, the Trace", in *The Arcades Project*: both speak of the individual's desire to protect himself or herself from the anonymous crowd of the city; moreover, the bourgeois interior becomes, so to speak, an occasion for the affirmation of individual personality.[18] Beyond Arendt and Benjamin's picture, one can also speak of a tension between the demands of public life and the home and domestic space – often associated with everyday life, passivity and, from a gendered perspective, femininity. As Rita Felski observes, the critical tradition of modernity is grounded in the "vocabulary of anti-home".[19] Given that political reflection on the city focuses mainly on the outward and "heroic" side, sometimes giving the impression of desperately wanting to rescue the common world from the shards of its fragmentation, how can we integrate the multiple aspects of domestic, ordinary and familiar places and experiences into a reflection on the potential of a city or community? And given that intimacy necessarily encompasses a series of specific relationships with people, objects and spaces, how can we think about it without falling into an absolute fragmentation of the common world? The domestic interior is thus a reflection, and in part an essential material and historical element, of a long process that helps us to understand the traits and ambivalences of modern subjectivity.

If Descartes played a central role in this process by giving priority to the thinking subject, it continued with Rousseau, who for Arendt is "the first articulate explorer and to an extent even theorist of intimacy".[20] It is worth stressing that in Arendt's reading the intimacy of the heart, as opposed to the intimacy of a private home, does not correspond to an objective place: it rebels against society, which is also much more difficult to locate than the public sphere. Furthermore, Rousseau's rebellion against the corruption of the human heart by society, and by urban life in particular, entailed a particular type of turbulence, an internal conflict in which Jean-Jacques seemed to rebel against Rousseau, the intimate man in conflict with the social man:

> The modern individual and his endless conflicts, his inability either to be at home in society or to live outside it altogether, his ever-changing moods and the radical subjectivism of his emotional life, was born in this rebellion of the heart.[21]

Symptomatically, this process was accompanied by a surprising flourishing of poetry and music from the mid-18th century onwards, as well as the advent of the novel. And the novel, as Benjamin shows, is deeply linked to the isolation of the protagonist, as opposed to the storyteller, who embodies a kind of collective, shareable teaching.[22]

It is important not to forget that, in the framework outlined by Arendt, all of this is also related to the multiple forms of alienation that arise in the passage from the Archimedean point to the interior of the human being. In terms of our urban concerns, and to summarise, we might say that the progressive abandonment of the Greek equation of the public realm with freedom, through the constitution of a modern social space in which the public and the private have become to a certain extent indiscernible, allows us to think of intimacy in at least three senses: i) as an instance of individual affirmation; ii) in relation to the domestic, familiar and everyday realms and iii) as an element that manifests itself in a complex way – because it is made up of enrichment and collapse – in the very self-absorption and withdrawal of city dwellers.

Withdrawal

According to Richard Sennett, who extends Arendt's framework by means of a more historical and sociological approach, beyond the major processes related to capitalism and secularisation, both the loss of the political value of private space and the respective expansion of the psychological dimension of intimacy are connected to a failure that generates many misunderstandings, one that is particularly pressing when it comes to thinking about political issues and the very power of community: if the notion of intimacy, and the psychological imagination of life that it summons, "connotes warmth, trust, and open expression of feeling",[23] then the impersonal and external world, which does not usually reward us in relation to this expectation, seems to fail us constantly. The growing preoccupation with inner life, in which what is meaningful seems to depend entirely on the expansion of our psyche and the expression of our personality, has consequences for how community ties are conceived, as we can be led to believe that "community is an act of mutual self-disclosure and to undervalue the community relations of strangers, particularly those which occur in cities".[24]

In *The Fall of Public Man*, but also in other works, Sennett seeks to broaden our understanding of these processes, intersecting the experience of the modern city with an analysis of the decline of the public realm and the "tyrannies of intimacy".[25] It is important to look at certain fundamental psychological dimensions that circumscribe what is at stake here:

> To speak of the legacy of the 19th Century's crisis of public life is to speak of broad forces such as capitalism and secularism on the one hand and of these four psychological conditions on the other: involuntary disclosure of character, superimposition of public and private imagery, defense through withdrawal, and silence. The obsessions with selfhood are attempts to work out these conundrums of the last century, by denial. Intimacy is an attempt to solve the public problem by denying that the public exists. As with any denial, this has only made the more destructive aspects of the past the more firmly entrenched. The 19th Century is not yet over.[26]

Clearly, these psychological conditions are not of the same order and do not necessarily operate simultaneously, but they contribute profoundly to the constitution of the sphere of intimacy, at least as we are conceiving of it here: in tension with the public and political realm and characterised by an ambivalence in which destructive elements coexist closely with an enrichment of the human soul. In this sense, it is also important to look at the notion of withdrawal, not only because it can be approached from various perspectives but also because it embodies the ambivalence that arises from the comingling of destruction and enrichment.

One of these perspectives is entrenched in philosophy's complex relationship with the city. If it is true that Western philosophy is deeply linked to the *polis*, it is no less true that, since ancient times, but also at various pivotal moments in Western thought, the city was seen as a place of corruption. In this sense, and with different tonalities that we cannot explore in depth here, we can even speak of an anti-urban tendency in philosophy, one that can be identified from the outset in Diogenes the Cynic, has a faithful representative in Rousseau and can also be found in Heidegger's hut in the Black Forest.[27]

When it comes to thinking about the city from a political and aesthetic standpoint, however, perhaps the most pertinent sense of withdrawal lies somewhere between the philosophical, the social and the psychological, as in Sennett's analysis of the "uncooperative self".[28] First, it is important to realise that in this case, the counterpoint to the anti-urban tendency in philosophy may be a need for solitude that can become highly productive from a spiritual or existential point of view. Solitude, as Arendt points out, should not be confused with loneliness, and only the former reveals the richness of the life of the mind as a reflective counterpoint to human plurality.[29] This reflexive dimension of our mental life, and in particular of thinking, accounts for the very Kantian original duality of the self, or in other words, "the split between me and myself which is inherent in all consciousness".[30] This unconsciously conscious self-awareness accompanies all our activities, even though it is not itself an activity. We access it through a withdrawal from appearances, which can also mean a withdrawal from the demands of present and everyday life.

From another perspective, closer to the aspects of the city addressed by Sennett, withdrawal instead implies a reaction to the anxiety generated by social interactions. A classic response that is deeply linked to metropolitan life is the defence mechanism described by Simmel, according to which anxiety is resolved through a mask that city dwellers use to cope with the hustle and bustle of street life. According to Sennett, "the richness of what's happening and who is in the street prompts urbanites to appear cool and impassive outside, while seething with stimulation inside. This is an all-important tool of character".[31] This seemingly banal experience has many consequences and, as we will see later, is problematically integrated into aesthetic and artistic experiences in and with the city. It implies a particular correlation or confrontation: human beings are torn by the confrontation between the world of appearances and the inner world in which the self folds in on itself.

Rather than philosophical or existential enlightenment, rather than a conception of the mask that can open productively to play and art, this more problematic sense of withdrawal, which implies voluntary action aimed at reducing anxiety, can lead to a kind of blindness that has two fundamental psychological ingredients: narcissism, in which the self becomes a mirror of reality, and complacency, the idea that everything is fine as it is (not to be confused with the human need to feel safe).[32] Along with vanity and indifference, these ingredients are part of a poisonous recipe that should be taken into account whenever we reflect on possible antidotes to individualism and thus on the importance of the creation or maintenance of communities, which is also Sennett's intention in *Together*: to work through the conditions in which human cooperation can function without disregarding the destructive elements of withdrawal. But let us now return to art, because many of the answers to these problems are made visible through artistic means, which have a unique ability to delve into paradoxes and ambiguities.

Art, action and performance: an open closure

> Walking, in particular drifting, or strolling, is already – within the speed culture of our time – a kind of resistance. Paradoxically it's also the last private space, safe from the phone or e-mail. But it also happens to be a very immediate method for unfolding stories. . . . There is no theory of walking, just a consciousness. But there can be a certain wisdom involved in the act of walking. It's

more an attitude, and it is one that fits me all right. It's a state where you can be alert to all that happens in your peripheral vision and hearing, and yet totally lost in your thought process.[33]

It is striking that Francis Alÿs, a Belgian artist who has lived in Mexico for many years, sees walking as a "private space" and as a form of resistance to the pressures of the social sphere. In many of his works, walking is a bodily rooted artistic procedure and a way of immersing oneself in contemporary cities through a combination of poetic and political elements. But what is also pertinent in the quote is the description of this particular mode of consciousness, which combines external attention and internal immersion (which can also be seen as a withdrawal or distraction). This is an ordinary and perhaps even prosaic detail, but it implies a certain wisdom and an attitude that can be enhanced and transfigured as an artistic procedure.

In fact, the dialectic between being present and being absent, between attention and distraction, has deep historical and psychological roots and has seminally entered the discussion on modern art's relationship with the city. At the same time, it allows one to understand that, paradoxically, working through withdrawal may also be a fertile form of action in an urban setting, one that recalls Arendt's sense of creation as a "second birth".[34] Art, obviously with different tools than those of philosophy, has the ability to turn the duality of consciousness into a form of action. In the section "Modernity" in the essay "The Paris of the Second Empire in Baudelaire", Benjamin introduces a small distinction which is of the utmost importance in this respect: his goal is to show that Baudelaire's remarks on the *flâneur* do not point to a self-portrait. In fact, the most meaningful descriptions of the city come not from the *flâneur*, whether he takes the form of the observer/detective or the rubbernecker/*badaud*, but from a particular form of distraction, the "absentmindedness" (*Geistesabwesenheit*) "of those who have traversed the city absently (*abwesend*) as it were, lost in thought or worry. The image of 'fantasque escrime' ('fantastical/absurd fencing') does justice to these individuals".[35] The "absentmindedness" (*Geistesabwesenheit*) of those who, in the midst of fencing, indulge in their own preoccupations appears as a counterpoint to the vigilant attention of the passer-by in the big city. In this sense, "being present" in the ordinary world is an ambivalent task and a problematic issue, not a given.

The path traced throughout this chapter relates in various ways, although not always directly, to the aesthetic dimension and trends of contemporary art itself, in particular to the latter's fascination with the self-absorption and inwardness of urban life. Interesting examples include Philip-Lorca diCorcia's photographs of passers-by in works like *Los Angeles*, *New York*, *Hong Kong* and *Paris* and in the (both appealing and disturbing) series *Heads*. These photographs reconfigure the traditional paradigm of street photography by focusing on the "expressions of intense inwardness" worn by people on the streets of big cities.[36] At the same time, they add a dramatic to-be-seenness that stems from the technical procedures themselves, including the use of hidden flashes that highlight the individuals in the crowd – detaching them from the lonely mass and, because they are unaware of being photographed, allowing their enigmatic expressions to move to the fore. If we compare Carla Filipe's artistic universe with the sense of self-absorption conveyed by the passers-by photographed by diCorcia, both of which are public in form and enter a "space of appearance", we will find ourselves in two completely different aesthetic and political realities. Nevertheless, both are at work on the "street", artistically reconfiguring the ambivalent and intimate experiences of city dwellers.

Let us return to Arendt: in the face of what appears, of what is seen and heard by all, intimate life, however rich in passion and thought and however much it delights in sensory life, usually has an uncertain and obscure existence. Although the transfiguration of this intimate life, through its deprivatisation and disindividualisation, can take many forms, the most common "occurs in storytelling and generally in artistic transposition of individual experiences".[37] In Arendt's work, it is difficult to circumscribe an aesthetic thought with clearly defined contours, but some of her observations go straight to the heart of significant tensions that are activated and performed by artistic works, first and foremost the tension between the common world and intimate life, which historically has different connotations with individualism, domestic space, family, and withdrawal. Elena Tavani's emphasis on the performative aspect of action and judgement in Arendt's "aesthetics and politics of appearance" is very convincing, as it allows us to deal with the artistic gesture in its intrinsic relationship with the world as a stage.[38]

In this sense, and to conclude this chapter, it is worth recalling both Carla Filipe's interview, in which she refers to a link between intimacy and plurality, and the play between exposure and concealment that takes on various forms in the six pieces analysed in the second section. Whether in the transfiguration of family experiences or in the viscera of the body-mind, they fruitfully perform the complex movement between the intimate and the political, the conceptual and historical framework of which was outlined in the previous sections.

Passions, thoughts, and the pleasure of the senses thus reach plurality. Community is not guaranteed; humour brings that note of modesty that strengthens the capacity of language to enter the double play of appearances, mobilising reality and theatre simultaneously. The common world remains a space for action, an ever-renewed actualisation of birth, a way of establishing the power of plurality between the intimacy of the self and the strangeness of the other.

Acknowledgements

This work was supported by the FCT – Fundação para a Ciência e a Tecnologia, under the Norma Transitória – DL 57/2016/CP1453/CT0040 (https://doi.org/10.54499/DL57/2016/CP1453/CT0040), and the projects UIDP/00183/2020 and PTDC/FER-FIL/32042/2017.

74 *Rethinking the City*

I would also like to thank Carla Filipe and the Serralves Foundation for their permission to reproduce the images that accompany this chapter.

Notes

1. Lima and Filipe, "Entrevista a Carla Filipe", 200. As with all other quotations in this chapter that do not refer to an existing translation, the translation is my own.
2. Counting from the top left to the bottom right, these are the fourth and sixth pieces. The fourth can be translated as: "The problem of post-merdinity is the fabrication of a sense of community where no community exists" (the typo in "merdinity" evokes the Portuguese word *merda*, shit). The sixth, although it mixes Portuguese and English, is easily understood.
3. See Canela and Filipe, "Actualizando passados esquecidos", 101.
4. Element six says:

    The ambiguity of the experience of the city re-emerges in the post-modern ambivalence of the stranger/foreigner. Two faces 1 attractive because it's mysterious = sexy bech promises joy without demanding an oath of loyalty, infinite occasion. The other is mysterious threatening. None can w[in].

5. Mourão et al., "João Mourão and Luís Silva in Conversation", 26.
6. Arendt, *The Human Condition*, 69.
7. See Ibid., 28–37.
8. Ibid., 178.
9. Ibid., 200.
10. Ibid., 43.
11. Ibid.
12. Ibid., 248.
13. This is not the place to analyse the various ramifications of this process and, specifically, the dialectical movement through which the Archimedean point is relocated to the interior of the human being, but it is nonetheless important to highlight that the Cartesian perspective leads to the equation of introspection and a loss of common sense, in which the latter is no longer conceived of as a sense "by which all other senses, with their intimately private sensations, were fitted into the common world . . ." and "became an inner faculty without any world relationship. This sense now was called common merely because it happened to be common to all" (Ibid., 283). It is within this problematic framework that Kant's *sensus communis*, and aesthetic judgement as a reflective judgement that implies communicability, should be considered. On this topic, see Arendt, *Lectures on Kant's Political Philosophy*.
14. Arendt, *The Human Condition*, 317.
15. Ibid., 257. This idea of the widespread phenomenon of loneliness, and its inhuman aspects, is also mentioned in the chapter Arendt devoted to the private realm (58–67).
16. Simmel, "The Metropolis and Mental Life".
17. Arendt, *The Human Condition*, 52.
18. See Benjamin, *The Arcades Project*, 212–227. Gaston Bachelard's analysis of familiar spaces and objects in *The Poetics of Space* allows for the drawing of connections between "small things" and intimacy while pointing in the poetic direction of reverie. Particularly interesting in this regard is the function of poetic images that revolve around "immensity" and the analysis of Baudelaire's use of the term *vaste*. Bachelard's argument can be summed up in the following passage: "It would seem, then, that it is through their 'immensity' that these two kinds

of space – the space of intimacy and world space – blend. When human solitude deepens, then the two immensities touch and become identical" (203).
19 Felski, "The Invention of Everyday Life", 86.
20 Arendt, *The Human Condition*, 38–39.
21 Ibid., 39.
22 Benjamin, "The Storyteller".
23 Sennett, *The Fall of Public Man*, 5.
24 Ibid., 4.
25 Ibid., 337–340.
26 Ibid., 27.
27 On Heidegger's hut and the philosophical, ethical and political implications of the escape from the city it represents, see Sennett, *Building and Dwelling*, 126–129.
28 See Sennett, *Together*, 179–195.
29 On this question, see in particular the chapter "Invisibility and Withdrawal" in Arendt's *The Life of the Mind*, which extends our understanding of the notion of appearance and at the same time works through the productive tension between thinking and the human condition of plurality:

> Since plurality is one of the basic existential conditions of human life on earth – so that *inter homines esse*, to be among men, was to the Romans the sign of being alive, aware of the realness of world and self, and *inter homines esse desinere*, to cease to be among men, a synonym for dying – to be by myself and to have intercourse with myself is the outstanding characteristic of the life of the mind Arendt, *The Life of the Mind*, p. 74.

30 Ibid., 75.
31 Sennett, *Together*, 181.
32 See Ibid., 182–190.
33 Alÿs and Ferguson, "Russell Ferguson in Conversation with Francis Alÿs", 31.
34 Arendt, *The Human Condition*, 178.
35 Benjamin, "The Paris of the Second Empire", 41. Although the English translation uses "distraction" for *Geistesabwesenheit*, and although the polarity between attention (*Aufmerksamkeit*) and distraction (*Zerstreuung*) is important in Benjamin's thinking, here a more literal translation such as "absentmindedness" is much more attuned to the polarity between presence of mind (*Geistesgegenwart*) and absentmindedness (*Geistesabwesenheit*), which also plays an important role in many aesthetic and historico-political considerations throughout his work.
36 Fried, *Why Photography Matters*, 253.
37 Arendt, *The Human Condition*, 50.
38 Tavani, "Hannah Arendt".

Bibliography

Alÿs, Francis and Russell Ferguson, "Russell Ferguson in Conversation with Francis Alÿs", in *Francis Alÿs*, edited by Cuauhtémoc Medina, Russell Ferguson e Jean Fisher, 7–55, London/New York: Phaidon, 2007.
Arendt, Hannah, *The Life of the Mind, Vol. 1: Thinking*, London: Secker & Warburg, 1978.
Arendt, Hannah, *Lectures on Kant's Political Philosophy*, edited and with an interpretative essay by Ronald Beiner, Chicago: The University of Chicago Press, 1992.
Arendt, Hannah, *The Human Condition*, Chicago/London: The University of Chicago Press, 1998.

Bachelard, Gaston, *The Poetics of Space*, translated by Maria Jolas, Boston: Beacon Press, 1994.

Benjamin, Walter, *The Arcades Project*, translated by Howard Eiland and Kevin McLaughlin, Cambridge, MA/London: The Belknap Press of Harvard University Press, 1999.

Benjamin, Walter, "The Paris of the Second Empire", in *Selected Writings, Vol. 4: 1938–1940*, translated by Harry Zohn, edited by Howard Eiland and Michael W. Jennings, 3–92, Cambridge, MA: Harvard University Press, 2003.

Benjamin, Walter, "The Storyteller: Observations on the Works of Nikolai Leskov", in *Selected Writings, Vol. 3: 1935–1938*, translated by Harry Zohn, edited by Howard Eiland and Michael W. Jennings, 143–166, Cambridge, MA, Harvard University Press, 2002.

Canela, Juan and Carla Filipe, "Actualizando passados esquecidos: uma conversa com Carla Filipe", *Dardo Magazine*, no. 91 (2016): 96–101.

Felski, Rita, "The Invention of Everyday Life", in *Doing Time: Feminist Theory and Postmodern Culture*, 77–98, New York/London: New York University Press, 2000.

Fried, Michael, *Why Photography Matters as Art as Never Before*, New Haven/London: Yale University Press, 2008.

Lima, Francisco Cardoso and Carla Filipe, "Entrevista a Carla Filipe", in Francisco Cardoso Lima, "O Artista pelo Artista na Voz do Próprio", PhD in Art Studies, Universidade de Aveiro, 2013.

Mourão, João, Luís Silva and Carla Filipe, "João Mourão and Luís Silva in Conversation with Carla Filipe", in *Amanhã não há arte*, Lisboa: Fundação EDP, 2019.

Sennett, Richard, *The Fall of Public Man*, Cambridge/London/Melbourne: Cambridge University Press, 1976.

Sennett, Richard, *Together: The Rituals, Pleasures and Politics of Cooperation*, New Haven/London: Yale University Press, 2012.

Sennett, Richard, *Building and Dwelling: Ethics for the City*, New York: Farrar, Straus and Giroux, 2018.

Simmel, Georg, "The Metropolis and Mental Life", in *The Sociology of Georg Simmel*, edited and translated by Kurt H. Wolff, 409–424, Glencoe, IL: The Free Press, 1950.

Tavani, Elena, "Hannah Arendt – Aesthetics and Politics of Appearance", *Proceedings of the European Society for Aesthetics* 5 (2013): 466–475. www.eurosa.org/volumes/5/TavaniESA2013.pdf

Part II
City, place and the political

6   From the *domus* to the *urbs*
The place of life

Andrew Benjamin

Opening

Questions arise once the city is taken to be an object of experience existing beyond the hold of mere empirical description.[1] One concerns the city as a possible locus of experience that is not delimited by simple acts of description. This question acquires acuity when it is also understood that integral to the city – sedimented into it – are the constitutive memories that form part of it.[2] Having acquired this level of complexity, the possibility of the city being an object of experience takes on a different quality, as does what counts as experience. As a result experience can no longer be equated with immediacy. A related question concerns the determinate elements of the subject/object relation itself; the subject and the object of experience. Who experiences? What is it that is experienced? Already present as part of the history of the city is a division – though one with its own internal forms of connection – between a history that has a literal archaeological presence and thus has an ineliminable material register and that which is there despite the absence of the material.[3] The latter is as relevant as the material insofar as those elements – for example, sites of the massacre of the indigenous occupiers of land that occurred during the process of settlement and of which there is no direct material evidence – are ones that are not simply forgotten, more significantly they are maintained as forgotten in the construction of the city. The latter point gives rise to the problem of what it is like to bring the question of memory and thus of remembering into the more general concern with the city as a locus of experience. There are, of course, no immediate or direct answers to these questions. Nonetheless, they are important precisely because they provide fundamental elements framing how the complex set of connections between the city as an object of experience and subjects of experience are to be conceived. There will always be the need to position these concerns within a delimited domain.

In this chapter, what is compressed into the questions noted earlier concerning the relationship between the city and experience will be taken up through an analysis of two related images, the foundation of Lavinium and the founding of Rome. Staged in both is the presentation of the founding of

DOI: 10.4324/9781003452928-8

80 *Rethinking the City*

the city and thus a presentation of a retrospective recreation of the origin. (This is the enacted presence of the myth of origin.) Part of the more general argument is going to be that analyses of this nature make a contribution to the question of how the city as a locus of experience may be understood since it will show how differentials of power are inscribed into the image of the city in acts of foundation. Differentials of power, as used in the argumentation of this chapter, is a term underscoring the recognition that differences are never pure. They are inevitably constructed in terms of diminished or augmented access to the benefits inherent in the organization of human life; they are not the product of human actions; on the contrary they position and determine actions.[4] In the context of this chapter, differentials of power are presented in terms of the differences between the slave and the citizen. In general terms, while the interrelationship between experience, memory and the city yields a point of departure, on its own that set of connections is not enough. There is a further aspect that forms an indispensable part of the project. The city as a locus of thought, its presence within the philosophical, is not exhausted by its literal presentation in an image. An engagement with what is represented – represented both within and equally beyond the image's ideational content – also has to occur. The argument however is a complex one.

What has to be taken into consideration is the relationship between the city and a conception of the philosophical that defines the latter in terms of its engagement with life. There is an important assumption at work here. To the extent that philosophy is defined in relation to life – in other words, to the extent that there is an affinity between the philosophical and the biopolitical – then what has to be noted, as a necessary correlate to that definition, is the claim that life is placed. While it can only be sketched in outline, what is meant by biopolitics does not have to do with the relationship between government and human populations emerging at a particular historical juncture (this is of course the argument of Michel Foucault in *Sécurité, Territoire, Population*).[5] The claim is not a historical one. Rather the biopolitical identifies the relationship between life understood as an activity which can only be addressed as always already placed. Aristotle's famous assertion in the *Politics* (1253a) that "the human is by nature and essentially a political animal" (ὁ ἄνθρωπος φύσει πολιτικὸν ζῶον) has to be understood as claiming that what human being is essentially (namely, the being of being human) is a *polis* dweller. In other words, human life cannot be separated from its location in the *polis*. The *polis* is the place of life. Such a positioning of human being – human being as being-in-place – is also signalled by Arendt:

> Men = earth bound creatures, living in communities, endowed with common sense, *sensus communis*, a community sense; not autonomous, needing each other's company even for thinking ("freedom of the pen") = first part of the *Critique of Judgment*: aesthetic judgment.[6]

Life necessitates a philosophical consideration of the place in which life is lived – in Arendtian terms human beings are "earth bound creatures" – since life is the process of its being lived out. As a result life has a necessary connection to place. Places are inhabited. The inhabitation of place establishes an ineluctable link to architecture (be the latter transitory or permanent). From within this framework architecture can be reconsidered not in relation to the creation of buildings but rather as the housing of life. This is the move from the *domus* to the *urbs*. Design as a process occurs within that particular setting. This redefinition of the architectural as the housing of life gives rise to a number of interrelated questions. They have to be addressed since they emerge once life is given centrality.

The point of departure for these questions is the proposition that life while placed cannot be essentialized in terms of activity. The implicit premise is that the regulative element in this claim is that housing be commensurate with the continuation of life as liveable. Hence, the first question to be posed in relation to any urban configuration is how it houses life. The second is this: what is the nature – the quality – of the life maintained through its being housed? Asking the questions posed earlier undoes the possibility of an abstract conception of activity since once what is emphasized is the continual presence of forms of life, then these questions bring into play the already present differential of power that defines and structures forms of life. Differing modes of inhabitation are to be defined in terms of the differentials of power that are articulated within them and that these modes sustain.

Towards Life

There is, at least since Arendt's *The Human Condition*, the continual identification of the project of human being with life. The latter needs to be developed since life is neither simple finitude nor is it delimited by the body in any direct way. Rather life within such a setting figures in terms of process; life as the *vita activa*. What this means is that life can be understood as the complex continuity of its being lived out. Underscoring the centrality of life, which here can be identified with the discontinuous continuity of its actualization, brings with it the possibility of the development of a non-anthropocentric conception of human life. This occurs by insisting on place – the world – as the necessary locus of life. Occurring as a result is an already present and thus constitutive and original relation between life and world. Holding to the centrality of that constitutive relation gives rise to the contemporaneous realization that the actualization of what philosophy has long thought of as the "good life" is far from necessary. There is only ever the actualization of different forms of life. That lack of the necessity of the "good life" is premised upon the inscription of what has already been identified as differentials of power within the placed nature of human being. While the first aspect of the discovery of life brings the originality of the relation that defines human being as being-in-place into play, opening up the need to incorporate the "good life" is already to have introduced the other aspect that forms part of the discovery of life.

The claim is straightforward. Philosophy has always been concerned with the possibility of the "good life". While that concern has not given rise to a unanimity of approaches – for example, Aristotle on "*eudaimonia*" is importantly different to Seneca's conception of the "*vita beata*" – it is nonetheless possible to discern within the presence of philosophy's continual engagement with life an opening to the good. The point here is that references to the "good life" are not to be understood in terms of an abstraction from life. Rather they attest to the presence of that which attends life as an immanent possibility. The "good life" becomes therefore that which allows the different ways in which being-in-place occurs to be judged. The locus of judgement is the differing ways in which forms of life are housed. Judgement is not the mere attribution of a quality to the given. Rather judgement presupposes a transformation of the given into that which can be judged. Judgement assumes therefore the judgeability of the given. And judgeability assumes the presence of immanent criteria of judgement.[7] In this context those criteria cannot be separated from the proposition that human being is being-in-place. The connection between the possibility of the "good life" and the housing of forms of life in creating a locus of judgement is that which allows for a productive link to be established between an analysis of the presentation of slavery in the ancient world (presentation since what will be analysed on the level of the image is the presence of slaves) and questions staged by the demand for hospitality within the contemporary.[8] Today, it is the combination of poverty and the continual creation of refugees that combines to refuse possible actualizations of the potential for the "good life".[9] Again, the "good life" is not just a quality that pertains in the abstract, it has to be thought in terms of the relation between lived possibilities and an immanent potential for the "good life".

To restate the opening that has already emerged; the identification of the "good life" as an immanently present potentiality intrinsic to the placed nature of human being as being-in-place provides a ground of judgement for the particularization of life on the level of the pragmatic instance. In other words, integral to the position to be developed is that the possibility of judgement is already there, given the necessity that life is always already housed (this is the case as much in pragmatic instances as it is in images). It is however essential to go further. The claim is that a concern with housing brings the architectural into play. To the extent that an insistence on lived possibilities, whether actualized or not, can be accorded viability, then as a result, architecture cannot be reduced to building nor equally can the architectural be conceived as a contingent concern of human being. As though life were only ever contingently housed. The presence of life as already housed – recognizing the possibility of both positive and negative determinations – and human being as being-in-place both ground and occasion judgement. That ground has a complex presence. It is both an *arché* and yet precisely because the presence of the "good life" is only ever an immanent potentiality, it is an-archaic. The actualization of the "good life" is not a founding state of affairs. Rather it is an-archaic because it is continuously present as immanent; therefore as a potentiality providing a continual ground of judgement. It is precisely this position that allows for the development of a philosophy of the city.

While David Harvey is correct to argue that

> the right to the city ... is to claim some kind of shaping power over the processes of urbanization, over the ways in which our cities are made and re-made and to do so in a fundamental and radical way,

the question to be addressed is, of course, how, what Harvey identifies as a "shaping power" is to be interpreted.[10] The question is more complex than first appears as any response has to include the way the presence of both active and repressed memories figures within "processes of urbanization". The question is central as it pertains to the presence of the city as an object to be experienced once it is understood as the place in which what is at work are the differentials of power that are of necessity operative within the placed nature of human being. Rather than suggest a simple response, a beginning will be made by analysing two images; one of the founding of Lavinium and the other of the founding of Rome. The choice is not arbitrary. These images of foundation, both in the mythic sense and in the literal building of walls, demonstrate the ways in which differentials of power are already at work in the representation of the construction of the foundation. The foundation is therefore a complex site.[11] While this approach underscores that the positing of both original singularity or purity is simply putative, it has the further value of allowing for a reconfiguration of hospitality – whether that is linked to the housing of refugees or in the case of Rome the presence and possibility of providing housing that was contemporaneous with the – "good life" – in terms of the relationship between modes of inhabitation and judgement. This is a complex and demanding point.

The presupposition underpinning it is that the systematic housing of slaves as free thus as bound to the possibility of the "good life" would be contemporaneous with the abolition of slavery. While there would be a necessary temporal lag, the two moments would have to be thought together. The housing of slaves that was in fact premised on the possibility of the "good life" presupposes the suspension of a logic that sustained slavery. A similar argument can be made in relation to the refugee. The accommodation of the refugee that is defined in relation to the possibility of the "good life" also has to be understood as predicated upon the suspension of the logics creating refugees. While again there would be a necessary temporal lag, what has to be undertaken both philosophically and architecturally is a mode of inclusion that is positioned in relation to the logics sustaining traditional urbanism.

84 Rethinking the City

Figure 6.1 Details from *Tomb of the Statili (Sepulcrum Statiliorum)*, Museo Nazionale Romano, Rome.
Source: Reproduced with the permission of Ministero della Cultura.

To the extent that the latter is the articulation of the interplay of the logics of carbon and capital which when taken together are inextricably bound up with the creation of refugees means that the adequate housing of refugees would be premised on an urbanism no longer explicitly defined in terms of those logics.[12] Raised here is a set of concerns that will guide the encounter with images of the foundation of Lavinium and Rome. (In interpretive terms what this means is that these images have a force that exceeds their specific historical location.)

The first image is the presence of a wall in a frieze from the *Tomb of the Statili (Sepulcrum Statiliorum)* (Figure 6.1). The overall significance of the element of the frieze to be discussed is that it recounts the story located in a number of sources, including Dionysus of Halicarnassus, (1.45.2) of the founding of Lavinium.[13] What matters therefore is that the frieze can be positioned as part of the presentation of a myth of origin. More generally, it concerns the presence of Aeneas. While other elements of the frieze deal with military battles between the Rutuli and the Trojans, what is of great and specific interest in the frieze is that it forms part of an Augustan engagement with both Roman identity and thus Rome's relation to Troy.[14] The seated woman in the frieze according to the analysis by Marini Recchia and Fausto Zevi is a "probable personification of a city".[15] The second is the image *Romulus und Remus bauen die Mauern von Rom, Unknown* (circa 1501–1625) located in

From the domus *to the* urbs 85

Figure 6.2 Romulus und Remus bauen die Mauern von Rom, Unknown (circa 1501–1625), Herzog August Bibliothek Wolfenbüttel: D 4 Geom. 2° (1–91).
Source: Authorized reproduction.

the Herzog August Bibliothek in Wolfenbüttel (Figure 6.2). With the juxtaposition of these images both historical and interpretive questions emerge. To invoke Aby Warburg's formulation, what form within these two images does the "afterlife of antiquity" take?[16] On one level, these images are separated by 1,500 years; on another, there is an important form of repetition. What, however, is being repeated? On what does a "nachleben" insist?[17] A return will be made to the questions. To begin, there is clearly another: what is a wall? Answering this question means staying with ancient sources.

The Philosophical and Literary Wall

In both the Roman and the Greek world it is inconceivable to think of the creation of a city independently of the creation of walls. Walls have a stark reality. That reality is, of course, the creation of the condition of both enclosure and exclusion. Walls have to be thought in relation to gates and thus threshold conditions. Vitruvius states that a new city begins with the building of its walls. And yet, in *De Architectura* Vitruvius wrote sparingly of walls. In recounting the move of the "city of Sapia" from one location to another, he noted that once a site was found "the walls were transferred" (*ad moenia transferenda*).[18] They were transferred because the initial setting for the city had become unliveable. On one level, the sequence is hardly remarkable. It is possible to detail the number of instances in which the wall figures as a significant and yet real occurrence. The wall however denotes far more.[19]

As a beginning the wall identifies what might be described as a specific conception of shared space. That conception of space is always linked to a sense of the regulative be that a sense theological or purely normative. While the example from Horace concerns the ancient world, it is not difficult to see that there is a contemporary force to this formulation. Horace rewrites the Greek poet Callimachus. In the Hymn to Demeter, Callimachus wrote that:

Δάματερ, μὴ τῆνος ἐμὶν φίλος, ὅς τοι ἀπεχθής,
εἴη μηδ᾽ ὁμότοιχος:
                    Hymn to Demeter. 116–7

Demeter, may the man you hate never be my friend nor share a wall with me.[20]

Both the shared wall and friendship are based on a specific reverence for the Gods and thus contextually on this sense of the regulative. As significantly, the wall in question is as much a literal object as it is a condition of the shared. It is not difficult to notice this doubled presence in Horace's rewriting of Callimachus. In *Odes* 3.2.26–8, Horace wrote,

vetabo, qui Cereris sacrum
volgarit arcanae, sub isdem
sit trabibus

I forbid the one who made public the secret rites of Ceres
be under the same beams (as me).[21]

What is important about Horace's rewriting of Callimachus is the way in which "shared beams" come to be substituted for the "same wall" (ὁμότοιχος). What is significant about his position emerges from the fact that the work synecdoche circumvents any straightforward reduction of the material to its mere physical presence. An opening of genuine importance is provided precisely because material presence now coincides with an evocation of the shared as that which both includes and excludes. Inclusion and exclusion are far from neutral terms. The doubled quality of the wall is thereby affirmed.

It is possible to continue to find points of intersection between the presence of the wall, moments of both constraint and control and what has already been rereferred to as a form of an-arché. Note Heraclitus DK 44:

μάχεσθαι χρὴ τὸν δῆμον ὑπὲρ τοῦ νόμου ὅκωσπερ τείχεος
The people must fight for its law as for its walls.[22]

Here what is significant is the connection between "law" (νομος) and the "wall" (τεῖχος).[23] The wall, while clearly to be identified with the literal wall, can also be interpreted as affirming not just the placed nature of human being – the wall as disclosing the space of human sociality – but equally the recognition that the wall both separates and joins, excludes and includes. These divisions are spatial to the extent that the spatiality in question cannot be separated from the enacted presence of differentials of power. Holding to the position necessitates that place – while an indispensable part of any definition of the being human being – is inevitably marked either by the differences it contains or by the differences maintained by exclusion. The wall constructs an inside and an outside that are occupied in differential terms. Henceforth, because this form of difference operates both materially and spatially – thus architecturally – it will be understood in terms of differential modes of territorialization. (The shift in terminology, while accepting the general claim that human being is being-in-place, marks the differential ways in which placedness is actualized. Thereby providing a way of opening up what Harvey first identified as "processes of urbanization". They become differential modes of territorialization.)[24]

The wall therefore functions to describe the being of being human while at the same time having particular specificity, one that always devolves into differing forms of territorialization. Once there is a move to a description of the disclosed place as that which involves different modes of territorialization, it follows that the space that is disclosed cannot be understood in terms of either unity or neutrality. Implicit in the fragment is the claim that there is no point at which it is possible to think of human being independently of being-in-place; namely, as always already situated within the space disclosed by the "wall". And thus it is an an-arché for the precise reason that it is always already in play. The same type of thinking can be brought to the term *nomos*. In this context, it refers both to the particularity of specific laws and conventions (the always contextual and potentially conflictual *nomoi*) and to the identification of *nomos* with what can be described as the already present immanent condition of human sociality. *Nomos*, thus construed, is continually positioned against the plurality of conflicting *nomoi*. The position is not arbitrary. It is also clear from the reiteration of the first line of Pindar Fragment 169a – Νόμος ὁ πάντων βασιλεύς ("nomos the king of all") which is taken as asserting the ubiquity of *nomos* in contradistinction to the plurality of *nomoi* – in both Herodotus and Plato.[25] In addition, the accompanying

88 *Rethinking the City*

claim is that in contemporary terms the relation between *nomos* and *nomoi* as it appears here can be mapped on to the distinction between unconditional justice and the pragmatic, the latter can be understood as contingent presence of specific statutes.

The Heraclitan fragment divides between that which addresses specificity and that which is always irreducible to it. There is therefore a form of an-archic excess. The excessive here is immanence. The argument is going to be that this element is there at the beginning, thus allowing the specific to be judged. The judgeability of the specific opens up to both negative and positive determinations. Removed as a result is the attribution to a wall, or a gate, or a threshold, of anything other than an always already determined set of possibilities that are themselves judgeable. It is the relationship between the immanent and the particular that needs to be demonstrated in relation to the already identified images. If there are going to be spaces of hospitality, then they are not going to be linked to the discovery or the creation of an "empty zone".[26] Rather they would arise from the suspension of pre-existing configurations of power.[27] That suspension then becomes the continual creation of openings to be lived out and thus to be housed. That is why Boano and Astolfo argue that "hospitality" once recast as what they call "inhabitation" has greater extension. They take it to refer

> to the way we exist in the city, particularly our ability to dwell, care for, repair, and imagine relationships and places and to constantly reposition ourselves according to a specific trajectory, both spatial and temporal, in a constant negotiation of life.[28]

It is this reference to the constancy of a "negotiation" with "life" to which a return will need to be made.

Presented Walls

The first image is from the *Tomb of the Statili* (*Sepulcrum Statiliorum*). It is a painted columbarium frieze. Created during the period in which Augustus was emperor (27BCE–14CE). (It is currently on display in the Palazzo Massimo alle Terme in Rome.) The frieze is part of a number that takes up the creation as much of Rome and its ensuing identity. As a whole, the friezes create what Peter J. Holliday in his analysis of the works in their entirety describes as offering "an extraordinary plea for inclusion in the energizing vision of a unified Rome, a powerful new rhetoric of *Romanitas*".[29] The posited recovery of specific "mores" forms an essential part of the creation of what *Romanitas* means. In part this is linked to the way Roman identity was not defined – in any direct sense – in racial or geographical terms. As Holliday points out, what continued to matter was not *nobilitas* but *virtus*. Inclusion is linked therefore to a projected universalizing tendency that delimits and creates a space in relation to which the particular presence of a myth of origin forms an essential part of the creation of a setting in which self-identity and thus the identity of selves can accord.

It is not difficult to see therefore that what is occurring in this setting is central to the universalizing of virtue. There is a relation of dependency. Virtue is connected to the creation of peace and the presence of peace ensures the continuity of virtue. It is at this precise point, of course, that the literal content of the image needs to be brought into play. As has already been noted the obvious presence of the seated figure of the woman ensures that what is at stake is the reiteration of the myth of origin. The building of the wall brings with it both the literal and the figural significance that wall construction entails. If the description of the frieze went no further, then what is seen is the relationship between the founding of Rome as the setting in which virtue becomes possible. However, the frieze contains more. Indeed, the vast majority of the image is taken up neither by the seated woman nor by the wall as though they were discrete entities. The contrary is the case. The wall is being built. There is literally the presentation of a dynamic process of wall creation. The question that has to be addressed therefore is the status of those building the wall. Before addressing this question, it is essential to remain with the presence of virtue.

One of the arguments developed by Seneca in a number of his texts concerns the relationship between slavery and virtue.[30] As part of the universalising project within Stoicism – though this will have extension elsewhere in Roman thought – Seneca leaves open the possibility of the virtuous slave.[31] In other words, the slave can be included within the realm of virtue. While Stoicism allows for the virtuous slave insofar as Stoicism's sense of the universal ignores the distinction between the slave and the freeman, it is unclear in what sense the so-called virtuous slave can actually function as a locus of virtue since acting in relation to virtue presupposes the possibility of being free.

At this point it is essential to turn to the frieze since what can be seen in the creation of the wall is the point at which the setting for the reiterated presence of the universality of virtue – namely, the place disclosed by the wall – is established by the very ones from whom that possibility is itself withdrawn. What this means of course is that if slavery can be equated with the creation of what Walter Benjamin called "mere life" (*bloßes Leben*), then it is also the case that fundamental to *Romanitas* is the denial, in precise and already calculated instances, of the very universality it sought to propagate.[32] The slave's body therefore is caught at the intersection between the creation of a civic space for the free and its disavowal through the recreation of "mere life". This accounts for why, for example, in the comedies of Plautus the slave can function as a comic figure precisely because the tension between "mere life" and a setting in which instances of civil life are projected back onto the slave continue to define the operative presence of the figure of the slave. It is only in comedy, thus as a joke, that a slave – here Leonida in Plautus's *Asinaria* – may say to the freeman, "tam ego homo sum quam tu" ("I am a human being as much as you").[33] The "quam" (as) announces a relation of equality and thus a freedom that is impossible. Unfreedom has to prevail. Again, this is the condition of the comedy. The slaves' presence within theatre – and the importance of the comedic should be noted – and, equally, within both Stoicism and the Epicurean definition of the "good life" in terms of *otium* (the latter is a condition that depends on slavery) are the presentation of sites of radical unfreedom.[34] This underscores the centrality of the proposition that the presence of life necessitates the continuity of "negotiation". (It should always be remembered that negotiation is "*nec otium*".)[35]

What occurs within the frieze therefore is the presentation of the complex set of connections between a myth of foundation, the creation of the literal wall that is simultaneously the affirmation of the placedness of human being – that is the being of being human as being-in-place – and the inscribed presence of those whose inclusion is maintained by their forced and continuously reinforced exclusion. If this final point were to be developed, then what has to be argued is that the creation of the setting of life cannot be separated from setting in which the equation of life with "mere life" is equally there as a possibility. The argument has to be presented in terms of the slaves' literal creation and what that creation then entails. The copresence of civic life and "mere life" defines the image. Different modes of territorialization are occurring; there is a doubling within the same place. Hence the need to move from place to differential modes of territorialization to account for lived reality of being-in-place. However, it is important that this positioning resists any form of naturalization. That resistance is provided by the possibility of a continual opening to judgement. While that opening could not have been recognized within the world in which the frieze was created – there was neither an explicit nor an implicit critical relation to slavery in the Roman world – once it is conceded that either an image of place, the building of walls etc. or the reference to walls and place in philosophical or literary texts brings into play both its own pragmatic determinations and an immanent presence that while related to the pragmatic cannot be reduced to it, what is opened is the possibility of judgement. That possibility is defined by the pragmatic and the immanent; in directly philosophical terms, what this means is that their anoriginal irreducibility is judgement's condition of possibility.

In the anonymous 16th-century engraving – *Romulus und Remus bauen die Mauern von Rom* – architecture is directly inscribed. The square in what might well have been Romulus's right hand presents architecture as a practice. This reiterates the presence of practice within architecture's representation in a number of Renaissance frontispieces, notably Serlio.[36] (This is radically distinct from the personification of architecture which appears in the 18th century in the frontispiece of Marc-Antoine Laugier's *Essai sur l'architecture* (2nd ed. 1755))[37] (Figure 6.3). In Laugier, architecture has a purely symbolic presence. In the other images, activity and practice predominate. This

From the domus to the urbs   91

Figure 6.3 Frontispiece of Marc-Antoine Laugier's *Essai sur l'architecture* (2nd ed. 1755).

Source: Photograph of author's copy.

is not just a difference on the level of meaning, it allows architecture's own activity to be understood as always already implicated in the creation of the disequilibria of power that is commensurate with the foundation of a city. This position is reinforced by the presence within the engraving of both the wall and the positioning of the gate as the threshold condition marking both entry and exit. The necessity of policing has now two modalities. The city is the site of both the free and the unfree, and equally the city gate is policed to both include and exclude. The presence of that possibility needs to be set against what has been identified earlier as that which allows for judgement. Again, this position can be maintained to the extent that architecture is understood as the housing of life. This position demands therefore a fundamental move away from the identification of architecture with the single house; an identification that in the end necessitates the conflation of architecture with real estate. It is only by moving to a relational conception of the architectural – again, from the *domus* to the *urbs* – that the complexities that define life can be linked to the necessity that life be housed.

As in the frieze what is occurring in the engraving is a specific presentation of the territorialization of life. The city is being constructed in relation to freedom as a result of the practices of the unfree. Despite the appearance of neutrality the disequilibria of power that is there at the origin brings with it – in part through its own form of refusal – the recognition that life is always already housed. A setting that once linked to the copresence of the wall and of *nomos*, which in their irreducibility to the purely material opens up and sustains the possibility of judgement.

Returning to the specific example with which these deliberations started, namely images presenting slavery, means noting that any attempt to address the problem of slavery would have to address the question of the housing of slaves. The "afterlife of antiquity" that occurs when these two images are juxtaposed is not of the movement of bodies, as though bodies merely moved, the afterlife is more emphatically of the construction of the city in a way that positions freedom and unfreedom as originally present within it. Once this position is opened up in the wake of a critical engagement with slavery, which within the realm of the strictly philosophical means relinquishing any link between the contemporary and both Stoicism and Epicureanism, then what becomes necessary is how the reterritorialization of a city or the reterritorialization of parts of the city would then occur. Again, this has to be understood not as an act of charity but as stemming from the recognition that life is already housed. (As a consequence *caritas* loses its hold as an operative ethico-political term. Emerging in its place is a position which, if only as a point of departure, can be defined in terms of "the right to the city".)[38] The move to addressing this question in terms of territorialisation is that this allows specificity to exert its hold. It is a form of specificity that has to address, on the level of housing, what different modes of inhabitation demand.

Experience and Differentials of Power

What has to occur now is a return to what has already emerged as the experience of the city. Once the city is no longer to be understood in terms of its pure givenness to experience, there will always need to be the recognition that the object of experience has inscribed within it differentials of power that are not literally superficial but were and remain constitutive. Whether that origin is equated with settler colonialism or constructed by a relationship between freedom and unfreedom, any concern with experience has to incorporate them into the object as a locus of experience. Such a locus cannot be experienced immediately, it has to come to be experienced. What is clear about the structure of both the Roman house and the Roman city is that slaves were housed in relation to their position as unfree.[39] While it is true that freed slaves occupied the "same" domestic and public space as citizens, what is left open as a question is the effect that the possible suppression of slavery would have had on both domestic and public space. Precisely because the slave is there at the origin in which the architect appears as a slave master, the overcoming of slavery would envisage a different relationship between architecture and the creation of both public and private space. Were there not to have been slaves then what counted as inhabitation would have been radically transformed. The housing of slaves would have had implications for how space was produced. The same claim can be made in terms of the housing of the refugee.

In his extended reflection on "negotiation", Derrida establishes a connection between what he calls in other texts "unconditional hospitality" and the question of action. He writes the following:

> Let us begin by distinguishing affirmation and position. I am very interested in this distinction. For me it is of the utmost importance. One must not be content with affirmation. One only needs position. That is, one must create institutions. Therefore, one needs position. One needs a stance. Thus, negotiation, at this particular moment, does not simply take place between affirmation and negation, position and negation: it takes place between affirmation and position, because the position threatens the affirmation. That is to say that in itself institutionalization in its very success threatens the movement of unconditional affirmation. And yet this needs to happen, for if the affirmation were content to – how shall I say it – to wash its hands of the institution in order to remain at a distance, in order to say, "I affirm, and then the rest is of no interest to me, the institution does not interest me . . . let the others take care of that", then this affirmation would deny itself, it would not be an affirmation. Any affirmation, any promise in its very structure requires its fulfilment. There is no promise that does not require its fulfilment. Affirmation requires a position.[40]

94 Rethinking the City

Taking a position is, of course, to take a stand. Stand taking can be equated with a mode of being. In this sense, negotiation delimits not just activity but activity that is premised upon the holding of an affirmed position that is linked to that which has unconditional force. Moving beyond the strict confines of Derrida's own argumentation, the contention here is that what has unconditional force is the description of human being as being-in-place. Acts of displacement, whether they be forced removal or the refusal to accept the arrival of the refugee, can be judged precisely because they stand opposed to that which has unconditional force. The space between the unconditional and the specific is the space of judgement. Action within that space is a type of affirmation. While Derrida is right to argue that "a promise requires its fulfilment", what is important is that action be linked to judgement. (That which makes judgement possible is, of course, the immanent presence of that which has unconditional force.) In his lectures on hospitality Derrida argues that all forms of calculation be excluded from the thinking of hospitality.[41] For Derrida, the copresence of "affirmation" and "position" does not amount to a form of calculation. And yet, it might be argued that something is missing from Derrida's argument. In the same way that the presence of slaves structures inhabitation within the city, the presence of the refugee and thus hospitality more generally cannot be separated from different ways of coming to inhabit the city. There is therefore an intrinsic spatial concern at work. Hospitality becomes a form of inhabitation. Inhabitation here must be thought in terms of a reterritorialization. That reterritorialization results from an understanding of the city and thus an experience of the city beyond immediacy, and thus it is a conception of experience that has to be connected to the structuring force of judgement.

In conclusion, therefore any genuine engagement with the city as a locus of experience has to separate experience from immediacy and connect it to the processes – be they architectural, philosophical or political – that are enacted as a result of the productive relation between experience and judgement. Only then is it possible to approach the city either as a topos within the philosophical or as a site for design. Judgement allows for the actualization of the city as a locus of potential re-inhabitation. The question of potentiality and thus the actualization of potentials is fundamental to projects of intervention within the city no matter how they are understood. Here it would be necessary to start from the recent conceptualization of the city as a "project" by Pier Vittorio Aureli. He argues that

> the city as a project is thus not only the possibility of radical change for the city, but also the possibility of maintaining the city project as pure potential, as a way of keeping the future of the city open ended.[42]

While this claim is accurate, it is essential to avoid the conflation of "the open ended" with the deregulated. Deregulation is no more than the projected freedom to further logics of both carbon and capital. A freedom that will always need its own form of policing. This is the reason why there needs to be a link, within both the philosophical and the architectural, between judgement and potentiality.

Notes

1 This is a slightly extended version of a lecture first given in the Dipartmento di Architectura in the Politecnico di Torino on October 26, 2023. I am grateful to the response of students and staff at the Politecnico, especially Camillo Boano and Marco Trisciuoglio. Also, I want to thank Ben Brown, Nathan Bell, Julia Thwaites, Desley Luscombe, and Lucy Benjamin, as well as the volume's editors, for their helpful and insightful comments on the chapter.
2 There is an important affinity here with the position developed by Aldo Rossi. Baukuh in their critical engagement with Rossi has provided a clear summary of his position: "The city is just the material trace of the events that have produced it, a deposit of contradictory ambitions, unfulfilled hopes, a collection of vanities and weaknesses, of petty compromises, glorious failures, true madness" ("The Broken Promises", 103).
3 Michel De Certeau makes a similar point. In his discussion of walking and thus the creation of the city as the locus of experience, he writes of the creation of "surface of projection" which "itself visible, it has the effect of making invisible the operations that made it possible". de Certeau, *The Practice of Everyday Life*, 97.
4 Part of what is intended by the formulation differentials of power can be explained in terms of structural injustice. The extension to the position is that structural injustice as historical ubiquity rather than being a simple explanation of the operation of power within the contemporary. The position indicated here alludes therefore to the work of Iris Marion Young. See Young, "Structural Injustice and the Politics of Difference".
5 Foucault, *Sécurité, Territoire, Population*.
6 Arendt, *Lectures on Kant's Political Philosophy*, 27. In addition, see Benjamin, "Thinking Life: The Force of the Biopolitical".
7 For a development of this position, see Benjamin, *Place Commonality and Judgement*.
8 For an important investigation of how the connections – in both a positive and negative sense – between ancient forms of citizenship and the contemporary predicament of the refugee can be understood, see Gray, "Citizenship as Barrier and Opportunity".
9 The most important philosophical analysis of the refugee is Bell, *Refugees*.
10 Harvey, "The Right to the City", 160.
11 In her analysis of the presence of architectural metaphors in Latin literature, Bettina Reitz-Joosse argues that "city-building was deeply relevant to Roman global politics in general as well as to the powerful contemporary Augustan discourse of re-foundation and *renovation*". Reitz-Joosse, *Building in Words*, 135. Reitz-Joosse's work is indispensable for any rethinking of the role of architecture in the analysis of literary text and by extension works of art. For another philosophical account of the foundation of Rome, see Serres, *Rome*.
12 For an analysis of the positioning of the logic of carbon, understood as "carbon form", as indicative of the current state of modernity and its implications for both architectural theory and design, see Iturbe, "Architecture and the Death of Carbon Modernity".
13 Though the position is slightly more complicated, as Dionysus of Halicarnassus refers more directly to Alba.

14 On the general question of the relationship between Rome and Troy during this period, see Finkelberg, "Roman Reception of the Trojan War".
15 Recchia and Zevi, "La storia più antica di Roma", 28. (My translation) In Daniela Bonanome's entry in the catalogue from the Palazzo Maximo, she writes the following: "Therefore the building of the walls represents the foundation of Lavinium by Aeneas, in the presence of the mythical personification". (My translation) Gaspari and Paris, *Palazzo Massimo alle Terme*, 376.
16 For an overview of Warburg's conception of art history within which the idea of the "afterlife of antiquity" plays a central role, see Johnson, *Memory, Metaphor, and Aby Warburg's Atlas of Images*, 2012.
17 Opened up here is of course the question of how to interpret Roman art. Clearly, what is being distanced, by bringing these images into a form of juxtaposition, is both the claim that meaning is determined either by the context of work's production, or it is linked to the work of rhetoric operative in the period under consideration. This is not an argument against recourse to both context and the use of rhetoric. It is merely to say that neither is sufficient precisely because slavery was normalized within this period and thus cannot be used to account for what is *now* clearly being staged in these images. Meaning cannot be separated from the work's afterlife. It is not located simply in its contextual life. While this necessitates far more detail what is being staged here is an opening towards the work of both Tonio Hölscher and Jas Elsner. See Hölscher, *The Language of Images in Roman Art* and Elsner, *Art and the Roman Viewer*.
18 Vitruvius, *On Architecture*, 44 [1.iv,.12].
19 In his study of walls within predominantly literary texts, Simon Goldhill has argued that the Long Walls that joined Athens to Piraeus "play a significant role in the conceptualization of Athens as a polis". Goldhill is of course correct. The project here however is to take the presence of wall less literally and thus allow another set of questions to emerge. See Goldhill, "What's in a Wall?".
20 Callimachus, *Hecale. Hymns. Epigrams*, 369.
21 My translation.
22 My translation.
23 The fragment is, of course, open to different interpretive possibilities. For another reading, see Papastephanou, "Walls and Laws".
24 For a more sustained development of this position, see Benjamin and Reinmuth, "The Architecture of the Counter-Measure".
25 For a discussion of the role of Pindar's fragment, see Benjamin, *Place Commonality and Judgement*.
26 See Agamben, *Quando la casa brucia*, 32.
27 While a specific argument is developed here, it should not be thought that this is the only approach. The recent analysis of sacred spaces by Pier Vittorio Aureli leads him to the conclusion that "the architecture of sacred space can offer a way of experiencing a 'different' temporality made of limits and stoppages". See his "Rituals and Walls", 24.
28 Boano and Astolfo, "Notes around Hospitality as Inhabitation", 226. Their work is indispensable for any attempt to take up housing and by extension the move from hospitality to inhabitation. Boano, *Projetto Minore* provides a sustained overview of his position. This book will be indispensable for any future thinking of the urban.
29 Holliday, "The Rhetoric of 'Romanitas'", 124. A further recent discussion of the frieze and the others related is provided by Brilliant, *Visual Narratives*, 30–36.
30 In this regard, see Benjamin, "Redressing the Metaphysics of Nudity".
31 Seneca's complex relation to slavery emerges most clearly in Letter XLVII. The claim made by others is that slaves are slaves (*Servi sunt*). This is counted by

Seneca's own formulation "by no means, they are men" (*Immo homines*). All Seneca is doing however is attributing a capacity for feeling and thus the possibility of virtue to slaves he is not in any sense calling into question the institution of slavery itself.

32 While Walter Benjamin argues that "man cannot, at any price, be said to coincide with the mere life *(mit dem bloßen Leben)* in him" (Benjamin, "Critique of Violence", 251), the argument has to be that any human can be reduced to "mere life". Slavery would be an instance of such a reduction. Moreover, it is a form of reduction that is never bare but always leaves a mark. For an account of the operative presence of systematic violence on all levels of Roman society against slaves, see Lenski, "Violence and the Roman Slave", 275–298.

33 Plautus, "Asinaria", 490 [Act II, Scene iv, Line 83]. For another reference to the way in which the comedies of Plautus work to reinforce the position of the slave and in addition establish a link between slavery and a specific conception of femininity, see: Jeremy Hartnett. *The Roman Street*, 95–97.

34 The failure of Epicureanism to develop a critique of slavery has been show, by Arenson "Epicurus on Pity, Slavery and Autonomy". Moreover, for an argument that demonstrates the link between the treatment of women and the treatment of slaves with Epicureanism, see Gordon, "Remembering the Garden".

35 Derrida in his approach to "negotiation" describes it as "un-leisure" and then further clarifies it as "the impossibility of stopping, of settling in a position. Whether one wants it or not, one is always working in the mobility between several positions, stations, places, between which a shuttle is needed". What he is describing is what is identified earlier as the continuity of "negotiation". Derrida, *Negotiations*, 16.

36 On the image of architecture in Serlio, see Luscombe, "The Architect and the Representation of Architecture".

37 The original drawing was by Charles-Dominique-Joseph Eisen and the subsequent engraving by Jean-Jacques Aliamet. For a detailed discussion of the frontispiece, see Williamson, "Other Lives: Charles Eisen and Laugier's *Essai sur L'architecture*", https://drawingmatter.org/other-lives-charles-eisen-and-laugiers-essai-sur-larchitecture/

38 The classic formulation of this position is found in Lefebvre, *Le droit à la ville*.

39 While there is a wealth of material on the topic, for an important overview of the housing of slaves in Greece and Rome, see Métraux, "Ancient Housing: 'Oikos' and 'Domus'".

40 Derrida, *Negotiations*, 26–27.

41 Derrida, *Hospitalité*, 179.

42 Aureli, "Means to an End", 38.

Bibliography

Agamben, Giorgio, *Quando la casa brucia*, Macerata: Giometti & Antonello, 2020.

Arendt, Hannah, *Lectures on Kant's Political Philosophy*, Chicago: University of Chicago Press, 1982.

Arenson, Kelley E., "Epicurus on Pity, Slavery and Autonomy", *Proceedings of the Boston Area Colloquium in Ancient Philosophy* 34, no. 1 (2019): 110–136. https://doi.org/10.1163/22134417-00341P11

Aureli, Pier Vittorio, "Means to an End. The Rise and Fall of the Architectural Project of the City", in *The City as a Project*, edited by Pier Vittorio Aureli, Berlin: Ruby Press, 2013.

Aureli, Pier Vittorio. "Rituals and Walls: On the Architecture of Sacred Space", in *Rituals and Walls: The Architecture of Sacred Space*, edited by Pier Vittorio Aureli and Maria Shéhérazade Giudici, London: The Architectural Association, 2016.

Baukuh, "The Broken Promises of *The Architecture of the City*", in *Two Essays on Architecture*, 63–119, Zürich: Kommode Verlag für Text und Bild, 2013.
Bell, Nathan, *Refugees: Towards a Politics of Responsibility*, London: Rowman and Littlefield, 2021.
Benjamin, Andrew, *Place Commonality and Judgement. Continental Philosophy and the Ancient Greeks*, London: Continuum Books, 2010.
Benjamin, Andrew, "Redressing the Metaphysics of Nudity: Notes on Seneca, Arendt, and Dignity", *Classical Philology* 113, no. 1 (2018): 39–52. https://doi.org/10.1086/695837
Benjamin, Andrew, "Thinking Life: The Force of the Biopolitical", *Crisis and Critique* 9, no. 2 (2022). www.crisiscritique.org/storage/app/media/nov-25/andrew-benjamin.pdf
Benjamin, Andrew and Gerard Reinmuth, "The Architecture of the Counter-Measure", in *On Power in Architecture*, edited by Mateja Kurir, London: Routledge, 2024. (Forthcoming).
Benjamin, Walter, "Critique of Violence", in *Selected Writings, Vol: 1, 1913–1926*, edited and translated by Marcus Bullock and Michael W. Jennings, 236–252, Cambridge: Harvard University Press, 2004.
Boano, Camillo, *Projetto Minore*, Siracusa: Lettera Ventidue, 2020.
Boano, Camillo and Giovanna Astolfo, "Notes around Hospitality as Inhabitation. Engaging with the Politics of Care and Refugees' Dwelling Practices in the Italian Urban Context", *Migration and Society: Advances in Research* 3, no. 1 (2020): 222–232. https://doi.org/10.3167/arms.2020.030118
Brilliant, Richard, *Visual Narratives. Story Telling in Etruscan and Roman Art*, Ithaca: Cornell University Press, 1984.
Callimachus, *Hecale. Hymns. Epigrams*, edited and translated by Dee L. Cayman, Cambridge: Loeb Classical Library, 2022.
de Certeau, Michel, *The Practice of Everyday Life*, translated by Steven Rendall, Berkeley: University of California Press, 2002.
Derrida, Jacques, *Negotiations. Interventions and Interviews, 1971-2001*, edited and translated by Elizabeth Rottenberg, Stanford: Stanford University Press, 2002.
Derrida, Jacques, *Hospitalité, Vol. 1: (Séminaire 1995–1996)*, Paris: Éditions du Seuil, 2021.
Elsner, Jas, *Art and the Roman Viewer*, Cambridge: Cambridge University Press, 1995.
Finkelberg, Margalit, "Roman Reception of the Trojan War", in *Rome: An Empire of Many Nations*, edited by Jonathan Price, Margalit Finkelberg and Yuvar Shahar, 87–99, Cambridge, Cambridge University Press, 2021.
Foucault, Michel, *Sécurité, Territoire, Population. Cours au Collège de France (1977–78)*, Paris: Éditions du Seuil, 2004.
Gaspari, Carlo and Rita Paris, eds., *Palazzo Massimo alle Terme (Catalogue)*, Rome: Electa, 2013.
Goldhill, Simon, "What's in a Wall?", in *Visualizing the Tragic. Drama, Myth and Ritual in Greek Art and Literature*, edited by Chris Krauss, Simon Goldhill, Helene P. Foley and Jas Elsner, 127–149, Oxford: Oxford University Press, 2007.
Gordon, Pamela, "Remembering the Garden: The Trouble with Women in the School of Epicurus", in *Philodemus and the New Testament World. Novum Testamentum, Supplements* 111 (2004): 221–243. https://doi.org/10.1163/9789047400240_011
Gray, Benjamin, "Citizenship as Barrier and Opportunity for Ancient Greek and Modern Refugees", *Humanities* 7, no. 3 (2018). https://doi.org/10.3390/h7030072
Hartnett, Jeremy, *The Roman Street. Urban life and Society in Pompeii, Herculaneum, and Rome*, Cambridge: Cambridge University Press, 2017.
Harvey, David, "The Right to the City", in *The City between Freedom and Security Contested Public Spaces in the 21st Century*, edited by Deane Simpson, Vibeke Jensen and Anders Rubing, 156–171, Berlin/Boston: Birkhäuser, 2016.

Holliday, Peter J., "The Rhetoric of 'Romanitas': The 'Tomb of the Statilii' Frescoes Reconsidered", *Memoirs of the American Academy in Rome* 50 (2005): 89–129. www.jstor.org/stable/4238830

Hölscher, Tonio, *The Language of Images in Roman Art*, Cambridge: Cambridge University Press, 2004.

Iturbe, Elisa, "Architecture and the Death of Carbon Modernity", *Log*, no. 47 (2019): 10–23. www.jstor.org/stable/26835026

Johnson, Christopher D., *Memory, Metaphor, and Aby Warburg's Atlas of Images*, Ithaca: Cornell University Press, 2012.

Lefebvre, Henri, *Le droit à la ville*, Paris: Economica, 2009.

Lenski, Noel, "Violence and the Roman Slave", in *The Topography of Violence in the Greco-Roman World*, edited by Werner Riess and Garrett G. Fagan, 275–298, University of Michigan Press, 2016.

Luscombe, Desley, "The Architect and the Representation of Architecture: Sebastiano Serlio's Frontispiece to Il ferzo libro", *Architectural Theory Review* 10, no. 2 (2005): 34–53. https://doi.org/10.1080/13264820509478540

Métraux, Guy P. R., "Ancient Housing: 'Oikos' and 'Domus'", *Greece and Rome. Journal of the Society of Architectural Historians* 58, no. 3 (1999): 392–405. https://doi.org/10.2307/991533

Papastephanou, Marianna, "Walls and Laws: Proximity, Distance and the Doubleness of the Border", *Educational Philosophy and Theory* 43, no. 3 (2011): 209–224. https://doi.org/10.1111/j.1469-5812.2009.00592.x

Plautus, Titus Maccius, "Asinaria", in *Oxford Classical Texts: T. Macci Plauti: Comoediae, Vol. 1*, edited by William M. Lindsay, Oxford: Oxford University Press, 1903.

Recchia, Filippo Marini and Fausto Zevi, "La storia più antica di Roma sul fregio della basilica di Ostia", *Atti della Pontificia Accademia romana di archeologia* 80 (2007–2008): 149–192.

Reitz-Joosse, Bettina, *Building in Words. The Process of Construction in Latin Literature*, Oxford: Oxford University Press, 2021.

Rossi, Aldo, *The Architecture of the City*, translated by Diane Ghirardo and Joan Ockman, Cambridge, MA: MIT Press, 1984.

Serres, Michel, *Rome. Le livre des fondations*, Paris: Éditions Grasset & Fasquelle, 1983.

Vitruvius, *On Architecture I*, translated by Frank Granger, Cambridge, MA: Harvard University Press, 1983.

Williamson, Rebecca, "Other Lives: Charles Eisen and Laugier's Essai sur L'architecture", *Drawing Matter*, accessed June 11, 2024. https://drawingmatter.org/other-lives-charles-eisen-and-laugiers-essai-sur-larchitecture/

Young, Iris Marion, "Structural Injustice and the Politics of Difference", in *Intersectionality and Beyond: Law, Power and the Politics of Location*, edited by Emily Grabham, Davina Cooper, Jane Krishnadas and Didi Herman, 289–314, London: Taylor & Francis, 2008.

7 Navigating Marx's collective *praxis* and Kierkegaard's individual *practice* in the swarming-dream city of capitalism

Bartholomew Ryan

This chapter analyses the tensions and challenges of applying philosophy to collective praxis and individual practice in the city environment via two philosophers of modernity: Karl Marx and Søren Kierkegaard. To travel with these two philosophers as urban thinkers and disruptive dialecticians in the wake of Hegel, who are writing in the middle of the nineteenth century, is to experience their attempt to emancipate the human being from abstraction and despair in a landscape where urbanity and modernity are intertwined. Both Kierkegaard and Marx write philosophical and social critiques of the modern age with streetwise verve and style and for an age in which we are still somewhat immersed.

I will offer three main points, via Marx and Kierkegaard, in showing the dynamic relationship between the philosopher and the city. First, the reality of the swarming and dream landscape of capitalism is observed and revealed in Kierkegaard's and Marx's writings in the city; two, Kierkegaard's individual practice and Marx's collective praxis are wedded and welded with their experience in the urban environment; and three, there emerges a tension and paradoxical interpenetration between certainty and doubt in modernity with these two philosophers. I propose that Marx and Kierkegaard move in opposite directions, in that Kierkegaard journeys from the stance of the personification of doubt and struggling history of a person to a ahistorical inner certainty that is manifested into action; while Marx moves from certainty on the historical destiny of the proletariat and the overturning of the bourgeois order to an increasing doubt, as capitalism expands, unfolds, and adapts.

Affinities Between Marx and Kierkegaard

In juxtaposing Marx and Kierkegaard, I find myself noting at least nine affinities between the two before setting out. First, they share the same birthday with a five-year difference in age: They were both born on 5 May, Kierkegaard in 1813 and Marx in 1818. Second, they studied ancient Greek thought in their dissertations: Marx on Democritus and Epicurean thought and Kierkegaard on Socratic irony. Third, they loved and were inspired by

DOI: 10.4324/9781003452928-9

literature, Shakespeare especially, and they applied and appropriated it into their thought which the reader can encounter through their rhetoric, use of quotation from poets, and literary style and mastering of language in their writings. Fourth, their work is full of sarcasm and jokes, sometimes crass, and sometimes highly effective as a weapon. Fifth, neither of them held an academic post. Sixth, their global influence properly began only during and after the First World War. Seventh, they are two of the most famous and influential critics of Hegel while, at the same time, profoundly influenced by Hegel. After the consolidation of Hegel in intellectual circles in Denmark, Kierkegaard was triggered to engage in individual transformation concretely rather than abstractly but paradoxically in moving towards the religious sphere; while for Marx, the task becomes collective transformation, to concretely change the world in the sociopolitical sphere. As Jamie Aroosi puts it in his book *The Dialectical Self: Kierkegaard, Marx and the Making of the Modern Subject* "self-transformation is a necessary condition for political transformation; and political transformation is a necessary consequence of self-transformation".[1] Eighth, theory must always be applied to concrete action and experience. Ninth, they are urban thinkers and modern city dwellers, with Kierkegaard forging his thought and writings from Copenhagen and Berlin, and Marx predominantly from Paris, Brussels, and London. This ninth point of affinity leads in to the first of the three points or aspects of this chapter. This is the existential religious philosopher of paradox and passion often in the guise of the flaneur on the city streets seeking to awaken the "single individual" [*Enkelte*] in his reader and the exiled revolutionary philosopher attempting to activate the consciousness of the proletariat in cities all over the world.

Experiencing Capitalism in the "Fourmillante cité, cité pleine de rêves"

Both Kierkegaard and Marx are urban writers, sometimes to the point of disdain for the rural life. In *The Communist Manifesto*, Marx and Engels write that:

> The bourgeoisie has subjected the country to the rule of the towns. It has created enormous cities, has greatly increased the urban population as compared with the rural, and has thus rescued a considerable part of the population from the idiocy of rural life.[2]

Thus, for Marx and Engels, it is the bourgeoisie that have been the innovators to building the modern city and not the proletariat. The proletariat was carried along by the bourgeois, the latter supposedly saving them from rural life. It must be remembered that the authors of *The Communist Manifesto* show admiration for many aspects of the achievements of the bourgeoisie in their push to overcome and destroy them.

Kierkegaard, on the other hand, has a more ambiguous relationship with the rural environment. Not unlike Marx and Engels, he also initially judges life outside the city as a kind of "idiocy of rural life". In 1840, before publishing any of his major works, Kierkegaard makes a trip across to Jutland to visit a village called Sæding where his father was from. As a city dweller, he makes a few derogatory observations in his diary on life outside the city, but he also feels quite lost, and one entry is revealing in showing how it is impossible for him to be a flaneur, where in the city, the urban environment can form a symbiotic relationship with his critical imagination. Here is an example:

> Simply because one has such a wide vista out on the heath, one has nothing at all to measure with; one walks and walks, objects do not change, since there actually *is* no *ob-*ject (an object always requires the other whereby it becomes and *ob-*ject. But the eye is not the other, the eye is the combinatory factor).[3]

As Kierkegaard matures as a writer, and as he feels forced to take his long walks further away from the centre of Copenhagen and to venture outside the city walls (when he begins to be looked out mockingly on the streets from the passers-by after caricatures of him appear in the weekly satirical magazine *Corsaren* [The Corsair]), his remarks and relationship with the countryside become more positive and are viewed as spaces for inspired spiritual guidance. One example is the discourse "The Lily of the Field and the Bird of the Air" (signed under his own name), written in the revolutionary year of 1848 like *The Communist Manifesto*. And in his earlier pseudonymous writings, echoes of the Romantic age in the treatment of nature are still consciously present, such as in the opening pages of the section "In Vino Veritas"[4] (from his pseudonymous work *Stages on Life's Way*), which is set in Gribskov – the large forest just outside Copenhagen.

Kierkegaard is forever associated with his city of birth, like many other modernists in literature – such as, for example, Baudelaire and Paris, Dostoevsky and Saint Petersburg, Cavafy and Alexandria, Joyce and Dublin, and Pessoa and Lisbon. Marx's city is more abstract as he moves from city to city while always fighting to speak and write to and for the urban masses. Moscow, Berlin, Paris, Havana, and Beijing can all claim him as their own. But it is in London, the centre of capitalism, where Marx lives the last three decades of his life and where he writes *Capital* and *Grundrisse*. The reader may not encounter the names of the various streets, parks, theatres, and cafés of the city that Marx is writing in as we find in Kierkegaard, but the urban configuration of the metropolis and being in the nexus of capitalism resonate throughout Marx's two great works that attempt to conceive of a new method and new way of critically interpreting the world and human beings' place in it.

Baudelaire's poem *Les Sept vieillards* begins with the words: "*Fourmillante cité, cité pleine de rêves* [Teeming, swarming city, city full of dreams]".[5]

The first part – *fourmillante cité* – can be translated as swarming or teeming but also "ant-like", as the word for "ant" in French is "*fourmi*". This line conjures up an image of swarms of faceless people moving quickly through the streets. Anyone who has experienced using public transport in the great capitalist cities such as New York and London knows this feeling very well of the *fourmillante cité*. In *Either/Or: Part I*, published 14 years before Baudelaire's poem, the *fourmillante cité* is present everywhere in which the pseudonymous aesthetic author thrives and submerges himself, in elation and despair, much like Baudelaire does as the magnificent poet-flaneur of the Parisian streets. They allow themselves to be both victim and conqueror of their own seductive intellect and demonic imaginative power. As George Pattison writes in his essay "Kierkegaard and Copenhagen", Kierkegaard uses a phrase, "the human swarm", to "describe the collective reality of the city".[6] The pseudonymous flaneur and seducer of *Either/Or* writes: "I was walking along Langelinie, seemingly nonchalantly and without paying attention to my surroundings, although my reconnoitering glance left nothing unobserved".[7]

The opening sentence of Kierkegaard's text *Fear and Trembling*, attributed to another pseudonym called Johannes de silentio, reads as follows: "Not only in the business world but also in the world of ideas, our age stages *em wirklicher Ausverkauf* [a real sale]".[8] In fact, *Fear and Trembling*, although one of Kierkegaard's most religiously focused philosophical texts by a pseudonym, begins and ends with a reference to the state of affairs of economics in Copenhagen. When thinking with Kierkegaard's and Marx's works via the city, this juxtaposition of the devaluing of money and ideas reveals the authors' embeddedness with the urban environment and anticipates the practice that is needed and presented in their later works. It is important to state that Kierkegaard wrote *Fear and Trembling* and *Repetition* and much of *Either/Or: Part I* in Berlin. These works are the product of a highly imaginative thinker located in the centre of the city, who takes long walks every day, following in the tradition of the flaneur, observing every detail, taking in every sound and gesture, reading the names of streets, moving in and out amongst the crowds, and hanging about outside places of evening entertainment – specifically the theatre. The city is the site of social, religious, and political participation and gatherings, and Kierkegaard makes the reader very aware of this fact while, at the same time, the city also informs his own reflections and observations. His pseudonyms are examples of multiple subjectivities which are influenced by the swarming city and to which they try to control and conquer. They are the watchers of the city, where even one of the pseudonyms explicitly carries the name of his vocation: Vigilius Haufniensis. This is the pseudonymous author of *The Concept of Anxiety*, whose name literally means "watchman of Copenhagen" in Latin. Kierkegaard's pseudonyms could well fit into Marshall Berman's definition of modernism in the first sentence of the second preface to his book *All That is Solid Melts into the Air*: "I define modernism as any attempt by modern men and women to become subjects as well as objects of modernisation, to get a grip on the modern world and make themselves at home in it".[9]

Marx also follows a vision of modernism in the everyday, "real" concreteness of life alongside the dream-like, ethereal, immaterial aspect following Baudelaire's description of modernity.[10] The modern city provides the landscape for clandestine meetings, pamphlet and newspaper distribution, posting slogans, a questioning and renaming of streets/signs, and guerrilla warfare, which the young Marx as a journalist was attuned to. The *fourmillante cité* of modernity is also the city of desire and dreams (*pleine de rêves*), relentlessly sending messages to our subconscious, convincing us that there is something that we are lacking and need to attain, and the capturing and controlling of time itself. Kierkegaard captures this dreamlike reality in the city through his pseudonymous authors who are the subjective observers. This dream world is what allows for what Marx calls the "sensuous supra-sensuousness thing" (*ein sinnlich übersinnliches Ding*)[11] or what Sami Khatib called "the *aesthetics of real abstraction*".[12] That "thing" is the commodity which begins *Capital*. So the first sentence reads: "The wealth of societies in which the capitalist mode of production prevails appears as an 'immense collection of commodities'; the individual commodity therefore begins with the analysis of the commodity".[13] As is well known, Marx's method is to begin by first focusing on the commodity, the finished product of the capitalist journey. The product, the commodity, is "an assemblage of social relations"[14] – which is how Marx defines "human essence" in his *Theses on Feuerbach*. Before writing *Capital*, Marx discovers, while studying and writing in the British Library in London, that "it is not individuals who are set free by free competition; it is, rather, capital which is set free".[15] Marx, as the great observer, is a kind of flaneur visualising the mode of production from the standpoint of production and then letting the capitalist system unfold before the reader's eyes over the course of a few thousand pages. What Marx in fact does is conceive of a phantasmagoria of the capitalist world which perhaps has not been surpassed. The ghost or spectre which was once communism, declared in the famous first sentence of *The Communist Manifesto*, is now capitalism. Marx was already acutely aware of this in describing modernity in *The Communist Manifesto*:

> All fixed, fast-frozen relations, with their train of ancient and venerable prejudices and opinions, are swept away, all new-formed ones become antiquated before they can ossify. All that is solid melts into air, all that is holy is profaned, and man is at last compelled to face with sober senses his real conditions of life and his relations with his kind.[16]

After the failure of the revolutions of 1848, Marx retreats to London to write *Grundrisse* and *Capital*, now completely immersed in the dream landscape of "appearances" and what "seems", where both space and time are being manipulated. This perception on the contortion of reality and non-reality and the dissolution of what "is" and what "seems" also occurs in the new approaches to representing reality in painting such as in Cubism and Expressionism. For example, Ernst Ludwig Kirchner's painting *Potsdamer Platz* from 1914 shows an urban landscape that is like a dream and which is fluid and where both human figures and buildings seem to be melting, where green pathways appear as rivers, and where prostitutes take centre stage and yet are isolated and cramped on an island. Churches appear as skyscrapers, where the sacred and the profane are no longer separate and, like being in a forest, the urban jungle is a place where the logic of distinction has fallen away. At the time of painting this work, Potsdamer Platz was the most densely populated part of Berlin. Kirchner said that he didn't want to portray the world as it was, but how he experienced it, that is what life in a metropolis felt like.[17]

An Age of Intensified Collective Praxis and Individual Practice

In his book *The Century*, Alan Badiou calls the twentieth century "a century of the demonstration",[18] and that it "is witness to a profound mutation of the question of the 'we'".[19] In this century, we witness the disappearance of God which was once "the opium of the people"[20] for Marx and also the possible threat to the individual. The city landscape is the space where both collective and individual revolt occur, whether that be in mass demonstrations and collective upheavals in the city, or in the urban loneliness and diverse subcultures emerging on the periphery and in the derelict impoverished centres. Benjamin wrote that "Streets are the dwelling place of the collective".[21] They are also the natural home of the individual flaneur and alienated subject in modernity, realised so often in literature, painting, and film – from Jean-Paul Sartre's novels to Munch's ghost-like persona on the bridge in *The Scream* in Oslo to Scorsese's Travis Bickle in the film *Taxi Driver* set in New York. Marx shows us the deceived, alienated, and abstracted proletariat of the city. For Marx, it is with the collective in the urban landscape where the revolution should happen and triumph to transform society. While Kierkegaard argues that the space of the passionate individual is being lost in the face of new forms of the public sphere and the increasing mediocrity of the established church and emptiness of its teaching.

Both Marx and Kierkegaard are philosophers of upheaval to different degrees. We may use the word "rupture" in regard to Marx and "unsettle" in regard to Kierkegaard. Both take their cue from a paragraph from Hegel's Preface to *The Phenomenology of Spirit* which begins: "Besides, it is not difficult to see that ours is a birth-time and a period of transition to a new era. Spirit has broken with the world it has hitherto inhabited and imagined".[22] But 14 years after this paragraph, Hegel is writing that philosophy "begins its flight only with the onset of dusk"[23] – implying that only after transformation has occurred can philosophy begin to decipher and interpret the world. But living through the Industrial Revolution which really began in England, Marx wishes to cause a massive rupture in history, to transform human history with the overthrow of the ruling classes and a complete smashing of the prevalent ideology of class led by the destruction of private property. Marx continues the earlier vision from *Phenomenology of Spirit* and is also still inspired by a destiny of history. Kierkegaard is disruptive in a different way. His prototypes are Christ and Socrates who, for him, unsettle and denigrate history. He wants to present a Christ and Socrates who are contemporaneous, shattering a historical place for them into something ahistorical. They are always to remain an offence and a paradox in the face of the established order and a model and guide for the "single individual" and subjective passion. To sum up, the revolutionary Marx and Engels signify rupture where they declare in *The Communist Manifesto*: "The Communist revolution is the most radical rupture with traditional property relations; no wonder that its development involves the most radical rupture with traditional ideas".[24] The rebellious Kierkegaard declares – via his most obvious philosophically inclined pseudonym Johannes Climacus – that "the most one person can do for another is to unsettle him".[25]

Collective Praxis

For Marx, individualism is a product of a kind of society and which, for our time, is a capitalist society. In *The German Ideology*, Marx writes that "consciousness is, therefore, from the very beginning a social product, and remains so as long as men exist at all".[26] The natural unit then is not individual but is a community or group. From a Marxist perspective, the goal of capitalist society and right-wing culture in general is to protect individual liberty. Marx is in favour of individual liberty, but the individual liberty he sees being promoted is actually being exploited by a capitalist society which is really driving separation, alienation, and appropriation. Individual liberty cannot be achieved for Marx without collective activity and possibility. Marx and Engels explicitly call for revolution in *The Communist Manifesto*, where they write at the end of their manifesto that their ends can only be attained by "the forcible overthrow of all existing social conditions".[27]

In this section, I include two Marxists of the twentieth century who powerfully and effectively merged theory and practice into praxis. The first figure is Leon Trotsky. In the opening page of *History of the Russian Revolution*, which was published in 1930 and to this day is still one of the greatest histories of an actual event written by one of its main actors, Trotsky writes: "The history of a revolution is for us first of all a history of the forcible entrance of the masses into the realm of rulership over their own destiny".[28] The stage is set immediately, and following Marx, Trotsky expresses precisely the fact and necessity of collective praxis over individual action. In this sentence, we find the essence of Marx's rupture. It is "the forcible entrance" or *irruption* – as it is translated in French – "of the masses", which it is at once the place of history and the formation of history. The stage is the city of St. Petersburg where the Bolshevik revolution takes place.[29]

The second figure is Georg Lukács, the writer who coined the term "romantic anti-capitalist"[30] when describing his pre-Marxist phase as a young man at a time when he wrote an essay on Kierkegaard and was also engrossed in writers such as Nietzsche, Ibsen, and Dostoevsky. He makes the journey from his two early seminal pre-Marxist books *Soul and Form* and *Theory of the Novel* to forging one of the key Western Marxist texts of the twentieth century: *History and Class Consciousness*. Published in 1923, this is one of the finest intellectual efforts to implement collective praxis and continue the historical destiny of the proletariat in the aftermath of the Bolshevik revolution. There are many fascinating aspects to this philosophical work, but the two most powerful aspects from it (from the two central essays in the book: "Class Consciousness" and "Reification and the Consciousness of the Proletariat") are highlighted here to cement the idea and activity of collective praxis. The first is a deepening of Trotsky's sentence of the irruption of the masses, in the goal and activity of "observing society *from a class standpoint other than that of the bourgeoisie*".[31] The bourgeoisie with its fetishisation of individual liberty will never budge for the proletariat because "with the bourgeoisie, also, class consciousness stands in opposition to class interest".[32] And as Marx had written in the middle of the dense notebooks that make up the *Grundrisse*: "The exact development of the concept of capital is necessary, since it is the fundamental concept of modern economics, just as capital itself, whose abstract, reflected image [*Gegenbild*] is its concept, is the foundation of bourgeois society".[33]

The second aspect of *History and Class Consciousness* is that of the famous term "*Die Verdinglichung*", which is translated into English as "reification" – literally "making into a thing". Lukács claims that reification "is the necessary immediate reality of every person living in capitalist society".[34] At the beginning of the essay, he states that "[r]eification requires that a society should learn to satisfy all its needs in terms of commodity exchange".[35] Lukács takes the idea of reification from Marx's concept and study of the commodity in *Capital* but in doing so anticipates Marx's comments on alienation in his earlier *Economic and Philosophical Manuscripts* which were only made known to Lukács in 1932 when they were first published – nine years after the publication of *History and Class Consciousness*. Also, one can see in his analysis of reification as to why Lukács was drawn to Kierkegaard before becoming a Marxist. For reification is the loss of selfhood, it is when the human self or essence becomes abstract and is abstracted from itself, when it is reduced or reified into an object such as in abstracted labour. Both the actual work of the human being and the human being itself are reified.

Lukács has highlighted the challenges faced by the proletariat in the reality of reification and in the obstacles in attaining class consciousness, while Trotsky has given a masterclass in narrating the success of an epic historical rupture in the forced entrance of the masses and thus grasping its own destiny. These elements that Lukács and Trotsky provide are the basis of Marxist praxis.

One of Marx's most famous sentences lays down the gauntlet of what praxis is and in entering metaphilosophy, in the final point of the *Theses on*

Feuerbach (written crucially before *The Communist Manifesto*): "the philosophers have only interpreted the world, in various ways; the point is to change it".[36] This is the starting point of praxis. Praxis is any social human activity that is attempting to change conditions. It is also the social activity in relationships between human beings. Thus, this particular section called "collective praxis" is in part due to the relationship between human beings and also to the idea that praxis is part of a universal historical narrative. As Lefebvre writes in *Metaphilosophy*: "All praxis is situated in a history; it is a creator of history".[37]

Individual Practice

In 1846, Kierkegaard publishes a short fascinating text known as *Two Ages. The Age of Revolution and the Present Age: A Literary Review*, probably his most explicitly critical analysis of culture and society, which was officially a review of a novel in Denmark. In the review, Kierkegaard differentiates "the revolutionary age" from "the present age". The former is defined as "a passionate, tumultuous age" which "wants to overthrow everything",[38] echoing the French Revolution. It is an age that has "form" and "culture" – which Kierkegaard says that "the tension and resilience of the inner being are the measure of essential culture". It is an age that "must be able to be violent, riotous, wild, [and] ruthless toward everything but its idea"; "has a concept of propriety"; has "immediacy"; is "essentially revelation"; and has "not nullified the principle of contradiction".[39]

The "present age", on the other hand, "is essentially a sensible, reflecting age, devoid of passion, flaring up in superficial, short-lived enthusiasm and prudentially relaxing in indolence".[40] It is an age of "publicity" and "anticipation"[41] and "has nullified the principle of contradiction".[42] It is recognised by traits of "chatter" – which "is the annulment of the passionate disjunction between being silent and speaking", "formlessness, "superficiality"; and "philandering" – which is "the annulled passionate distinction between essentially loving and being essentially debauched".[43] It is the Age of Restoration and the Industrial Revolution. Kierkegaard's critique of the present age is that it is mediocre and lukewarm, the opposite to a revolutionary age. But it is also an age without faith, because faith for Kierkegaard embodies passion, decision, and inwardness. Finally, the present age is an age which embraces the "public" or "the crowd person [*Mængden*], which is synonymous with untruth for Kierkegaard[44] and which is guided by "the press". Kierkegaard writes:

> Together with the passionlessness and reflectiveness of the age, the abstraction "the press" (for a newspaper, a periodical, is not a political concretion and is an individual only in an abstract sense) gives rise to the abstraction's phantom, "the public", which is the real leveller".[45]

The idea of levelling in *Two Ages* is what makes Kierkegaard profoundly distrustful of the collective. The collective comes in the form of "the crowd person", the masses, or "the public" and is articulated through the modern "the press" which bears no responsibility. As Benjamin writes in *The Arcades Project*: "within the labyrinth of the city, the masses are the newest and most inscrutable labyrinth".[46] In *Two Ages*, Kierkegaard distinguishes between the modern and ancient forms of the public:

> The public is a concept that simply could not have appeared in antiquity, because the people were obliged to come forward *en masse in corpore* [as a whole] in the situation of action, were obliged to bear the responsibility for what was done by individuals in their midst, while in turn the individual was obliged to be present in person as the one specifically involved and had to submit to the summary court for approval or disapproval.[47]

As Pattison puts it in his book *Kierkegaard, Religion and the Nineteenth-Century Crisis of Culture*,

> [T]he public is actually a manifestation of social disintegration and of the individualizing fragmentation of life typical of the present age. The unity figured in the public is the illusory unity that is all that levelling is able to produce.[48]

Levelling is also primarily very dangerous for Kierkegaard because it negates the individual and the responsibility of the individual. In *The Arcades Project*, Benjamin quotes from Karl Korsch, who writes that "the commodity is a born leveller".[49] For Kierkegaard, levelling "is not the action of one individual but a reflection-game in the hand of an abstract power".[50] Like Marx, Kierkegaard is equally critical of emerging modern democracy, but Kierkegaard is scathing towards any form of "a people's government", which he describes in his diary in the revolutionary year of 1848 as "the true picture of hell".[51] The difference between Marx and Kierkegaard is that, for Marx, democracy is a falsehood governed by the ruling classes; while for Kierkegaard, democracy is a falsehood ruled by mediocrity, abstraction, the disappearance of the individual, and the universal acceptance of the lukewarm. When Kierkegaard uses the word "lukewarm", he is thinking of the passage that he likes to quote (as does Dostoevsky) from the final section of the Bible – *The Book of Revelation*: "I know they works, that thou art neither cold nor hot: I would thou wert cold or hot./So then because thou art lukewarm, and neither cold nor hot, I will spue thee out of my mouth".[52]

In Kierkegaard's individual practice, there are two prominent critical figures in the city: the all-observing aesthetic flaneur of the earlier pseudonymous works and later psychologist of despair and militant Christian called Anti-Climacus (Kierkegaard's last pseudonym). Their dwelling place is Copenhagen, which literally means "market [*Køben*]-harbour [*Havn*]". It does not have the same size and depth as the cities of London, Paris, and Berlin, but Kierkegaard, with the imagination of a poet and the dialectical skill of a philosopher, is able to transform this market-harbour of the urban masses into a city landscape. Kierkegaard's flaneur wanders the city as dreamscape and who calls himself not only a "flaneur"[53] but also a "*Dagdriver*" and "*Lediggænger*".[54] These latter two words are the Danish for loafer or idler and literally mean "day-drifter" and "light-walker" respectively. They are to be an affront to the busyness of city life and also of settled and fashionable philosophical ideas. Kierkegaard's loafer has a vocation that fits well with the expression by the poet Edward Clarke, in his book *The Vagabond Spirit of Poetry*, in what he calls "these oxymoronic states" which are an "industrious indolence and indolent industry".[55] As Benjamin writes, "The idleness of the flaneur is a demonstration against the division of labour".[56] Kierkegaard's flaneur, *Dagdriver* or *Lediggænger* is the "single individual" as subversive figure sauntering the streets of Copenhagen, donning masks and disturbing the pillars of the bourgeoisie – such as church, state philosophy, and newly emerging democratic politics and media. For example, the large chapter or quasi-novella "The Seducer's Diary" inside Kierkegaard's book *Either/Or* (which represents the beginning of his authorship), Kierkegaard's enigmatic pseudonym "Johannes" creates a phantasmagoric landscape, naming various streets, making symbols of quotidian events, and providing images of thought in his voyeuristic view of the city. He comes across as a shadowy Byronic-bohemian-bourgeois vampiric figure with a cape. The references to this image of being a kind of vampire deftly moving in and out of the city streets are numerous in *The Seducer's Diary*, such as "living in a kingdom of mist", "eyes in a cape", and "continually seek my prey".[57] The vampire image is also apparent in *Repetition* where, in Berlin, the pseudonym Constantin Constantius relishes watching the city by a window at moonlight, and desiring to throw on a cape after midnight, looks out his window and "sees the shadows of passersby hurrying along the walls" where a "dreamworld glimmers in the background of the soul".[58] It is the radical individual vision of the all-observing aesthetic city dweller – being both supremely bourgeois and deeply critical of the new bourgeoisie of modernity. Benjamin later writes: "The flaneur is the observer of the marketplace. . . . He is a spy for the capitalists, on assignment in the realm of consumers".[59]

But it is Kierkegaard's final pseudonym who articulates an ethico-religious individual practice in the urban environment in the face of the established order, the self-satisfied Hegelianism of Copenhagen, and the mediocre "present age" led by bourgeois Christendom. This final pseudonym, Anti-Climacus, wrote two books: *The Sickness unto Death* (1849) and *Practice in Christianity* (1850). The word that Anti-Climacus uses in the title of the second book, which is translated as "practice", is *Indøvelse* in Danish, which has a connotation for military training in Danish. But "practice" works here too as it also keeps the sense in English of continual trying or a regular practising of a musical instrument or a sport. It is the process of the ongoing activity.

The primary target is "the crowd person" and present-day Christendom, and the reader they wish to reach is "the single individual" and wrench it out of the crowd. This is what Anti-Climacus has to say about the "crowd person" in *The Sickness unto Death*:

> He now acquires a little understanding of life, he learns to copy others, how they manage their lives – and he now proceeds to live the same way. In Christendom he is also a Christian, goes to church every Sunday, listens to and understands the pastor, indeed, they have a mutual understanding; he dies, the pastor ushers him into eternity for ten rix-dollars – but a self he was not, and a self he did not become.[60]

The Sickness unto Death reveals the sickness in losing the self; while *Practice in Christianity* provides the cure in becoming a self. Both books have the word "Awakening" in their subtitles, showing again this attempt to awake from the dreamscape of the crowd in the urban jungle where the logic of distinction no longer applies. Kierkegaard demands that his "single individual" will have to both suffer and flourish in the city. It is easier to find faith and to be spiritually awake in a monastery or in the wilderness, but to be awake in the city is the real task for individual practice. Anti-Climacus writes:

> in the actuality of daily life, to see this loftiness in Copenhagen, in the market on Amagertorv, in the middle of the daily bustle of weekday life! . . . But to see it in actuality *everyday*![61]

Climacus had already explicitly pointed out that Christianity is not a doctrine;[62] it is rather an everyday ordeal and task. For Anti-Climacus and for Kierkegaard, the two most important prototypes for individual practice are Socrates and Christ. The prototypes as they live and act remain an offence to the established order, as they interact in the public arena. The first is Socrates. In *The Sickness unto Death*, Anti-Climacus explains clearly what is needed: "Popular opinion maintains that the world needs a republic, needs a new social order and a new religion but no one considers that what the world, confused simply by too much knowledge, needs is a Socrates".[63] The second is Christ. Throughout *Practice in Christianity*, the exceptionality and non-systematic activity of Christ are emphasised, how he is an offence to the philosopher, the statesman, the clergy, the citizen, and the scoffer[64] and what kind of company Christ keeps in the city. Anti-Climacus is at pains to show that to become a self is to become spirit[65] and that spirit is "always critical".[66] Thus, to be a self is to be spiritual; and to be spiritual is to be polemical.

Conclusions and Inconclusions: Paths Towards Doubt and Certainty

In 1865, Marx filled in a questionnaire or "Confessions" with his family. For the question for the "favourite motto", Marx jotted down: "De omnibus dubitandum", meaning "everything must be doubted".[67] This is also the title of an unfinished pseudonymous work by Kierkegaard. *De omnibus dubitandum* is a philosophical journey into total doubt. Hegel attributed this sentence to Descartes in his *Lectures on the History of Philosophy*,[68] and Marx and Kierkegaard probably took the sentence from there. Johannes Climacus's *De omnibus dubitandum* was most likely written between *Either/Or* and *Fear and Trembling* and *Repetition*. Previously, in *Either/Or*, the aesthete wrote on "the courage to doubt everything".[69] I make the case here that in the modern city of capitalism, Kierkegaard makes a journey through the process of doubt and despair towards decision and faith as a form of inner certainty. While Marx's thought moves from certainty and decisionism to a shifting space of increasing doubt, ambiguity, and openness in the increasing awareness of the unfolding totality and increasing agency of capitalism, as he forges both *Grundrisse* and *Capital* in London.

Benjamin points out in the notes for *The Arcades Project* that "doubt appears to be that of the flâneur".[70] In the last two years of his life, Kierkegaard publishes a broadsheet called *Øieblikket* (translated as "The Moment", but literally means "blink of the eye"),[71] which he hands out on the street in the centre of Copenhagen and which runs through nine issues before Kierkegaard collapses on the street. The tenth issue, which is practically complete, is published posthumously as Kierkegaard dies six weeks later. Kierkegaard's watchman, in his *Øieblik* – as moment of vision and moment of decision, makes the leap and overcomes the flaneur's ambiguity and Kierkegaardian doubt and despair.

If Kierkegaard is the watchman of the market-town that is Copenhagen; then Marx is the all-seeing critical observer of the entire capitalist world. One of Marx's primary goals is to ensure the emergence of the proletariat's awakening to class consciousness and to act with certainty. But something happens. After the failed proletariat revolutions and moderately successful bourgeois revolutions of 1848, Marx has to flee mainland Europe where he is ensconced in London for the rest of his life while he watches the age of capitalism flourish, poverty in the industrial cities increase, and modern colonialism outside Europe expand. Marx begins to understand that the subject he is surgically examining is constantly growing and evolving. David Harvey writes that Marx's process of representation is an unfolding, where he discovers, in *Capital*, that capitalism is in a "perpetual state of contradictory unity and, therefore, in perpetual motion".[72]

One of the most fascinating theoretical works of the nineteenth century is written during this time of exile, which is his *Grundrisse*. Published for the first time only in 1939, it begins with an analysis of material production, a critique of liberal individualism, and a reflection of political economy, and then shows the becoming of capital as an "organic system" and "historically how it becomes a totality",[73] and reveals the fragmentation and reconfiguration that is happening before his eyes in modernity. One could start with the meaning of the word "Grundrisse" when reflecting on fragmentation and reconfiguration. In a presentation on *Grundrisse*, J. D. Mininger points out that "Risse" can mean crack, tear, fissure, or breach and that "Grund" could be translated as "cause" or "reason" or, in its adjectival function, as "fundamental" or "basic". Building from that, Mininger then suggested that one could thus translate the title of *Grundrisse* as Cracks in the Fundament, Fundamental Cracks, The Fundamental Grounds/Reasons for Scissure, and even perhaps The Cause of Crisis.[74] This is an unfolding text if ever there was one.

I have tried to think about Marx and Kierkegaard together in their embodiment and actualisation of what Aroosi calls a "philosophy of emancipation" and "praxis of freedom"[75] in his book *The Dialectical Self*. These parallel journeys in the city are intermingling. One strives to go from doubt to certainty via the single individual and towards an ethico-religious practice or training [*Indøvelse*]; while the other moves from certainty to doubt in the unfolding world of capitalism. Totality and fragmentation may not in fact be opposites but rather interpenetrating elements of each other. Totality is an assemblage of concepts and fragmentation a shattering of these concepts. Together they make up the city landscape of Kierkegaard and Marx.

Notes

1 Aroosi, *The Dialectical Self*, 6.
2 Marx, "The Communist Manifesto", 225.
3 Kierkegaard, *Papers and Journals*, 135 [July 1840 III A 68].
4 Kierkegaard, *Stages on Life's Way*, 16–17.
5 Baudelaire, *Complete Poems*, 230.
6 Pattison, "Kierkegaard and Copenhagen", 53.
7 Kierkegaard, *Either/Or I*, 323.
8 Kierkegaard, *Fear and Trembling*, 5.
9 Berman, *All that is Solid Melts into the Air*, 6.
10 Baudelaire famously writes: "By modernity, I mean the ephemeral, the fugitive, the contingent, the half of art whose other half is eternal the and the immutable". See Baudelaire, *The Painter of Modern Life and Other Essays*, 13.
11 Marx, *Capital*, 163.
12 Khatib, "Sensuous Supra-Sensuous", 50.
13 Marx, *Capital*, 125.
14 Marx, "Theses on Feuerbach", 147.
15 Marx, *Grundrisse*, 650.
16 Marx, "The Communist Manifesto", 224.
17 See https://frenchquest.com/2015/12/25/my-art-review-potsdamer-platz-1914-by-ernst-ludwig-kirchner/
18 Badiou, *The Century*, 106.
19 Ibid., 96.
20 Marx, "Towards a Critique of Hegel's *Philosophy of Right*", 64.
21 Benjamin, *The Arcades Project*, 423 [M3a, 4].

114 Rethinking the City

22 Hegel, *Phenomenology of Spirit*, 6.
23 Hegel, *Elements of the Philosophy of Right*, 23.
24 Marx, "The Communist Manifesto", 237.
25 Kierkegaard, *Concluding Unscientific Postscript*, 387.
26 Marx, "The German Ideology", 167.
27 Marx, "The Communist Manifesto", 246.
28 Trotsky, *History of the Russian Revolution*, xv.
29 Fifty years after this historical moment, Guy Debord writes in *The Society of the Spectacle*: "the city is the *locus of history* because it embodies at once a concentration of social power, which is what makes the historical enterprise possible, and a consciousness of the past" (Debord, *The Society of the Spectacle*, 125). Another Marxist and writer of the city Henri Lefebvre writes that the city, like human essence for Marx, is also "an ensemble" with its "great social categories: artisans, workers, women – and then ideologies" (Lefebvre, *Metaphilosophy*, 81).
30 Lukács, *Theory of the Novel*, 19.
31 Lukács, *History and Class Consciousness*, 54.
32 Ibid., 61.
33 Marx, *Grundrisse*, 331.
34 Lukács, *History and Class Consciousness*, 197.
35 Ibid., 91.
36 Marx, "Theses on Feuerbach", 158.
37 Lefebvre, *Metaphilosophy*, 7.
38 Kierkegaard, *Two Ages*, 77.
39 Ibid., 61–66.
40 Ibid., 68.
41 Ibid., 69–70.
42 Ibid., 97.
43 Ibid., 102.
44 Kierkegaard explicitly states near the end of *The Point of View*, in what he calls his "report to history", that "the crowd is untruth" (Kierkegaard, *The Point of View*, 110).
45 Kierkegaard, *Two Ages*, 93.
46 Benjamin, *The Arcades Project*, 446 [M16, 3].
47 Kierkegaard, *Two Ages*, 91.
48 Pattison, *Kierkegaard, Religion and the Nineteenth-Century Crisis of Culture*, 64.
49 Benjamin, *The Arcades Project*, 664 [X9].
50 Kierkegaard, *Two Ages*, 86.
51 Kierkegaard, *Papers and Journals: A Selection*, 302 [Pap. VIII I A 667].
52 *The Holy Bible*, 302 [Book of Revelation 3, 15–16].
53 Kierkegaard, *Papers and Journals: A Selection*, 351 [1848 IX B 63: 7]; *The Point of View*, 61.
54 For more on Kierkegaard's *Dagdriver*, see Ryan, "Kierkegaard's *Dagdriver*".
55 Clarke, *The Vagabond Spirit of Poetry*, 12.
56 Benjamin, *The Arcades Project*, 427 [M5, 6].
57 See Kierkegaard, *Either/Or I*, 310, 314, 321, 323, 352, 363, 441.
58 Kierkegaard, *Fear and Trembling*, 151.
59 Benjamin, *The Arcades Project*, 427 [M 5,6].
60 Kierkegaard, *The Sickness unto Death*, 52.
61 Kierkegaard, *Practice in Christianity*, 59–60.
62 Kierkegaard, *Concluding Unscientific Postscript*, 379.
63 Kierkegaard, *The Sickness unto Death*, 92.
64 Kierkegaard, *Practice in Christianity*, 46–52.
65 Kierkegaard, *The Sickness unto Death*, 13.
66 Ibid., 25.
67 www.marxists.org/archive/marx/works/1865/04/01.htm.

68　Hegel, *Hegel's Lectures on the History of Philosophy*, Vol. 3, 224.
69　Kierkegaard, *Either/Or I*, 23.
70　Benjamin, *The Arcades Project*, 425 [M4a, 1].
71　In Western thought, *Øieblikket* has a rich history as a temporary messianic interruption going back to St. Paul's *rhipé* [twinkling of the eye] (*Corinthians I*, 15:52), which Martin Luther translated into the word *Augenblick* in his translation of the *New Testament*, and was subsequently utilised again and modified in their own way by Kierkegaard and then Heidegger.
72　Harvey, *A Companion to Marx's Capital*, 26.
73　Marx, *Grundrisse*, 278.
74　Mininger expressed these points in a talk called "Crisis and Ambivalence: A Close Reading of Marx's 'Fragment on Machines'". See bibliography for more information.
75　Aroosi, *The Dialectical Self*, 190.

Bibliography

Aroosi, Jamie, *The Dialectical Self: Kierkegaard, Marx and the Making of the Modern Subject*, Philadelphia: University of Pennsylvania Press, 2019.
Badiou, Alain, *The Century*, translated by Alberto Toscano, Cambridge/Malden: Polity, 2007.
Baudelaire, Charles, *The Painter of Modern Life and Other Essays*, translated and edited by Jonathan Mayne, London: Phaidon Press, 1995.
Baudelaire, Charles, *Complete Poems*, translated by Walter Martin, Manchester: Carcanet, 1997.
Benjamin, Walter, *The Arcades Project, 1927–1940*, translated by Howard Eiland and Kevin McLaughlin, Cambridge, MA: Harvard University Press, 2002.
Berman, Marshall, *All that is Solid Melts into the Air: The Experience of Modernity*, Verso: London, 1982.
Clarke, Edward, *The Vagabond Spirit of Poetry*, Winchester: Iff Books, 2014.
Debord, Guy, *The Society of the Spectacle*, translated by Donald Nicholson-Smith, New York: Zone Books, 1995.
Harvey, David, *A Companion to Marx's Capital*, London/New York: Verso, 2010.
Hegel, G. W. F., *Hegel's Lectures on the History of Philosophy*, Vol. 3, translated by E. S. Haldane and Frances H. Simson, New York: Humanities Press, 1955.
Hegel, G. W. F., *Phenomenology of Spirit*, translated by A. V. Miller, Oxford: Oxford University Press, 1977.
Hegel, G. W. F., *Elements of the Philosophy of Right*, translated by H. B. Nisbet, Cambridge: Cambridge University Press, 2011.
The Holy Bible, Authorised King James Version, Oxford: Oxford University Press, 2008.
Khatib, Sami, "'Sensuous Supra-Sensuous': The Aesthetics of Real Abstraction", in *Aesthetic Marx*, edited by Samir Gandesha and Johan F. Hartle, 49–72, London: Bloomsbury, 2017.
Kierkegaard, Søren, *Two Ages. The Age of Revolution and the Present Age: A Literary Review*, translated by Howard V. Hong and Edna H. Hong, Princeton, NJ: Princeton University Press, 1978.
Kierkegaard, Søren, *The Sickness unto Death*, translated by Howard V. Hong and Edna H. Hong, Princeton, NJ: Princeton University Press, 1980.
Kierkegaard, Søren, *Fear and Trembling/Repetition*, translated by Howard V. Hong and Edna H. Hong, Princeton, NJ: Princeton University Press, 1983.
Kierkegaard, Søren, *Philosophical Fragments/Johannes Climacus*, translated by Howard V. Hong and Edna H. Hong, Princeton, New Jersey: Princeton University Press, 1985.
Kierkegaard, Søren, *Either/Or I: A Fragment of Life*, translated by Howard V. Hong and Edna H. Hong, Princeton: Princeton University Press, 1987.

Kierkegaard, Søren, *Practice in Christianity*, translated by Howard V. Hong and Edna H. Hong, Princeton, NJ: Princeton University Press, 1991.

Kierkegaard, Søren, *Concluding Unscientific Postscript to the Philosophical Fragments*, translated by Howard V. Hong and Edna H. Hong, Princeton, NJ: Princeton University Press, 1992.

Kierkegaard, Søren, *Papers and Journals: A Selection*, translated by Alastair Hannay, London: Penguin Classics, 1996.

Kierkegaard, Søren, *The Point of View*, translated by Howard V. Hong and Edna H. Hong, Princeton, NJ: Princeton University Press, 1998.

Lefebvre, Henri, *Metaphilosophy*, translated by David Fernbach, London/New York: Verso, 2016.

Lukács, Georg, *History and Class Consciousness*, translated by Rodney Livingstone, London: Merlin Press, 1971a.

Lukács, Georg, *The Theory of the Novel*, translated by Anna Bostock, Cambridge: The MIT Press, 1971b.

Marx, Karl, *Grundrisse*, translated by Martin Nicolaus, London: Penguin Books, 1973.

Marx, Karl, "The Communist Manifesto", in *Selected Writings*, edited by David McLellan, 221–247, Oxford: Oxford University Press, 1977a.

Marx, Karl, "The German Ideology", in *Selected Writings*, edited by David McLellan, 159–191, Oxford: Oxford University Press, 1977b.

Marx, Karl, "Theses on Feuerbach", in *Selected Writings*, edited by David McLellan, 156–158, Oxford: Oxford University Press, 1977c.

Marx, Karl, "Towards a Critique of Hegel's Philosophy of Right: Introduction", in *Selected Writings*, edited by David McLellan, 63–74, Oxford: Oxford University Press, 1977d.

Marx, Karl, *Capital: A Critique of Political Economy*, Vol. 1, translated by Ben Fawkes, London: Penguin Books, 1982.

Miéville, China, *A Spectre, Haunting: On the Communist Manifesto*, London: Head of Zeus, 2022.

Mininger, J. D., "Crisis and Ambivalence: A Close Reading of Marx's 'Fragment on Machines'", in *Multitude: The Present State of Labor and the Future of Political Praxis*, Vilnius, Lithuania: A Public Seminar Hosted by DEMOS Institute of Critical Thought, February 17, 2010.

Pattison, George, *Religion and the Nineteenth-Century Crisis of Culture*, Cambridge: Cambridge University Press, 2002.

Pattison, George, "Kierkegaard and Copenhagen", in *The Oxford Handbook of Kierkegaard*, edited by John Lippitt and George Pattison, 44–61, Oxford: Oxford University Press, 2015.

Ryan, Bartholomew, "Kierkegaard's *Dagdriver*: Loafing as a Means of Resistance to the Technological, Media, and Consumer System", in *Kierkegaard and Political Theology*, edited by Roberto Sirvent and Silas Morgan, 307–326, Eugene, Oregon: Pickwick, 2018.

Trotsky, Leon, *History of the Russian Revolution, 1932*, translated by Max Eastman, London: Penguin Books, 2017.

8 Contemporary identity politics and the city

More than fragmentation

Irandina Afonso

Introduction

Our lives are grounded in a complex set of variables and in a wide array of interactions and mediations that were not an eminent feature of urban experience in the ancient and the modern world. Complex layers of time and space configure the political, social and power relations in which we stand with others, a constellation that is particularly evident in urban contexts. Space relates to social dynamics, to changes, to polarised visions and to new representations; time, in turn, consolidates meanings and narratives, highlights stability and establishes powers and dominant identities.[1] One important feature that epitomises the interdependence of time and space is globalisation – its multiform reflexes produce new vulnerabilities, reinforce social injustices, and threaten the city and democracy in unforeseen ways. Globalisation engenders highly selective and spatially encapsulated forms of connection combined with widespread disconnection and exclusion, resulting in large pockets of privilege set alongside untold misery.[2]

This inequality pertains not only to material deprivation, lack of security, and lack of dignity but also to exclusion from debates on the terms of recognition and participation in collective life – that is, the ability or capacity to voice one's opinions, to discuss and to be involved in positive social transformations. When it comes to recognition, one central objective stands out in particular: individual autonomy or personal self-realisation.[3] Only those who feel (at least somewhat) recognised by others can relate to themselves rationally and thus be called "free" in the complete sense of the word.[4] Arguably, this is not an individual matter; the individual and the collective reinforce and constitute each other in the

> process by which all members of a community experience a gain in personal autonomy in virtue of having their rights expanded. [At the same time,] [t]he community is "enlarged" in the internal sense that the measure of individual liberty in that society increases.[5]

DOI: 10.4324/9781003452928-10

118 *Rethinking the City*

This resonates deeply with Maurice Merleau-Ponty's[6] observation that recognising the subject as fully immersed and implicated in the world frees him from absolute determinism and enables a continuous production of what it means to be human – through relations established in co-construction with others and with objects. Today, this perspective stands alongside the Cartesian subject of modernity with which the neoliberal image of self-creation is connected: how, then, can we build bridges between the subject, who thinks of himself as his own origin and as pre-existing the object,[7] and the contemporary subject, who emerges as both product and producer of his worldly condition? Questioning this dichotomous framework puts us on the path to comprehending that the modes through which we conceptualise subjectivity and processes of political subjectivation have a significant impact on the democratic exercise. This framework connects with conflicts between individual autonomy and the common good. At the same time, however, we are searching for the "how" – how this impact can favour the ethical dimension of the political (versus moralisation and the depoliticisation of public spaces), thus promoting a deeper, more diversified type of democratic participation.

Reframing difference, the city and democracy

Cities are paradoxical places where freedom and domination, progress and violence, evolve side by side. Strength and resilience, but also fragmentation and conflict, remain variables of existential incompleteness. As such, efforts to reconceptualise, raise awareness of and encourage political participation must be validated, in an endeavour to create, preserve and imagine the city as a condition of the possibility of more responsive and integrative ways of living and thinking. Difference may be considered a constituent of urbanity and a driving force of politics, specifically of democracy,[8] of which the city is the epitome. Contemporary identity politics can contribute critically to the deepening of democracy and urban experience. Ironically, serious damage can be caused to public space[9] by criticisms that do not recognise the implicit ambiguous dialogue between attraction and fear in the processes of creating subjectivity and social ties – a dialogue that may be represented as a form of eroticism:

> The erotic dimension of the city has always been an aspect of its fearfulness, for it holds out the possibility that one will lose one's identity, will fall. But we also take pleasure in . . . being drawn out of oneself to understand that there are other meanings, practices, perspectives on the city, and that one could learn or experience something more and different by interacting with them. . . . The erotic meaning of the city arises from its social and spatial inexhaustibility.[10]

These increasingly urban times and spaces bring together people and groups with disparate personal narratives, sociopolitical contexts and worlds of thought. Philosophy re-enters the city to articulate insights not only from social and political philosophy, epistemology, ontology and ethics but also from "new" philosophical interests, such as identity theory, technology, mobility phenomena and ecology. Rather than mere historical events, these have become structuring constituents of human life; they denote, in its complexity and with its diverse consequences, the multidimensional problematisations and mediations of contemporary urban life, as well as its potential to transform sociocultural paradigms. One relevant aim is to understand the city as a material and immaterial common good,[11] where the frontiers between private and public, urban and rural, economic and cultural are gradually being eroded. These are preponderant efforts to reformulate and devise new concepts and expose new subject positions,[12] to redefine reality within a deeper democratic matrix – "deeper" in the sense of being radical, that is, in the sense of diversifying democratic participation by allowing the margins (or what is excluded from the abstract notion of the human) to inhabit the real.[13] Particularism, pluralism and antagonism need not be absolute impediments to the promises of the universal, of democracy and the common good; rather, they are constituent – and productive – parts of the inexhaustibility of the social world. They are the raw material and fertile ground for positive transformations.[14]

This democratic matrix is deeper also in the sense that we must give voice to those who are not present – the dead and the yet to be born – including them in our current deliberations. We must do so by mobilising the non-representational, the sensible or, in other words, a "gnoseological maturity"[15] a broader framework of comprehension, with more potentialities than that of representation or the "rational", because it encompasses spaces of appearance.[16] As such, gnoseological maturity is "attentive to the meaning of what gives itself and of what becomes, as well as to what is absent, or denied, by the impossibility of accessing the realm of words".[17] Although the temporal and intentional character of the human being is evident in the actual discourses and concepts we use, as well as in the institutions we idealise, any consequent revisions to (or innovations within) democracy and fair democratic institutions must therefore involve the perception that "here and now" is not all there is.

Iris Marion Young's ideal city, in her words, "affirms", "represents" and "celebrates" group difference and advocates empowerment over mere autonomy.[18] Yet attending solely to "group differences" (an approach that presumes homogeneity and a coincidence of interests within groups) and "political representation" (which focuses on institutional and ideological means of recognising and affirming diverse social groups) is not sufficient to mitigate inequality in the sphere of political participation. Young's approach excludes those who cannot resort to institutional means or who do not have access to such means to negotiate the terms of recognition, the conditions of one's own future realisation and perspectives for conceiving of a better city. In many cases, there are no established means available to the "invisible", the undesired, those who do not count (displaced people, "illegal" migrants, clandestine workers, those who identify as non-binary and all those whom society does not recognise as valuable). Insofar as they do not benefit from the protection and recognition of established institutional and legal rights, how can they gain recognition?

One critical task consists, then, in validating apolitical, or otherwise extra-political or pre-political, forms of participation[19] – forms that the right to the city should accommodate, thus enabling the notion of extra-legal rights, or in other words, the exercise of the right to have rights, an exercise that is made visible through collective action in the public space of the city, with those who are "foreign" or "strange", at the margins of the essentialist "we" discourse.[20] Such forms of protest may also emerge in waiting spaces, in heterogeneous and heterotopic spaces, such as detention centres, refugee camps and displaced persons camps,[21] allowing for new approaches to political agency and calling for alternative modes of protection, solidarity, and emancipation.

Between what *is* and what *could be*

The new social and political actors stand on the fringes of the "universal", contributing to acknowledging the contingency of democratic foundations, the equivocal homogeneity of society and the difficulty of articulating particularisms through universal representation or, in other words, of articulating the normative and ethical orders. This reverberates with Ernesto Laclau's idea of incommensurability or "the gap between the ethical moment and the normative order"[22] – meaning that, in a democratic community, the total correspondence between ethical and normative orders "can lead only to totalitarian unification or to the implosion of the community through a proliferation of purely particularistic identities".[23] Thus, in a democratic community, it is desirable to bridge the gap, that is, to impede its foreclosure and negotiate incommensurability via the political, proposing diverse contexts and deconstructing the "facts" that sustain social structures and the epistemic frameworks that underlie them.

The emergence of new social and political actors energises the dynamic relation between the ontological question concerning what *is* and the ethical question concerning what *ought* to be, working our way through Laclau's pinpointing questions:

> Is a proliferation of particularisms – or their correlative side: authoritarian unification – the only alternative in a world in which dreams of a global human emancipation are rapidly fading away? Or can we think of the possibility of relaunching new emancipatory projects which are compatible with the complex multiplicity of differences shaping the fabric of present-day societies?[24]

Contemporary identity politics has the tools to critically scrutinise the gap that Laclau identifies, and its translation into social movements gains emancipatory potential by seeking to conquer new spaces.[25] To properly manage these tools, these movements must be conscious of systemic and global structures and the injunctions of the social world, bringing the members of (seemingly) different struggles together as part of the solution, embracing diverse modes of thinking and configuring methodological approaches[26] and strategies.[27] These are the conditions for extrapolating a mere tolerance of the "unintelligible" within the acceptable, or for accommodating it within dominant norms; by contrast, acknowledging the increasing complexity of social systems, their overlapping networks, opens the way to the disruptive competences of alterity, other modes of life and daily practices of resistance to capitalist rationality. We can say that the advantage lies in the ability to break the confidence of the dominant, to show how equivocal its pretensions to universality are.[28] At the same time, it is a way of thinking about the future that does not limit itself to our lifetime. In this way, we can relativise the privilege of the state and of the juridical dimension as a mediator in the articulation of the universal. Concrete human experience is re-established as the condition of this articulation, a place which formalisms, over time, have tried to occupy.[29]

Cities provide spaces (e.g., squares, parks, streets) where people gather, protest and demonstrate. We usually refer to these spaces as public spaces, but in a political sense "space of presentation"[30] seems more suitable, not only for capturing the nexus of speech and action but also for capturing what the classic space of political debate tends to neglect: "the equally valid and creative participation of those who resist hegemony".[31] Such emphasis on spaces of appearance helps to reveal the limits of the political. Spaces of presentation are where action may emerge "between bodies", that is, "a space that constitutes the gap between my own body and another's. . . , a spatial figure for a relation that both binds and differentiates".[32] This results in potential political action that neither liberalism (with the idea of the individual merit of pursuing one's own interests) nor Marxism (with the reduction of all subjective positions to those of "class") could ever have considered,[33] since the space of appearance is constituted by bodies acting politically together, performatively emerging "between" – between identities, between classes, genders, races, religions, political affiliations and so on. Historical–material matters and abstract–subjective questions are here intermingled, and thus, in their emancipatory struggle, these identities embody intersectional politics, laying bare the limitations of debates grounded in recognition *versus* redistribution.

This is why these problematisations require the investigative, revisionary and relational methods of philosophy,[34] as well as its ability to translate concepts, discourses and practices and to critically examine the relationship between the legitimacy and responsibility of power and proclamations of self-determination or freedom. The body, as the *locus* of subjectivity and lived experience, materialising discourses and practices of power,[35] is becoming an inexhaustible political argument, a force for transforming contemporary public spaces, the city and social institutions. As a reflexive, deliberative and organisational activity, politics depends not only on the existence of public and presentation spaces but also on people's access to and active participation in those spaces. It is here that certain aspects of the philosophical debate on identity politics and on the effectiveness of the multiple nature of demands, social movements and political agents converge.

Identity politics is viewed by some critics as a politically counterproductive, anti-democratic or simply inconsequential species of particularism.[36] This becomes all the more apparent if the particularities of identity translate to criteria of discursive authenticity and veracity, that is, when they limit access to spaces of debate and presentation to those who experience oppression "in the flesh" or share a specific, essential identity (only gay people can speak to homosexuality; only women can speak to gender discrimination; only Black people can speak to racism; only residents can speak to a city's affairs, etc.). This may also occur when those who do not constitute the "universal subject" (i.e., those who are not assimilated into the normative) or who lack the conceptual framework necessary for recognising their own experience as discrimination are obliterated or rendered invisible by modes of epistemic injustice.[37] And finally, there are criticisms of identity politics in general, which discredit identity-based social movements and blame minority movements for the weakening of the political left or for undermining the expectation of unity between so-called majorities and minorities.[38]

Importantly, however, these critiques indicate the power of processes of naturalisation, of false conceptual oppositions, of hegemonic dispositions when it comes to organising and managing the social world; they dangerously hinder the innovative and transformative potential of many social agents who are exposed to the same structures that govern interactions and exchanges.[39] Due to the complex interdependence of human lives and the transversal effects of globalisation, the issues and problems of one group are the issues and problems of all.

Intersection and equivalence

To understand the nature of current struggles and the diversity of social relations that the democratic dynamic has yet to embrace, we need a theory of subjectivity that addresses the multiplicity of subject positions. The very idea of community – which has been connected to conceptions of the city or the urban from antiquity to the modern era – can be used to devalue, deny or repress ontological differences between subjects and seeks to dissolve social inexhaustibility in the comfort of a self-enclosed whole.[40] Ultimately, we are multiple and contradictory subjects, inhabiting as many communities as there are social relations (and the subject positions they define), constituted by a variety of discourses.[41] Indeed, "[w]hile communities can be closed, those that thrive do so in the act of transforming encounters with strangers into meaningful relationships. And it is in this transformation that ethical life becomes possible".[42]

As such, conceiving of the community in an essentialist sense, as a collective subject with homogeneity, unity and coherence, is usually "antiurban" – especially now, in a time marked by multiculturalism shaped by displacement and migration, where contemporary cities and social life are "structured by vast networks of temporal and spatial mediation among persons, so that nearly everyone depends on the activities of seen and unseen strangers who mediate between oneself and one's associates, between oneself and one's objects of desire".[43] Identity politics, when it addresses intersectionality, acknowledges the reinforcement of inequalities through the overlapping of class-based, racial, economic, environmental and cultural disparities (to mention but a few). Attempts to conceive of alternative ways of mobilising new political and social imaginaries – new solidarities according to embodied experiences that ultimately reconfigure traditional political subjects – must ultimately take the systemic nature of discrimination into account. New political subjects, other modes of resistance and political formulations of subjectivity put into practice "an idea of liberty that transcends the false dilemma between the liberty of the ancients and the moderns and allows us to think individual liberty and political liberty together".[44] They reflect a diversity of political spaces and multiple belongings, confronting us with the possibility of active political participation and the full realisation of the individual.

On this theme, Kimberlé Crenshaw's work on intersectionality, Laclau and Mouffe's work on radical democracy, Amartya Sen's identification of the risks of identity illusion in "Identity and Violence" and the model of political performativity proposed by Judith Butler are all instructive. Within these conceptual frameworks, collective democratic engagement establishes practices of translation between notions of the "universal"[45] and connect the particular to the universal by proposing a democratic translation or equivalence of struggles, which is decisive for transforming "subversions" into instituted and democratised politics and forms of agency that persist over time. For this, it is important to underscore that a relation of equivalence is not a tautological relation of identity between objects,

> since the substitutability it establishes between certain objects is only valid for certain positions within a given structural context. In this sense, equivalence shifts the identity that founds it from the objects themselves to the contexts of their appearance or presence.[46]

To make discursive forms equivalent – or in other words, to allow negativity, or antagonism, to acquire a kind of presence – is to reveal the "impossible" as a constituent part and catalyst of what we call reality:

> It is because the social is penetrated by negativity – that is, by antagonism – that it does not achieve the status of transparency, of full presence, and that the objectivity of its identities is permanently subverted. From here the impossible relation between objectivity and negativity has become constitutive of the social.[47]

Struggles that do not spontaneously converge, such as anti-racism, anti-sexism and anti-capitalism, can establish stronger alliances when they let go, in a given context, of a specific identity ladder (which tends to enclose members' views and increase intolerance to difference) and embrace democratic principles and the values of radical freedom and equality.[48] Moreover, let us not ignore the fact that democratic rights, "while belonging to the individual, can only be exercised collectively" and "presuppose the existence of equal rights for others".[49] From here, we highlight the possibility of moving from a dated notion of universalism (i.e., the universalisation of a specific group's values) towards universality reconfigured from particularism.[50] In this way, although diverse social struggles may appear incompatible, they problematise and expose systemic causes and common problems (having the potential to go beyond mere alliances) and seek structural change. For example, while there is no necessary link between the struggles of the working class and the environmental movements, they are related due to the capitalist relations of production that underlie various relations of subordination. Deconstructing the relations of capitalist production therefore requires the participation of all concerned in decisions about what will be produced, how it will be produced and how it will be distributed.[51] In this way, the interests of those who produce (such as factory workers) intersect with those who are affected by production decisions (e.g., environmental and anti-capitalist activists). This may be precisely what it means "to see what basis of commonality there might be among existing movements without recourse to transcendental claims".[52]

The idea of the subject as a "pure and universal human essence" who, in its particularity, embodies the universal – like the "universal class" in Marx – is in decline and is profoundly anti-democratic.[53] This does not mean that we must reject universalism, but we do need "a new kind of articulation between the universal and the particular".[54] Societies are confronted with radically new political spaces, which means that we must abandon the idea of a single constitutive space of political power, as well as the idea of a unitary subject.[55] We have in fact been given a glimpse of the dilution of epistemological and ontological limits that social struggles incarnate in the form of protests and uprisings such as those in Tahrir Square (2012), Puerta del Sol (2011), Tunisia (2010–2011), Zucchotti Park (2011), Taksim Square (2013) and Syntagma

Square (2015). Broadcasted on television and mobile phones – and hence multiplying solidarities – these protests combine (or intersect) different kinds of claims, including economic and political–ideological claims, and cannot be reduced to just one kind of struggle: people fight for democracy against authoritarian regimes, against racism and sexism (including when directed towards immigrants and refugees), against corruption in city administration and business, for the welfare state against neoliberalism, against the privatisation of public space and for participation in democracy that goes beyond party affiliation.[56] At the same time,

> when we think of the impact of these imaginative and innovative actions and these moments where people learned how to be together without the scaffolding of the state, when they learned to solve problems without succumbing to the impulse of calling the police, that should serve as a true inspiration for the work that we will do in the future to build these transnational solidarities.[57]

We stand before an important philosophical responsibility: the construction of a just city. The impact, on individual and collective well-being, of philosophical neglect is not just about the perpetuation of violence, discrimination and injustice based on identity but also about the threats to or dismantling of collective democratic projects, of just institutions that allow for different conceptions of meaningful life and a sense of the future for the individual, the collective and the exercise of the common good.

Final remarks

When we address the city on the basis of only local and internal premises, the determining participation of "the global flow of persons, ideas, and commodities" remains invisible to us.[58] However diverse, the variables that reverberate with individual and collective existence nonetheless have an interdependent, overlapping and global character,[59] which further reinforces the complexity of city dwelling. The multiform reflexes of globalisation end up producing new vulnerabilities, reinforcing social injustices and threatening the city and democracy in ways that neither the ancient thinkers of the *polis* nor the utopian intellects of modernity were prepared to consider. The multidimensional intricacy of our societies and global cities exceeds the traditional terms of the debate on recognition and redistribution. It reminds us every day that new political imaginaries and heterogeneous, heterotopic spaces combine to question, reconfigure and dynamise citizenship, social bonds, power relations and democracy itself.

Following a post-metaphysical framing of identity[60] – an alternative to notions such as "unity", "essence" and the ontological priority of the subject – identity politics bridges the particular and the universal, materialising our common future in present ethical commitments and new modes of political legitimation. All along this path, however, we must expose and avoid "false radicalism" (the prioritising of a given struggle over all others) and "false gradualism" (the triaging of struggles, embodied in the thought: "now we must fight against the military dictatorship and for grassroots democracy, leaving aside all dreams of socialism for the time being").[61] In fact, the ethical dimension of politics that germinates from this framework of equivalence is ambitious and complex, but it is in line with the demands and perils of the fragmenting circumstances in which we live: cities are an amalgam of multiplicity, difference, identity, attraction, fear, excess and exclusion. They are places of temporal and spatial mediations between ideas and goods and between the familiar and the "strange" (in the form of the living, the dead or those yet to come).

The city and the political subject exist along a line of tension between what they have been, what they are and what they can and wish to be. It is up to everyone – individuals, communities, institutions – to preserve this tension responsibly and critically for the sake of something more than fragmented views of liberty and social justice.

Acknowledgements

This publication is funded with National Funds through the FCT/MCTES – Fundação para a Ciência e a Tecnologia/Ministério da Ciência, Tecnologia e Ensino Superior (Foundation for Science and Technology/Ministry for Science, Technology and Higher Education – Portugal) in the framework of the Institute of Philosophy, Project UIDB/00502/2020. Irandina Afonso is a PhD scholarship holder (DOI 10.54499/UI/BD/150998/2021) financed by FCT, I.P (the Portuguese national funding agency for science, research, and technology), ref. UI/BD/150998/2021, at the Philosophy & Public Space RG of the Institute of Philosophy (UIDB/00502/2020) of the Faculty of Arts and Humanities, University of Porto. The editing of this chapter was supported by funds from the FCT – Fundação para a Ciência e a Tecnologia, under the project UIDP/00183/2020.

Notes

1 Pereira and Afonso, "Other Spaces and Peripheral Urbanities", 78.
2 Nuttall and Mbembe, "Introduction: Afropolis", 5.
3 Honneth, *The Struggle for Recognition*, 82–85.
4 Ibid., 174–175.
5 Ibid., 85.
6 Merleau-Ponty, *Phénoménologie de la perception*, 399–410.
7 Ibid., 55, 230–231.
8 As Chantal Mouffe explains:

> I believe . . . that it is the existence of this tension between the logic of identity and the logic of difference that defines the essence of pluralist democracy and makes it a form of government particularly well-suited to the undecidable

character of modern politics. Far from bewailing this tension, we should be thankful for it and see it as something to be defended, not eliminated.

Mouffe, *Return of the Political*, 133

9 For the purposes of this chapter, "public space" is understood as space that is necessary for the functioning of democracy, for the performance of democratic roles. It has a fundamentally physical dimension (with some important exceptions, as it can nowadays be virtual/online) and is freely accessible to all, allowing people to debate and participate in collective decision-making on matters of common interest. It is a space where we are exposed to alterity, to those with whom we exercise the politics of difference: to the diversity of other points of view and modes of life (see Pereira, *A Filosofia e a Cidade*; Parkinson, *Democracy and Public Space*).
10 Young, *Justice and the Politics of Difference*, 241.
11 Pereira, "City and Common Space", 259.
12 Mouffe replaces the term "subject" with "subject positions". The social agent is not a homogenous and unified entity; he or she occupies various *subject positions* resulting from articulatory practices and discourses (class, nationality, gender, profession, social role, ethnicity, . . .) which constantly transform and subvert the subject. These positions do not express an *a priori* or necessary relation to the other (*The Return of the Political*, 12).
13 Mouffe, *The Return of the Political*, 13.
14 Afonso, "Na antecâmara da catástrofe", 203.
15 Afonso and Pereira, "Da reconstrução do sujeito", 170 [footnote 8]. Translated by the author.
16 As Hannah Arendt explains:

> It is the space of appearance in the widest sense of the word, namely, the space where I appear to others as others appear to me, where men exist not merely like other living or inanimate things but make their appearance explicitly. . . . To be deprived of it means to be deprived of reality which, humanly and politically speaking, is the same as appearance.
>
> Arendt, *The Human Condition*, 198–199

17 Afonso and Pereira, "Da reconstrução do sujeito", 170 [footnote 8]. Translated by the author.
18 In Young's words,

> [a]utonomy is a closed concept, which emphasizes primarily exclusion, the right to keep others out and to prevent them from interfering in decisions and actions. . . . It should be distinguished from empowerment, which I define as participation of an agent in decision-making through an effective voice and vote. . . . Empowerment is an open concept, a concept of publicity rather than privacy. Agents who are empowered with a voice to discuss ends and means of collective life, and who have institutionalized means of participating in those decisions, whether directly or through representatives, open together onto a set of publics where none has autonomy.
>
> Young, *Justice and the Politics of Difference*, 251

19 See Mouffe, *The Return of the Political*; Butler, *Notes Toward a Performative*.
20 See Arendt, *The Human Condition*; Butler and Athanasiou, *Dispossession: The Performative*.
21 See Agier, *Gérer les indésirables*; Foucault, "Of Other Spaces"; Pereira and Afonso, "Other Spaces and Peripheral Urbanities". Recall, for example, the protests in the Moria Camp for refugees in 2019 www.euromesco.net/news/refugees-protest-at-poor-living-conditions-after-a-deadly-fire-in-moria-camp-lesbos/.

128   *Rethinking the City*

22 Laclau, "Identity and Hegemony", 81. Here, the ethical moment is "the moment of madness in which the fullness [homogeneity] of society shows itself as both impossible and necessary" (Ibid.), whereas the normative order is "an ontic raw material incarnating, in a transient way, that universality" (Ibid.).
23 Ibid., 86.
24 Ibid.
25 See Habermas, "New Social Movements".
26 For example, to understand racism we need to understand the history of capitalism and colonialism. Angela Davis notes in this regard that "[o]ur histories never unfold in isolation. We cannot truly tell what we consider to be our own histories without knowing the other stories. And often we discover that those other stories are actually our own stories" (Davis, *Freedom is a Constant Struggle*, 135–136).
27 See Davis, *Freedom is a Constant Struggle*.
28 Butler, "Competing Universalities", 179.
29 See Ibid.
30 Or of "appearance", following Hannah Arendt, a term that highlights the association of speech with action (see also note 16). In Arendt's view, this space is not necessarily a physical dimension; it "predates and precedes all formal constitution of the public realm and . . . the various forms in which the public realm can be organized" (*The Human Condition*, 199). Thus, in an ontological sense, the political space is a potential space which, in contrast to material, constructed spaces, will exist and survive only if people act and speak together, "no matter where they happen to be" (Ibid., 198).
31 Resistance is understood here not in terms of some plane of negation but as transformative action that takes place in an essential dynamic with power relations, as explained by Foucault in "Sex, Power, and the Politics of Identity" (Pereira and Afonso, "Other Spaces Peripheral Urbanities", 78).
32 Butler, *Notes Toward a Performative*, 77.
33 Mouffe, *The Return of the Political*, 12.
34 By "revisionary" I mean the process of capturing, for example, common-sense concepts, institutions and vocabularies and trying to transform and improve them, whereas by "relational" I mean the ability to interconnect and articulate diverse concepts, problems, contexts, domains of enquiry and the like, even if they have no apparent relation to each other.
35 Materiality can be reformulated so as to accommodate the observation that the matter of the body is also the effect of power dynamics that are inseparable from norms and regulations, thus moving beyond a reductionist philosophy of the body and matter – as a "limit" or an "essence" – and instead conceiving of it as a "perspective" and a "situation" (the body that is already situated in a specific cultural and social context, the body as a dimension for the interpretation, reappropriation and rewriting of that context) (see Butler, "Sex and Gender", 48).
36 See Fukuyama, *Identity*; Habermas, "New Social Movements"; Rorty, *Achieving Our Country*.
37 See Butler et al., *Contingency, Hegemony, Universality*; Fricker, *Epistemic Injustice*; Spivak, "Can the Subaltern Speak?".
38 Fukuyama, *Identity*; Alcoff, *Visible Identities*.
39 See Fraser and Honneth, *Redistribution or Recognition?*.
40 Specifically, if we think of community as "a desire for social wholeness, symmetry, a security and solid identity which is objectified because affirmed by others unambiguously" (Young, *Justice and the Politics of Difference*, 232). This idea of community also hints at a metaphysics of presence by collapsing the temporal difference that is intrinsic to language and experience into a totality that can be encompassed by a single point of view (Ibid., 230–231). However, I agree

with Young's claim that this sense of community has serious political consequences: "it often operates to exclude or oppress those experienced as different" (Ibid., 234).
41 Mouffe, *The Return of the Political*, 20.
42 Meagher, "Pretend It's a City", n/p.
43 Young, *Justice and the Politics of Difference*, 237.
44 Mouffe, *The Return of the Political*, 19. Generally, and put simply, on the ancient view liberty consists in active participation in collective power, whereas on the modern conception it consists in the "peaceful enjoyment of private independence", a shift away from the subordination of the individual to the community (Ibid., 37). Following Chantal Mouffe, both alternatives share a similar problem: the idea of a unitary subject, whether a "unitary situated self" or a "unitary unencumbered self". This dilemma dissolves, however, once we "abandon the abstract universalism of the Enlightenment, the essentialist conception of a social totality, and the myth of a unitary subject" (Ibid., 21).
45 See Butler, "Competing Universalities", 167.
46 Laclau and Mouffe, *Hegemonía y estrategia socialista*, 109–110. Translated by the author.
47 Ibid., 220–221. Translated by the author.
48 For example, defending the right of national minorities to self-determination involves the assertion of a universal principle grounded in universal values (Laclau, *Making of Political Identities*, 4).
49 Mouffe, *The Return of the Political*, 19.
50 Butler, "Competing Universalities", 167.
51 Laclau and Mouffe, *Hegemonía y estrategia socialista*, 294.
52 Butler, "Competing Universalities", 167.
53 Laclau, *Making of Political Identities*, 4.
54 Mouffe, *The Return of the Political*, 13.
55 Ibid., 20 (see also note 44); see also Parkinson, *Democracy and Public Space*.
56 See Žižek, "Trouble in Paradise"; Butler and Athanasiou, *Dispossession: The Performative*.
57 Davis, *Freedom is Constant Struggle*, 144.
58 Nuttal and Mbembe, "Introduction: Afropolis", 15.
59 See Coate and Thiel, *Identity Politics in the Age*.
60 See Heyes, *Anaesthetics of Existence*; Butler, *Notes Toward a Performative*; Benhabib, "Strange Multiplicities".
61 Žižek, "Trouble in Paradise", 5.

Bibliography

Afonso, Irandina, "Na antecâmara da catástrofe ou pensar o presente a partir do impensado", *Filosofia. Revista da Faculdade de Letras da Universidade do Porto* 39 (2022): 199–214. https://ojs.letras.up.pt/index.php/filosofia/article/view/13398/12094

Afonso, Irandina and Paula Cristina Pereira, "Da reconstrução do sujeito e da vulnerabilidade como força", *Argumentos de Razón Técnica* 22 (2019): 162–176. http://doi.org/10.12795/Argumentos/2019.i22.07

Agier, Michel, *Gérer les indésirables, Des camps de réfugiés au gouvernement humanitaire*, Paris: Éditions Flammarion, 2008.

Alcoff, Linda Martin, *Visible Identities: Race, Gender, and the Self*, New York: Oxford University Press, 2006.

Arendt, Hannah, *The Human Condition*, Chicago: The University of Chicago Press, 1998.

Benhabib, Seyla, "Strange Multiplicities: The Politics of Identity and Difference in a Global Context", *Macalester International* 4 (1997): article 8. http://digitalcommons.macalester.edu/macintl/vol4/iss1/8

Butler, Judith, "Sex and Gender in Simone de Beauvoir's Second Sex", *Yale French Studies*, no. 72 (1986): 35–49. https://doi.org/10.2307/2930225

Butler, Judith, *Gender Trouble: Feminism and the Subversion of Identity*, New York, NY: Routledge, 1989.

Butler, Judith, "Competing Universalities", in *Contingency, Hegemony, Universality. Contemporary Dialogues on the Left*, edited by Judith Butler, Ernesto Laclau and Slavoj Zizek, 136–181, London/New York: Verso, 2000.

Butler, Judith, *Notes Toward a Performative Theory of Assembly*, Cambridge, MA/London, UK: Harvard University Press, 2018.

Butler, Judith and Athena Athanasiou, *Dispossession: The Performative in The Political*, Cambridge, UK: Polity Press, 2013.

Butler, Judith, Ernesto Laclau and Slavoj Žižek, *Contingency, Hegemony, Universality. Contemporary Dialogues on the Left*, London/New York: Verso, 2000.

Coate, Roger and Markus Thiel, eds., *Identity Politics in the Age of Globalization*, Boulder, CO: Lynne Rienner, 2010.

Crenshaw, Kimberle, "Mapping the Margins: Intersectionality, Identity Politics, and Violence against Women of Color", *Stanford Law Review* 43, no. 6 (1991): 1241–1299. https://doi.org/10.2307/1229039. www.jstor.org/stable/1229039

Davis, Angela Yvonne, *Freedom is a Constant Struggle. Ferguson, Palestine, and the Foundations of a Movement*, Chicago: Haymarket Books, 2016.

Foucault, Michel, "Of Other Spaces: Utopias and Heterotopias", translated by Jay Miskowiec (Originally a Conference at the Cercle d'études architecturales on 14 March 1967 and published in *Architecture, Mouvement, Continuité*, no. 5 (1984): 46–49). http://web.mit.edu/allanmc/www/foucault1.pdf

Foucault, Michel, "Sex, Power, and the Politics of Identity", in *Ethics, Subjectivity and Truth, Essential Works of Foucault 1954–1984*, edited by Paul Rabinow, 163–173, New York: The New Press, 1997.

Fraser, Nancy and Axel Honneth, *Redistribution or Recognition? A Political-Philosophical Exchange*, translated by Joel Golb, James Ingram and Christiane Wilke, New York: Verso, 2004.

Fricker, Miranda, *Epistemic Injustice. Power and the Ethics of Knowing*, Oxford: Oxford University Press, 2007.

Fukuyama, Francis, *Identity: Contemporary Identity Politics and the Struggle for Recognition*, London: Profile Books, 2018.

Habermas, Jürgen, "New Social Movements", *Telos*, no. 49 (1981): 33–37. https://doi.org/10.3817/0981049033

Heyes, Cressida J., *Anaesthetics of Existence: Essays on Experience at the Edge*, Durham, NC: Duke University Press, 2020.

Honneth, Alex, *The Struggle for Recognition: The Moral Grammar of Social Conflicts*, translated by Joel Anderson and Thomas McCarthy, Malden, MA: Polity Press, 1996.

Laclau, Ernesto, ed., *The Making of Political Identities*, Malden, MA: Verso, 1994.

Laclau, Ernesto, "Identity and Hegemony: The Role of Universality in the Constitution of Political Logics", in *Contingency, Hegemony, Universality. Contemporary Dialogues on the Left*, edited by Judith Butler, Ernesto Laclau and Slavoj Zizek, 44–89, London/New York: Verso, 2000.

Laclau, Ernesto and Chantal Mouffe, *Hegemonía y estrategia socialista. Hacia una radicalización de la democracia*, translated by Ernesto Laclau, Madrid: Siglo XXI, 1987.

Meagher, Sharon, *Pretend It's a City': Urban Foundations for Ethical Life*, Gotham Philosophical Society, 2021, [online], accessed February 17, 2022. https://philosophy.nyc/2021/02/23/pretend-its-a-city-urban-foundations-for-ethical-life/

Merleau-Ponty, Maurice, *Phénoménologie de la perception*, Paris: Gallimard, 1976.

Mouffe, Chantal, *The Return of the Political*, London/New York: Verso, 1993.

Nuttall, Sarah and Achille Mbembe, "Introduction: Afropolis", in *Johannesburg, The Elusive City*, edited by Sarah Nuttall and Achille Mbembe, 1–33, Durham, NC: Duke University Press, 2008.

Parkinson, John R., *Democracy and Public Space. The Physical Sites of Democratic Performance*, New York, NY: Oxford University Press, 2012.

Pereira, Paula Cristina, org., *A Filosofia e a Cidade*, Vol. II, Porto: Edições Afrontamento, 2010.

Pereira, Paula Cristina, "City and Common Space", in *The Routledge Handbook on Philosophy of the City*, edited by Sharon M. Meagher, Samantha Noll and Joseph S. Biehl, 253–262, London/New York: Routledge, 2019.

Pereira, Paula Cristina and Irandina Afonso, "Other Spaces and Peripheral Urbanities", in *Differences in the City: Postmetropolitan Heterotopias as Liberal Utopian Dreams*, edited by Jorge L. Casero and Julia Urabayen, 73–86, New York: Nova Science Publishers, 2020.

Rorty, Richard, *Achieving Our Country: Leftist Thought in Twentieth Century America*, Cambridge, MA: Harvard University Press, 2000.

Sen, Amartya, *Identity and Violence. The Illusion of Destiny*, New York: W. W. Norton & Company, 2006.

Spivak, Gayatri Chakravorty, "Can the Subaltern Speak?", in *Colonial Discourse and Post-Colonial Theory. A Reader*, edited by Patrick Williams and Laura Chrisman, 66–111, New York: Columbia University Press, 1994.

Young, Iris Marion, *Justice and the Politics of Difference*, Princeton, NJ: Princeton University Press, 1990.

Žižek, Slavoj, "Trouble in Paradise: The Global Protest", *London Review of Books* 35, no. 14 (2013), [online], accessed February 25, 2022. www.lrb.co.uk/the-paper/v35/n14/slavoj-zizek/trouble-in-paradise

Part III
Urban experience, aesthetic concepts

9 Towards a political ecology of urban ambiances

Jean-Paul Thibaud

1. Our ways of being sensitive to the spaces we inhabit are undergoing profound changes. Not only is the world itself in the throes of change, but our sensitive relationship with it is also undergoing major transformations. The question of sensitivity is a particularly relevant and operative entry point for thinking about current and future changes in our living environments. In other words, sensitivity cannot be reduced to passive reception; it instead has the power to intensify and reconfigure our relationship with the world. Walter Benjamin masterfully demonstrated the fundamentally socio-historical nature of the forms of perception:

> During long periods of history, the mode of human sense perception changes with humanity's entire mode of existence. The manner in which human sense perception is organized, the medium in which it is accomplished, is determined not only by nature but by historical circumstances as well.[1]

Changes in the socio-technical and urban environment go hand in hand with transformations in the conditions of sensitive experience. Georg Simmel emphasises the hyperstimulation of the urban environment and the lessening of sensory capacities of city dwellers; Walter Benjamin highlights the aesthetics of shock and the loss of aura; Siegfried Kracauer reveals in great detail the culture of distraction and the sensationalism of mass leisure. All these authors show how the birth of modern metropolises has been accompanied by changes in modes of attention and the conditions of sensitive experience. Stéphane Füzesséry and Philippe Simay[2] sum up this process of the fragmentation of sensitivity as follows: "By constantly soliciting the senses of the city-dweller, the metropolis paradoxically enacts a regression in the order of visual perception, from sign to simple signal and from signal to undifferentiated nervous stimulation". With Walter Benjamin, it is the art of storytelling that tends to go lost, and with it, the ability to articulate, exchange, and transmit experiences.[3] Communicable experience (*Erfahrung*) is replaced by a lived experience (*Erlebnis*) composed of shocks and dispersed excitations that elude our capacity for synthesis.

DOI: 10.4324/9781003452928-12

2. Are we not currently witnessing another turning point in sensitivity, in which the contemporary world is creating a new distribution of the sensible and giving rise to new modes of feeling? Are we not witnessing an unprecedented reconfiguration of the forms of sensitivity? In this respect, one could talk of "ambiental sensitivity",[4] that is, a diffuse and ordinary sensitivity, collective and discreet, open to the tonal dimensions of situated experience, embedded in diverse forms of life, and imbued with the socio-ecological mutations of the contemporary world. In other words, the ambient is becoming a vector of experience from which new modes of existence open up and new ways of relating to the sensible world unfold. It gives rise to a singular form of sensitivity, irreducible to artistic, aesthetic, landscape, or environmental sensitivities. Rather, they are ways of being sensitive to the precariousness of living environments, to changes in climatic conditions, and to the nuances of atmospheric impregnations in everyday life. Always situated and circumstantial, ambiental sensitivity concerns the content and quality of the elements in which we are immersed on a daily basis. It stems less from attention to clearly identifiable objects than from a diffuse sense of the environments that envelop, permeate, and radiate through us. It is a discreet sensitivity that tests the vitality and vulnerability of the world's ecology.

3. How is it possible to test and implement this hypothesis of ambiental sensitivity? How does it reconfigure ordinary forms of sensory experience? What does it tell us about the fragmentation of the contemporary sensorium and the recomposition of the sensitive spaces we inhabit? Jacques Rancière's thinking is particularly relevant and operative in this line of questioning. He formulates the issue of sensitivity and aesthetics in a new way. According to this perspective, if the sensible is closely linked to the political, it is because it distributes places and identities, establishes the visible and the invisible, and carves out space and time:

> I call the distribution of the sensible the system of self-evident facts of sense perception that simultaneously discloses the existence of something in common and the delimitations that define the respective parts and positions within it. A distribution of the sensible therefore establishes at one and the same time something common that is shared and exclusive parts.[5]

Dissensus and disagreement thus constitute the distribution of the sensible and the way in which the common is configured and reconfigured. With modernity, Rancière identifies an aesthetic revolution that redistributes the order of the perceptible. Ordinary life enters the world of art, against the grain of the classical world of fine art. A new form of perception emerges that acknowledges the most banal events and the most trivial details of everyday life. Jacques Rancière analyses the emergence of what he calls the *aesthetic regime of art*.[6] If we follow Rancière's philosophy, with ambiental sensitivity we also need to uncover the way in which today's world appears in a new light, the way it opens up a new regime of perceptibility, with its discordances and disagreements as well as its concordances and resonances.

4. Several clues lead to this hypothesis of ambiental sensitivity. First of all, the modern experience of hyperstimulation and shock aesthetics seems to be giving way to other characterisations of late modernity. Various authors have attempted to re-specify the terms of contemporary sensitive experience, describing it more in terms of a loss of contact with reality and resulting in a hallucinatory experience,[7] a preponderance of weak and distended sensations[8] or perception under anaesthesia.[9] François Bonnet insists also on the anaesthesia that afflicts today's societies, noting the loss of a pathic relationship with the world:

> Numerous attempts have been made to establish a symptomatology of post-industrial society, particularly its spectacular dimension. Through these various approaches, though paradoxically rarely called upon, a phenomenon seems to be emerging that embraces a broad spectrum of behaviours linked to the dominance of the intangible (images, knowledge, information) in social organisation. This phenomenon is anaesthesia . . . It describes a deficit of sensations and a growing inability to feel.[10]

As we shall see, one of the challenges of a political ecology of urban ambiances is precisely to restore the place of feeling and resonance in ordinary experience. Everything seems to indicate that we are witnessing the emergence of a new regime of perceptibility in which immersion and attention to low-intensity background phenomena prevail. The second clue to this transformation of the human sensorium can be seen in the growing importance accorded in English-speaking social sciences to the category of the *ambient*. Cheryl Foster thus proposes a fundamental distinction between a narrative and an ambient approach to environmental aesthetics. If ambiance connotes the feeling of being immersed, enveloped, and infused by a living environment,

> the ambient dimension of aesthetic value can act as a catalyst for the inculcation of a sensitivity toward the environment: ecological, political, economic, or recreational kinds of concern often grow out of this more isolated and yet fundamental kind of environmental experience.[11]

Most of the time, the term ambient is used to designate the diffuse, discreet, tacit, and unnoticed dimension of sensitive experience that which lies "beneath interpretation".[12] But then, if the ambient is increasingly becoming an explicit category to account for contemporary sensitivity, we still need to uncover its various meanings and uses. In a way, it is becoming a battleground of the distribution of the sensible, in which the fragmentation and reconfiguration of sensitivity is being played out afresh.

5. Three major trends mark our time: the growing influence of neoliberal policy on everyday lived spaces, the increasing presence of digital technologies in urban space, and the growing awareness of the transition to the Anthropocene era. These far-reaching processes pave the way for a renewed urban ecology that is more attentive to the ambient, affective, and existential conditions of contemporary experience. The first trend is mainly economic and concerns *the aestheticisation of urban spaces*. One can observe a tendency to design the sensory world for commercial purposes. This major process entails the commodification of urban space. An extensive literature exists in this regard which talks about *aesthetic capitalism*,[13] *sensory marketing*,[14] *experience economy*,[15] or *emotional commodity*.[16] A process of aestheticisation of everyday life is taking place, which involves a very large number of devices, ranging from scenography to landscaping, through sensory design, the illumination, sonification, or conditioning of spaces. Such processes are at work in various urban domains: the gentrification of historical town centres, the climatisation of underground spaces, new scenes of the creative city, the functional design of transport amenities, and the design of shopping malls or theme parks. Everything happens as if it were a matter of producing attractive ambiances and appealing sensitive worlds. Yves Michaud[17] speaks in this respect of the "hyper-aestheticisation" of the contemporary world, of a generalised aestheticisation based on the design of ambiances in all areas of life. In this respect, it is nothing less than sensitivity itself that is being transformed:

> In depth, this ambient evolution is inseparable from that of contemporary sensitivity. A new regime of sensitivity – of aesthetics in the etymological sense of "feeling" – is at stake. That the world is now perceived in the form of sensitive experiences rather than objects, in the form of lived experiences rather than substances or even people, has a scope that goes far beyond the realms of art and luxury alone.[18]

Feeling tends to become the primary condition of our relationship to the world, but this kind of feeling relates primarily to conditioned ambiances and a commodity aesthetic. We need to open up a whole new field of research in this area, distinguishing between different forms of urban ambiance and specifying how the realm of the sensory is embedded in the processes of urban transformations. For example, one could question the asepticisation of our living environment,[19] the urban programming of animation,[20] the emergence of a guaranteed city,[21] the spectacularisation of the urban,[22] and the reign of clean urbanism.[23] These are all proposals that attempt to describe the shortcomings and derivative forms of urban aestheticisation. It is as if today's city forms part of a process of the impoverishment of sensitive experience and reduction of the field of perception. Various research projects are empirically investigating these contemporary trends, drawing on concrete case studies to describe a new regime of sensitive experience: the Disneyfication of Times

Square shows how an urban landscape is transformed into imagescapes with commercial value, giving rise to a feeling of re-enchantment, of the order of simulation and suspension of disbelief;[24] the privatisation of public spaces in Berlin's Potsdamer Platz illustrates how ambiance is part of a new power strategy that plays on inclusion, seduction, and a veritable economy of affect;[25] the arrangement of various ambiances in Singapore's gigantic ION Orchard shopping mall reveals how each one is aimed at a particular segment of society while helping to forge the affective identity of this city-state.[26] In such instances, it is as if these ambiances are part of a certain derealisation of the urban experience, a distancing of the relationship with reality of the floating and marvellous kind, in some way a "platform for dreaming".[27]

6. The second trend is mainly technological and concerns the *digitalisation of the urban world*. The rise in power of embedded technologies, smartphones, sensors, and other mobile digital tools can no longer be considered an epiphenomenon of transformations in the urban environment. It deserves to be questioned in its own right. The same is true of a whole field of research that is transforming ordinary urban life and which comes under the heading of ambient intelligence.[28] Another aspect of ambiance bursts onto the scene here that focuses more on new technologies and augmented perceptions. The measure of the dissemination and growing influence of such digital environments must be taken. Whether we are talking about augmented cities, urban computing, or smart cities, city dwellers are living in an increasingly technological world which makes demands on them and profoundly affects their experience. The development of these new information and communication technologies influences not so much the physical and built form of cities as the experience of city dwellers and the formation of new sensory relationships with living environments.[29] In this context, the category of ambient is increasingly used to designate the diffuse and omnipresent informational flows that permeate the daily experience of city dwellers and to highlight the ubiquitous and integrated nature of this type of artificial environment. The scale of these ambient reconfigurations of the urban environment is such that they seem to affect the worlds of commerce and consumption, surveillance and militarisation, and art and creation.[30] All areas of urban life are affected by the growing influence of the digital world. What then of the socio-aesthetic consequences of the digital revolution which we are witnessing? The sheer scale of this upheaval has given rise to an in-depth critical analysis that raises the very question of aesthetics anew. Theoretical critique war machines are emerging to describe the complexity of perceptual mutations and deconstruct the structures of contemporary sensitivity. Aesthetic warfare[31] as well as the conflict of perceptions[32] are the themes here. Elsa Boyer describes the conditions for the emergence of artificial perception at the crossroads of perception, imagination, and technology. Through a close critical reading of Husserlian phenomenology, she shows how new technologies mobilise an underground economy of perception that grows past the distinctions between reality and fiction, sensation and *phantasma*, and

perception and imagination. For his part, Bernard Stiegler takes a long look at the transition from technical to technological sensitivity. He describes the "machinic turn of sensitivity" that tends to transform aesthetic experience into aesthetic conditioning. He notes the refunctionalisation of aesthetics and the externalisation of human faculties, which in a way leads to a deficit of sensitivity. This kind of work once again sounds the alarm of the tendency of post-industrial societies towards anaesthesia and amnesia and a growing inability to feel. Returning more directly to the ambient ecology of the urban environment, it is undoubtedly the question of attention that lies at the heart of the issue.[33] While technical interfaces play a fundamental role in our sensitive relationship with the urban environment, the most advanced developments in urban computing are aimed precisely at reducing their cognitive load and increasing tacit knowledge in their use. Ambient intelligence must be as invisible and integrated as possible, involving a minimum of effort and conscious deliberation and relying on implicit processes of habituation and incorporation. Sensitivity thus plays as much as possible on backgrounds and distraction to go unnoticed and encourage a sense of flow. This ecology of attention[34] helps question these new ways of being sensitive to what surrounds us. The aim is to describe the ways in which attention is captured, channelled, and structured and to give full scope to floating, distributed, and peripheral perceptions. Such perspectives take us directly back to ambiances, in that they argue for a political ecology of floating attention and question afresh the common ground and perceptual backgrounds that set the tone for urban experience. We face here a major challenge in reconsidering the close connection between the technical and aesthetic registers of urban experience. Gilbert Simondon's notion of techno-aesthetics[35] would then be of invaluable help in accounting for the unprecedented processes of psychic and collective individuation with which we are dealing nowadays. From this perspective, new forms of sensitivity are emerging in close relation to these new associated milieus. This exploration of the sensitive background of cities – the ambient commons – would enable us to understand how singular attentional regimes deal with the over-solicitation of the human sensorium.

7. Last but not least, the third trend is mainly ecological. This *ecologisation of living environments* relates to our growing concern with the current socio-environmental crisis. Ecological issues call for profound changes in our sensitivity. They point to the precariousness of living and the fundamental vulnerability of human existence. Human beings are affected by a diffuse feeling of being less and less at home on Earth and the impression that the ground is slipping away under their feet. Glenn Albrecht forged the concept of "solastalgia"[36] to account for the eco-anxiety induced by global climate change. It refers to a form of homesickness one gets when one is still at "home", a loss of comfort (or *solace*) from the familiar world, a feeling of distress related to the degradation of a place for which we care. As of now, not only do we acknowledge that our existence is precarious, but we feel and experience it as well. The coronavirus epidemic is a perfect example of

this common feeling of vulnerability. In his spherologic philosophy, Peter Sloterdijk[37] developed a whole theory of immunology and atmospheric design as life support. Atmosphere – and even more ambiance – also leads to the fundamental question of the Anthropocene, climate change, and biodiversity. It requires rethinking our attachment to the world, underpinning a non-instrumental approach to nature, and contributing to the development of an ecological aesthetic.[38] It may even be that attention to atmosphere/ambiance[39] can help relearn how "to listen to the Earth".[40] This is the atmospheric feature of ambiance and, more generally, the various natural elements (air, water, earth, fire). When we speak of ambiance as a medium of perception, when we emphasise the flows, radiations, and other emanations that pass through us, we are dealing precisely with the elemental[41] and with the flesh of the world.[42] According to this perspective, we are not in the world, but of the world, of its same fabric and texture. The dichotomy of object and subject is then irrelevant, as the body is so porous to its surroundings and permeable to the elements (i.e., the air we breathe or the sound that makes us vibrate, the smell or the heat that invades us).[43] A new way of thinking about ecology requires us to clarify what the world is made of. Following in the footsteps of the pre-Socratic Ionians, ambiance calls into question an ontology of the object, moving more readily towards an ontology of the element.[44] The question then is what the urban environment does to the elements and how it transforms them. From green-blue grids to air pollution, from eco-neighbourhoods to contaminated land, from hydropolitics to heat islands, a whole political ecology of the elements is implicitly at work. On an architectural scale, original proposals[45] are put forward for designing with and according to temperature, humidity, wind, and other ambient factors. On an urban scale, we need to understand how the city contributes to the experience and modulation of the weather, whether in terms of air flow, radiation, humidity, precipitation, or air quality.[46] But we should also talk about urban air in the plural, taking into account the different qualities of different neighbourhoods, depending on their proximity to industrial areas and their ability to protect themselves from all kinds of noxious substances. The same is true of atmospheric inequalities – particularly pronounced in megacities[47] – which are expressed in both physical (health and toxicity) and sensory terms (unbreathable air, nauseating odours, and the fog of smoke and particles). The ambient approach to such phenomena offers a new perspective on the subject. It helps to question the great divide between nature and culture, between physical and psychic entities. Alfred North Whitehead's critique of the bifurcation of nature can be implemented here.[48] After all, elements as diverse as air, water, and vegetation are as much ambient factors as they are environmental resources. They contribute to our sensory experience while nourishing our living environment. Atmosphere thus has both a meteorological and an affective side, a physical side (gaseous envelope) and an aesthetic side (affective tonality).[49] A new research theme is emerging in this area, giving weather its rightful place. Rain, wind, sun, snow, and fog are all examined through the prism of the history of sensitivity[50] and meteorological culture.[51] Thus, urban environment is not reducible to its built and material characteristics, nor indeed to its technological components. If it tries to domesticate the elements, this can only be partial and incomplete. The city is not just made up of confined, hermetically sealed spaces; it remains exposed to the seasons and the weather, to climatic variations and meteorological modulations, to a relative impermanence[52] and form of mixture. The ambient conditions in which we live are therefore partly beyond our control, challenging our sheer will to master them. In a way, weather unknowingly affects the city, tempering and enlivening it, colouring everyone's day-to-day experience. Reintroducing the elements into the sensitive transformation of inhabited spaces opens the way to an ecology of life[53] that is attentive to our atmospheric condition.

8. Various diverging forces are at play in the transformation of contemporary sensitivity, which are of an economic, technological, and ecological nature. These three underlying trends initiate a sensitivity that can be described as ambiental, although appearing very different – sometimes opposed and in dispute – in their societal stakes, political implications, and ecological consequences. Indeed, each of them operates diffusely and discreetly, often at an infra-conscious level, imprinting their mark on sensitive spaces and transforming the very mediums of perception. But while I have distinguished these three tendencies for analytical purposes, in everyday experience they are at work simultaneously, combining and intertwining closely in specific local ambiances. Ambiental sensitivity, then, can be said to be a sensitivity to the ambient situations in which we are immersed, or even more precisely, a sensitivity to everyday ambiances. To put it briefly, an ambiance can be defined as a space–time continuum experienced in sensitive terms. In John Dewey's terms, it refers to the diffuse quality of a situation,[54] its affective tonality. If I insist on *ambiance*, it is because it has the capacity to inscribe sensitivity within any ordinary situation, to articulate the passive and active features of situated experience, and to infuse daily life through and through. In other words, ambiance and situation are coextensive. With ambiance, it is not only a question of perceiving a landscape, evaluating the aesthetic value of a place, or measuring a physical environment. It is all about feeling ordinary situations, sensing the affective tonality of a place, and bodily experiencing the sensory fabric of social life.[55] Whereas atmosphere is more akin to a disseminated and delocalised affect – "floating in the air" – ambiance always relates to a concrete sensitive and affective situation that is embedded in a material world, infused with a specific weather, and indissociable from social practices. From this point of view, an ambiance constitutes the basic unit from which our sensitivity is configured, modulated, and transformed in everyday life.

9. The notion of medium is of prime importance for understanding the very sense of ambiance. We should remember that ambiance is not what one perceives, nor is it an object of perception (such as a landscape or a painting).

Ambiance is the very condition of perception. It makes perception possible and opens up the perceptibility of the world; no vision is possible without a light environment and no audition without a sonic field. One does not see the same way in a thick fog or under a blazing sun, in a uniform lighting of a shopping mall, or in the darkness of a street at night. Hence, we do not perceive an ambiance. We perceive *according to* an ambiance, depending on the quality of the medium at a given time. As Fritz Heider so aptly put it, the medium is not a thing but the means through which things can be apprehended.[56] Consequently, we are led to revisit our categories of thought with an interest in the immaterial,[57] the incorporeal,[58] and the ephemeral,[59] by focusing on porous envelopes, quasi-things,[60] and hyperobjects[61] as much as solid objects. We go from an ontology of the substance to an ecology of the elements and an ethology of the affects. It is important to understand that ambiance is not a sensitive domain among others but rather what makes the world perceptible, what gives an existence to the sensitive. One could say that ambiental sensitivity is a sensitivity to ambient worlds that inhabit us as much as we inhabit them. It is a sensitivity to the medium itself, a sensitivity to the sensitive milieu in which we are immersed.

10. To clarify the notion of ambiance further, it is important to recognise its transformative and permeating powers, its capacity to exert forces and to produce effects, to infuse experience, to establish and maintain habits, and to induce common behaviours in a very discreet manner. An ambiance is fragile and precarious, ephemeral and evanescent. A simple whisper, a small gesture, or a quick glance can be enough for an ambiance to take hold, transform itself, or vanish. It often takes very little for an ambiance to lose its consistency, to deteriorate, or to alter. But even if its existence is never completely assured, this does not mean that it is without effect and without consequences. On the contrary, an ambiance exists only in action, when it exerts its influence and authority.[62] Rather than dissociating the cause from the effect, ambiance confuses, entangles, and assimilates them. It is not the cause of an influence but rather the influence itself. An ambiance is an operating mode that is even more efficient precisely because it is discreet and unnoticed. These remarks have serious consequences. They consider ambiance the domain *par excellence* for forming perceptual habits and for activating sensory-motor schemes as well as a socio-aesthetic engagement with the world. Ambiance permeates everyday life, infuses common sensitivity, and transforms experience discreetly and continuously. It filters what is perceptible and imperceptible, distributes what is habitual or not in terms of perception, and sets what is to be taken for granted in ordinary experience. In French language we use the word *imprégnation* to illustrate the way a specific milieu spreads, infuses, and transforms its surroundings with low-intensity dynamics and molecular phenomena.[63] It involves a continuous process of familiarisation with an environment. This performative power of ambiance operates most of the time at a pre-reflective level, at the level of body experience, by suggesting movements and inciting motor tendencies, modulating ways of being

and feeling, and by activating past experiences and involuntary memories. We are dealing here with the framing of the sensory world as specific ambiances. That is to say, when anonymous percepts and impersonal affects are formed and transformed, when ways of being and feeling become ordinary, are naturalised and given in the mode of evidence. In other words, ambiance is a powerful domain which participates in the distribution of the sensible. It shows a power of immersion, infusion, and contagion that shapes our body schemes and our very capacities to feel. Whether we notice it or not, sensitivity is affected and shaped by the various ambient situations experienced every day. As mentioned earlier, ambiental sensitivity is a sensitivity to the medium. It is also a sensitivity to the nuances, attunements, and micro-variations of sensitive experience. In other words, ambiental sensitivity is a hypersensitivity to the permeating power of ambiance, to the way in which sensory worlds infuse and transform everyday experience at a subconscious level.

11. Ambiental sensitivity opens up a new avenue for political ecology and sheds new light on the reconfiguration processes of the human sensorium. Although ambiance is diffuse, it nonetheless remains framed and channelled. The sensitive domain is never naked or pure. On the contrary, ambiance is always filtered, domesticated, and normalised by social life. It would be a mistake to view the sensitive independently of the conditions that inform it and the contexts that specify it. If ambiance proves to be particularly relevant in political ecology, it is because it postulates sensitivity embedded in forms of life: a sensitivity that intertwines materialities and climates, narratives and activities, weathers and sociabilities, social norms and background affects. We are then led to conceive of the urban as the site of installation of various ambient situations as the locus for the production and transformation of sensitive worlds. An ambiance does not make the world perceptible in a generic and undifferentiated way, rather it specifies how territories and atmospheres hold together. Ambiental sensitivity opens an ecosensitivity that cannot be reduced to a new sense of nature[64] but rather a sensitivity that enhances a new consistency and porosity of ambient worlds. This reconfiguration of sensitivities also involves affect and resonance. The urban operates as a formidable inducer, activator, and resonator of affective tonalities. It establishes ambient situations by setting the tone to spaces and giving a feel for a specific *Stimmung*. The urban demonstrates a tonalising power which frames and conditions collective affects. It can take the form of warm conviviality or insecurity, alleged hospitality or strangeness. Another important issue is that of "ontological security".[65] To be habitable a space has to convey a basic trust which maintains a sense of security and familiarity by ensuring the continuity of everyday experience. Ambiances contribute to this basic trust we have in the world as it appears, exists, and continues. One is certain to find the world as it was left the day before without even having to question it. In other words, ambiances tend to reinforce what is taken for granted by installing and maintaining a familiar environment over time. Jeffrey Courtright names "existential trust"[66] as this atmospheric form of trust

that takes the form of a generalised ambient and diffuse trust. But sometimes this feeling of reliability in everyday life is challenged. This is the case of certain catastrophic situations, natural disasters, large-scale pandemics, or terrorist attacks that contribute to the loss of natural evidence and reveal the precariousness of life by defamiliarising our relationship to the world. This is also the case now with current socio-ecological problems and the related eco-anxiety they induce. This issue concerns the habitability of the world; ambient sensitivity tests our very sense of familiarity and security and involves a basic existential dimension. Various theories seek to account for these transformations: a crisis of resonance[67] that is at once psychic, ecological, and democratic; a crisis of sensitivity[68] to lifeworlds; an extinguishing extinction of experience[69] that increases our sense of estrangement from the natural world. This aspect of a political ecology of ambiances concerns an enlarged sensitivity which restores the living world to its full place. From this perspective, ambiental sensitivity can be understood as an attempt to restore a vibrant link between the world of humans and non-humans. It is a form of sensitivity where nature is no longer kept at a distance. On the contrary, it is about exploring new ways of being affected and acting accordingly. This affect is not about melancholy, dread, or denial – even though they are very present nowadays – but about what we could provisionally call an affect of a *strange wonder*. A paradoxical mixture of strangeness and wonder: strangeness for being open to the otherness of the non-human and the singularity of every living being and wonder because unexplored living worlds and unusual atmospheres are yet to discover, encounter, and amaze. In a way, ambient sensitivity consists of intensifying our ways of feeling alive and enhancing our attunements to lifeforms.

Notes

1 Benjamin, *The Work of Art*, 222.
2 Füzesséry and Simay, *Une théorie sensitive*, 30–31, my translation.
3 Benjamin, "Le conteur".
4 I prefer to use the term *ambiental sensitivity* rather than *ambient sensitivity*, insofar as it is not just a matter of sensitivity to what surrounds us but more precisely a sensitivity to *ambiances*. Throughout the text, I've also retained the French word *ambiance* rather than its English translation *ambience*, as ambiance is now a notion – difficult to translate – that has been widely developed, specified, and theorised within the French-speaking humanities and social sciences.
5 Rancière, *The Politics of Aesthetics*, 12.
6 Rancière, *Aisthesis*.
7 Bégout, *Zéropolis*.
8 Koolhaas and Mau, *S, M, L, XL*.
9 Ingersoll, *Sprawltown*.
10 Bonnet, *Après la mort*, 14–15, my translation.
11 Foster, "The Narrative and the Ambient", 134.
12 Shusterman, *Sous l'interprétation*.
13 Böhme, *Critique of Aesthetic Capitalism*.
14 Rieunier, *Marketing sensoriel*.

15 Pine and Gilmore, *The Experience Economy*.
16 Illouz, *Emotions as Commodities*.
17 Michaud, *L'art, c'est bien fini*, 38.
18 Michaud, *Le nouveau luxe*, 131, my translation.
19 Sennett, *Flesh and Stone*. Thomas et al. *L'aseptisation des ambiances piétonnes*.
20 Hajer and Reijndorp, *In Search of New Public Domain*.
21 Breviglieri, "Une brèche critique", 213–236.
22 Jeudy and Berenstein-Jacques, *Corps et décors urbains*.
23 Dolle, *Le territoire du rien*.
24 Boyer, "Twice-Told Stories", 30–53.
25 Allen, "Ambient Power", 441–455.
26 Hudson, "ION Orchard", 289–308.
27 Ratouis, *La plateforme du rêve*.
28 Aarts and Marzano, *The New Everyday*.
29 Wachter, "La ville numérique".
30 Crang and Graham, "Sentient Cities", 789–817.
31 Stiegler, *De la misère symbolique*.
32 Boyer, *Le Conflit des perceptions*.
33 McCullough, *Ambient Commons*.
34 Citton, *Pour une écologie de l'attention*.
35 Simondon, "Sur la techno-esthétique", 391–392.
36 Albrecht, "Solastalgia: A New Concept", 41–55.
37 Sloterdijk, *Foam. Spheres, Vol. III*.
38 Rigby, "Gernot Böhme's Ecological Aesthetics", 139–152.
39 The notions of *ambiance* and *atmosphere* are, in a way, very close (albeit different) and share many of the same issues related to ecology.
40 Abram, *The Spell of the Sensuous*.
41 Macauley, *Elemental Philosophy*.
42 Merleau-Ponty, *Le Visible et l'invisible*.
43 Thibaud, "The Atmospherization of Everyday Life", 163–173.
44 Barbaras, *Le tournant de l'expérience*.
45 Rahm, *Architecture météorologique*.
46 Tixier et al., *L'ambiance est dans l'air*. Janković and Hebbert, "Hidden Climate Change", 23–33.
47 Adey, "Air/Atmospheres of the Megacity", 291–308.
48 Whitehead, *The Concept of Nature*.
49 McCormack, "Engineering Affective Atmospheres", 413–430. Ingold, "The Atmosphere", 75–87.
50 **Corbin**, *La pluie, le soleil et le vent*.
51 *Ethnologie française*, Special issue *Météo*.
52 Saito, "The Aesthetics of Weather".
53 Ingold, *Being Alive*.
54 Thibaud, "De la qualité diffuse", 227–253.
55 Thibaud, "A Brief Archaeology".
56 Heider, "Thing and Medium", 1–34.
57 Lyotard, *Les Immatériaux*.
58 Cauquelin, *Fréquenter les incorporels*. Grosz, *The Incorporeal*.
59 Buci-Glucksmann, *Esthétique de l'éphémère*.
60 Griffero, *Quasi-Things*.
61 Morton, *Hyperobjects*.
62 Griffero, *Atmospheres: Aesthetics of Emotional Spaces*.
63 Thibaud, "The Lesser Existence of Ambiance", 175–187.
64 Collot, *Un nouveau sentiment de la nature*.
65 Giddens, *Modernity and Self-Identity*.

66 Courtright, "Is Trust Like an 'Atmosphere'?", 39–51.
67 Rosa, *Resonance*.
68 Mengual and Morizot, "L'illisibilité du paysage", 87–96.
69 Pyle, "The Extinction of Experience", 64–67.

Bibliography

Aarts, Emile and Stefano Marzano, *The New Everyday: Visions of Ambient Intelligence*, 010 Publishers, 2003.
Abram, David, *The Spell of the Sensuous: Perception and Language in a More-than-Human World*, Vintage Books/Random House, 1996.
Adey, Peter, "Air/Atmospheres of the Megacity", *Theory, Culture & Society*, 30, no. 7/8 (2013): 291–308.
Albrecht, Glen, "Solastalgia: A New Concept in Human Health and Identity", *Philosophy, Activism, Nature* 3 (2005): 41–55.
Allen, John, "Ambient Power: Berlin's Potsdamer Platz and the Seductive Logic of Public Spaces", *Urban Studies* 43, no. 2 (2006): 441–455.
Barbaras, Renaud, *Le tournant de l'expérience*, Paris: Vrin, 1998.
Bégout, Bruce, *Zéropolis*, Paris: Allia, 2002.
Benjamin, Walter, "The Work of Art in the Age of Mechanical Reproduction", in *Illuminations*, edited by Hannah Arendt, translated by Harry Zohn, from the 1935 essay, 217–251, New York: Schocken Books, 1969.
Benjamin, Walter, "Le conteur", in *Expérience et pauvreté. Suivi de Le conteur et La tâche du traducteur*, 51–106, Paris: Editions Payot et Rivages, 2011.
Böhme, Gernot, *Critique of Aesthetic Capitalism*, translated by Edmund Jephcott, Mimesis International, 2017.
Bonnet, François J., *Après la mort. Essai sur l'envers du présent*, Éditions de l'éclat, 2017.
Boyer, Christine, "Twice-Told Stories: The Double Erasure of Times Square", in *The Unknown City. Contesting Architecture and Social Space*, edited by Iain Borden, Joe Kerr, Jane Rendell and Alicia Pivaro, 30–53, Cambridge: The MIT Press, 2000.
Boyer, Elsa, *Le Conflit des perceptions*, Editions MF, 2015.
Breviglieri, Marc, "Une brèche critique dans la 'ville garantie'?", in *De la différence urbaine*, edited by Elena Cognato Lanza, Luca Pattaroni, Mischa Piraud and Barbara Tirone, 213–236, Genève: MétisPresses, 2013.
Buci-Glucksmann, Christine, *Esthétique de l'éphémère*, Paris: éditions Galilée, 2003.
Cauquelin, Anne, *Fréquenter les incorporels. Contribution à une théorie de l'art contemporain*, Paris: PUF, 2006.
Citton, Yves, *Pour une écologie de l'attention*, Paris: Le Seuil, 2014.
Collot, Michel, *Un nouveau sentiment de la nature*, Paris: Editions Corti, 2022.
Corbin, Alain, ed., *La pluie, le soleil et le vent. Une histoire de la sensibilité au temps qu'il fait*, Paris: Aubier, 2013.
Courtright, Jeffrey, "Is Trust Like an 'Atmosphere'? Understanding the Phenomenon of Existential Trust", *Journal for Philosophy in the Contemporary World* 20, no. 1 (2013): 39–51.
Crang, Mike and Stephen Graham, "Sentient Cities: Ambient Intelligence and the Politics of Urban Space", *Information, Communication Society* 10, no. 6 (2007): 789–817.
de Cauter, Lieven, *The Capsular Civilization. On the City in the Age of Fear*, NAI Publishers, 2004.
Dolle, Jean-Paul, *Le territoire du rien, ou la contre-révolution patrimonialiste*, Paris: Lignes, 2005.
Ethnologie française, Special issue *Météo. Du climat et des hommes*, Tome XXXIX, no. 4, 2009.

Foster, Cheryl, "The Narrative and the Ambient in Environmental Aesthetics", *The Journal of Aesthetics and Art Criticism* 56, no. 2 (Spring, 1998): 127–137.
Füzesséry, Stéphane and Philippe Simay, "Une théorie sensitive de la modernité", in *Le choc des métropoles. Simmel, Kracauer, Benjamin*, edited by Stéphane Füzesséry and Philippe Simay, 30–31, Paris: Editions de l'éclat, 2008.
Giddens, Anthony, *Modernity and Self-Identity. Self and Society in the Late Modern Age*, Cambridge: Polity Press, 1991.
Griffero, Tonino, *Atmospheres: Aesthetics of Emotional Spaces*, translated by Sarah De Sanctis, Burlington, VT: Ashgate, 2010.
Griffero, Tonino, *Quasi-Things. The Paradigm of Atmospheres*, translated by Sarah De Sanctis, Albany: SUNY Press, 2017.
Grosz, Elisabeth, *The Incorporeal. Ontology, Ethics, and the Limits of Materialism*, New York: Columbia University Press, 2017.
Hajer, Maarten and Arnold Reijndorp, *In Search of New Public Domain: Analysis and Strategy*, NAI Publishers, 2001.
Heider, Fritz, "Thing and Medium", in *On Perception, Event Structure, and Psychological Environment, Psychological Issues*, Vol. 1, no. 3, 1–34, New York: International Universities Press.
Hudson, Chris, "ION Orchard: Atmosphere and Consumption in Singapore", *Visual Communication* 14, no. 3 (2015): 289–308.
Illouz, Eva, ed., *Emotions as Commodities. Capitalism, Consumption and Authenticity*, London: Routledge, 2017.
Ingersoll, Richard, *Sprawltown: Looking for the City on its Edges*, New York: Princeton Architectural Press, 2006.
Ingold, Tim, *Being Alive. Essays on Movement, Knowledge and Description*, New York: Routledge, 2011.
Ingold, Tim, "The Atmosphere", *Chiasmi International* 14 (2012): 75–87.
Janković, Vladimir and Michael Hebbert, "Hidden Climate Change – Urban Meteorology and the Scales of Real Weather", *Climatic Change* 113 (2012): 23–33.
Jeudy, Henri-Pierre and Paola Berenstein-Jacques, eds., *Corps et décors urbains*, Paris: L'Harmattan, 2006.
Koolhaas, Rem and Bruce Mau, *S, M, L, XL*, New York: Monacelli Press, 1995.
Lyotard, Jean-François, ed., *Les Immatériaux*, Paris: Centre Georges-Pompidou, 1985.
Macauley, David, *Elemental Philosophy. Earth, Air, Fire and Water as Environmental Ideas*, Albany: State University of New York Press, 2010.
McCormack, Derek, "Engineering Affective Atmospheres on the Moving Geographies of the 1897 Andrée Expedition", *Cultural Geographies* 15, no. (4) (2008): 413–430.
McCullough, Malcom, *Ambient Commons. Attention in the Age of Embodied Information*, Cambridge: The MIT Press, 2013.
Mengual, Estelle Zhong and Baptiste Morizot, "L'illisibilité du paysage. Enquête sur la crise écologique comme crise de la sensibilité", *Nouvelle revue d'esthétique* 22 (2018): 87–96.
Merleau-Ponty, Maurice, *Le Visible et l'invisible*, Paris: Gallimard, 1964.
Michaud, Yves, *Le nouveau luxe. Expériences, arrogance, authenticité*, Paris: Stock, 2013.
Michaud, Yves, *"L'art c'est bien fini". Essai sur l'hyper-esthétique et les atmosphères*, Paris: Gallimard, 2021.
Morton, Timothy, *Hyperobjects. Philosophy and Ecology after the End of the World*, Minneapolis: University of Minnesota Press, 2013.
Pine, Joseph, and James Gilm *The Experience Economy*, Boston: Harvard Business School Press, 1999.
Pyle, Robert, "The Extinction of Experience", *Horticulture* 56 (1978): 64–67.

Rahm, Philippe, *Architecture météorologique*, Paris: Archibooks + sautereau éditeur, 2009.
Rancière, Jacques, *The Politics of Aesthetics. The Distribution of the Sensible*, edited and translated with an introduction by Gabriel Rockhill, London: Continuum International Publishing Group, 2004.
Rancière, Jacques, *Aisthesis: Scènes du régime esthétique de l'art*, Paris: Galilée, 2011.
Ratouis, Olivier, *La plateforme du rêve. Figures américaines de la fonction de loisir*, Strasbourg: Ecole supérieure des arts décoratifs, 2004.
Rieunier, Sophie, ed., *Marketing sensoriel et expérientiel du point de vente*, Paris: Dunod, 2017.
Rigby, Kate, "Gernot Böhme's Ecological Aesthetics of Atmosphere", in *Ecocritical Theory: New European Approaches*, edited by Axel Goodbody and Kate Rigby, 139–152, Charlottesville: University of Virginia Press, 2011.
Rosa, Hartmut, *Resonance: A Sociology of Our Relationship to the World*, Cambridge: Polity Press, 2019.
Saito, Yuriko, "The Aesthetics of Weather", in *The Aesthetics of Everyday Life*, edited by Andrew Light and Jonathan M. Smith, 156–176, New York: Columbia University, 2005.
Sennett, Richard, *Flesh and Stone: The Body and the City in Western Civilization*, London: Faber and Faber, 1994.
Shusterman, Richard, *Sous l'interprétation*, translated by Jean-Pierre Cometti, Combas: édition de l'éclat, 1994.
Simondon, Gilbert, "Sur la techno-esthétique", in *Sur la technique (1953–1983)*, 391–392, Paris: PUF, 2014.
Sloterdijk, Peter, *Foams. Spheres, Vol. III: Plural Spherology*, translated by Wieland Hoban, Semiotext(e), Cambridge: The MIT Press, 2016.
Stiegler, Bernard, *De la misère symbolique. La catastrophe du sensible*, Paris: Galilée, 2005.
Thibaud, Jean-Paul, "De la qualité diffuse aux ambiances urbaines", in *Raisons Pratiques 14. La croyance et l'enquête*, edited by Bruno Karsenti and Louis Quéré, 227–253, Paris: EHESS, 2004.
Thibaud, Jean-Paul, "The Lesser Existence of Ambiance", in *Atmosphere and Aesthetics. A Plural Perspective*, edited by Tonino Griffero and Marco Tedeschini, 175–187, New York: Palgrave Macmillan, 2019.
Thibaud, Jean-Paul, "A Brief Archaeology of the Notion of Ambiance", *Unlikely. Journal for Creative Arts*, no. 6 (2020). Translating Ambiance. https://unlikely.net.au/issue-06/notion-of-ambiance
Thibaud, Jean-Paul, "The Atmospherization of Everyday Life", in *Breathe. Investigations into Our Atmospherically Entangled Future*, edited by Klaus K. Loenhart, 163–173, Basel: Birkhäuser, 2021.
Thomas, Rachel, Suzel Balez, Gabriel Bérubé and Aurore Bonnet, *L'aseptisation des ambiances piétonnes au XXIe siècle, entre passivité et plasticité des corps en marche*, 78, Grenoble: CRESSON [Rapport de recherche], 2010. hal-00596914. https://shs.hal.science/halshs-00596914
Tixier, Nicolas, Damien Masson, Cintia Okamura, Pascal Amphoux, Laure Brayer, Sandra Fiori, Guillaume Meigneux et al. *L'ambiance est dans l'air: la dimension atmosphérique des ambiances architecturales et urbaines dans les approches environnementalistes*, 81, Grenoble: CRESSON, [Rapport de recherche], 2011. hal-00993840. https://hal.science/hal-00993840
Wachter, Serge, "La ville numérique: quels enjeux pour demain?", *Métropolitiques*, 2011. https://metropolitiques.eu/La-ville-numerique-quels-enjeux.html
Whitehead, Alfred North, *The Concept of Nature*, Cambridge: Cambridge University Press, 1920.

10 Urban life scenes in Georg Simmel

Passages between house and city

Adriana Veríssimo Serrão

A philosophy of the city

> Irrespective of whether one considers philosophy in general a science, the philosophy of society has no right not to avail itself of the advantages or disadvantages of belonging to philosophy in general through the creation of a particular science of sociology.[1]

To read Georg Simmel's 1903 "Die Großstädte und das Geistesleben" as a *stricto sensu* social analysis or as a study in urban sociology is to gain only a partial understanding of it, one that does not take into account the theoretical principles Simmel attributed to this science, which was still seeking its own epistemological place and status within the human sciences (*Geisteswissenschaften*).

The question "How is society possible?", which guides the excursus of the 1908 *Sociology* – along with its correlate: "Under what conditions is sociology possible as a science?" – is Kantian in form. According to Simmel, this area of knowledge did not possess the required epistemological boundaries to become a special science, on the same level as those already in existence. The question derives from "philosophical matters" that in this case encompass the wider field of "society" as a theoretical object. The methodological distinction between form and matter is equally Kantian. The philosophy of society need not take into consideration everything that belongs to the chaos of the social (as not every movement of the soul belongs to psychology), but it must isolate what is "specifically social in society", that is, the formations that come into being through relationships established among individuals, abstracting from private motivations and intentions.[2]

Reciprocal actuation (*Wechselwirkung*) is the moving principle of the dynamics that are at work in social forms. It is not the simple combining of interests and objectives among neighbours, which occurs in the fortuitous encounters of *some with others*, but rather a movement of causation and effectuation in both directions, with an ultimately organic matrix: social phenomena must be understood as simultaneous causes and effects, exercised by some on others, just as occurs in the case of organisms. *Wechselwirkung* operates in coexistence, in *Mitdasein, being among others*, originating new formations according to procedures that are reversible but not symmetrical or equivalent, procedures that may be either balanced and adequate or generators of dissonance and conflict. It is an operating principle of a non-disjunctive logic: the third is not merely the *terminus medius* that links two separate terms (as in Aristotelian logic) but incorporates itself in the relation and transforms it, generating different properties. Social, cultural and economic formations arise from relationships among individuals and gain objectivity, gaining a configuration (*Gestalt*) that is defined independently of their subjective origins; to be preserved, however, they must be reactivated by individual subjectivity. Their duration may be more or less long, they may have different intensities and scales, but they lead to the appearance of new forms or to the obsolescence of previously existing forms, in a permanent process of differentiation, through either complexification or disaggregation. Interpretative sociology deals with this circuit of synthesis between subjectivity and objectivity, between individuality and supra-individuality, in a never-ending dialectic of formal dissolution and reconfiguration (*Umformung*).

The Simmelian conception of social life is a hermeneutics of synthesis, not in the Hegelian sense of overcoming contradictions but in the Kantian sense of a copula or "third",[3] not of compact entities, as if they were cohesive unities but of forms with internal forces. It is also not limited to structuring macro-formations in social organisation on a more general level (political, economic, juridical, institutional). As a historical formation, the city owes its continuity and changes to modes of socialisation (*Vergesellschaftung*) that stabilise interactions between individuals and groups, but there are also more transient motives and energies that sprout from person to person, passing through the social tissue, recovered or disappearing, sometimes with explicit surface manifestations, sometimes acting on a more subtle level:

> If the science of sociology deals with the consequences of the fact that each singular human being is not alone in the world but is determined by the coexistence (*Mitdasein*) of others, then its gaze cannot be restricted to the large collective formations that are circumscribed by politics and the economy, by law and the church, by family and civilisation in general. It must also focus on the finer, more fleeting relationships that develop between people, determining our lives in a thousand interwoven ways, threads that are frequently abandoned, only to be taken up anew and woven in a different way, ultimately uniting with others the internal vitality and stability of our existence.[4]

It is notable that Simmel uses "gaze" (*Blick*) to refer to the movement that takes place both on the horizontal plane – in the evolving series of phenomena – and on the vertical plane, uniting in the same phenomenon surface and depth, in a superposition of different layers. To understand the modern city longitudinally is to understand it as resulting from historical movements; to understand it transversely is to identify a path between the highest spheres of *Geist* and the most common daily expressions.

Equally noteworthy are the similarities between Simmel's descriptions of the sociologist's and the philosopher's gaze, which use the same metaphors of intertwining, intervals and subtle signs, in a course of thought that rejects the closed solidity of a system:

> The world is given to us as a sum of fragments, and the endeavour of philosophy consists in putting the whole for the part; and this is achieved by putting the part for the whole. Among the numberless threads which form the intertwining of reality and whose totality constitutes the philosopher's problem, the specificity of his spiritual kind allows him to grasp a single one; he declares this to be the one that keeps the whole cohesive, from which all others derive; while on the surface it may appear only fragmentary and often covered by others, he follows it as the unique continuum through the whole network; he weaves it beyond the relative measure of its finite manifestation into the infinite and the absolute.[5]

It would be reductive to consider each of the subjects that awakened Simmel's philosophical interest – fashion, ruins, the face, landscape, among many others – as a dilettante's exercise or to try to classify them according to specific disciplines. Each describes a "point of existence" (*Punkt des Daseins*),[6] a fragment of reality in which forces are concentrated with great intensity and which maintains, with more or less coherence, the threads connecting it to other fragments and to the always sought-after wholeness. From the exhaustive explicitness of a phenomenon-fragment it becomes obvious that its impulses and energies (pre-forms) converge and become objective upstream, at which point they are released and diverge, sometimes complementing each other, sometimes contrasting, from a relational perspective which aims at an inaccessible wholeness. As an adventurer, the philosopher circulates in a unitary vital process and "deals with unsolvable problems as if they had a solution".[7] He or she charges into the unknown, aware that it will not become known but deriving from each detail an intuition of the whole of its sense and of life's deep currents, which arise from the contingent intersections of phenomena.

The difference between a "part" and a "fragment" of a whole is illustrative of the typically philosophical topic of the unity of the real. The fragment is neither a loose piece of a mechanism nor a self-contained part, isolated from others. It presupposes a previous unity and maintains threads that tie it to the vital course. It is "a portion [*Stück*] that remains when the parts [*Teile*] of a pre-existing whole have entered into decline".[8]

Relativism (*Relativismus*) stands in solidarity with the fragmentary character of life, offering "a metaphysical image of the world" that shifts the traditional search for a substantial basis of reality through an organic vision of the flux of time.[9]

Metropolises and the tragic condition of modernity

> The *a priori* of empirical social life consists in the fact that life is not wholly social.[10]

Late historical formations, metropolises are the point where multiple longitudinal and transversal processes intensify – what Simmel calls a "tragedy of culture", from a cultural point of view, and a "tragic fate", from a metaphysical point of view: the conflict between and dissociation of life and forms.

A fundamental and insurmountable tragedy in the human condition accompanies the entire path of civilisation (*Kultur*): the opposition between man and world, subject and object. The human being enters the world as a counterpoint to surrounding natural existences, in a dualism that constitutes an indefinitely occurring movement, turning all of history into a struggle (one of violence and resistance) between spirit and nature.[11]

The second tragic instance occurs within spirit itself, that is, from the interior life movement to exteriorisation: the internal psychic energies expand through language, expressiveness, creativity and actions. The soul – like the current of natural phenomena – is one of life's manifestations: pure temporality, uninterrupted succeeding, a continuum devoid of parts. By contrast, the forms it produces are always limited and finite realisations, tending towards stability.

It would be impossible to understand the dynamic of forms, which are human products, if they were not rooted in a subjacent stratum. It is from this tension between life and forms – between mobility and permanence – that Simmel proceeds to his concept of culture (*Bildung*). Culture is a bilateral mode of coordination: when subjectivity is exteriorised it becomes objective in innumerable forms, of which it takes hold again, to complete its formation. Culture is then an eminently synthetic concept: it turns the subjective into the objective and the objective into the subjective, in a process that moves from itself to itself through the appropriation of objective entities: "Culture is the path from closed unity to blossomed unity through the blossoming of multiplicity".[12]

The tragic becomes more serious when it is no longer possible to return to oneself. This may happen through the multiplication of innumerable productions that have lost their original meaning and have become devoid of their cultural function or through the evolution of those contents themselves, which tend to obtain an independent existence in an automatism that has its own movement and its own logic:

> The great enterprise of the spirit to overcome the object as such in order to create itself as an object, and to return again to itself through

the enrichment of such creation, is very often a success; but this self-completion comes at the cost of the tragic risk of witnessing the emergence, within the intrinsic autonomy of the world which it created and which conditions it, of a logic and a dynamic that separate the contents of culture from the ends of culture with ever increasing speed and to an ever greater extent.[13]

This is then the ineluctable destiny of forms: a freezing and petrification occurring in the technical field but also in political institutions, moral codes, religious dogmas and philosophical systems. Ultimately, however, it is still and solely a manifestation of life, which is in itself life and death. So the tragedy of culture leads back to metaphysical tragedy: the paradox of life's producing that which is no longer alive but dead.

Such is the tragedy inherent in culture. In fact, and unlike a destiny completely made up of sadness or destruction brought from outside, we call the following a tragic destiny: the forces of annihilation directed against an entity come precisely from the deepest layers of that entity itself.[14]

In light of the dissonance between subjective spirit and objective spirit, let us briefly indicate the main lines that determine the functioning of big cities, in which an exterior body and an interior soul are intertwined, using the Berlin of Simmel, the illustrious Berliner, as an example. To function on a large scale, the metropolis requires a division of labour, industrialisation, the global circulation of money and the mechanisation of many sectors of life, all of which shape the urban condition, including daily and public behaviour, in addition to moulding thought, psychology and sensibility.

i) The complexification of an economy based on the division of work demands the specialisation of tasks, which renders individuals economically indispensable while nonetheless making them ever more dependent on the supra-individual gear of a "socially technical mechanism".[15]
ii) The monetisation of life, as well as the cause and effect of production and increasing consumption, entails the predominance of the culture of things over the culture of people. Monetary economy replaces inherent qualitative values with exchange quantitative values, replacing the question "What is it?" with "How much does it cost?" It thus annuls individual qualities and reduces each object to being "one more".
iii) Close relationships among people and direct exchanges between local, small-scale producers and their clients give way to relationships that follow patterns, in the context of a manufacturing market economy. The more the public sphere grows, the more the sphere of private relations is diminished. More than the inhabitants of villages or the rural world,

who are involved in always concrete experiences, the inhabitant of the metropolis perfects abstract comparison in a strengthening of intellectual faculties and analytical capabilities at the cost of sensibility.[16]

The speed and intensity of rhythms, the compartmentalisation of timetables – the metropolis is guided by the automatism of clocks – engenders a state of permanent sensory stimulation, a psychic nervousness from which the citizen defends himself by withdrawing: *Blasiertheit*. The one who is *blasé* is not indifferent to what surrounds him, but he becomes capable of reacting mentally, not epidermically, almost anaesthetising his hyper-sensibility, and through private acts he manages to attain some measure of stability in the midst of instability.[17]

The inversely proportional relation between nearness in space and distance from the world – whether objects or other people – contributes to creating a metropolitan condition that differs from what governs the existence of the inhabitants of small communities: the metropolitan resident faces the challenge of finding means of preserving his individuality, his margin of free action and expression, without relinquishing the multiple spheres of insertion that offer him greater opportunities for personal development.

The essay on metropolises ends with a diagnosis of fighting and reconciliation and resumes the tragic dimension at the individual level. Modern man views himself as standing at a crossroads, a pair of widely diverging paths: on the one hand, indispensable participation/insertion in ever more varied and disparate totalities, which enlarge the scope of the orientations at his disposal; on the other, the need to maintain his personal identity, to secure ever more elaborate resources. The destiny of the individual is a recurring topic for Simmel, who often reflects on different historical conceptions of individualism:

> The great task for the future, however, is that of achieving an organisation of life and society that creates a positive synthesis of both kinds of individualism; of conceiving of the eighteenth-century ahistorical ideal, with its equal and equally justified individuals, solely united by universal and merely rational law, in a superior unity with nineteenth-century individualism, which found its achievement in the history of ideas in the differences between individuals, in the inherent legality of each personality, and in their organisation through historic life.[18]

From the point of view of historical awareness encompassing categories, Simmel proposes a new understanding of individualism, with enough flexibility to reconcile equality and difference, freedom and self-determination – a task which is ultimately among "life's final questions": how to resolve the dilemma between "the individual subjectivity that modern man does not want to relinquish and the supra-individual community of all, which is no

156 Rethinking the City

less necessary for him"?[19] From the point of view of real existence, the only path open to this antagonistic condition presents itself as the *art of living*, the task of giving oneself a law: a (free) individual configuration within a (shared) multiple community.[20]

From the city to the house: passages from the outside to the inside

The changes that took place inside houses at the beginning of the 20th century were not simply an antidote to the dispersal of public existence but also reflected a dualism within the private sphere between the tendency towards individuality and the feeling of solitude, of being alone in the multitude. The house represents an extension of what the individual owns, organising a space as *his* house, *his* home, preserving areas of individuality from the threat of dissolution in impersonality. At the same time, however, to furnish the various rooms he uses artefacts that were not manufactured or created by him: they are technical products and industrial objects, bringing into the highly individual "inside" the impersonal and mechanical "outside" of which the inhabitant wishes to free himself. The inside of the house is a meeting of two opposites: in the same physical space, the tendency towards individuality meets the opposite tendency towards generality.

The tension between subjectivity and objectivity reaches its extreme here. On the one hand, the subjectivity of the inhabitant is heightened to the level of hyper-subjectivism, resulting in a claim not just to the physical individuality of his residence but to a personalised and original environment. On the other hand, the dependence on the influence of social models is reinforced by the sophistication of the styles used in each room: furniture, artefacts, decorative elements, and appliances, themselves endowed with numerous variants.

The chapter in *Philosophie des Geldes* dedicated to "The Style of Life", written at the turn of the century, describes the "objectification of cultural contents, setting between the subject and his creations a growing otherness, which extends down to the intimacy of daily life". Whereas in the first decades of the 19th century interiors were characterised by the simplicity and durability of crafted artefacts, passed down from parents to children, guaranteeing habitual contact and easy integration – "a marriage between the personalities and their objects" – the clutter of intricately made objects began to hinder this nearly personal relationship. What was once a continuous relationship with small elementary appliances was broken; in its place, a gap, a hostility arose: "an abundance of objects facing me . . . form a sort of party".[21]

Although in opposition to ways of being that are considered obsolete, and demanding free choice, modern individualised taste nonetheless incurs another paradox: the tragedy of freedom. In small communities, freedom consisted in the "extension of the I", acting on docile forms that easily accepted manipulation, whereas an environment stuffed with innumerable rigid details that we cannot assimilate into ourselves gives rise to a feeling of servitude, of facing an adverse presence. The impression of being buried under technical exteriorities, technically reproduced things, "is not only the consequence but also the origin of the fact that they confront us as autonomous objects".[22]

What meaningful configurations of taste preside over the desire to give personal, different styles to the various rooms in the house? What is the aesthetic status of the mass-produced artefacts that so entice the city dweller, as opposed to the old-fashioned objects of our forefathers, cloaked as they are in family histories? Can these new variants – industrially produced, commercially exhibited in shops and suggestive shop windows, and bought with money that moves swiftly from hand to hand – really be called *styles*?[23]

In his most clarifying essay on this subject, "The Problem of Style", Simmel asserts the following principle: the more a production is singularised, the less one cares about its style. This is not a characteristic of all works of art but only of those that are truly original. In the case of Michelangelo and Rembrandt, the style to which they belonged – Mannerism or the Baroque – is irrelevant, because they transcend style, whereas so many Baroque statues and neoclassical buildings, if nothing in them really impresses us, if nothing about them stands out, are simply inserted in a common type: in a *style*. And this is sufficient for us to locate and order them.

In the artistic field, the gradation from particular to general obeys an inversely proportional law of compensation: the more, the less. The less there is of the peculiar in a particular, the more there is of what is common to all particulars: "we can only access what is typical in it". The style, or what is typical, comes before the weak or almost non-existent peculiarity. This law acts as a criterion for evaluating the immanent quality of works of art on a scale that culminates in uniqueness (*Einzigkeit*). In exceptional cases the creative soul, "the mysterious particularity of an artist", gives rise to a style (not the other way around): a previously unprecedented mode is subsequently resumed, and that first gesture becomes a style through imitation.[24] Only in this case is the equivalence of style and man pertinent.

The defence of Simmel's concept of the internal sovereignty of art – the view that art should not depend on extrinsic (moral, political, religious etc.) or intrinsic (artistic norms and precepts) values but must solve a problem posed by itself – clearly has a philosophical basis and does not arise from classification by art history or critique.[25] Simmel, who, even when diagnosing the most dramatic consequences of the crisis of culture and the tragedy of modernity, adopts a neutral position, here displays an unusual severity in denouncing the confusion between the living forms of art and the lifeless forms of technical objects, resuming the crucial distinction in his metaphysics of life: that between the *more life (Mehr Leben)* of lively forms and the *more-than-life (Mehr-als-Leben)* of industrial objects.

The peremptory stance against a rising trend towards decorating houses, multiplying and diversifying their elements, is directed not solely against quantity but mainly against the confused mixing of essences and purposes. The artefact is a means to an end beyond itself, whereas the work of art is autotelic, an end in itself. Pieces of furniture (chairs, tables, beds etc.) and decorative objects (lamps, glasses, crockery etc.) with exclusively practical purposes are meant to fulfil the teleology of the useful, as in traditional settlements domestic needs were met with stylised and lasting patterns, replicated generation after generation.

In his observations on modern interiors, Simmel identifies two further diverging effects which border on the banality of the false: these consist on the one hand in displaying simply functional things *as if they were artworks*, using precious materials and recurrently altering forms to individualise what is merely typical, and on the other hand in using *in a functional way* what is artistic in itself, for example sitting on or drinking from a crafted object, which is an act of "cannibalism" that "demot[es] the master to the condition of a slave".[26] Adulterated taste, devoid of critical judgement, oscillates between *Blasiertheit* and superficiality; modern man's unilaterality is compensated for by multilateralism.

This compensation had already been noted in writings from the 1890s on the phenomenon of the grand universal exhibitions which the European capitals of London (1851) and Paris (1889–1890) – great cities that sought to become universal cities, world centres – competed with each other to host. In his observations on the *Gewerbe-Ausstellung*, an industrial exhibition in Berlin which he attended in 1896, Simmel mentions some of the pernicious effects that mass movements have exerted on art appreciation: the concentration of a great number of products exhibited in a limited space; the mixture of styles of unequal aesthetic quality (unique works of art set side by side with crafted artefacts and industrial products); changes in sensibility (cluttered with stimuli they must absorb quickly, the visitors' brains are in no condition to quietly contemplate a unique artwork).[27]

More than the adulteration of taste, Simmel targets the entry into the world of art of such movements as the *Jugendstil* and the *Arts and Crafts* movement, which were widespread from the mid-19th century on and aimed to replace erudite salon art with functional art that was accessible to all classes. Simmel, who also thought about aesthetics and contributed significantly to the establishment of new categories – gravity, quantity, vivacity, height – beyond the artwork's beauty,[28] sensed that the difference between the artefact and the work of art was in the process of being lost, and thus he did not contest the aesthetic value of functionalism nor did he place it at an inferior level. Instead, he defended a strict distinction between both aesthetic spheres: one artistic and the other practical.[29]

The height of discredit is attained when the applied arts, whose essence is type/style, produced in multiple series and reproducible prototypes, are signed as if they were individual and original creations, which cannot exist but once. Such actions erase the distinction between being one among many and being unique because one's qualities are unique.

In decorative matters, Simmel is partial to more stylised and cohesive environments – rooms full of historically "heavy" objects are rather unpleasant – although he accepts the presence of works of art in people's homes.

To surround oneself with antiques, paintings or decorative objects, if of exceptional quality (such as a Lalique crystal glass), is not necessarily a species of snobbery; it moderates the excesses of the vicissitudes of fashion, but such objects must be given prominence. However, drinking from such a glass or sitting on an ancient sofa compromises aesthetic appreciation free of all empirical interest.

It is essential that a unique work be able to show its specific self-sufficient wholeness without being disturbed, kept safe from the interference of practical life; it is convenient to give it prominence through a frame, a delimitation, which prevents the confusion of the world of the artwork with the empirical world.[30]

From the house to the city: passages from the inside to the outside

There is another point of view from which Simmel takes a vehement stand against mixing aesthetic genres. If handcrafted artefacts are to be part of daily life and must have a style that corresponds to basic uses, the uniformity of that style must also effect a sense of safety, providing moments of tranquillity and suspending nervous unrest outside, where everything is entangled, relative and conflicting.

As a protective refuge that provides a break from having to perform social roles and from social and professional competition, the house provides tranquillity, unifies animic energies and pacifies psychic layers. The house is to be a personal space, but it is not supposed to elicit too much effort in the search for new trends; in a possible balance between an exaggerated subjectivism and generality, at home the soul recovers the unity of life, and man finds peace within himself.

Precisely where the Ego reinforces its most intimate personal core, it may also admit inter-subjectivity. The harmony of the environment is a *third*, where convivial relationships are strengthened, where acquaintances and strangers are welcome to feel at home. In the peacefulness of the dining room, meals taken together surpass the mere naturalism of the biological act of eating, and isolation gives way to exercises in socialisation and sharing.[31] The house is a place of privacy but also a place of hospitality.

> It is an unspeakable happiness to be at home in any foreign place – it is really a synthesis of both of our nostalgias: for wandering (*Wanderschaft*) and for home (*Heimat*) – a synthesis of becoming and being.[32]

Besides the aesthetics of art and the aesthetics of objects for daily use, urban culture is permeated by signs of a diffuse aestheticism which uses the body as a support for ornamentation. Among these transitory manifestations from the inside to the outside, two stand out: the desire to cut a public figure by wearing more common clothing, on the one hand, and the desire to care for and embellish oneself, on the other.

Fashion, in the wider sense of sartorial typologies and codes, has always been a social phenomenon par excellence, even before the modern era. Simmel provides examples from the Renaissance and the centuries that followed, underlining the essentially distinctive social status associated with clothing. Industrial society (and its accompanying individualism) diversified ways of dressing, with industry, trade and *designers* following suit. Many are the levels covered by one of Simmel's most developed essays dedicated to this social manifestation, "Die Mode". Fashion differentiates individuals according to class and economic possibilities, but it also allows for differentiation within a class unlike the rigid stratification of past eras.

As for "the passage from the house to the street", in preparation for going out again, there are two relevant aspects: belonging to or following a *type* (or a pattern) while at the same time maintaining a certain *distance* between the I and the others.

To follow a specific style and be "in fashion", or on the contrary, to create a fashion and to continuously innovate (not forgetting that innovation and the capacity to continuously change one's style "come from above", from the wealthy bourgeois élites or the vanguard) is to enter a cover that creates a protective barrier, a distancing from others.[33] Mediating between individualisation and equalisation, the covering of an individual body according to a predetermined form that imitation disseminates is the visible symbol of a generality that is shown without exhibiting interiority. Clothes serve as a mask, protecting their bearer from complacent gazes, from reproach, from shame.[34] When we are covered, we do not show ourselves; we are noticed due to physical impressions translated into symbolic meanings: this may be thanks to the most impersonal harmony or extravagance, either by approaching the general or by reacting to conformity.

Ornaments and jewels mediate between the self and others as well, but they have a more personal character. They magnify the personality, idealising the image one has of oneself, but at the same time they carry an irradiating gleam, a *Radioaktivität*[35] that amplifies the sphere of influence of subjectivity: "We adorn ourselves for ourselves, and we are only capable of doing so in so far as we adorn ourselves for others".[36] The fundamental principle of *Wechselwirkung*, reversibility without parity, presides over the ornament: centrifugally (from the being who becomes richer in the extension from the centre to the periphery) and centripetally (receiving attention and recognition from others). The for us/for others opposition, the synthesis of egoism and altruism, is interpersonal but not symmetrical. The person who does not use ornaments renounces the claim to individuality, accepting the slide into impersonality. The person who uses ornaments disseminates a pleasant sensorial effect and, in return, experiences a feeling of gratitude for receiving something beautiful:

> It is one of the most noteworthy sociological combinations: that an act intended to give relevance exclusively to the bearer and to increase his

or her importance does not reach its goal but through the eye candy it offers others, exclusively through a sort of gratitude from those others.[37]

The brightness of a jewel, the radiance of an ornament, more than the type of clothes or hairstyle one sports, is in fact an excess – an unnecessary everyday element, chosen for special occasions – although an "excess [that] flows over" ("das Überflüßige fließt über"),[38] in direct proportion to the fineness of the material. Superseding the colourfulness of gold, sapphires or emeralds, the discrete transparency of the diamond emits a sensible radiation that prolongs the corporeal, transforming it into the spiritual. Because of the consideration it receives – at the limits of a social concept of formal elegance and the opposite of extravagance – the ornament gives what is otherwise completely impersonal a mark or measure of individuality. The nature of the ornament, leading the eyes of others to the bearer and being worthy of attention, is the opposite of a secret: in this case, one deserves attention precisely because of what one hides.[39]

From the human condition: man as "bridge and door" between two worlds

The border between the house and the city is not a rigid barrier. It is marked by the swinging of the door, which is alternately open(ed) and closed. Allowing unhindered circulation between spaces, passage inside and outside, the movement of the door easily reveals different intentions and different routes, from seeking to enter to seeking to exit: the easy articulation of interiority and exteriority. On the other hand, the function of the window is chiefly unilateral, permitting one to peer from inside out but not vice versa, from outside in. It opens to the world but still from an enclosed space.

The door is the image of that "border point" (*Grenzpunkt*) where man may be in permanence but without settling, where the physical finite opens to the metaphysical infinite, where the threshold neighbours the presentiment of many possibilities: "the door is therefore made to allow life to spread through it, from the limitation of the isolated being-for-oneself to the unlimitedness of all orientations in general".[40]

The door symbolises both the connection and the separation of spaces, space being a precondition of sociability. Concentric, it may close upon itself (isolate); centrifugal, it may open and escape its centre. A further symbol of human existence is the solidity and security of the bridge, a "third" connecting two fixed points, previously separated from the rest of nature. The bridge implies a division in space, the violence of opposing the world; only later is there a new connection from here to there, on the trail from the finite to the finite. The bridge allows for circulation, but always on the same route, from here to there and from there to here; it remains within the circumscribed domain of the finite.

Devoid of essence, the human being shares the flexible condition of the bridge and the door, in a limitless dialectic between connection and separation: "he is the being who connects, who always has to connect, and without separating he cannot connect". The bridge and the door are metaphors that have a categorial function, portraying the dualism at the heart of the human condition and its peninsular situation, neither a continent nor an island but rather an isthmus between worlds. As a door, however, the human being has the privilege of transgressing limits and venturing into freedom. Transgression joins fragmentation and recomposition:

> The human being is the border being (*Grenzwesen*) who has no borders. The enclosure of his being-at-home by means of the door signifies his snatching of a portion of the uninterrupted unity of natural being. But just as the formless infinity of being only takes shape in its capacity to be limited, so its limitedness only finds its meaning and dignity in what becomes perceptible through the mobility of the door: in the possibility of stepping out of that limitation at any moment and entering freedom.[41]
> (English Translation by Helena Leuschner).

Acknowledgements

This work is funded by Portuguese national funds through the FCT – Fundação para a Ciência e a Tecnologia, I.P., within the project UIDB/00310/2020. The editing of this chapter was supported by funds from the FCT – Fundação para a Ciência e a Tecnologia, under the project UIDP/00183/2020.

Notes

1 Simmel, *Soziologie*, 41. As with all other quotations in this chapter, the translation is my own, together with Helena Leuschner.
2 Simmel, *Soziologie*, 42–61.
3 On the multiple functions of the *third* in Simmel's work, see the exhaustive study by Thomas Bedorf, "Georg Simmel: Der Dritte", 101–154.
4 Cf. Simmel, "Die Gesellschaft zu zweien", 348. I agree with Lucien Freund, according to whom Simmel's focus was not so much "society" as permanence and change, the elasticity and the firmness of socialisation (*Vergesellschaftung*) ("Questions fondamentales de la sociologie", 90–91). This confirms the affinity of the problems of sociology with at least two of the main problems of philosophy identified by Simmel in *Hauptprobleme der Philosophie*: being and becoming, subjectivity and objectivity. Two other problems are specifically philosophical: the essence of philosophy and ideal demands.
5 Simmel, *Hauptprobleme der Philosophie*, 32.
6 Simmel, "Philosophie der Mode", 9.
7 Cf. Simmel, "Das Abenteuer", 173. This may be the key to tackling the controversial matter of unity in Simmelian multimodal production, which sociologists viewed as philosophical and as permeated with psychological characteristics and which academic philosophers viewed as proof of impressionism, eclecticism and wandering. On this subject, see Rammstedt, "Il saggio di Georg Simmel", 101–116.

8 Simmel, "Das Fragment Charakter des Lebens", 202.
9 Simmel often had to clarify what he meant by *Relativismus*, justifying it to the philosophers of the absolute. In a letter to his teacher Heinrich Rickert from 15 April 1916, for example, he writes:

> [I]t is frequently meant by relativism . . . that all truths are relative, that they are probably errors, that all morals are relative, . . . and similar trivialities. What I understand by relativism is an absolutely positive metaphysical image of the world, and therefore it is no more sceptical than Einstein's and Laue's [Max von der Laue] physical relativism. . . . [I]t does not mean that, for me, truth and untruth are relative to one another but that truth means a relation of contents to each other, none of which possesses truth by itself, as no body is heavy in itself but only in the reciprocal relation of one with another".
> Simmel, "Brief an H. Rickert", 637–638.

Consider also the following statement: "My own concept of metaphysics is connected with this relativism as a cosmic and gnosiological principle that uses the *Wechselwirkung* organic image as a substitute for the substantial and abstract unity of the world image"; Simmel, "Fragment einer Einleitung", 305.
10 Simmel, *Soziologie*, 53.
11 Simmel, "Der Begriff und die Tragödie der Kultur", 385. This idea is reiterated in Simmel, "Die Ruine", 288, concerning culture in general and architectonic art in particular.
12 Simmel, "Der Begriff und die Tragödie der Kultur", 387.
13 Ibid., 415–416.
14 Ibid., 411. Cf. the discussion of the metaphysical tragedy of being in the first essay of *Lebensanschauung* ("Die Transzendenz des Lebens").
15 Simmel, "Die Großstädte und das Geistesleben", 116.
16 This is a summary of some of the theses of *Philosophie des Geldes*, which are further dealt with in Simmel's philosophical and metaphysical writings. For a wide-ranging study of this work (which is one of Simmel's most important contributions), see Felizol, "A Tragédia da Liberdade". For a sociological interpretation, see Freund, "Questions fondamentales", 18–33. For more on the relation between money and technology, see Garcia, "Simmel on Culture", 123–178.
17 Simmel, "Die Großstädte und das Geistesleben", 122. See the analysis of Frisby, "Simmels Theorie der Moderne", 35–40 and 41–49.
18 Simmel, "Die beiden Formen des Individualismus", 56. On this subject, see Andolfi, "Simmel e la sensibilità alle differenze", 7–29.
19 Simmel, "Kant und die moderne Ästhetik", 271–272.
20 This is the path of Simmelian ethics, dealt with in the last chapter of *Lebensanschauung* ("Das individuelle Gesetz. Ein Versuch über das Prinzip der Ethik"). On the art of living, see the analysis in Andolfi, "L'etica di Simmel", 7–33.
21 Simmel, *Philosophie des Geldes*, 637–638.
22 Ibid., 638.
23 On our fascination with commodities, the habit of window shopping and going to shops and stores, see Portioli, "La fascination des sens", 50–59; "La performance des objets", 110–115.
24 Simmel, "Das Problem des Stiles", 374–376.
25 His most relevant essays on the autonomy of the work of art achieved by artistic vanguards and emancipation from the rigid codes of academia are "L'art pour l'art" and "Gesetzmäßigkeit im Kunstwerk".
26 Simmel, "Das Problem des Stiles", 379.
27 Simmel, "Berliner Gewerbe-Ausstellung", 33–38; "Über Kunstausstellungen", 242–250. Museums are sites of accumulation as well, but the works are exhibited

for long stretches of time, enabling a type of serene contemplation that is impossible in more ephemeral exhibitions that last for just a few weeks. See Harrington, "Introduction", 30–38.

28 On the necessary separation of art and beauty, breaking with the traditional concept of the fine arts, see Simmel, "Kant und die moderne Ästhetik" and "Jenseits der Schönheit".
29 Simmel, "Das Problem des Stiles", 381. Simmel uses the same arguments for the distinction between shapers and creators in "Gestalter und Schöpfer". Different interpretations of Simmel's concept of style are offered by Harrington, "Introduction", 38–47, and Vargiu, "Artigianato o cannibalismo". On Simmel as an art collector, see Rammstedt, "L'arte nella vita", 163–174.
30 On the boundary function of the frame, delimiting the work of art as a world apart, see "Der Bildrahmen. Ein ästhetischer Versuch", 101–108, which returns to the contrast between the functional piece of furniture and the insular character of the picture. On this problem, see Vargiu, Insularità, 53–58.
31 The social aspects of meals are explored in "Soziologie der Mahlzeit", 140–147.
32 Simmel, "Aus dem nachgelassenen Tagebuche", 273.
33 Simmel, "Philosophie der Mode", 12–13.
34 Ibid., 25–26.
35 Simmel, "Psychologie des Schmuckes", 386.
36 Ibid., 385.
37 Ibid., 385.
38 Ibid., 387.
39 This oscillation between showing and concealing is described as the (mainly feminine) dialectic of *coquetterie*, revealing a typically feminine, urban culture which reconfigures the traditional relations between the sexes. On *coquetterie* as a modality of seduction, see Simmel, "Die Koketterie", 256–277. For a comparison of the ornament and the secret, cf. Simmel, *Soziologie*, 414.
40 Simmel, "Brücke und Tür", 58.
41 Ibid., 60–61. On Anthropology in Simmel, see Serrão, "Condição humana", 45–55.

Bibliography

Andolfi, Ferruccio, "L'etica di Simmel ovvero l'individuo come dover essere", in *Georg Simmel. La legge individuale*, edited by Ferruccio Andolfi, 7–33, Roma: Armando Editore, 1995.

Andolfi, Ferruccio, "Simmel e la sensibilità alle differenze", in *Georg Simmel. Forme dell'individualismo*, edited by Ferruccio Andolfi, 7–29, Roma: Armando Editore, 2001.

Bedorf, Thomas, "Georg Simmel: Der Dritte in einer Grammatik des Sozialen", in *Dimensionen des Dritten: Sozialphilosophische Modelle zwischen Etischem und Politischem*, 101–154, München: Wilhelm Fink Verlag, 2003.

Felizol, Francisco, "A Tragédia da Liberdade na Filosofia do Dinheiro de Georg Simmel", Master diss., University of Lisbon, 2011.

Freund, Julien, "Questions fondamentales de la sociologie", in *Georg Simmel. Sociologie et Épistémologie*, 7–78. Paris: PUF, 1981.

Frisby, David, "Simmels Theorie der Moderne", in *Georg Simmel und die Moderne*, edited by Hein-Jürgen Dahme und Otthein Ramstedt, 9–79, Frankfurt am Main: Suhrkamp, 1984.

Garcia, José Luís, "Simmel on Culture and Technology", *Simmel Studies* 15, no. 2 (2005): 123–178. Bielefeld: Universität Bielefeld.

Harrington, Austin, "Introduction", in *Georg Simmel. Essays on Art and Aesthetics*, edited by Austin Harrington, 1–92, Chicago/London: The University of Chicago Press, 2020.

Papilloud, Christian, "Georg Simmel. La dimension sociologique de la Wechselwirkung", *Revue européenne des sciences sociales* 38, no. 119 (2000): 103–129.
Portioli, Claudia, "La fascination des sens par la marchandise entre anesthésie et hyperesthésie. Sur l'une des acceptions de l'esthétique chez Simmel", *Revue des Sciences Sociales*, no. 40 (2008): 50–59.
Portioli, Claudia, "La performance des objets chez Simmel. Architecture, artefacts et interaction", *Revue des sciences sociales*, no. 59 (2018): 110–115.
Rammstedt, Angela, "L'arte nella vita quotidiana di Simmel", in *Georg Simmel e l'estetica*, edited by Claudia Portioli and Gregor Fitzi, 163–174, Milan: Mimesis, 2006.
Rammstedt, Otthein, "Il saggio di Georg Simmel. Un tentativo di avvicinamento", in *Georg Simmel e l'estetica*, edited by Claudia Portioli e Gregor Fitzi, 101–116, Milan: Mimesis, 2006.
Serrão, Adriana Veríssimo, "Condição humana e individualidade em Georg Simmel", *Philosophica*, no. 42 (2013): 45–55.
Simmel, Georg, *Philosophie des Geldes: Gesamtausgabe*, Vol. 6, edited by David P. Frisby and Klaus Christian Köhnke, 7–716, Frankfurt a. M.: Suhrkamp, 1989 [1900].
Simmel, Georg, *Soziologie. Untersuchungen über die Formen der Vergesellschaftung* in *Gesamtausgabe*, Vol. 11, edited by Otthein Rammstedt, 7–875, Frankfurt a.M.: Suhrkamp, 1992 [1908].
Simmel, Georg, "Das Problem des Stiles", in *Gesamtausgabe*, Vol. 8, edited by A. Cavalli and V. Krech, 374–384, Frankfurt a. M.: Suhrkamp, 1993a [1908].
Simmel, Georg, "Die Gesellschaft zu zweien", in *Gesamtausgabe*, Vol. 8, edited by A. Cavalli and V. Krech, 348–354, Frankfurt a. M.: Suhrkamp, 1993b [1908].
Simmel, Georg, "Psychologie des Schmuckes", in *Gesamtausgabe*, Vol. 8, edited by A. Cavalli and V. Krech, 385–393, Frankfurt a. M.: Suhrkamp, 1993c [1908].
Simmel, Georg, "Die beiden Formen des Individualismus", in *Gesamtausgabe*, Vol. 7, edited by Rüdiger Kramme, Angela Rammstedt and Otthein Rammstedt, 49–56, Frankfurt a. M.: Suhrkamp, 1995 [1901].
Simmel, Georg, "Der Bildrahmen. Ein ästhetischer Versuch", in *Gesamtausgabe*, Vol. 7, edited by Rüdiger Kramme, Angela Rammstedt and Otthein Rammstedt, 101–108, Frankfurt a. M.: Suhrkamp, 1995 [1902].
Simmel, Georg, "Kant und die moderne Ästhetik", in *Gesamtausgabe*, Vol. 7, edited by Rüdiger Kramme, Angela Rammstedt and Otthein Rammstedt, 255–272, Frankfurt a. M.: Suhrkamp, 1995a [1903].
Simmel, Georg, "Die Größstädte and das Geistesleben", in *Gesamtausgabe*, Vol. 7, edited by Rüdiger Kramme, Angela Rammstedt and Otthein Rammstedt, 116–131, Frankfurt a. M.: Suhrkamp, 1995b [1903].
Simmel, Georg, "Philosophie der Mode", in *Gesamtausgabe*, Vol. 10, edited by Michael Behr, Volkhard Krech and Gert Schmidt, 7–37, Frankfurt a. M.: Suhrkamp, 1995 [1905].
Simmel, Georg, *Kant und Goethe. Zur Geschichte der modernen Weltanschauung*, *Gesamtausgabe*, Vol. 10, edited by Michael Behr, Volkhard Krech and Gert Schmidt, 119–166, Frankfurt a. M.: Suhrkamp, 1995 [1906].
Simmel, Georg, "Die Ruine. Ein ästhetischer Versuch", in *Gesamtausgabe*, Vol. 14, edited by Rüdiger Kramme and Otthein Rammstedt, 124–130, Frankfurt a. M.: Suhrkamp, 1996 [1907].
Simmel, Georg, *Hauptprobleme der Philosophie* in *Gesamtausgabe*, Vol. 14, edited by Rüdiger Kramme and Otthein Rammstedt, 7–157, Frankfurt a. M.: Suhrkamp, 1996 [1910].
Simmel, Georg, "Der Begriff und die Tragödie der Kultur", in *Gesamtausgabe*, Vol. 14, edited by Rüdiger Kramme and Otthein Rammstedt, 194–223, Frankfurt a. M.: Suhrkamp, 1996a [1911].

Simmel, Georg, "Die Koketterie", in *Gesamtausgabe*, Vol. 14, edited by Rüdiger Kramme and Otthein Rammstedt, 256–277, Frankfurt a. M.: Suhrkamp, 1996b [1911].

Simmel, Georg, "Das Abenteuer", in *Gesamtausgabe*, Vol. 14, edited by Rüdiger Kramme and Otthein Rammstedt, 168–185, Frankfurt a. M.: Suhrkamp, 1996c [1911].

Simmel, Georg, "L'art pour l'art", in *Gesamtausgabe*, Vol. 13, edited by Klaus Latzel, 9–15, Frankfurt a. M. Suhrkamp, 1996 [1914].

Simmel, Georg, "Gestalter and Schöpfer", in *Gesamtausgabe*, Vol. 13, edited by Klaus Latzel, 184–189, Frankfurt a. M.: Suhrkamp, 1996 [1916].

Simmel, Georg, "Gesetzmäßigkeit im Kunstwerk", in *Gesamtausgabe*, Vol. 13, edited by Klaus Latzel, 382–394, Frankfurt a. M.: Suhrkamp, 1996 [1917/18].

Simmel, Georg, "Das Fragment Charakter des Lebens. Aus den Vorstudien zu einer Metaphysik", in *Gesamtausgabe*, Vol. 13, edited by Klaus Latzel, 202–216, Frankfurt a. M. Suhrkamp, 2000 [1916].

Simmel, Georg, "Brücke and Tür", in *Gesamtausgabe*, Vol. 12, edited by R. Kramme and A. Rammstedt, 55–61, Frankfurt a. M.: Suhrkamp, 2001 [1909].

Simmel, Georg, "Soziologie der Mahlzeit", in *Gesamtausgabe*, Vol. 12, edited by R. Kramme and A. Rammstedt, 140–147, Frankfurt a. M.: Suhrkamp, 2001 [1910].

Simmel, Georg, *Lebensanschauung. Vier metaphysische Kapitel*, *Gesamtausgabe*, Vol. 12, edited by R. Kramme and A. Rammstedt, 209–425, Frankfurt a. M.: Suhrkamp, 2001a [1918].

Simmel, Georg, "Die Transzendenz des Lebens", in *Lebensanschauung. Vier metaphysische Kapitel*, *Gesamtausgabe*, Vol. 12, edited by R. Kramme and A. Rammstedt, 212–235, Frankfurt a. M.: Suhrkamp, 2001b [1918].

Simmel, Georg, "Das individuelle Gesetz", in *Lebensanschauung. Vier metaphysische Kapitel*, *Gesamtausgabe*, Vol. 12, edited by R. Kramme and A. Rammstedt, 346–425, Frankfurt a. M.: Suhrkamp, 2001c [1918].

Simmel, Georg, "Aus dem nachgelassenen Tagebuche", in *Gesamtausgabe*, Vol. 20, edited by Torge Karlsruhen and Otthein Rammstedt, 261–296, Frankfurt a. M.: Suhrkamp, 2004a [n/a].

Simmel, Georg, "Fragment einer Einleitung", in *Gesamtausgabe*, Vol. 20, edited by Torge Karlsruhen and Otthein Rammstedt, 304–305, Frankfurt a. M.: Suhrkamp, 2004b [n/a].

Simmel, Georg, "Über Kunstausstellungen", in *Gesamtausgabe*, Vol. 17, edited by K. C. Köhnke, C. Jaenichen and E. Schullerus, 242–250, Frankfurt a. M.: Suhrkamp, 2005 [1890].

Simmel, Georg, "Berliner Gewerbe-Ausstellung", in *Gesamtausgabe*, Vol. 17, edited by K. C. Köhnke, C. Jaenichen and E. Schullerus, 33–38, Frankfurt a. M.: Suhrkamp, 2005 [1896].

Simmel, Georg, "Jenseits der Schönheit", in *Gesamtausgabe*, Vol. 17, edited by K. C. Köhnke, C. Jaenichen and E. Schullerus, 353–356, Frankfurt a. M.: Suhrkamp, 2005 [1897].

Simmel, Georg, "Brief an Heinrich Rickert", in *Gesamtausgabe*, Vol. 23, edited by Otthein and Angela Rammstedt, 637–638, Frankfurt a. M.: Suhrkamp, 2008 [1916].

Vargiu, Luca, *Insularità. Una metafora per l'opera d'arte*, Milano/Udine: Mimesis, 2020.

Vargiu, Luca, "Artigianato o cannibalismo. Georg Simmel e il dibattito coevo sulle arti applicate", in *Georg Simmel. Variazioni estetiche*, edited by Federica Pau and Luca Vargiu, 153–187, Milan: Meltemi, 2024.

11 The art of dwelling as tacit *philia*

Tiago Mesquita Carvalho

Introduction

Gaining clarity on what dwelling is about, why it is in crisis and its possible relation to the built environment is one of the central tasks of this chapter. Another is to suggest that by acknowledging how things and communities shape one another, dwelling can acquire new importance as a means of reigniting the dwindling sense of community that presently defines public life in cities. Overall, I will argue for a moderate technocratic principle by asserting that dwelling cannot and should not be the exclusive concern of experts. Although I rely on historical references, I will not be arguing for a return to dwelling *stricto sensu*. By observing its current transformations and marginality, I aim to provide an account of why it continues to offer valuable lessons towards an understanding of the built environment that allows for the emergence of the social bonds that both constitute communities and tie them together. For this, I will elaborate on the work of a set of authors who identify and discuss a long-held diagnosis of what is missing in cities today and what can be done about it. I aim to advance the concept of dwelling either as an art or, negatively, as something that is missing.

I will begin by exploring two common-sense insights. The first is that historical centres and ancient towns, built by anonymous craftsmen and often nestled within the more expansive, newer parts of a city, tend to have a more generally inviting atmosphere than their "new town" counterparts, even though the latter are the result of far more intentional professional design processes.[1] I am here referring to the general impression given by these public spaces and the buildings that surround them, as well as their streets, alleys, and squares. Their aesthetic features ground their lasting appeal as sites for gathering and strolling; indeed, visiting them is often synonymous with "being in a city", while visiting the "generic city" beyond them is not.[2] The modern city lacks a fundamental quality that ancient cities, as a rule, cultivated naturally.[3] Nevertheless, due precisely to the immanent and striking qualities of such areas, they are currently under financial, touristic and real estate stress and have become something other than sites of gathering and community.[4] Generic cities are now being built for generic men. Tourism

DOI: 10.4324/9781003452928-14

is a weapon of mass destruction,[5] and what it destroys will become clearer in the course of my argument.

In my view, much of the social and psychological fragmentation that cities exhibit can be attributed to the dissolution of dwelling and to the development of professional power and expertise. Urban planning, as a proxy for economic ideology, aspires to the total management of cities under the parameters of a logistical approach that seeks to ensure the optimal circulation of goods, labour and information. Social issues have become largely solvable problems and are addressed through the improvement of spatial organisation, where the assumption of a functional determinism looms.[6] In this way, urban form and social organisation are viewed as things that can be *made*. This notwithstanding, such a loss triggers an awareness of what is missing that offers opportunities for assessing the extent to which buildings and places are the material ground for human flourishing.

The second insight that I intend to stress is the paradoxical observation that forsaken and depressed areas currently, and unmistakably, enjoy a more pronounced liveliness and sense of community than other areas, which in turn is reflected in how the built environment is approached. Catastrophes usually trigger altruistic endeavours that unite both strangers and neighbours under the common aim of jumpstarting the rebuilding of one's own world. Barbarism – the Hobbesian *Homo homini lupus* – is not an *a priori* given.[7] Traces of dwelling and its ingenuity can be seen in the inventiveness of those who build vegetable gardens at the inner edges of cities. Marginal people in shanty areas continue to carve out both their built environment and their existence through the use of their creative powers. Any account of what dwelling is ought to show why this is the case.[8] Moreover, there are striking similarities between this insight and how the houses of old were unwittingly erected with locally available materials, perfected according to a background of collective experiences. The cumulative outcome of such situated knowledge often corresponded to the more encompassing body of traditional cultures. For Pietro Belluschi, vernacular architecture is a "communal art not produced by a few intellectuals or specialists but by the spontaneous and continuing activity of a whole people with a common heritage, acting under a community of experience", where a rare good sense in the "handling of practical problems" is displayed.[9]

These two insights are related. Both point to what dwelling is about, the extent to which cities were once tacitly built around a notion of public life and the role of professionals in this transformation. The current relevance of dwelling is undoubtedly related to the uprooting that has resulted from the unbridled rationalisation and commodification of urban life. Unlike other areas where one can clearly state that progress of some sort has been made (e.g., the theoretical and applied sciences), the present lived, built environment has largely been an unsuccessful endeavour, despite our improved technical mastery. Its success would seem to depend less on "state-of-the art" knowledge than on a local and deeply contextualised understanding (or know-how) of what makes for a successful built environment. The latter type of knowledge would seem to be more directly available to those who dwell in a given place.

Dwelling as a skill

Aristotle famously included house building as an example of *techne*[10] and the house as an example of what sustains human flourishing in a community.[11] The root of the Greek *ethos* points to dwelling as the space of social reality, of customs and habits that give order to life.[12] Community involvement strengthens the sense of the intricate connection between individual flourishing and the flourishing of the whole and allows for the emergence of *philia* between its members.[13] For Aristotle, *philia* is an association that is enabled by the virtues and that contributes to the common good of a community, which in turn promotes individual flourishing. It is in this sense that dwelling expresses a background agreement regarding the nature of the shared aim of the human good. *Philia* is a bond that runs through a community, independent of kinship and other contractual relations. The claim that dwelling and other skills hinge on such a bond is nevertheless foreign to the liberal world view, in which friendship is generally relegated to the private sphere or understood as an emotional state.[14] It is in this sense that dwelling assumes that, to become good practical agents, honour commitments and be responsible, human beings must become involved in various types of obligations towards what is given: towards the family, the place, and the community itself – elements that make them who they are and that draw on a notion of what is good.

Roger Scruton uses the term *oikophilia* to describe a love that arises from the natural rootedness of the human being not only in a home but in a place and a community.[15] The *oikos* is where everything happens, where human beings grow. Although the city offers anonymity, there is always a need for community, a form of life and a setting that allows for a certain measure of stability, or as Berleant puts it, a place.[16] In this sense, dwelling is about the full sense of what matters in life, about the primal meaning of "home". Dwellers make a space their own, as a place of engagement, of direct lived experience and memory, as where and how one's life is shaped.[17]

The examples of marginal urban areas, vernacular architecture and the built environment of old towns have something in common. They contribute to expanding the concept of dwelling as a skill that comprises "a set of practices and technologies that evolve in response to a specific place".[18] Dwelling accounts for a type of care that attends to the "expectations" of a place.

With the help of Michael Polanyi, I wish to further consider dwelling as a tacit, inarticulate skill that expresses an embeddedness in the particulars of a given situation, which are subsidiarily integrated in the focal attention of dwellers.[19] Aristotle said more or less the same of virtuous action and the role of practical reason.[20] The human good is not given beforehand in settled rules or principles, as methodological procedures are.[21] The elements that constitute a context are crucial to understanding how to act well. Doing good, like proper building and dwelling, is contingent on various salient contextual singularities and on what is appropriate to them in each case. In this sense, due to its ineffable content, a general science of ethics or of dwelling is untenable from the outset. One learns to dwell by being with others in a place. Dwelling is rooted in a praxis within a place and the problems it poses. It proceeds and is constituted not by rule-like structures but by listening for what a place demands, as passed on through example. Its tacit dimension means that it uses a shared background that cannot be made explicit. Just as no two communities are alike, the skills of dwelling are multifarious and cannot be taught. They therefore escape the architect, as they can be picked up only from the inside, through personal experience with those who live in a place, just as to learn and master a language one must enter its world.[22]

By contrast, progress in science and technology is based on a knowledge type the truth and applicability of which, its social and historical origins notwithstanding, are independent of such backgrounds. Furthermore, they can be laid down in abstract laws, principles and prescriptions. These can further be translated into all sorts of general devices, structures and schemes for building. Such decontextualised knowledge is easily transmitted and can hence become increasingly available as it is easily stored and applied without any bearing on community experience or personal interpretations. Such universal and causal scientific explanations have since become a world view but have also fostered design approaches in fields where tacit knowledge once reigned supreme. This consigned the tacit dimension of dwelling to oblivion, as reason became equated with certainty and lawfulness.

The diremption of dwelling today as a contextual and site-specific form of engagement and the decline of both places and communities are two sides of the same coin. By structuring the built environment, architecture, urban planning and civil engineering frame our experience of being in the world. They can either support our sense of being or weaken it.[23] The design of the built environment has a clear normative bearing on human flourishing and how it allows one to experience oneself as a completely embodied and social being. Urban forms play a role in how various social needs are expressed in public life, along with a sensible acquaintance with the natural scale of human sense perception.[24] Such social needs have an anthropological grounding that can be nourished or hindered by urban forms: the need for security and openings, the need for certainty and adventure, for work organisation and play, for predictable and unpredictable events, isolation and encounter.[25] Simultaneously, negative aesthetics point to instances that shrink life, leaving one confused, adrift, perhaps rootless.[26] Ugliness, chaos and incoherence are then experiences that help to raise criticism and value judgements.

The rise of professionalisation

Experts in the built environment are thus prone to become acutely specialised in a knowledge type that is accepted as a proper replacement for and even improvement on the tacit skill of engaging with the contextual circumstances and expectations of a place. The professionalisation of architecture and urban planning brought about by abstract rules and procedures learned by routine has provided much efficiency in meeting housing demands within the critical urbanisation of the post-War period but has also pushed these fields further away from the lifeworld. They have developed into an industry aimed at manufacturing apartments. Lefebvre rightly translates this relationship when he contrasts *inhabit* (in French *habiter*) with *habitat*.[27] Illich draws the same contrast between the resident and the dweller.[28] Just like any other commodity, contemporary architecture and urban planning are mostly concerned with manufacturing habitats and functional neighbourhoods as quickly as possible. The Cartesian isomorphic space, assumed from the outset, has gradually been superimposed on the intricacy of places, where dwellers once shaped their own worlds. In the name of order, cleanliness, security, and other technologically procured commodities and industrially defined needs, dwelling was replaced with the apartment, measured in a certain number of square feet. Residents have lost contact with a primal art of living and must in turn accept a world that has been made and planned for them.

The establishment of professional urban planning, by which experts resort to visual models, is ultimately the result of two historical shifts in how cities have been conceived since the Middle Ages. During the Renaissance, the city became an end in itself, a complete work of art to be made according to an overall plan and aesthetically pleasing visual features based on geometrical forms.[29] In the past, however, the overall form of a city or town was determined by its anonymous dwellers, without any overall intentionality; its growth was organic, thanks to a multiplicity of vicinal, spontaneous actions in the handling of practical problems. Save for the intentions embedded in the accumulated experiences of tradition, cities and towns were not centrally or explicitly designed.[30] It is important to stress that I do not mean to imply that dwellers were necessarily wiser in the past or that they deliberately avoided conceiving of the city as an end in itself. In the absence of both powerful technological means and a wide range of available foreign materials and techniques, buildings and cities grew spontaneously through a slow evolutionary process that spanned hundreds of years.[31] In such conditions, the steady adaptation of the built environment to city functions can be understood only according to the previous definition of dwelling: a highly contextual collective skill that attends to the particularities of a place and that both reinforces and is reinforced by *philia*, by which a shared notion of the common good within a community expresses itself in the forms of the built environment.

172 Rethinking the City

The idea that the organic and consistent structure of various medieval towns and cities emerges from uncoordinated collective actions is one that cuts across various knowledge fields, from economics to politics. I do not mean to assert that such a principle is valid across the board, but I do want to claim that it is worth considering that the transformation to the built environment that professional urban planning brought about is ultimately based on an epistemic shift and a narrow version of rationality. Such an enquiry may at least provide an account of why the cities and towns of yesteryear still offer excellent conditions for life between buildings without having been planned or designed by professionals. It suggests that a general Promethean control over matter does not necessarily imply a better lived experience in public space and that dwelling managed to strike a balance between means and ends while strengthening communities.

What the first shift suggests is that there are at least some *emergent structures*, such as medieval towns and cities, the economy and society, that are the result of human action but not of a deliberate, centralised design. Dwellers of yore, for instance, used an accumulated situated knowledge in the form of building traditions, shared practices and cultural expectations, which, although tacit and inarticulate, amounted to effective responses to recurring problems transmitted over generations.[32] On the other hand, attempting to reach a certain outcome by resorting to explicit and instrumental "rational" principles often results in failure. In the case of such "geometric" approaches to city planning, an epistemic replacement occurs by which tacit knowledge gives way to abstract, articulated, routinisable knowledge on the basis that it will lead to a better result.

The second shift developed out of the first but instead adapted the growing and encompassing charisma of scientific and applied knowledge, finding a fruitful analogy in the activity of physicians. Urban planners and architects became akin to surgeons confronting a malfunctioning urban body; both were ascribed thaumaturgic powers that could purportedly improve its health. Buildings and urban forms were then constructed with the expectation of delivering a function. The Modern Movement in architecture ended up building the same geometric forms everywhere, resulting in ever-increasing uniformity and impoverishment, with rampant psychological and social consequences.[33] Indeed, it reflected its epoch in a special sense: it is the form of contemporary alienation and disorientation that gives rise to a fragmented city. The arrival of bureaucratic expertise and its reliance on the criterion of efficiency as the way to manage, organise and improve society is a fallacy that has affected both the social sciences[34] and overall urban planning. Historically, as more abstract universal principles, procedures and methods in the image of the scientific world view gained momentum, they ended up affecting views on how cities ought to be designed. The split between fact and value assisted the birth of science. With the loss of such a link, praxis has gradually been subsumed under the same lawful accounts of objects according to their physical and material features.[35] Functionalism does not consider the bearing that forms have on the good and public life between buildings and has therefore failed in its attempt to create cities that anchor communities. The rise of a professional class tasked with designing cities corresponds to this general loss of the authority of the tacit, contextual skill implied in dwelling. The process by which dwellers became individual residents and that by which *philia* bonds were shattered reveal themselves to be one and the same.

The loss of place

The Modern Movement's assumption of cultural neutrality and homogeneity is not only historically exceptional but, judging by its ubiquity, a sign of its supposed success. Its buildings are the result of sterile and narcissistic assumptions, aspiring to formal perfection but remaining, like the modern self, decontextualised, floating in a vacuum, disconnected from their surroundings. The functionalist shift held universal space as a default, thus paving the way for a contextless urban design. In its forms, it expressed a late development of Western philosophy: a commitment to the analytic, the universal and the a priori, which surfaces in ahistorical approaches that underestimate the role of place.

The ontological link between forms, places and subjects was lost in the process because what forms do can allegedly be known in advance and anticipated through a technical calculus,[36] as the modern self knows by transcending place and establishing a view from nowhere. The intimate bond between place and persons, on the other hand, expresses itself in dwelling. Given their epistemic and ontological significance, places are therefore constitutive of dwellers. In a sense, places are only truly knowable in their depth, not by a disinterested hovering subject but by an immersion that allows them to unfold.[37] Human beings cannot avoid belonging to a place: "a place contributes to the process of becoming that must include the material as well as the spiritual work that sustains human life".[38]

These remarks permit a better understanding of the consequences of the implied epistemic shift brought about by professionalised urban planning. Once embedded in communities as a set of practices that ruled over the organic upkeep of neighbourhoods, dwelling became objectified and further commodified as the purview of professionals. Polanyi's insight about the tacit dimension suggests that being familiar with a place means internalising its contextual features. As an art, it cannot be equated with a fixed methodology and thus becomes especially prone to vanishing, since it prevails only when communities last and preserve a sense of belonging by which unspecifiable knowledge can be transmitted via examples.[39] It thus holds a fragile status, being subject to upheavals that unravel the social fabric.

On the other hand, by resorting to detached knowledge acquired through explicit, transmissible rules, urban planning established itself as a straightforward endeavour, but one that expressed a disembodied form of being in the world. Architects build but no longer abide in what they build; their space and time are the abstract background of the abstract needs of the generic individual. In his attempt to identify a timeless way of building and to capture the essence of such a process, Christopher Alexander notes that urban design has become simplified. This contrasts with those cities that, either old or new, display a thicker, complex structure.[40] In an attempt to deal with complexity and ambiguity, professionals reduce them in their minds to manageable categories, which are subsequently projected onto the concrete city. A strict separation of activities results in a loss of coherence and variety.

Furthermore, since dwelling hinges on the *philia* background that pervades a community, it depends on much more than the appropriate built environment. Form alone does not determine meaning, and nor does it induce a more communal configuration of the social fabric. This is why, although historical city centres can currently host either long-term or short-term residents, the outcome will never be dwelling. The personal freedom of dwelling is lost to the contemporary resident and the tourist because, like so many other community bonds, it has been exposed as a burden on the detached autonomy of the modern subject. The unity of dwelling was shattered into a means-end distinction, and thus it became something to be enhanced through a technology-procured disburdenment that exposed cities and places to the larger commodification pattern of contemporary life that is technology.[41]

Lastly, many of the expert practices of today are also digitally mediated by CAD software, which makes visualising and designing buildings easily achievable but which also blurs the imagination and multisensory embodied aspects of *in situ* conception or drawing. The built environment has been affected by experts' digitally mediated practices: the design process has become a passive form of visual manipulation, an intellectually learned retinal journey,[42] straying from a tacit, embodied skill. When digitally available, models, sketches and blueprints flow without friction in cyberspace, rendering design processes otherworldly. The generic city becomes a standard that in turn emerges from such practices. Buildings and public spaces become progressively phantasmatic and dreamlike, made not to be lived but to be appreciated by the immaterial eye of a disembodied subjectivity.

Here, negative aesthetic judgements[43] can join a critical assessment of experts' assumptions, which derive from late-19th-century scientific views about subjectivity, knowledge and the role of human minds as data receivers. Subjects, after all, are largely embedded in their corporeal, social and cultural backgrounds. Environmental aesthetics[44] and the philosophy of technology have shown that artefacts and the built environment have a normative bearing on agency and the kinds of goods one pursues to flourish. Thus, in a message of hope in a bomb-ravaged London, Winston Churchill addressed Parliament regarding the reconstruction of the House of Commons as follows: "We shape our buildings, and afterwards our buildings shape us".[45]

Towards a hermeneutics of urban forms

The importance of dwelling encompasses the way in which it establishes *philia* bonds between communities and how it can assist the practices that comprise contemporary architecture and urban planning. I would now like to bridge the gap between dwelling and the design of the built environment by relying on concepts from the philosophy of technology. First of all, approaching cities as large technological systems seems somewhat plausible as it accepts the growing importance of technology in its mutations.[46] Networked infrastructures that sustain everyday life are a central part of cities. I am not arguing that cities can be entirely reduced to such systems, but only that their design and maintenance cannot be ignored. One of the tasks with which the philosophy of technology has been occupied is that of unearthing the black box of artefacts and infrastructures so as to make manifest their embedded moral, social and political assumptions. Following Churchill's dictum, Albert Borgmann, for instance, advanced a "real ethics" that recognises that moral life and the structure of everyday praxis maintain a direction provided by the shape of public space.[47] The general point is to see that while the built environment does not determine life between buildings, it undoubtedly conditions its structure. Redesigning urban forms has a bearing on the nature of public life and constrains how social bonding unfolds. Although the notion that material settings influence public life and community may sound technocratic, acknowledging – rather than denying – this connection allows us to consider ways to harness this influence. The design of the built environment comprises practices that have a bearing on social ontology, that is, what people are and how they relate to each other, how they cultivate their individual and collective self-images.

By contrast, if we accept that technology plays a defining role in mediating the nature of public life, urban planning may be able to develop a sounder relation to it, in a way that pays greater mind to how roads, cars, buildings and streets mediate the field of experiences and social relations.[48] Taking this into account, I wish to propose that the deliberate transformation of the city by experts is not and should not be the only way to transform public life. The emergence of the professional class notwithstanding, the meaning of dwelling can still be grasped today. Namely, the fact that the inconspicuous bond between marginal communities and places blooms in an underdetermined or frugal built environment suggests that leaving room for configurations to surface is worthwhile.

The extent to which our lifeworld is rooted in artefacts becomes apparent when one of them breaks down or malfunctions.[49] These are instances where the artefact's function is put on hold. In semiotic terms, the connection between the artefact and its meaning is shaken. A blackout seems to make dinner at home impossible but unfolds other possible engagements. The "buried substance"[50] that artefacts concoct becomes explicit, and everyday life reveals its former, taken-for-granted dependence on the built environment.

Following a breakdown, however, artefacts can take on other meanings. Besides sudden catastrophic events, there are other ways to upturn the context of use:[51] an everyday artefact in a museum, for instance, can generate a different atmosphere. In Cuba, an economic embargo led islanders to engage in "technological disobedience"[52] by employing spare parts and subverting technologically predesigned meanings to overcome everyday impairments. In the parlance of the philosophy of technology, the built environment displays multistability.[53] Similarly, when drawing the contrast between *habitat* and *inhabit*, Lefebvre pointed out that, despite the former's abstract forms, there is still room for groups to appropriate habitat.[54]

In its critique of technological determinism, the philosophy of technology goes beyond the perspective that users are pushed to unremittingly adapt to the intentions of engineers or designers.[55] By entering the lifeworld of users, artefacts become interpretable, whereby their proper function is usually subverted. Technology does not afford necessity, and it is not merely the sum of rational means. Feenberg uses the term "democratic rationalisation" to extend the Frankfurt School argument against "an exclusive monopoly on rationality" and to depict interventions "that challenge undemocratic power structures in modern technology".[56] Like Ihde's multistability, the principle is that function is contingent on a fixed use which actually conceals a plural potentiality. Of course not everything goes, but the point is to stress interpretation and to highlight that function is not fixed.

Given the encroaching, large technological systems of contemporary cities, the active engagement by which groups of people explore other meanings within the built environment to expand the conditions of their existence – how they playfully assemble to unfold other uses beyond the primacy of proper function – is where dwelling can currently be grasped. It can be intrinsically subversive, as it does not impose a fixed meaning on the built environment. Moreover, the ephemeral, provisional character of dwelling can strengthen existing forms of *philia* or even fashion new bonds of mutual agreement. This is how abandoned factories become squats or temporary settings for parties, ruins become vegetable gardens, squares become skateparks and streets become playgrounds for games. The anonymity of public space recedes, and through dwelling community life is amended and expresses itself by exploring the multistability of artefacts' functions.[57]

The point is to recognise that the imaginative and improvised ways in which technological objects and infrastructures are read "in order to", that is, repaired, tinkered and appropriated by users in a given place, are at odds with the expectations of experts about what the built environment ought to accomplish. As a bundle of large technological systems, the city seeks to impose singular functions on spaces, thus achieving closure.[58] However, offhand and makeshift uses challenge the monopoly of the socio-technical order of the city and the implicit spatial determinism of rational organisation.[59] Understood as such, dwelling stresses the contingency of the built environment by rendering it with a personal sense according to the demands of community life. In view of these remarks, this leads us back to our initial observation that dwelling thrives in impoverished areas and has prospered in the cities and towns of old. Also, it leads us to a reframing of the role of the expert.

Ruins, vacant lots and public housing areas usually display traces of dwelling due to an absence of urban policies and technological improvements. An underdetermination of the built environment can be found in these settings, which triggers the appearance of a lively resourcefulness. In the same way, cities and towns of old allowed dwelling to surface by likely displaying a multifarious ambiguity by which several activities were able to arise, overlap[60] and coexist. The multistability of technology points to how surroundings are used according to a practical context that holds several "possibilities for" that transgress the meanings of the generic city. By using them, dwellers unreflectively recognise that artefacts and urban forms are "alive" and radiate other functions. Affordances other than those provided by the generic city can appear through either a playful or a defying interpretation, but they can also be embedded in public space. An approach that regards dwelling as both foreseeable and inchoative can in fact be purposely assumed at the outset. The point is that professionals can permit the shaping and use of public space according to what residents hold as good. The design of the built environment can thin out *philia* bonds by expelling ambiguity, but it can also stimulate its rekindling, although it cannot determine its arrival.

Public and democratic deliberation regarding the design of the built environment is especially relevant today as cities are more prone to breakdowns, dissolutions and general decay, all of which are more or less kept at bay through local and collective efforts. Ultimately, an examination of these processes points to the insufficiency of science and technology when it comes to providing a complete, rational plan for social life.[61] The many systematic failures and flaws of urban forms and infrastructures emphasise the extent to which the longing for dwelling perseveres, along with the unavoidable role played by its contextual tacit rationality in summoning collective engagements of care, by which people with different skillsets and from different walks of life gather to deal with recurring practical problems. The fact that this longing customarily surfaces to fill in the gaps and defects of urban planning speaks to a longing for a more active approach to the interplay between human flourishing, social relationships, and materiality. The point is to acknowledge how relationships between things and people intertwine with and flow back to *philia* bonds between individuals and to their expanded embodied skills.

Conclusion

This points to certain conclusions regarding the perseverance and significance of dwelling. Today, wherever the built environment is not subjected to continuous maintenance or refurbishment, it is prone to become an object of reconfigurations and tweaks that nudge it towards fulfilling the needs of whoever lives in it. For such interventions to occur, a context-bonded community must already be in place, along with room for interpretation that hinges on the ambiguity of the built environment. Such ambiguity is linked to an incompleteness that allows collective actions to arise with the unintended result of tying communities together. Notions of the common good are expressed through a contextual material hermeneutics.

The overall argument of this chapter thus views dwelling as an art that necessarily draws on contextual knowledge emerging from site-specific practices. This skill discloses itself either as building, improving or appropriating places, that is, a collective interpretation of the surroundings and whereabouts of one's home which both expresses community needs and contributes to caring for a place. Thanks to a diminishing sense of community and an overdetermined built environment, dwelling now tends to be mostly ephemeral, episodic and performative, although it continues to draw upon and strengthen existing *philia* bonds and to bolster other relationships. This supports the observation that the practices at the heart of professional urban planning have replaced the art of dwelling with the provision of residences. The fragmentation of dwelling is accompanied by a thinning of social *philia* bonds that support a shared notion of a common good and is tantamount to the broader pattern of individualisation associated with the detached modern self.

There is reason to think that the fall of the art of dwelling is just one of the many radical transformations that have resulted from the extension of instrumental reasoning to various areas of human activity. As far as professional practices regarding the built environment go, this chapter points to opportunities open to experts who seek to immerse themselves in the fine-grained rationality that a sense of place provides and who wish to create spaces where residents can actively attribute meaning to their public surroundings by meeting and joining with others. Overall, this would be in line with the larger tendency to consider the design of the built environment and technological innovation not as given facts provided by experts but as endeavours with a strong impact on praxis, and hence as subject to public democratic scrutiny and responsibility.[62]

Acknowledgements

The editing of this chapter was supported by funds from the FCT – Fundação para a Ciência e a Tecnologia, under the project UIDP/00183/2020.

Notes

1 Gehl, *Life Between Buildings*, 41.
2 Koolhaas, "The Generic City", 1249. This term describes an overall pan-urban global phenomenon whereby rapid urban expansion makes cities more alike,

The art of dwelling as tacit philia 179

liberating them from the straitjacket of identities tied to historical city centres. For Koolhaas, airport environments offer the neutrality of the generic city.
3 Alexander, "The City is Not a Tree", 118.
4 Lefebvre, "Right to the City", 73.
5 Rebelo et al., "Capitalist Visuality", 244.
6 Lefebvre, "Right to the City", 99.
7 Solnit, *A Paradise Built in Hell*, 2.
8 Delmar et al., *Notes from the Underdog*, 8.
9 Belluschi quoted in Rudofsky, *Architecture without Architects*, 3–4.
10 Aristotle, *Nicomachean Ethics*, 11 and 119 [1097a20 and 1140a6].
11 Aristotle, *Politics*, 1 and 68 [1252a1–10 and 1278b15].
12 Pereira, *Modernidade e Tempo*, 237.
13 Aristotle, *Nicomachean Ethics*, 181 [1161b11].
14 MacIntyre, *After Virtue*, 156.
15 Scruton, *How to be a Conservative*, 32.
16

> In its most basic sense, place is the setting of the events of human living. It is the locus of action and intention, and present in all consciousness and perceptual experience. This human focus is what distinguishes place from the surrounding space or from simple location".
> Berleant, *Aesthetics and Environment*, 76.

17 Berleant, *Living in the Landscape*, 12.
18 Thompson, "Farming as Focal Practice", 168.
19 Polanyi, *Personal Knowledge*, 50 and 55.
20 Aristotle, *Nicomachean Ethics*, 120 [1140a20–21].
21 Vallor, "Moral Deskilling", 109.
22 Illich, "Dwelling", 56.
23 Pallasmaa, *The Eyes of the Skin*, 12.
24 Gehl, *Life Between Buildings*, 62–68.
25 Lefebvre, "Right to the City", 147.
26 Berleant, *Living in the Landscape*, 15.
27 Lefebvre, "Right to the City", 79.
28 Illich, "Dwelling", 57.
29 Gehl, *Life Between Buildings*, 39–41.
30 Ibid.
31 Alexander, "A City is Not a Tree", 118.
32 Scruton, *How to be a Conservative*, 28–29.
33 Lefebvre, "Right to the City", 127–128.
34 MacIntyre, *After Virtue*, 86 and 107.
35 Ihde, *Technology and the Lifeworld*, 97. Lefebvre, "Right to the City", 99.
36 Augustin Berque describes this incoherence of things within the world of human beings as *décosmisation* – a loss of a sense of the interconnection between the human environment and the broader cosmos, a human environment that is viewed as neutral and geometric rather than concrete, outside of one's existence. Berque, *La pensée paysagère*, 78–79.
37 As Preston states, insofar as epistemology "since Descartes has almost always been done internally, it is not surprising to find the external environment treated as largely irrelevant to knowledge claims". Preston, "Moral Knowledge", 175 and 184.
38 Thompson is mainly addressing farming as a set of practices that define a place, but I would argue that this also holds true for dwelling. Thompson, "Farming as Focal Practice", 174–177.

180 Rethinking the City

39 Polanyi, *Personal Knowledge*, 53.
40 Alexander, "A City is Not a Tree", 128.
41 Borgmann, "The Design of Public Space", 179.
42 Pallasmaa, *The Eyes of the Skin*, 14.
43 "The normative range of aesthetics has also been extended to allow for negative values: a significant part of the criticism by the environmental movement is aesthetic in character". Berleant, *Living in the Landscape*, 25.
44 Ibid., 32.
45 Winston Churchill quoted in Borgmann, "The Design of Public Space", 175.
46 Hughes, "The Evolution of Large Technological Systems", 51.
47 Borgmann, "The Design of Public Space", 175.
48 Verbeek, "Tecnopólis", 1118.
49 Ihde, *Technology and the Lifeworld*, 32.
50 Winner, *Autonomous Technology*, 330.
51 Ihde, *Technology and the Lifeworld*, 32–33.
52 Oroza, *Rikimbili*, 20.
53 Ihde uses the term as a way to question the view that technology is marked by a single trajectory and by autonomy. Technologies are ambiguous and show a range of embeddedness across cultures. The polymorphy in visual perception displayed by images like the duck-rabbit, and the Necker cube is expanded to highlight the fact that artefacts are also multistable regarding the possible relationships that humans can establish with them. Ihde, *Technology and the Lifeworld*, 144–146.
54 Lefebvre, "Right to the City", 79.
55 Feenberg, *Questioning Technology*, 82.
56 Ibid., 108.
57
> Our actions are embedded in the multiple ways we interact with and presuppose our technologies, yet this multiplicity remains perceptually and praxically ambiguous. What is there about the artefacts we employ? . . . What is the object? The object is or could be any of the things named, or it could become how it is used. That, too, is an ambiguity essential to technologies.
>
> Ihde, *Technology and the Lifeworld*, 68–69

58 "When the social groups involved in designing and using technology decide that a problem is solved, they stabilize the technology. The result is closure". Bijker et al., *The Social Construction of Technological Systems*, 6.
59 "Thus what essentialism conceives as an ontological split between technology and meaning, I conceive as a terrain of struggle between different types of actors differently engaged with technology and meaning". Feenberg, *Questioning Technology*, xiii.
60 That a semi-lattice structure allows many more systems to overlap than a tree-like structure was one of the points of Alexander's seminal essay. Cities based on the former model allow a variety of activities to emerge by promoting function overlap. Alexander, "A City is Not a Tree", 136.
61 Henke and Sims, *Repairing Infrastructures*, 13–16.
62 Vallor, "Moral Deskilling", 122.

Bibliography

Alexander, Christopher, "A City is Not a Tree", in *The City Reader*, edited by Richard T. LeGates and Frederic Stout, 118–131, New York/London: Routledge, 1996.
Aristotle, *Aristotle's Nicomachean Ethics*, translated with an interpretive essay, notes, and glossary by Robert C. Bartlett and Susan D. Collins, Chicago/London: University of Chicago Press, 2011.

Aristotle, *Aristotle's Politics*, edited by Jonathan Barnes with an introduction by Melissa Lane, Princeton/Oxford: Princeton University Press, 2016.
Berleant, Arnold, *Living in the Landscape*, Kansas: University Press of Kansas, 1997.
Berleant, Arnold, *Aesthetics and Environment. Variations on a Theme*, New York/London: Routledge, 2018.
Berque, Augustin, *La pensée paysagère*, Paris: Archibooks, 2008.
Bijker, Wiebe, Thomas Hughes and Trevor Pinch, eds., *The Social Construction of Technological Systems. New Directions in the Sociology and History of Technology*, Cambridge, MA: MIT Press, 1987.
Borgmann, Albert, "The Design of Public Space", in *Real American Ethics: Taking Responsibility for Our Country*, 175–188, Chicago: University of Chicago Press, 2006.
Delmar, Alexandre, Luís Ribeiro da Silva, Margarida Quintã and Joaquim Moreno, *Notes from the Underdog – Anotações sobre o Abaixo de Cão. A agricultura de subsistência do Porto*, edited by John Wriedt, Leipzig: Spector Books, 2021.
Feenberg, Andrew, *Questioning Technology*, London/New York: Routledge, 1999.
Gehl, Jan, *Life Between Buildings. Using Public Space*, translated by Jo Koch, London: Island Press, 2011.
Henke, Christopher R. and Benjamin Sims, *Repairing Infrastructures. The Maintenance of Materiality and Power*, Massachusetts: The MIT Press, 2020.
Hughes, Thomas Parke, "The Evolution of Large Technological Systems", in *The Social Construction of Technological Systems. New Directions in the Sociology and History of Technology*, edited by Wiebe E. Bijker, Thomas Parke Hughes and Trevor Pinch, 51–82, Cambridge, Massachusetts/London, England: MIT Press,1987.
Ihde, Don, *Technology and the Lifeworld: From Garden to Earth*, Indiana: Indiana University Press, 1990.
Illich, Ivan, "Dwelling: Address to the Royal Institute of British Architects. York, U.K.", in *In the Mirror of the Past: Lectures and Addresses 1978–1990*, 55–64, New York and London: Marion Boyars, 1992.
Koolhaas, Rem, "The Generic City", in *S, M, L, XL*, 1248–1264, New York: The Monacelli Press, 1998.
Lefebvre, Henri, "Right to the City", in *Writings on Cities*, translated and edited by Eleonore Kofman and Elizabeth Lebas, 63–181, Oxford: Blackwell Publishing, 1996.
MacIntyre, Alasdair, *After Virtue: A Study in Moral Theory*, Notre Dame, IN: University of Notre Dame Press, 2007.
Oroza, Ernesto, *Rikimbili. Une étude sur la désobéissance technologique et quelques formes de réinvention*, Saint-Étienne: Publications de l'Université de Saint-Étienne, 2009.
Pallasmaa, Juhani, *The Eyes of the Skin: Architecture and the Senses*, NJ: John Wiley & Sons Ltd, 2005.
Pereira, Miguel Baptista, *Modernidade e Tempo: Para uma Leitura do Discurso Moderno*, Coimbra: Minerva, 1990.
Polanyi, Michael, *Personal Knowledge*, London: Routledge, 1998.
Preston, Christopher J. "Moral Knowledge: Real and Grounded in Place", *Ethics, Place & Environment* 12, no. 2 (2009): 175–186. https://doi.org/10.1080/13668790902863390
Rebelo, Ana Miriam, Heitor Alvelos and Álvaro Domingues, "Capitalist Visuality: Branding, Architecture, and Its Visual Reproduction. A Case Study in the City of Porto", in *Perspectives on Design and Digital Communication III, Springer Series in Design and Innovation*, Vol. 24, edited by Nuno Martins, David Brandão and Francisco Paiva, 241–253, New York: Springer, Cham, 2023. https://doi.org/10.1007/978-3-031-06809-6_16
Rudofsky, Bernard, *Architecture without Architects: A Short Introduction to Non-pedigreed Architecture*, New York: Doubleday, 1964.

Scruton, Roger, *How to be a Conservative*, London: Bloomsbury Continuum, 2014.
Solnit, Rebecca, *A Paradise Built in Hell: The Extraordinary Communities That Arise in Disasters*, New York: Viking, 2009.
Thompson, Paul B. "Farming as Focal Practice", In *Technology and the Good Life?*, edited by Eric Higgs, Andrew Light and David Strong, 166–181, Chicago: University of Chicago Press, 2000. https://doi.org/10.7208/9780226333885-012
Vallor, Shannon, "Moral Deskilling and Upskilling in a New Machine Age: Reflections on the Ambiguous Future of Character", *Philosophy & Technology*, no. 28 (2015): 107–124. https://doi.org/10.1007/s13347-014-0156-9
Verbeek, Peter-Paul, "Tecnopólis: a vida pública dos artefactos tecnológicos", *Análise Social* 41, no. 181 (2006): 1105–1125.
Winner, Langdon, *Autonomous Technology. Technics-Out-of-Control as a Theme in Political Thought*, Cambridge: MIT Press, 1977.

Part IV
Cities, fragments and the arts

12 Odysseus impounded

Lost sailors, lost times, lost loves

Graeme Gilloch

***

If on a summer's day a traveller . . .

Mid-summer. Mid-afternoon. A third-floor apartment on the Place des Moulins in Marseilles. When the doorbell rings, Mariette is busy looking for more cigarettes in the bedroom, so Diamantis gets to his feet and, leaving Lalla in the kitchen, heads for the door. He recognises Cephea immediately, even though he has never seen her before. Her flight got in at 10.55 that morning; she has been in the city a few hours. But long enough. She knows. He notices the tears in her eyes. He invites her in, offers her a coffee, and taking her by the shoulders, holding her for a moment, looks to console her.

Thus ends Jean-Claude Izzo's 1997 novel *Les marins perdus* (*The Lost Sailors*). It is a scene, a denouement – seemingly ordinary, banal, humdrum – that belies the dramatic events that have unfolded over the previous hours and days, incidents that have brought these individuals together for this improbable and wholly unexpected rendezvous in Mariette's kitchen. We can imagine some of the conversations that will ensue, the stories and sorrows that will be shared over yet more cups of coffee and cigarettes because, of course, they have in part already been recounted: they constitute the novel. And so, as the book concludes, the reader is invited to think back, to reflect on, to (re-)imagine all that has gone before and led up to this moment, this encounter, this particular collection of characters. How has it come to this? How could things have panned out differently? What if? If only?

And so, as I read these final pages, came upon this curiously anti-climactic ending to a most curious novel, I was reminded of Walter Benjamin's essays from the late 1930s on Brechtian "epic theatre"[1] and the significance of the interruption[2] of action: when, for example, as a door is suddenly opened at the side of the stage and a stranger looks in upon the scene, the assembled characters are momentarily distracted, arrested in their gestures and attitudes, frozen in a composition or tableau, an image, that allows itself to be read and deciphered. The unanticipated intrusion has occasioned a cessation in the

DOI: 10.4324/9781003452928-16

conversation, a pause in proceedings that constitutes a critical moment of recognition and re-cognition, not only for the characters on stage themselves but most importantly for the hitherto "relaxed" but now "astonished" audience.[3] This chance to draw breath, to take stock, is the instant in which they become witnesses to a particular "situation"[4] and, above all, to its social, political and economic significance and ramifications. Benjamin terms this didactic moment: "dialectics at a standstill"; the configuration formed – of bodies, objects, of light and shade, of times past and present – corresponds to the "dialectical image",[5] Benjamin's key historiographical/epistemological category for the redemption of the "tradition of the oppressed",[6] of the catastrophic discontinuity of history,[7] of stories (the German term *Geschichte* here is provocatively, productively ambiguous).[8]

Cephea's unexpected arrival is an exemplary instance not only of this interruption-as-illumination but also of termination. The novel concludes. *Fin*. And she certainly could not have imagined that things would end up like this. It is her first time in Marseilles. She has only just arrived. Tired of waiting at home, unprepared to play the part of Penelope, she has flown in from Dakar with high hopes of a long-delayed and loving reunion with her estranged husband, Abdul Aziz, the 55-year-old Captain of an ageing freighter, the *Aldebaran*. The ship has spent the last five months rusting at the end of a long sea wall, impounded by the port authorities on account of some dubious accounts, some unpaid – in all likelihood never to be repaid – shipping debts accrued by the ship's invisible, untraceable owner. As the taxi from the airport follows the costal road:

> She [Cephea] watched as the city advanced towards her. She was dazzled. Why had she never come here before? And why just now? She started to feel she was going to enjoy her stay in Marseilles. Abdul, who was so good at telling stories, would show her around. Make her love the city, maybe. If he hadn't suffered too much by not being at sea.[9]

Perhaps, as Benjamin notes in his "One-Way Street" collection under the rubric "Articles Lost", "what makes the very first glimpse of a village, a town, in the landscape so incomparable and irretrievable is the rigorous connection between foreground and distance".[10] In any case, whatever these initial inviting prospects and perspectives of the city promise, these inklings of a "love at first sight" for Marseilles will not last long. Aziz has indeed "suffered too much", and it has driven him to violence, to the senseless killing of Nedim, the ship's young radio operator – naïve Nedim, who has fallen in love with Lalla, the girl from the sleazy Habana Bar, and who desperately tries to free her from his Captain's predatory sexual grip.

No, one thing is certain: Cephea will not enjoy her stay in Marseilles. She will not come to love this city. But then this is not her story. Nor one of her husband's many sagas. Rather, it is the loyal second-in-command, the Greek first-mate Diamantis, the man who opens the door, who is at the centre of this tale, this story of men lost, not at sea but on land, sailors who are all at sea when not at sea, if you follow my drift. As the *Aldebaran* has been forbidden to leave port, there is nothing to be done except play out, play act, the routines of life aboard ship or find other ways to while away the dreary days. After five months, these "other ways" have dried up: there is nothing left to do but endure the slow passage of time. And it is this that Diamantis, a *Grübler*, a brooder at the best of times, finds insufferable. For these are certainly *not* the best of times. As the hours creep by, there is nothing to distract him from revisiting, reimagining and replaying his past missteps and mistakes and, above all, the acts of betrayal that haunt him: the failure of his marriage to Melina, a woman he had known from their childhood days and who had once brushed off the taunt of another erstwhile suitor, Dimitri, that "She'd grow old like Penelope, waiting for him to return";[11] his absence as a father to their son, Mikis, now 18 years old and studying in Athens; and his abandonment without a word of goodbye some 20 years earlier of a young woman he had loved and left in Marseilles, Amina. Six days of his shore-leave they had spent together. He had told her he loved her. He had said he would be back in two weeks. He had lied. Indeed, although he had been in this port, this city, many times since that long-ago love affair, he had never once enquired after her, looked her up, sought her out. But now, after five months of going nowhere, that is to change: Diamantis resolves to find her. Why? Why *now*? Perhaps to discover how that particular "if only" may have unfolded, may yet have something still to unfold. And it does. There will be discoveries: Diamantis will find Amina; he will learn, not from her but from her "husband", Ricardo, the owner of the *Habana*, that he has a daughter – Lalla, of course. And there will be death: for while Nedim and Abdul fight it out on board the *Aldebaran* with fatal consequences, Diamantis drives out to Amina's house only to find that Ricardo has shot her dead in the upstairs bedroom. Back in the lounge, Ricardo sits on a sofa, finishes a drink and lights himself a cigarette as Diamantis picks up the gun, points it towards him and pulls the trigger again and again. From one murder scene to another: Diamantis drives back to the ship to find Lalla "huddled in a corner under the ships rail", screaming, sobbing and poor Nedim "skewered" on a piece of metal carelessly left on deck, on "some fucking thing that Diamantis couldn't identify".[12]

As the door of Mariette's apartment opens, the characters who confront each other have taken very different paths to this threshold, this moment: Diamantis has spent his time wandering the city of Marseilles, circling, searching, finding and eventually killing a murderer; filled with hope, Cephea has just arrived from Senegal, taken the flight from Dakar to Marseilles, travelled from A to B, left through "departures" and entered through "arrivals" to reach her destination. But as soon as Cephea finds herself in Marseilles, she is blown off course, sent hither and thither in the search for her husband: airport to the port authority; port authority to police station; police station to Mariette's flat via a detour/tour of the city, courtesy of a swindling taxi driver who takes the scenic route to inflate the fare. All this to find that her husband has murdered a young man. As soon as you arrive in Marseilles, the labyrinthine stage begins, as Benjamin might have said.[13] And the art of navigation has to be relearnt, how to navigate life, that is, how to find one's way in life, how to live and live on. Yes, indeed: that innocent, hopeful, first image of the city is soon gone and will never be restored.

Itineraries

The line and the labyrinth: direction and destination versus digression and detour. There are those for whom these contrasting ways of journeying, these conflicting itineraries, are not mutually exclusive but rather combine, coalesce, co-constitute each other: they do so, archetypically, in the figure of Odysseus. And this is apposite, for Odysseus is a recurrent motif, indeed I would argue the *leitmotif*, the red thread running through all of Izzo's writings, not just *The Lost Sailors*, where the parallels and correspondences are perhaps most evident – rueful Greek seafaring protagonist, abandoned wife, seductive former lovers, violence and vengeance. Yes, Diamantis may incarnate a modern-day Odysseus, Odysseus impounded, but the mythological mariner appears elsewhere, everywhere in fact, in Izzo's novels: in the "Marseilles trilogy" – *Total Chaos* (1995), *Chourmo* (1996), *Solea* (1998) – foundational texts of "Mediterranean noir" featuring the ill-fated ex-police officer Fabio Montale, the Odysseus myth is repeatedly invoked, not least in the title of the second volume, *Chourmo*, part of the city's argot and an explicit reference to the camaraderie of the galley slaves who for centuries rowed the ships of the "middle sea" and, in his final masterpiece, *A Sun for the Dying* (1999), a dying old man makes one final weary journey cross-country from Paris to Marseilles in search of a long-lost but never forgotten former lover and a final resting place under a cloudless sky overlooking the blue water.

Izzo returns time and time again to Odysseus, takes him as a guiding spirit. Perhaps this is because, for him, the Greek hero embodies a certain version of what one might term "Mediterranean masculinity": quick-witted and quick-tempered; passionate and violent; sentimental and seductive; lured by adventure but longing for home; faithful to friends but not to lovers; jealous, guilt-ridden. Nostalgic, homesick, but only in a particular, peculiar way. Odysseus, Aziz and Diamantis: these three wayward seafarers all share the same affliction: the incessant longing to be somewhere other than here-and-now, to be "elsewhere". They have sailed so far and for so long because they are animated by a common restlessness that has grown into a common rootlessness. Charles Baudelaire had a word for this melancholy condition: *spleen*. If such unfortunates belong anywhere, it is here in Marseilles, a homely–unhomely setting, an uncanny city for those who cannot remain still, who cannot be at peace.[14]

Odysseus is much more than just a figure of interrupted itineraries, but I will confine myself here to the following. As the crafty warrior who, before the seemingly impregnable walls of Troy, conceives of the wooden horse; as the "Nobody" who deceives and confounds the blinded cyclops Polyphemus, eluding his voracious clutches; as the captain who stops the ears of his crew with wax and has himself tied to the mast of his own ship so as to hear, yet escape, the seductive songs of the Sirens, it is Odysseus who outwits and circumvents the overpowering forces of nature, myth and fate, eluding death and destruction through the exercise of his intellect, cunning and ingenuity. In his 1934 essay on Franz Kafka, Benjamin writes:

> Ulysses stands at the dividing line between myth and fairy tale. Reason and cunning have inserted their tricks into myths; their forces cease to be invincible. Fairy tales are the traditional stories about victory over these forces, and fairy tales for dialecticians are what Kafka wrote when he went to work on legends.[15]

Indeed, one might argue that the figure of Odysseus embodies the emancipatory spirit and promise of the fairytale when Benjamin notes two years later in "The Storyteller" (1936): "The wisest thing – so the fairy tale taught mankind in olden times and teaches children to this day – is to meet the forces of the mythic world with cunning and with high spirits".[16]

But Izzo's *The Lost Sailors* is far from such "high spirits", its calamitous events, murderous violence and sombre tone much more in keeping with the darker, bleaker reading of the Homeric hero offered by Theodor Adorno and Max Horkheimer in *Dialectic of Enlightenment*, written some ten years after Benjamin's essays[17] and in the wake of his untimely death. Yes, in the figure of Odysseus, for them the prototypical modern subject, one can see that "the self represents rational universality against the inevitability of fate", but all this is at a cost. They write:

> Renunciation, the principle of bourgeois disillusionment, the outward schema for the intensification of sacrifice, is already present *in nuce* in that estimation of the ratio of forces which anticipates survival as so to speak dependent on the concession of one's own defeat, and – virtually – on death. The nimble-witted survives only at the price of his own dream, which he wins only by demystifying himself as well as the powers without. He can never have everything; he has always to wait, to be patient, to do without; he may not taste the lotus or eat the cattle of the Sun-god Hyperion, and when he steers between the rocks he must count on the loss of the men whom Scylla plucks from the boat. He just pulls through: struggle is his survival; and all the fame that he and the others win in the process serves merely to confirm that the title of hero is only gained at the price of the abasement and mortification of the instinct for complete, universal, and undivided happiness.[18]

Artful Odysseus lives by living through the sacrifice of pleasure. He confronts the word of myth with cynical calculation and low spirits. He is a figure of disenchantment or disillusionment in the dual senses of these words:

freed from mystification and denied fulfilment. He is not deceived by dreams because, as the arch-deceiver himself, he is simply bereft of dreams. And he is alone. Adorno and Horkheimer tellingly compare him to another unfortunate seafarer many centuries later:

> Both Odysseus and [Robinson] Crusoe, the two shipwrecked mariners, make their weakness (that of the individual who parts from the collectivity) their social strength. Delivered up to the mercy of the waves, helplessly isolated, their very isolation forces them recklessly to purse an atomistic interest.[19]

Odysseus and Crusoe, then, exist "only in complete alienation from all other men, who meet the two protagonists only in an alienated from – as enemies or points of support, but always as tools, as things".[20]

Let us add a third to this doleful duo: Diamantis. It is his misfortune to be "shipwrecked", stranded at least, in a wreck of a ship, not on an island but in a city, here in Marseilles. He will thread his solitary way through its streets and alleyways, its bars and clubs, in pursuit of his own "atomistic interest", an anachronistic interest indeed, 20 years too late. He will encounter and slay a monster, a mobster. But again, too late. He will survive, he will live to tell the tale. He is a survivor. But not all the crew will make it. And there is no happiness to be had, no "happy ever after". Lost sailors in Marseilles are not like lost children in the enchanted forest. This is no fairytale. There is only the consolation, if indeed it is any consolation, of not grieving alone. Diamantis, Lalla, Cephea – the novel ends with a sharing of sorrows as well as coffee and cigarettes. It is a gathering of mourners on a summer's afternoon in a city of strangers.

Marseilles: fabulous fragments

In Izzo's writing, and in *The Lost Sailors* in particular, Marseilles appears as a mosaic-in-motion composed of intensely coloured and vivid fragments, configured in three ever-shifting patterns: as a site of tales and storytelling; as a locus of aesthetic experiences (*terroir*); and as a space of hybridity, difference, otherness, of the elsewhere. Marseilles, then, assumes three (dis)guises: the (con)fabulous city; the sensuous city; the promiscuous city.

The (con)fabulous city: As a port city, home to itinerants of all kinds, Marseilles is a city of stories and storytelling. Adapting Henri Lefebvre, we might consider it as a triad of "narrations of space", "spatial narratives" and "narrational spaces".[21] And Izzo's novels are both a capturing of and a contribution to this rich fabulation and confabulation of this city, albeit not of the fairytale kind.[22]

Fabulation: the weaving of stories, spaces and moments, half-real, half-magical, experienced and imagined. Italo Calvino's *Invisible Cities*[23] would be exemplary here. And Marseilles is a worthy rival to Venice in this. William Firebrace (2010) begins his eclectic and kaleidoscopic *Marseille Mix*, with:

> Marseille is a series of invented cities, living as stories and images, sometimes original, sometimes borrowed, strung together without too much concern for the joints and overlaps. . . . Marseille more than most cities lends itself to myth and exaggerations. With every characterisation the feel of Marseille turns and shifts, the city moves from dangerous to harmless, from healthy to sick, from light to dark. Each of these images creates a different city, a city that is never precisely sited, a city that is always elsewhere.[24]

For Izzo, such tales, such "myths and exaggerations" are manifold, multiple and multi-layered. There are stories nested within stories, like a Russian doll, or Pandora's box (for they are all ultimately catastrophic, all leading to death); or like an old sea-chest filled with the long-forgotten bric-a-brac recalling voyages and ports-of-call from yesteryear: a few precious souvenirs half-hidden amidst a lot of old junk.

As soon as one arrives in Marseilles, the narrative stage begins – well, perhaps not immediately but eventually, inevitably. And this is true even for the key protagonists of *The Lost Sailors* who have been hitherto and otherwise taciturn figures, reluctant storytellers. As the waiting drags on and on, Aziz surprises Diamantis by telling him of his wife Cephea, confessing that she has left him on account of his serial infidelities and constant time away and asking for advice. Diamantis is taken aback because these two have been shipmates for 15 years, and in all that time they have exchanged few words and certainly nothing intimate, nothing personal, nothing of any real significance. After 15 years of workaday chit-chat interspersed with bragging about sexual exploits, Captain Aziz turns to his first mate and describes Cephea so clearly and tenderly that Diamantis will recognise her immediately upon opening the door of Mariette's apartment.

It is surprising, too, because Diamantis is hardly best placed to give any advice on such delicate matters of the heart. And Aziz knows it. Diamantis has (had) more than enough of his own disorientations and disillusionments to deal with, adrift as he is not just in this city but more intractably in his thoughts, his memories, his mistakes, his equivocations, his casual cruelty to Melina, his cowardly lie to Amina. He is lost: in his past, in this port. And as he ventures out to find Amina, to discover what has become of her, what might have become of them, so his footsteps in the city will coincide and cross with those of his ill-fated shipmate Nedim. It is Nedim who, on the lookout for love and sex, winds up in the Habana Club where Amina presides, finds himself cheated into debt and besotted with Lalla, the young woman who, after playing her part in swindling him, takes pity on and then falls for him, this gullible young man so clearly out of his depth, so close to death. Izzo's principal protagonists come and go, moving between ship and city, between different moments of the labyrinth: as a space of convolution and circulation; as a site of imprisonment; as a trap for the unwary. In so doing, they criss-cross and double-cross each other, desire, deceive and desert each other, tell each other stories blended of truth, falsehood, self-pity and self-justification. We find stories not simply aligned side by side like ships anchored in a port but entangled, twisting and twining like ropes, more knots than narratives, leading towards, tying us into, the final denouement of violence and murder.

"Confabulation" *could* mean these interweavings, the spinning of stories *with*. Indeed, this is its etymology: "Con-fabulation": from Latin: "a talking together, chatting, familiar talk". Is this not precisely what Aziz and Diamantis have shared these long years and here now in Marseilles, this confabulous city?

But the word also has another usage in psychology: here it refers to a particular pathological condition involving lapses of memory, slippages between what was and what one remembers of it, confusion of "real" and "false" memories but all without any intended deception. So not lying as such, but lying to oneself without even knowing it. One is misled by one's own memories. "Confabulation" then is the fabrication of memories and then the forgetting of their fabrication, akin perhaps to fetishism, to reification, as Adorno would have it.[25]

After a few drinks with Aziz, Diamantis tries to recall Melina but as he does so "another face loomed", Amina: "Her face was in his head, and it was too late now to blot it out".[26] Diamantis can imagine Cephea; he can envisage Amina; but he cannot recall the face of his own wife. Confabulation as a conflation of countenances. The "Marseilles mix" is a memory mix, too. A memory mix-up. Another swindle.

Marseilles: the sensuous cityscape

"History decays into images, not into stories", Benjamin famously claims.[27] Stories [*Geschichten*], these stories at least, break down, too, but not into pictures. Rather, they fracture, fragment into moments that appeal to other senses: taste, smell, touch, hearing. Izzo's writings on Marseilles are evocative, above all, of the ambience and atmosphere of the city, of its *aesthetics* understood here in the wider sense of "to do with the senses". And so, for example, at every opportunity in his novels – and *The Lost Sailors* is no exception – Izzo is at pains to describe the local cuisine with extraordinary specificity and precision. The characters that people his writings seldom, if ever, simply eat and drink in this or that bistro, grab a snack, gulp a beer: rather, we, the readers, are treated to the minute details of Provençal ingredients, herbs, sauces, wines. These grilled aubergines served with this kind of goat's cheese go best with a chilled Bandol rosé from this particular estate. Basil, mint, thyme, garlic, olive oil – these in combination with the vegetables and fish and seafood of the locality form a rich and enticing menu iterated and reiterated by Izzo.[28] And importantly, this has nothing to do with the snobbish gourmet or well-heeled restaurateur, nor with pricey tourist spots. Quite the opposite: in conjuring up these flavours and smells, Izzo foregrounds humble backstreet eateries, cheap bistros and unpretentious cafes, simple pleasures, everyday food cooked and served with love and care but without show and theatricality. Here you might find the best ratatouille, over there the freshest "catch of the day". The house white by the carafe in this seemingly down-at-heel place is particularly good. It comes from the vineyards in and around wherever. One of the most characteristic features of Izzo's stories is this continual attentiveness to the sensory experience of the cityscape and its particularity and distinctiveness, this local inflection. Only here do you find *this* fish cooked in *that* way. For me, the word that best captures this preoccupation with this micrological level of specific tastes and aromas is a term from oenology, from discussions of wine: *terroir*. *Terroir* refers to the distinctive and defining features of microclimate, soil, drainage, elevation and inclination that impart to the grapes of whichever variety they may be a highly specific character, one discernible by a sensitive palate in the wine glass. It is not just that each vineyard will have its own *terroir*; different plots, different parcels of the same vineyard will yield subtle differences, notes and accents. And so it is with Izzo. What distinguishes his work is precisely this special evocation of the *terroir* of Marseilles, *Marseilles as terroir*. This is all rather ironic in *The Lost Sailors*: *terroir* is, of course, "land", the very one on which our protagonists find themselves hopelessly stranded. Nevertheless, if there is a home for these seafarers, it is to be found at a modest bistro table. So it seems for Diamantis at least. He himself is smitten by Mariette, the daughter of the owner of a local café on the Place de Lenche, a small family run establishment that welcomes and embraces this particular lost sailor as one of their own. She, Mariette, is the very embodiment of the city: "a real Marseillaise. Cheerful and self-confident, with hazel eyes that weren't easily fooled".[29] They like each other; they begin an affair.

Indeed, we are told, Diamantis "likes Marseilles",[30] and perhaps this is because it is both *like* and *unlike* home, strangely familiar, uncanny. Here the notion of *terroir* is important: for this term does not refer to some Provençal chauvinism or parochialism. *Terroir* is paradoxical: it is the unique expression of a particular environment but one that makes connections. If each locality has its own *terroir*, then what they have in common is the very idea of *terroir* itself. *Terroir* is shared not through identity but through *difference*. This is why a Greek sailor can feel at home, part of the family, eating local cuisine in a bistro in Marseilles. The flavours are individual, but these are familiar, common ingredients. This is fundamental for Izzo: the tastes of Marseilles are variations on those of the whole Mediterranean region. And by this "pan-Mediterraneanism" he includes not just Europe but the coasts and hinterlands of the Middle East and of North Africa. Indeed, his love of this city, a love which runs through each and every line of his writing, is inspired by the multiculturalism and diverse communities of Marseilles drawn from this entire region, its embrace through centuries of trade, migration and exchange of travellers, passers-by and passers-through, outsiders, immigrants, strangers, itinerants, exiles, asylum-seekers and others; not just the "wretched of the earth", to borrow Frantz Fanon's (2001) famous phrase and title, but the wretched of the sea, too. Those who are lost. Those who can go no further. This is Marseilles's *terroir*, this is the "Marseilles mix".

Marseilles: the "promiscuous" city

Izzo is not alone in his recognition and exposition of Marseilles as a city of sensuous experiences, of aesthetic experiences, of a reawakening of otherwise and elsewhere dulled or diluted sensitivities: nor in his vision of the city as a site of cosmopolitanism and multiplicity. As I have suggested elsewhere,[31] the essays of Benjamin, Joseph Roth and Siegfried Kracauer from the 1920s all stress how in Marseilles there is an overloading, an overwhelming of the senses and a mixing of bodies, peoples, foodstuffs, flavours, smells and music. This is not so much a *melting* pot, in which differences are brought together and assimilated, dissolved into one another to create a blend, but a *mixing* pot where "otherness", alterity, is recognised and remains distinct. Like the food: a few strong distinctive flavours, not every herb in the kitchen cancelling each other out. Taste as openness to otherness.

On a visit to his cousin, Dimitri Venetsanou, who lives in a nouveau-riche part of Marseilles, Diamantis is disgusted by the man's racist contempt for "foreigners", for "Arabs". They argue over the dinner table. It nearly comes to blows. Diamantis gets up and leaves. The food has hardly been touched; "A Greek meal", specially prepared by Dimitri's wife Nena, Izzo informs us, but "Neither the sauce nor the cuttlefish had any taste".[32]

Marseilles is a city of promiscuity in its literal form: from the Latin, *pro-miscere*, for mixing.

Indeed, the crew of the *Aldebaran* are a microcosm of, or a metaphor for, such a city: "there were two Burmese, an Ivorian, a Comorian, a Turk, a Moroccan, and a Hungarian. Abdul Aziz was Lebanese, and he [Diamantis] was Greek".[33] They are all stuck here too. Like so many seafarers, wayfarers, before them.

Marseilles: not so much a destination as a city where those passing through have come to a standstill, their passage interrupted, cut short. Or a point of departure for those who can never get going, sailors unable to set sail. Seafarers who inevitably fare less well on land. Odysseus impatient, Odysseus impounded.

And this returns us, after many digressions, to the start of this essay and the end of the book: in Izzo's novel we experience a city as a site of interruption, of encounters and disturbances, of things chanced upon in *media res*, of incomplete stories, of unfinished business. We find ourselves in a city of improvisation and the staccato, of jazz, Montale's favourite and the cool music that provides a perennial soundtrack to Izzo's writings.

The Lost Sailors is a story born of an ongoing going nowhere, of unending disruption and interminable interruption. The *Aldebaran* is at a standstill. It will never set sail, never leave port; the very antithesis of *The Flying Dutchman*.

In Izzo's novel, the lives of some – Nedim, Amina, Ricardo – are terminated, cut short. The lives of others are interrupted. And such interruptions are opportunities: they are distractions, seductions, leadings astray, chances to look elsewhere, moments to reflect and think back. The importuned have an opportunity.

In *The Lost Sailors*, Izzo presents us with Marseilles as a city of "situations", scenes at a standstill chanced upon by a melancholy Greek sailor whose own destiny is to be endlessly deferred, whose destiny is deferral. Perhaps. Perhaps his future lies with Mariette and with Lalla. On the final page, after a fateful, fatal night, Diamantis stands like Janus on a threshold and opens a door to welcome, to console, a tearful traveller. And what now? What next?

And what of Marseilles, this cosmopolis of these washed-up remnants and fragments – stories, senses, peoples, the flotsam and jetsam of the Mediterranean world? How is this city configured in Izzo's writings? As ever-mobile mosaic? As perpetually turning kaleidoscope? Yes, both of these metaphors serve us well. But perhaps Benjamin's writings offer us a more powerful and appropriate image: the city of Marseilles as constellation.[34] Looking upwards, stargazing at the night sky, the constellation is a spatial-temporal complex of myriad glittering points and imagined lines, a fantastical geometry of elements and moments traced by the ancients into legible figures and patterns. And the reverse? Looking downwards from on high, a bird's-eye view, the nocturnal city is perhaps not so very different (or indeed, ships on night-time seas): it also appears as a manifold of pinpricks and ribbons of light set in darkness. Constellations are heavenly maps by means of which sailors, celestial cartographers par excellence, once navigated their way across the featureless expanses of the sea. In this city, by contrast, our sailors have no stars to guide them. It is no wonder that they are lost. And, though to be sure Odysseus has his ruses, this calls for the ingenuity of Ariadne. Indeed, it is the very trickery of the constellation to which Diamantis and his shipmates are now subject. It is, after all, the most deceptive of figures: stars that seem adjacent are the ones furthest apart; those that appear closest to us often prove to be the most far-flung, the most remote. What once seemed fixed in place and trusted in meaning now reveals itself to be shape-shifting, contingent, contestable, utterly unreliable. The constellation is always legible *differently, otherwise*. Terra firma proves to be anything but for those with sea-legs. And, importantly, constellations are imbued with mythological significance and productive of stories. The sky becomes a vast screen onto which figures, creatures, characters are projected and from which their archetypical dramas and narratives are seen to play out. The heavens are populated, they are alive, or so they seem. *They are to be read*.[35] And so, too, is the city, Izzo's city, Marseilles, this city from which he has derived and into which he has inscribed so many characters and episodes, so much passion and pain, so much misfortune and melancholy. This is his city, a city of fabulations and confabulations; of memories and meanderings; of brooding and brutality; of the senses and the sensual; duplicity and deceit; of life – vital,vibrant, vivid – but with death never far away. This, then, is the "Marseilles mix". Faint flickerings of light against a dark, sombre backdrop, it has an uncanny, haunting beauty. And it has its own distinctive *terroir* for which there is no better word than this: *noir*.

Notes

1. See, for example, Benjamin, "What is the Epic Theatre? (II)" [1939], 302–309.
2. See Ibid., 304–305.
3. See Ibid., 302 and 304.
4. Benjamin writes of this moment of witness: "the stranger is confronted with the situation: troubled faces, an open window, the furniture in disarray. But there is a gaze before which even more ordinary scenes of middle-class life look almost equally startling" (Benjamin, "What is the Epic Theatre? (II)", 305).
5. See Benjamin, *The Arcades Project*, 462 [N 2a,3].
6. See Thesis VIII of Benjamin's 1940 "On the Concept of History", 392.
7. On historical discontinuity, see Benjamin, *The Arcades Project*, 474 [N 9a,6]. On history as catastrophe, see Benjamin's famous invocation of Paul Klee's painting *Angelus Novus* in Thesis IX (Benjamin, "On the Concept of History", 392).
8. On the historian as chronicler and storyteller, see, for example, Thesis III, Ibid., 390).
9. Izzo, *The Lost Sailors*, 259.
10. Benjamin, "One-Way Street", 468.
11. Izzo, *The Lost Sailors*, 30. This has become precisely her fate.
12. Ibid., 248.
13. Benjamin writes of his 1926–1927 visit to Moscow that "the instant you arrive, the childhood stage begins. On the thick sheet ice of the street, walking has to be relearned. . . . Now the city turns into a labyrinth for the newcomer" (Benjamin, "Moscow", 23–24).
14. The first section of William Firebrace's *Marseille Mix* is tellingly titled "Elsewhere". He writes:

    Marseille becomes elsewhere because of the feeling it gives to outsiders of being different, unfixed. As to why one should want such an elsewhere to exist, this surely has something to do with the relentless inability to be content with where one is and the associated need to invent somewhere else – positive or negative, a place of hope or fear, alluring or repulsive, it doesn't really matter because elsewhere is always pulling, always leading one on.
    Firebrace, *Marseille Mix*, 19

15. Benjamin, "Franz Kafka", 799.
16. Benjamin, "The Storyteller", 157.
17. Adorno and Horkheimer, *Dialectic of Enlightenment*, 58.
18. Ibid., 57.
19. Ibid., 61.
20. Ibid., 62.
21. Henri Lefebvre famously looks to three dimensions of lived space: "representations of space" (how space is conceived, conceptualised and configured by

architects, planners etc.); "spatial practices" (the everyday physical organisation of spaces and routines) and "representational spaces" (subjective perceptions and experiences of a space). See Lefebvre, *The Production of Space*, 33–39.
22 Izzo's writings certainly offer no happy endings in this city, only death. In *Solea*, for example, the characters we have come to know in the first two volumes of the trilogy are shockingly murdered one by one until even Montale himself, the flawed but super-cool protagonist, is shot down and lies bleeding, dying, on a drifting boat. These are fairytales in reverse.
23 The English translation, published in 1974, is by the felicitously named William Weaver.
24 Firebrace, *Marseille Mix*, 10. He quite rightly sees Izzo's novels, especially the Montale trilogy, as a key part of the mythologisation and romanticisation of Marseilles. "The stories of Izzo", he writes, "are the classic Marseille *polars* [crime novels]" and "created a boom" in the genre (Ibid., 173). Although these are now somewhat *passé* (Ibid., 175), Firebrace notes:

> Readers enjoyed Izzo's vision of Marseille, believing that he was portraying an actual place rather than a fantasy. The city also began to follow the fantasy, to think of itself as a romantic location rather than a doomed port, and at the same time to consider the *cités* as even more disturbing than they are in reality.
> Ibid., 173

25 Among the "Notes and Drafts" of *Dialectic of Enlightenment* one finds, in a section titled "Le Prix du Progrès", the famous formulation: "All objectification [*Verdinglichung*] is a forgetting" (*Dialectic of Enlightenment*, 230).
26 Izzo, *The Lost Sailors*, 23.
27 Benjamin, *The Arcades Project*, 476 [N 11,4].
28 Originally titled *Marseilles* (2000), his little collection of non-fiction essays and fragments comes to bear the names of three of his favourite regional ingredients in the Italian and then English translations: *Garlic, Mint and Sweet Basil: Essays on Marseilles, Mediterranean Cuisine, and Noir Fiction* (2020).
29 Izzo, *The Lost Sailors*, 28.
30 Ibid., 16.
31 See Gilloch, "Sunshine and Noir" and "Fragments. Cityscapes. Modernity".
32 Izzo, *The Lost Sailors*, 30.
33 Ibid., 29.
34 Stars and constellations figure prominently in Izzo's novel: Cephea is named after a star; Aziz's new girlfriend is Stella; and his ship, the *Aldebaran* (Arabic: "the follower") shares its name with the brightest star in the constellation of Taurus. For Benjamin on the constellation, see, for example, the "Epistemo-Critical Prologue" to his *Trauerspiel* study (*German Tragic Drama*, 34–35); "On Astrology" from 1932 and "On the Mimetic Faculty" from 1933.
35 "'To read what was never written'. Such reading is the most ancient: reading prior to all languages, from entrails, the stars or dances", writes Benjamin in his 1933 fragment "On the Mimetic Faculty", 722.

Bibliography

Adorno, Theodor W. and Max Horkheimer, *Dialectic of Enlightenment*, translated by John Cumming, London: Verso, 1997.
Benjamin, Walter, *The Origin of German Tragic Drama*, translated by John Osbourne, London: Verso, 1985.
Benjamin, Walter, "One-Way Street", in *Selected Writings, Vol. 1: 1913–1926*, translated by Edmund Jephcott, edited by Marcus Bullock and Michael W. Jennings, 444–488, Cambridge, MA: The Belknap Press of Harvard University Press, 1996.

Benjamin, Walter, *The Arcades Project*, translated by Howard Eiland and Kevin McLaughlin, Cambridge, MA: The Belknap Press of Harvard University Press, 1999a.
Benjamin, Walter, "Moscow", in *Selected Writings, Vol. 2: 1927–1934*, translated by Edmund Jephcott, edited by Michael W. Jennings, Howard Eiland and Gary Smith, 22–46, Cambridge, MA: The Belknap Press of Harvard University Press, 1999b.
Benjamin, Walter, "On Astrology", in *Selected Writings, Vol. 2: 1927–1934*, translated by Rodney Livingstone, edited by Michael W. Jennings, Howard Eiland and Gary Smith, 684–685, Cambridge, MA: The Belknap Press of Harvard University Press, 1999c.
Benjamin, Walter, "On the Mimetic Faculty", in *Selected Writings, Vol. 2: 1927–1934*, translated by Edmund Jephcott, edited by Michael W. Jennings, Howard Eiland and Gary Smith, 720–722, Cambridge, MA: The Belknap Press of Harvard University Press, 1999d.
Benjamin, Walter, "Franz Kafka", in *Selected Writings, Vol. 2: 1927–1934*, translated by Harry Zohn, edited by Michael W. Jennings, Howard Eiland and Gary Smith, 794–818, Cambridge, MA: The Belknap Press of Harvard University Press, 1999e.
Benjamin, Walter, "The Storyteller. Observations on the Works of Nikolai Leskov", in *Selected Writings, Vol. 3: 1935–1938*, translated by Harry Zohn, edited by Howard Eiland and Michael W. Jennings, 143–166, Cambridge, MA: The Belknap Press of Harvard University Press, 2002.
Benjamin, Walter, "What is the Epic Theatre? (II)", in *Selected Writings, Vol. 4: 1938–1940*, translated by Harry Zohn, edited by Howard Eiland and Michael W. Jennings, 302–309, Cambridge, MA: The Belknap Press of Harvard University Press, 2003a.
Benjamin, Walter, "On the Concept of History", in *Selected Writings, Vol. 4: 1938–1940*, translated by Harry Zohn, edited by Howard Eiland and Michael W. Jennings, 389–400, Cambridge, MA: The Belknap Press of Harvard University Press, 2003b.
Calvino, Italo, *Invisible Cities*, translated by William Weaver, San Diego, CA, New York, NY/London: Harcourt Brace and Co., 1974.
Fanon, Frantz, *The Wretched of the Earth*, translated by Constance Farrington, Harmondsworth, London: Penguin Classics, 2001.
Firebrace, William, *Marseille Mix*, London: The Architectural Association, 2010.
Gilloch, Graeme, "Sunshine and Noir: Benjamin, Kracauer and Roth visit the 'White Cities'", in *Walter Benjamin and the Aesthetics of Change*, edited by Anca Pusca, 82–94, London: Palgrave, 2010.
Gilloch, Graeme, "Fragments. Cityscapes. Modernity. Siegfried Kracauer on the Cannebiere", *Journal of Classical Sociology* 13, no. 1 (2013): 20–29. https://doi.org/10.1177/1468795X12461410
Izzo, Jean-Claude, *Total Chaos*, translated by Howard Curtis, New York, NY: Europa Editions, 2005.
Izzo, Jean-Claude, *Chourmo*, translated by Howard Curtis, New York, NY: Europa Editions, 2006.
Izzo, Jean-Claude, *The Lost Sailors*, translated by Howard Curtis, New York, NY: Europa Editions, 2007a.
Izzo, Jean-Claude, *Solea*, translated by Howard Curtis, New York, NY: Europa Editions, 2007b.
Izzo, Jean-Claude, *A Sun for the Dying*, translated by Howard Curtis, New York, NY: Europa Editions, 2008.
Izzo, Jean-Claude, *Garlic, Mint and Sweet Basil: Essays on Marseilles, Mediterranean Cuisine, and Noir Fiction*, translated by Howard Curtis. New York, NY: Europa Compass Editions, 2020.
Lefebvre, Henri, *The Production of Space*, translated by Donald Nicholson-Smith, London: Wiley-Blackwell, 1991.

13 Drifting through Lisbon in a home movie archive

Inês Sapeta Dias

Drifting on a ruined map

In *Streetwalking on a Ruined Map*, Giuliana Bruno reflects on the limitations of the archive encountered while attempting to trace an Italian woman filmmaker's lost films. Researching (and digging up) the documentation that opens up the possibility of writing the history of Elvira Notari's (1875–1946) cinema, she both encounters and draws a ruined map ("ruined" insofar as it is fragmentary and filled with holes). An overlapping of paths sustains this map, which is a diagram of both her method and her subject: Bruno follows cinema along the streets of Naples, as a site of both production (the cinematic image of Naples) and projection (the sites of movie-going, which she localises in transitory venues – the arcade and the train station – expanding on the implications of transitoriness for defining a cinematic vision).

This text also deals with a lost archive, or an archive filled with blanks and voids, and this is primarily why it begins with a reference to Bruno's enquiry. It deals with a lost or ruined archive in two senses: first, it engages with home movies, which have long been left out of film archives, their preservation deemed unimportant (which has led to their being, to a great degree, lost); second, even within home movies there are certain situations and spaces that are recurrently filmed and others that are not filmed at all. Although home movies still constitute an unstable category in film studies (due in part to their archival status), they can roughly be defined as a subcategory of amateur filmmaking, a defining feature of which is that they are both made and intended to be viewed in private contexts. Home movies are made for recording present moments and determining how these will be remembered in the future, which results in a recurrence of some situations and an absence of others (those that are ugly, sad, or angry are usually lacking). The same can be said of city spaces: certain spaces are recurrently filmed while others are largely considered unfilmable. The word "lost" here refers, then, to issues of both memory (what has been forgotten) and representation (what remains invisible). In this chapter, I will try to show how they are related as the absences that, in part, found and define the archive.[1]

DOI: 10.4324/9781003452928-17

200 Rethinking the City

There is a parallel between the status of home movies in film archives and history (where they are blind spots) and the status of home movies in the history of images and representation (where they produce, or reproduce, blind spots). The second reason why this chapter begins with a reference to *Streetwalking on a Ruined Map* is a methodological one: in Bruno's research there is an overlapping of paths; she walks through the archive, where she follows the paths of cinema in Naples (in particular, the obliterated and censored filmic paths of Elvira Notari), speaking of her work as an endeavour for the "reappropriation of geography in history".[2] Following the fragments of Lisbon found in a home movie archive, and observing the particular paths these fragments draw, this chapter also aims to both traverse the archive and the city and account for the affinities between the two strolls.

An archival *topos*

There is an original disorder at the beginning of the archive I will be working with. Or better, this archive builds upon an original disorder.[3] When I began working as a film programmer at Lisbon's Video Library, a video and digital moving image archive integrated in the city's Municipal Archive, I encountered a strange set – "strange" because the images gathered there were very different from all the others in the archive, which is mainly composed of professional and commercial films or rushes of the archive's own video productions but strange also because these images, unlike all the others, were neither described, nor indexed or even identified in terms of their origin. They were orphans and foreign, their source unknown, portraying unknown people in undefined places, images left outside the scope of the archive and its defining tasks: identification, indexation, description – acts of "consignation".[4]

These silent images (clearly digitised from small-gauge formats such as 8mm or super8) unrolled on the computer screen in front of me, carving out their own particular paths. I began to recognise places: streets in Lisbon, buildings in other Portuguese cities, alongside images filmed in Madrid, Toledo, New York, Moscow, Berlin; an unknown beach and forest, with different people smiling and gesticulating to those filming them. Because of their composition, and because of the different people appearing in the shots, it was clear that I was seeing images filmed by different hands, belonging to different sets or, we might say, families (an emotional grouping and network of people). The images unrolled in a horizontal line – called a "timeline" in film editing – continuously substituting each other, without relief.[5]

I start to recognise certain people as they reappear on this disordered line of time. They gradually become characters, familiar not only because I see them in private situations (celebrations, gatherings, car trips, strolls, games and plays, and everyday activities such as reading and cooking) but also because I can watch them grow: I recognise a man in his twenties in a clip from when he was nine, playing at the beach, or from when he was four, making faces at the camera at a picnic. I begin tracing families.

Today, eight years after this first viewing, these images have been integrated in the Video Library archive (they are no longer strange). Almost all of the filmmakers and characters in the images have now been identified and contacted for information on dates, places, and names. The few images whose origin remains unknown maintain their orphan status.[6] They were identified and labelled as home movies, and they are now organised by family – each family constitutes a particular, indexed collection, identified by the name of its *author*.

Patricia Zimmerman defines home movies as a branch of amateur filmmaking: home movies are amateur films, but unlike other types of amateur films, which have their own specific, (semi)public exhibition circuits, home movies are exclusively made to be seen by those who make and appear in them. Even so, they are "amateur" in their making, a term Zimmerman traces back to nineteenth-century capitalism: opposed to "professional", which was reserved for describing the desirable attributes of workers, "amateur" referred to those features and activities that were excluded from the scope of work:

> In the nineteenth century, amateurism of all forms – bicycling, painting, drama – emerged as a zone for all the corporate capitalism expelled from the workplace: passion, autonomy, creativity, imagination, the private sphere, family life. Professionalism was linked with rationalized work, the public sphere, and exchange relations. Amateurism was located within leisure, the private sphere, and hobbies. Corporate capital exiled the ragged remains of bourgeois individualism into amateurism.[7]

Zimmerman concludes that this conception has influenced the view that defines amateur filmmaking and home movies as irrelevant pastimes, nostalgic mementos of the past, dismissed as insignificant by-products of consumer technology and often defined by negation: non-commercial, non-professional, unnecessary[8] – a perception that marked their irrelevance to film archives until at least the 1990s (although they are still mainly considered unprogrammable, excluded from the history currently being written by cinematheques all over the world).

In a text in which he reflects on his own cinematic practice, the American filmmaker Stanley Brakhage (1933–2003) reclaims the term "amateur", challenging the negative connotations it took on in the labour context by reminding us of its Latin origin. He recalls this root, *amator*, to defend amateur filmmaking as an act of love towards a subject and towards cinema, finishing by saying that he himself is an amateur filmmaker, as he makes cinema only to film what he loves:

> It is because an amateur is one who really lives his life – not one who simply "performs his duty" – and as such he experiences his work while he's working – rather than going to school to learn his work so he can spend the rest of his life just doing it dutifully -; and the amateur, thus, is forever learning and growing thru his work into all his living in a

"clumsiness" of continual discovery that is as beautiful to see, if you have lived it and *can* see it, as to watch young lovers in the "clumsiness" of their lack of knowing and the joy of their continual discovery of each other, if you have ever loved and can appreciate young lovers without jealousy.[9]

Taken in itself, and not as a comparative term, "amateur" designates a particular cinema, moved by the will to capture a subject, a cinema that acts through *e-motion*, moved by what is filmed, and a cinema made outside the logic of commodities, a cinema without products (or films) – in such a way we can ask whether we are talking about films when referring to home movies, as they are rarely edited and thus free of the sense and the *path* that film, through montage, defines.

> The substance of cinema is therefore an endless long take, as is reality to our senses for as long as we are able to see and feel (a long take that ends with the end of our lives); and this long take is nothing but the reproduction of the language of reality. In other words, it is the reproduction of the present. But as soon as montage intervenes, when we pass from cinema to film (they are very different, just as *langue* is different from *parole*), the present becomes past: a past that, for cinematographic and not aesthetic reasons, is always in the present mode (that is, it is a historic present).
>
> It is thus absolutely necessary to die, because while living we lack meaning, and the language of our lives (with which we express ourselves and to which we attribute the greatest importance) is untranslatable: a chaos of possibilities, a search for relations among discontinuous meanings. Death performs a lightning-quick montage on our lives; that is, it chooses our truly significant moments (no longer changeable by other possible contrary or incoherent moments) and places them in sequence, converting our present, which is infinite, unstable, and uncertain, and thus linguistically indescribable, into a clear, stable, certain, and thus linguistically describable past (precisely in the sphere of a general semiology). It is thanks to death that our lives become expressive. Montage thus accomplishes for the material of film (constituted of fragments, the longest or the shortest, of as many long takes as there are subjectivities) what death accomplishes for life.[10]

In his "Observations on the Long Take", the Italian filmmaker Pier Paolo Pasolini (1922–1975) begins with a reference to a home movie: the Zapruder film, which captures the assassination of John F. Kennedy in 1963 in Dallas, Texas. Because it was filmed from a single point of view, this long take corresponds to the *place* where the cameraman stood while filming – which is why Pasolini calls it a "subjective" shot. Pasolini relates the long take to cinema, opposing it to the film *per se* (which usually involves the montage of different points of view – or standpoints, perspectives). He relates cinema to the unstoppable, permanent, ongoing flux of life, opposing it to the death operated by montage – when life becomes fixed in a film.

It is not by chance that Pasolini begins his text with a reference to a home movie: again, insofar as they are rarely edited, home movies do not interfere with the flow of filming; they are closer to the flow of events as they unfold. Without the killing operated by montage, each shot is an installation, an autonomous whole (independent of what comes before and after) that condenses an ineffaceable connection to a particular space at a precise and present moment – a paradoxically fixed and permanent present (or an a-historical past). Even if images appear in a sequence, due to this connection (shot-space-present) it is a sequence that corresponds to the actual sequence of steps taken in life: unlike the paths edited in a film, the paths filmed in home movies are connected to the paths taken in space. There is thus a coincidence between the space of the film strip and the space covered by the body that sees and films. In home movies, to follow the path of the images is to follow the paths of this filming body.

Time, of course, participates in cinematic image construction but not in the usual way: home movies do not create an illusory time (like the time produced by montage in a film);[11] they capture and record present moments (in their present while they are being lived), usually so as to determine and control how they can be remembered in the future (as Roger Odin has underscored).[12] The cut corresponds to the closing of this filming eye, which leaves out what is not considered worthy of being remembered.

Blind fields

I return to the viewing and concentrate on paths and space, extracting images (shots and sequences) filmed in Lisbon. I extract them and arrange them in a line, organised by space: a single city space, filmed by different people, at different times, and on different occasions. I mark the spaces on a map of Lisbon: a different colour for each family or collection.

The map shows intense colour overlays in some spaces, while other spaces remain blank. It was drawn based on a small sample of nine collections (from an archive that includes over one hundred), with home movies made between the 1940s and the late 1970s. Although only the first nine collections I encountered with shots filmed in Lisbon were considered in this small exercise, the descriptions of the other archived films confirm the absent spaces in the map shown in Figure 13.1: the spaces left blank correspond to places where the amateur filmmakers gathered in this archive (as a whole) did not film. The majority of these blank spaces (or blind spots) correspond to unstable areas: territories intersected by large highways (and thus not easily traversed on foot), suburban areas, or what we might, following Ignasi Solà-Morales, call a *terrain vague*.

The 1990s (precisely the decade when attention to home movies began to rise) saw an intensification of interest in, and a boom of literature on, the

Figure 13.1 Map of Lisbon with spots for the spaces found in the home movie archive.
Source: Author.

new, growing cities and the consequent formation of suburbs.[13] These are described as resulting from the disordered growth and consequent fragmentation of urban spaces, defined as peripheral spaces (always standing in relation to a centre, on which they are dependent), as unrationalised abscesses in urbanistic planning, and therefore in urban organisation and order that gradually appear as the city grows beyond its established limits.

Ignasi Solà-Morales defines the *terrain vague* – a term for which he could not find a satisfactory translation – as the permanence (or resistance) of empty and unprogrammed spaces in the interior and in the folds of the ordered city: *inhabited, insecure, unproductive, indetermined, imprecise*, and *uncertain* are words that Solà-Morales uses to describe how the *terrain vague* is perceived in relation to the ordered city. Strange spaces (strange to the urban system), they place the negative of the city at the very core of what they deny.

Inhabitance of an archival city

There are recurrences, repetitions, and absences when it comes to which places in the city are filmed and how they are filmed. I return to the timeline and begin to see how these recurrences echo in the shots' frames (*cadres*). I start asking about what is filmed in each space, and how it is filmed, and whether there are recurrences in this regard. I start to ask about the performative aspect of what I am seeing – and under "performance" I include both the gestures made in front of the camera and the gesture of the camera itself.[14] I begin to realise that following the representation of space in this home movie archive allows us to see how physical spaces change over time, but it also allows for an account of the performative transformation of one particular space: how it is filmed and how bodies occupy and act in it (how they inhabit it).

The first thing that stands out is the repetition at the level of shot composition: the same perspectives on the same place, the same camera movements over the same subjects.

In the repetition of the frame, I begin by noticing the city's transformation: the same take on the same statue, in shots taken 30 years apart, allows us to witness the rising of new buildings in a once open and clear area.[15]

I notice a change in the types of vehicles circulating around this statue, situated at the intersection of some of the biggest avenues in Lisbon (Marquês de Pombal). I notice one or two bicycles and the absence of crosswalks, due to which pedestrians walk in a disordered way in the older collections – an absence of order of which the city of today has no memory – except, I suddenly realise, in some of the areas of which there are no images in this home movie archive, in the eastern part of Lisbon, which is known for being interrupted by large highways and where walkways are carved out by pedestrians' footsteps and do not appear on official maps.

Several sequences filmed around the same statue draw my attention not only to the transformations undergone by the city but also to transformations in terms of composition: the insistent vertical panoramic movements

Figure 13.2 Two shots of the same detail of Marquês de Pombal statue filmed in different decades.

Source: Author.

Figure 13.3 Frames of similar camera movements found in different home movies.
Source: Author.

in the older collections give way to zooming out in the images taken around the 1970s.[16]

I begin to pay attention to the inhabitation of space.[17] Around the same statue, I see the quiet traffic, a big empty garden, a green boulevard that occupies one of the axes flowing out into the intersection (Parque Eduardo VII), replaced by a disorderly occupation in the 1970s, particularly in the time surrounding the Revolution (around 1974).

In the images taken in 1974, we see an inscription on the statue of which there is no sign today ("No one can silence the voice of the working class").

One of the most intense colour overlays on the map drawn in Figure 13.4 signals the territory of the so-called New Avenues (Avenidas Novas) in Lisbon, built around the 1940s under the rule of Estado Novo ("New State"), the fascist regime that governed in Portugal from 1933 to 1974. We see strolls and leisurely, happy times, as well as recurrent shots of family members rowing around the lake in Campo Grande Garden, which lies at the centre of the New Avenues.

Trips to foreign places are one of the most recurrent themes in this home movie archive. People tend to film outside their homes, in extraordinary moments and situations, in times of fun, leisure, and rest (interruptions). When it comes to the city of Lisbon, this exact impulse finds its expression in the New Avenues: the same themes and situations repeat themselves in the images taken in this area, filmed as if it were a space in a foreign city, with portraits of people touring in a leisurely atmosphere. To visit the New Avenues is to make an exception: it is a space for the amateur.

A more thorough and broad analysis of these home movies would shed important light on the ways in which, and the extent to which, the city's

Drifting through Lisbon in a home movie archive 207

Figure 13.4 Frames of the same space filmed in different decades.
Source: Author.

design influences how it is inhabited. Even if in this methodological exercise I must restrict myself to the level of questions, I return to the images, looking for traces of this pressure.

The unrolling images remind me of a film that played an important role in the fixation of a certain image of Lisbon (one that remains quite dominant to this day, as most postcards sold in the city confirm): *Lisboa, Crónica Anedótica*, made in 1930 by Leitão de Barros, a filmmaker but also a choreographer of public demonstrations during Estado Novo – choreographic work that has driven a Portuguese researcher, Afonso Cortez, to sharply propose that at this time the country itself was turned into a film by Leitão de Barros in which the Portuguese people were stage-managed as extras. During the Estado Novo regime, the real city, the streets, was treated as an enormous set or studio.[18] An order was evident in these designed public demonstrations but also in Leitão de Barros's film: a sequencing of picturesque scenes, announced in an intertitle as documental and starring what, thanks in part to the film, have come to be viewed as "typical" Lisboetas.

Not only are there recurrences in terms of the spaces filmed and the perspectives from which they are filmed, but certain themes and atmospheres repeat themselves as well: the shots taken from the Santa Justa Lift over Rossio; the narrow, oblique streets with laundry hung from one side to the other; elderly people dressed in black; poor and transient people in the old downtown; men and women selling fish near the river at Cais do Sodré; modern public transport in the newer parts of town; the gardens and organised streets in the New Avenues. The places portrayed and the path through the city carved out by *Lisboa, Crónica Anedótica* are very much the same as those found in this home movie archive.

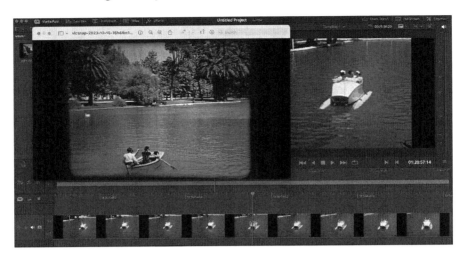

Figure 13.5 Shots of people rowing at Campo Grande Garden's lake, from two different home movie collections.
Source: Author.

This exercise would have to be extended further to allow for sustained conclusions, but from this small sample and exercise in montage we can identify traces of the picturesque,[19] which indicates the perseverance of a hegemonic image of the city that is sustained over time. The absence of suburbs or *terrains vagues* in this home movie archive, associated with the search for the picturesque, suggests an expansion of the notion of the "centre" to the scope of image construction: the hegemony of ordered city spaces finds a parallel in a hegemonic mode of representation. While it is difficult (and perhaps even unfruitful) to try to understand whether it is the image that establishes the centre (or what is central) or the other way around (whether people tend to film in an established and official urbanistic centre), there is in any case a close connection between the two.

Montage, access to an unconscious city

There is an exception in the sample used to design the map shown in Figure 13.8, however, that corresponds to an exception in the archive as a whole: marked in black are images that, even though they are produced in the same spaces as all the others, are concentrated in the folds of this centrality (both spatial and imagetic). This becomes clear when we consider a space such as Monsanto (a big forest area located on one of Lisbon's hills, planted by the Estado Novo regime). In most of the images filmed there, the filmmakers are looking for particular, wide (and picturesque) views over Lisbon: they film the landscape. They do not *film* Monsanto; they film *from* Monsanto. This exceptional collection on the other hand captures the inhabitants of this

Drifting through Lisbon in a home movie archive 209

Figure 13.6 Frames taken from home movie collections and *Lisboa, Crónica Anedótica*.
Source: Author.

Figure 13.7 Frames taken from home movie collections and *Lisboa, Crónica Anedótica*.
Source: Author.

green and (also) exceptional space, mostly removed from the daily life of the city. The filmmaker captures the sex workers and the furtive encounters that take place there, precisely removed and out of sight. The same happens in the rest of this collection: the filmmaker concentrates on what remains invisible, even if it inhabits the centre of the city.

210 *Rethinking the City*

Figure 13.8 Views over Monsanto taken from home movies and *Lisboa, Crónica Anedótica*.

Source: Author.

It is the montage, the juxtaposing of images shot in the same place or area, that makes this exception visible. The succession of repetitions makes the exceptional clearer. It reveals the city's unconscious, an unconscious in its inhabitancy and in its representation, and the unconscious of the archive.[20] The possibility of seeing recurrences, radical differences, absences that wouldn't otherwise be visible is made possible by montage: it is a heuristic tool, here, as it is in an atlas.

With regard to the sequencing principle of the atlas, authors such as Georges Didi-Huberman, Philippe-Alain Michaud, Christian Jacob, and Teresa Castro tend to consider the atlas a mechanism founded in movement – especially in their commentaries on Aby Warburg's *Atlas Mnemosyne*. Although atlases were initially a way of organising geographic reasoning through images (a sequence of maps), they have become a particular way of mapping (a space, more or less abstract) through images, a mechanism characterised by accumulation and sequencing which results in a *table* – the atlas maintains the diagrammatic root of the map. As a way of thinking through space, a voyage of vision,[21] the atlas is also a way of creating a path among images. It is a way of dealing with the immensity, the virtual infinity, of the archive,[22] a way of creating a path through this immensity, a way of dealing with chaos.[23]

In *Atlas Mnemosyne*, Aby Warburg researches the permanence of certain forms (the *(e)motion(al)* forms of *pathos*) in Western culture. To this end, he engages in a radical exercise: he takes pictures (from very different sources – painting, photography, publicity, his own personal archive)

Drifting through Lisbon in a home movie archive 211

and fragments of pictures and displays them on blackboards, shifting their arrangement according to a particular argument (the *Atlas* was never closed or fixed; in Warburg's lifetime, it was arranged according to his current reasoning or the current phase of his ongoing research). The act of extracting an image from its context, fragmenting it, and arranging it among others was key to fulfilling his desire to write a "history of art without text".[24] His method – seeing through montage – is described by Didi-Huberman as a way of putting images and thought back into movement where history has stopped[25] and by Nélio Conceição as a potential tool for accessing what can be called an "unconscious life of culture".[26] Fragmentation and montage are, in the atlas, a way of accessing what would otherwise remain under the surface of the unstoppable flux of images and life.

The same kind of extraction was key to the exercise described earlier:[27] the observed recurrences and repetitions would remain invisible if the images assembled here did not gain autonomy in relation to the sequences and film reels from which they come and in relation to the discourses families produce about them.

Drawing emotional maps of a past city

Following the impulse of the path that the identification of the atlas opens up (a voyage in images), I turn to the first map I have drawn and again follow the images to which it points. This time, I begin to attend not so much to those spaces that were repeatedly and recurrently filmed (and those that are

Figure 13.9 Frames with different views of and from Monsanto.
Source: Author.

absent) but to the connections between them. When different spaces appear contiguously in one and the same sequence (one reel in the original material), I signal this on the map – I draw the circulation in the film strip as if it were a circulation in a particular, specific, filmic city. I traverse the filmed city following the filmic (and filming) bodies in transit. I draw a (visual) path using the filmed (material) paths.

I begin to imagine a new map of Lisbon, made up of these connections, wondering if a psychogeographic map could be drawn on the basis of the materials provided by this archive: a map that is attentive to the relations that people – who both film and are filmed – establish with the spaces captured and the affinities they themselves establish between them.

In 1968, Guy Debord systematised his "theory of drifting", a fundamental situationist procedure. He defines drifting as a technique used for identifying the psychogeographic reasons that lead an individual to choose one path through a city over another. This theory is based on the observations of an experiment (a situational experiment, which literally starts with a created situation): a group of people are gathered in a certain space of the city and are left to circulate from that spot without a pre-defined path or endpoint (the group members are invited to leave to the side the considerations that would usually guide their decision to choose one direction over another). Guy Debord proposes that we examine the choices made by this group as they circulate and that we account for the influence of the ecology, microclimates, design, and environments of particular neighbourhoods (cuts in the urban texture), paying special attention (he says) to the overwhelming attraction of city centres for urban inhabitants and strollers. Maps are drawn out of these drifts, and new, transitory cities are imagined and designed on their basis. This is a technique for studying the psychogeographic textures of the city, a way of observing the city's fixed points and what Debord calls its "whirlpools", those points that make it difficult for one to get out. It is a way of observing the emotional (Debord uses the word "*passionel*") links an individual establishes with urban space – links that constitute emotional maps in which the real buildings appear closer, or further apart, and certain zones are extended, shrink, or are absent.

Although, as a method for studying the city of the present, psychogeography can influence how we design the cities of the future (particularly as practised by Guy Debord and his situationist companions), in light of the earlier experiment I began to wonder whether the same method couldn't be used to study an archival city, a city of the past, and whether, on the basis of this study, the same desire Debord expresses here could be projected onto a city of the present:

> The comrades who call for a new, free architecture must understand that this new architecture will primarily be based not on free, poetic lines and forms . . . but rather on the atmospheric effects of rooms, hallways, streets – atmospheres linked to the activities they contain. Architecture must advance by taking emotionally moving situations,

Figure 13.10 Map of the routes identified in the home movie archive.
Source: Author.

rather than emotionally moving forms, as the material it works with. And the experiments conducted with this material will lead to new, as yet unknown forms.[28]

The atlas is a psychogeographic map (and vice versa)

The home movie archive is made up of silent moving images that, while not arranged in a film, take up the length of a film reel. The images are sequenced as they were filmed, close to the particular path carved out by the filmmaker in the reality of space. Each cut is the eye closing – *this I don't want to see, this I don't want to remember, this is not worth remembering*. There is thus a psychogeographic principle that organises these paths, this closing of the eyes.

Only because of this closeness between the act of filming and the order we see in the filmed images can we consider the possibility of drawing a psychogeographic map using the materials provided by this archive. Although they are not drifting in Debord's strict sense of the term, the repetition of some spaces and the absence of others account for the emotional ties filmmakers have with the spaces they film. Connecting psychogeography to the atlas may allow us to realise the way in which the representation of a city (the hegemonic mode of representation of the city) influences how it is inhabited.

Drifting, for its part, is a suitable word to describe my own movement through the images of this home movie archive – a path constructed by the images I see, by the jumps I make in the disordered timeline, guided by memory and by chance – *this image reminds me of that one* (in this archive or in another). The atlas is a psychogeographic map, and vice versa – both are based on an act of fragmentation and a re-mapping. They join the two parallel strolls undertaken in this exercise – the one drawn using the materials in the archive and the one found within it.

Acknowledgements

The editing of this chapter was supported by funds from the FCT – Fundação para a Ciência e a Tecnologia, under the project UIDP/00183/2020.

Notes

1. In the introduction to *Uplift Cinema*, Alyson Field reads Giuliana Bruno's *Streetwalking on a Ruined Map* to examine the archaeological impulse of "digging through layers of sediment left by time; excavating among ruins; reconstructing fragments; and imagining the past through its artifacts, detritus, and ephemera". She invites us to stay with "the presence of absence" to address what has been lost. Researching the emergence of Black filmmaking around the 1910s, she discovers a nonextant film history. As she concludes: "[f]or those of us who study nonextant films, absence is the archive" (Field, *Uplift Cinema*, 24–25).
2. Bruno, *Streetwalking on a Ruined Map*, 4.
3. Exploring the archive of the term at the origin of the word "archive" – the Greek term *arkhe* – Jacques Derrida proposes a systematisation that remains influential to this day. He describes the archive as the *place* "where things commence" and in "which order is given". In his lecture, published under the French title "Mal d'archive", Derrida underscores terms related to place, defining the archive as the site of a particular *topology*. He defines it as "a house, a domicile, an address". This identification of archive with place (or *topos*) relates to Bruno's wish to situate geography at the core of history and sustains the possibility of conceiving of the archive as something that is likely to be traversed, as articulated in this chapter. See Derrida, "Archive Fever", 9–63.
4. Ibid., 10.
5. In *Le Temps Exposé: le cinéma de la salle au musée*, Dominique Païni uses the word "fatality" to describe what the regime of projection imposes on the cinematic image, which is linked, ontologically, to a narrative sequencing: cinematic images *kill* each other as they unroll on the screen on which they are projected (my words); the illusion of movement that defines the cinematic image is produced by the sequencing of frames, and the film is a sequence of shots.
6. The term "orphan film" was coined in the 1990s and was used in the film archival milieu to refer to moving images produced outside the commercial or professional sphere and without a known copyright holder. The first Orphan Film Symposium took place at the University of South Carolina in 1999 and was organised

by Dan Streible, who is mainly responsible for the stabilisation of the term (see Streible, "The State of Orphan Films"). Around that time, Eye (Vienna's Film Museum) initiated the project and collection "Bits and Pieces", in which short bits of unknown films are preserved and sometimes worked with in different montage exercises: www.eyefilm.nl/en/collection/collections/film/bits-pieces (accessed October 2023). It was also in the 1990s that home movies began to be considered by film scholars and archivists as a material bounty to be studied and preserved. By that time, around 99 per cent of these films had already been lost.
7 Zimmerman and Ishizuka, *Mining the Home Movie*, 278.
8 Ibid., 1.
9 Brakhage, "In Defense of Amateur", 165.
10 Pasolini, "Observations on the Long Take", 6.
11 Theorists and historians of the primitive moving image have thoroughly examined the consequences of montage for the creation of an illusory or fictional filmic time and space. For an introduction to this theme, see, for instance, Noël Burch's, *La lucarne et l'infini*.
12 Odin, *Le film de famille*.
13 Álvaro Domingues, a Portuguese anthropogeographer, systematised both this notion and the literature on this theme, enumerating some of the most influential publications from these years (in a text written (also) in 1995): *Disappearing City* (Peter Hall, 1990), *Edge City* (J. Garreau, 1991), *100 Mile City* (Deyan Sudjic, 1992), *Non-Place* (Marc Augé, 1992), *Fractured Metropolis* (Jonathan Barnet, 1995), and *Metropolis* (François Ascher, 1995). See Domingues, "(Sub)úrbios e (sub)urbanos".
14 If the gesture is key to understanding the cinematic image, particularly concerning interferences between what is in front and what is behind the camera (something that is stressed by João Mário Grilo in a wonderful text titled "Proposições para um cinema do gesto. O corpo do cinema a partir de uma leitura de Giorgio Agamben", where he comments on the discoveries Jean Rouch made when he lost his tripod at a shoot in Africa), it becomes an even more productive category in home movies, where the interaction with the subject is particularly strong. The pose is a knot in this interaction, as it makes visible how in some measure the image is also constructed and controlled by those who are filmed, not only by the person filming them. Related to their *amator* root, there is a predominance of subject over creation in home movies (which, alongside the absence of montage, may lead us to question the use of the category of the "author" to refer to this cinema).
15 François Penz and Andong Lu point out the importance of amateur filmmaking as an archaeological source for the study of the transformation of space and its representation. Although their reflection is an important reference for this chapter, my aim here is to try to understand whether we find in home movies traces of the emotional relationship that individuals maintain with city spaces – and the ways in which this relationship is influenced by urban design and modes of representation.
16 Both types of camera movements are ways of drawing a path of vision (*déroulement*) in space and in time, a drawing that Teresa Castro describes in her *La pensée cartographique des images*. They are both ways of "touching space with the eyes" (Castro, *La pensée cartographique des images*, 71 – my translation) and of traversing space without moving or shifting one's axis. Both are based on a "desire to appropriate the world through image", which Castro (Ibid., 51) associates with the first of these movements in particular (the panoramic). And if filming one's own family can be described as a way of controlling (a future) discourse (on the past), a way of imposing order on memory, the same can be said of

216 Rethinking the City

space: filming is a way of controlling space, first and foremost by framing. Both the panoramic and the zoom contribute to an expansion of this control over space by the eye.

17 At a conference held by the Faculty of Architecture of the University of Rome in 2018, Giorgio Agamben defined inhabiting as an act of creation, of conservation, and of intensification of habits and ways of being (the word "inhabit" stems from the Latin term *habitare*, which has its roots in *habeo*, "to have"). Agamben destabilises the meaning of this verb and, reading Émile Benveniste, underscores the languages in which this verb does not exist and is substituted by expressions such as "to be/being at" or "be from". To inhabit, here, is to create and to belong to a space that, through inhabitation, comes close to being a territory, even if an ephemeral one. A parallel can be drawn between space and the shot: the latter contributes to transforming space into territory, which we can relate to what Susan Sontag says about family photography in the hands of the tourist: the camera becomes a mechanism of power and control over the anxiety of being in a foreign, strange, insecure space (Sontag, "In Plato's Cave", 8). Agamben's conference can be found at: www.quodlibet.it/giorgio-agamben-abitare-e-costruire (accessed October 2023).

18 These images, taken at the same location at different times, show that the city now bears greater resemblance (in terms of its organisation) to the images taken during the Estado Novo regime, where the occupation of public space was ordered and choreographed, than to those taken during the revolutionary times of 1974 (when people occupied the streets and open spaces in a disordered way).

19 The picturesque is closely related to the "invention of landscape" (see Cauquelin, *L'invention du paysage*). Its constitution depends on an act of recognition and so on memory (Castro, *La pensée cartographique des images*, 71). It is a way of seeing and of recognising the picture in the land – the same type of vision movement that makes a space a landscape. It is a way of turning space into spectacle and of projecting art into nature (the garden is a concrete actualisation of this projection). On the garden, see Assunto, *Il paesaggio e l'estetica*. In one of its intertitles, *Lisboa, Crónica Anedótica* explicitly mentions that it is portraying the picturesque aspects of the city.

20 I consider the city's unconscious in Sapeta Dias, "Os baldios de *O fantasma*".

21 Castro, *La pensée cartographique des images*, 166 (quoting Christian Jacob).

22 This is pointed out by Teresa Castro in the interview included in *Atlas de um cinema Amador – cartografia do descartado* (Atlas of an amateur cinema – cartography of the discarded) (2021), the first episode of a series I directed with Luisa Homem (produced by Terratreme), which premiered at Cinema Batalha, Porto (May 2023).

23 Conceição, "The Productive Disorder of the Atlas", 135 (quoting Gilles Deleuze and Felix Guattari).

24 Castro, *La pensée cartographique des images*, 171.

25 Didi-Huberman, *Atlas, or the Anxious Gay Science*, 12.

26 Conceição, "The Productive Disorder of the Atlas", 148.

27 In *Lost Landscapes*, Paolo Simoni (one of the founders of the Archivio Nazionale dei Film di Famiglia (Home Movie National Archive), Bologna, one of the few archives in the world exclusively dedicated to the preservation and study of these films) poses a question that I am also posing here: which city appears in a home movie archive? Paolo Simoni reclaims and preserves the authorship of the home movies he analyses in his study, which is one of the main differences between his work and the exercise I am conducting here.

28 Debord, *Rapport sur la construction des situations*, 34–35 (my translation).

Bibliography

Assunto, Rosario, *Il paesaggio e l'estetica*, Palermo: Novecento, 2005.
Brakhage, Stan, "In Defense of Amateur", in *Brakhage Scrapbook: Stan Brakhage, Collected Writings 1964–1980*, edited by Robert Haller, 162–168, New York: Documentext, 1982.
Bruno, Giuliana, *Streetwalking on a Ruined Map: Cultural Theory and the City Films of Elvira Notari*, Princeton University Press, 1998.
Burch, Nöel, *La lucarne et l'infini (naissance du langage cinématographique)*, Paris: L'Harmattan, 2007.
Castro, Teresa, *La pensée cartographique des images*, Lyon: Aléas, 2011.
Cauquelin, Anne, *L'invention du paysage*, Paris: Plon, 1989.
Conceição, Nélio, "The Productive Disorder of the Atlas", in *Conceptual Figures of Fragmentation and Reconfiguration*, edited by Nélio Conceição, Gianfranco Ferraro, Nuno Fonseca, Alexandra Dias Fortes and Maria Filomena Molder, 131–154, Lisbon: IFILNOVA, 2021.
Cortez, Afonso, "Portugal (1928–1968): Um Filme de J. Leitão de Barros", PhD thesis, Nova University of Lisbon, 2015.
Debord, Guy, "Théorie de la dérive", *Les Lèvres nues*, no. 9 (1956): 251–257.
Debord, Guy, *Rapport sur la construction des situations et sur les conditions de l'organisation et de l'action de la tendance situationniste internationale*, Paris: 1001 nuits, 1997.
Derrida, Jacques, "Archive Fever: A Freudian Impression", *Diacritics* 25, no. 2 (1995): 9–63.
Didi-Huberman, Georges, *Atlas, or the Anxious Gay Science*, translated by Shane Lillis, Chicago/London: The University of Chicago Press, 2018.
Domingues, Álvaro, "(Sub)úrbios e (sub)urbanos – o mal estar da periferia ou a mistificação dos conceitos?", *Revista da Faculdade de Letras – Geografia, I série* 10, no. 11 (1994): 5–18.
Field, Alyson, *Uplift Cinema: The Emergence of African American Film and the Possibility of Black Modernity*, Durnham: Duke University Press, 2015.
Grilo, João Mário, "Proposições para um cinema do gesto. O corpo do cinema a partir de uma leitura de Giorgio Agamben", in *Cinema & Filosofia: Compêndio*, edited by João Mário Grilo and Maria Irene Aparício, 267–282, Lisboa: Colibri, 2013.
Jacob, Christian, *The Sovereign Map: Theoretical Approaches in Cartography throughout History*, translated by Tom Conley, Chicago: The University of Chicago Press, 2006.
Michaud, Phillippe-Alain, *Aby Warburg et l'image en mouvement*, Paris: Macula, 1998.
Odin, Roger, *Le film de famille. Usage privé, usage public*, Paris: Méridiens Klincksieck, 1995.
Païni, Dominique, *Le Temps Exposé: le cinéma de la salle au musée*, Paris: Cahiers du Cinéma, 2002.
Pasolini, Pier Paolo, "Observations on the Long Take", translated by Norman MacAfee and Craig Owens, *October* 13 (1980): 3–6. https://doi.org/10.2307/3397696.
Penz, François and Andong Lu, "Introduction: What is Urban Cinematics?", in *Urban Cinematics: Understanding Urban Phenomena through the Moving Image*, edited by François Penz and Andong Lu, 7–19, Bristol: Intellect, 2011.
Sapeta Dias, Inês, "Os baldios de *O fantasma*, ou da natureza como inconsciente (reprimido) da cidade", in *Cinema e Natureza*, edited by Filipa Rosário and José Duarte, Lisbon: Sistema Solar, 2024.
Simoni, Paolo, *Lost Landscapes: Il cinema amatoriale e la città*, Turim: Edizioni Kaplan, 2020.

Solà-Morales, Ignasi, "Terrain Vague", in *Anyplace*, edited by Cynthia Davidson, 118–123, Cambridge: MIT Press, 1995.

Sontag, Susan, "In Plato's Cave", in *On Photography*, 3–26, London: Penguin books, 2008.

Streible, Dan, "The State of Orphan Films: Editor's Introduction", *The Moving Image* 9, no. 1 (2009): vi–xix. www.jstor.org/stable/41167314

Zimmerman, Patricia, *Reel Families: A Social History of Amateur Film*, Indianapolis: Indiana University Press, 1995.

Zimmerman, Patricia and Karen L. Ishizuka, eds., *Mining the Home Movie: Excavations in Histories and Memories*, Berkeley: University of California Press, 2008.

14 The periphery is not where the city ends but where it begins to unfurl

Contributions to an architecture of the metropolis from Renaudie and Gailhoustet to Druot, Lacaton and Vassal

João Gonçalves Paupério

Introduction

What does it mean to live in the periphery? Are there specific forms of life arising from *or* within urban peripheries? Is it possible for these cultural specificities to inform new approaches to architecture? And finally, in a dialectical inversion, is it possible for these architectures to activate new forms of life? The aim of this chapter is to address these questions without necessarily formulating definitive answers by framing within the *longue durée* of history two relevant case studies that belong to the history of Parisian urbanism and architecture, namely the work of Jean Renaudie and Renée Gailhoustet during the 1960s and 1970s and the work of Frédéric Druot, Anne Lacaton and Jean-Phillipe Vassal since the early 2000s. Although these examples are considerably distant from each other both temporally and geographically, both address and rely on a finer reading of reality in their approaches to architectural design, which are largely a response to the social, political and ecological issues of the contemporary metropolis.

The invention of the *banlieue(s)*

Translations of the French term *banlieue*, which generally refers to the peripheries or suburban areas in the outskirts of cities, are often unsatisfactory from a conceptual point of view, in particular given that its meaning has changed throughout history and according to the geographical context to which it refers. Urban peripheries, namely those of the metropolitan agglomeration of Paris, are complex, fragmented and heterogeneous, from both a social and a spatial point of view. Historically, however, the word *banlieue* has consistently evoked an entity that is *in continuity* with the city yet *other* than itself and is often imbued with a pejorative connotation. This negativity has characterised perceptions of French urban peripheries: as the areas surrounding the gates of city walls became increasingly urbanised, earning them the moniker *faubourgs*,[1] these urban fringes were increasingly "perceived by the people of the city as a distant and particular territory".[2] Under the seal of rurality, one could

> begin to see the images of the periods to come taking shape: that of the mother-city, whose decisions weigh heavily on local life, and that of a very useful appendage to this city, but one that is discredited, and considered to be without qualities.[3]

In reality, the landscape of urban peripheries is complex and contradictory, which means that a strictly negative understanding of urban peripheries is a simplification and does not wholly correspond to their concrete reality. Located between the city and the countryside, *banlieues* were places of ambivalence from the early days. Their consolidation was carried out at the expense of populations that migrated both *from* and *into* city centres. The former concerned not only the lower classes in search of labour but also the upper classes, who found in the picturesqueness of certain *banlieues* an appealing place to spend their weekends or holidays,[4] building second homes there and contributing to the contradictory nature of the outskirts of Paris. While the ambiguous character of the *banlieue* is a topic of great interest, in this chapter I will focus particularly on another type of working-class periphery, known to have formed a *ceinture rouge* (red belt) around Paris.

At least until the mid-19th century, the perception of the *banlieue* as a mostly rural space prevailed.[5] As the Industrial Revolution took hold, however, the morphology and social composition – that is the landscape – of the Parisian outskirts began to transform. Despite the historical ambiguity at the heart of the use and perception of the periphery of Paris – its dual nature as a spot of both leisure and misery – from early on this was where the city put what it considered undesirable (from the perspective of both the hygienist ideology and an endeavour to maintain political stability) while equally remaining indispensable to the economic development and sociotechnical progress of the city proper.

In the final years of the *Ancien Régime*, plans were made to build cemeteries, hospitals, slaughterhouses, prisons, and other hotbeds of infection and pollution on the fringes of the urban fabric.[6] As the Industrial Revolution progressed, a similar criterion was applied to the establishment of large industrial facilities.[7] As a result, the negative connotations of the urban peripheries were amplified by the development of capitalism and the rise of a new industrial working class that would come, in centrifugal and centripetal migratory waves, to settle and live in the outskirts of the city. The urban reorganisation of the Parisian fringes was accentuated and accelerated from the 18th century onwards. Migratory waves were triggered both by renovation works (referred to as *embellissement*), such as that undertaken by Baron Haussmann in the city centre[8] and by a growing rural exodus which led masses of people from the provinces to industrialised cities in search of work. This urbanisation process resulted from a simultaneous concentration and "deconcentration" of employment within the Parisian agglomeration.[9]

These fluxes, the "demographic explosion"[10] they provoked and the precarious working and living conditions in which these populations found themselves consolidated the peripheries' reputation as places of poverty and deprivation. Populated by flows of people from different places and cultures (both in France and abroad), this reorganisation resulted in a significant level of social diversity, generating a mixed social geography composed of the original inhabitants of local communities (essentially devoted to cultivating and providing for the subsistence of Paris), sectors of the working class who had been expelled from the city centre, and an uprooted rural population who, no longer able to live off the land, were forced to join the ranks of a new industrial working class known as the "proletariat".[11] This social heterogeneity was reflected in the fragmented landscape that resulted from the urbanisation of once rural villages, making it difficult to ascribe a single meaning to the spaces of the *banlieue*. On the contrary, urban peripheries were places where rurality and urbanity met, and the city began to unfurl. For our purposes here, it is thus useful to consider this phenomenon through the lens of three intertwined images: (1) a *banlieue noir* (a dark periphery); (2) a *banlieue rouge* (a red periphery) and (3) a *banlieue verte* (a green periphery).[12]

The first of these refers to the importance of industrial activities and facilities in the configuration of suburban landscapes and to the slums, shantytowns and other forms of cramped and undignified housing that these industries mobilised around themselves. The second refers to the forms of social and political organisation, both socialist and communist in nature, which resulted from the former and which were instrumental to reorganising the landscape in more equitable terms. Finally, the latter refers not to the public parks created by Napoléon III or to the gardens in the "bourgeois" suburbs but, first and foremost, to the productive "working-class gardens" that arose from popular culture in the interstices of industrial peripheries and their suburban misery.

When the metropolis shatters, roots begin to grow

> These evocations have the character of a cry for help. Terraces have sprung up above some low-income neighbourhoods, where the tradition of working-class gardens is once again taking root.[13]

As the demography of Paris and its outskirts progressed at the pace of this industrial reorganisation of the landscape, working-class housing, that is, its scarcity and precariousness, became a pressing matter. Until the first years of the 20th century, the problem of housing was delegated to the workers themselves.[14] Solutions ranged from the construction of shacks in derelict areas to tenancy in unfit, overpopulated dwellings built by real estate speculators in more or less consolidated areas of the city.

In search of more space (i.e., of more square metres, but also more light and air), urban peripheries further from the city centre became a promised land for the fulfilment of this aspiration. At the turn of the century, housing became a concern not only of the workers themselves but of political leaders across the spectrum, from left, to right, from revolutionary syndicalism[15] to social Catholicism.[16] For both, the question of housing had parallels with the question of land. To address the social and moral implications of capitalism for a dispossessed working class, patronage and paternalistic politicians felt an urgent need to reconcile workers with the factory, through securing them not only a house of their own but also a piece of land they could farm in their spare time.[17]

Alongside the house itself, this piece of land would acquire both an ideological and a material importance. On the one hand, it fulfilled the moralising goal of keeping the working class away from the café and the cabaret, as well as from the political radicalisation that was growing in the peripheries.[18] On the other hand, it met hygienist concerns[19] regarding the increasing pollution of the city. Finally, it allowed patronage to reduce salaries by minimising the existential precariousness of workers through food and self-sufficiency.

To counterbalance the inability of both employers and the state to address the true scale of the housing problem, "working-class gardens" were created by religious and philanthropic institutions, as well as other forms of civic association,[20] as a palliative measure. Combining a form of collective property with personal ownership, these allotments became, as Cabedoce describes, places of strong sociability and popular culture which were "part of the landscape of these peripheries and of the space of the people who lived there". They represented,

> for people who had recently emigrated from rural areas, a means of maintaining contact with the land and, for them as for the Parisians driven out of the capital, a means of adapting to a new space, both urban and rural.[21]

Moreover, apart from their contribution to subsistence, these gardens served as an outdoor space where workers could spend their free time,[22] using the pavilion or the self-built pergola as an extension of their own home.

This in-between culture left its mark on the housing aspirations of the working class, and the correlation between the house and the garden became instrumental to the reorganisation of the suburban landscape.[23] In the early decades of the 20th century, allotments were set up by private initiatives for the construction of workers' pavilions in the outlying peripheries. Later, in response to the crisis of defective allotments, the *Office Public de Habitation Bon Marché* was created, and, under the influence of English garden cities and the direction of socialist politicians such as Henri Sellier, the first garden cities for the French working class were built during the interwar decades.[24]

The city and combinatorics: a geometry of fragmentation

Conversely, during the years following World War II, the issue was far from resolved. The urgent need to address housing and the scale of the problem shifted the ideological pendulum, guiding social housing towards the spheres of rationalisation, standardisation and normativity. These were materialised in towers and long housing blocks known as "grands ensembles",[25] mostly inspired by the modernist principles of the Athens Charter.[26] Over the following three decades, the average quality of popular housing increased, but its production conditions were bureaucratised and incorporated rationales that were similar to ongoing state-led capitalist developments. This meant respecting the principles of analytical and economic reasoning, such as the typification and division of functions, on both a domestic and an urban scale, with material implications for the landscape of the *banlieues*.[27]

It was in this context of promoting the construction of large housing estates on the outskirts of Paris that the work of Jean Renaudie, Renée Gailhoustet and Nina Schuch found fertile ground in Ivry-sur-Seine, an important commune in the history of both the *banlieue rouge*[28] and the *banlieue verte*.[29]

A masterplan for the urban renewal of the city centre was initially carried out by Roland Dubrulle, who developed his work along the functionalist typological guidelines of the *grands ensembles*. When Dubrulle stepped down, the post was taken up by Renée Gailhoustet, who in turn convinced the city administration to invite Jean Renaudie to be the person responsible for continuing the project in 1970. The latter had been part of *Atelier de Montrouge*,[30] from which he had split after political disagreements in May 1968, exacerbating ideological conflicts which became clear during the drafting of the proposal they designed in the same year for the new town of Le Vaudreuil.[31]

As Scalbert observes, to be a communist at the time was to belong to the avant-garde. Therefore, communist municipal management provided the ideal objective and subjective conditions in which communist architects could develop their designs.[32] Following the theoretical principles he had been germinating in his later years at *Atelier de Montrouge*, Renaudie sought to incorporate into his architecture the complex and intricate nature of the city, the design of which was meant to combine and superimpose the multiplicity of human needs, including indeterminate ones. In light of this end, the principle of separation promoted by zonal planning in the Athens Charter was considered obsolete.[33]

The design process for the urban renewal of Ivry involved the participation of the local population,[34] whom Renaudie believed to be perfectly capable of critically judging the outcome of collective housing projects, popularly known as "rabbit cages".[35] For Jean Renaudie, who led this process, architecture and urbanism were inseparable. Against this logic of rationalising and designing for just one type of person or family, the result of which was the aforementioned "rabbit cages", Renaudie and Gailhoustet's masterplan aimed to produce an architecture that was capable of responding to and combining popular diversity. From Renaudie's perspective, it is a mistake to suppose that people come in just one type. Thus, he claimed,

> [i]t is impossible to imagine that there is a single solution, a standard solution, which responds to such concerns. The need for diversity must be satisfied as much as possible: no two identical families will live in these dwellings, and the inter-family relations or relations between inhabitants do not correspond to simplistic, pre-determined models.[36]

In the design for Ivry, every apartment expresses its singularity, and the interior of each provides access to at least one individual garden. From the outside, in a tension between order and disorder, their oblique forms allow these outdoor spaces to communicate with each other while ensuring the necessary distance from their neighbours. Inside, these enable compartments to interconnect, making spaces with reduced surfaces feel larger and allowing them to escape predetermined functions. This amplitude of space is strengthened by the fact that most apartments are duplexes, with perforations in the slab that allow light and air to circulate through double-height ceilings.[37]

The grandson of peasants, Renaudie was not a stranger to the roots of popular culture.[38] In 1980, as the urban renewal of another working-class town was being completed in Givors, on the outskirts of Lyon, he wrote a text on the importance of garden terraces in these buildings.[39] According to him,

> practically all the inhabitants of these apartments have wanted a terrace, in so far as the idea of a garden is connected to all sorts of childhood. . . . It's an extraordinary experience to see a plant you yourself have chosen, grow or die.[40]

For the author, these terraces connected the apartments to the city. This was true not only from a formal point of view but in the sense of providing an intimate space between the individual and the collective. Their geometry sought to foster a sociability that resonated with the working-class gardens rather than the drawer-like urbanism of towers and bars that was so typical of the post-war era. Its concrete design acted as the support (or structure) upon which citizens could participate in the construction of the city itself. In fact, according to the author, there was "another ambition for the terraces, which takes time to realise: that the inhabitants can transform the building through the things they plant"[41] – a structure, he continued, which "must be the support for imagination".[42]

The same attitude would later be replicated by Renée Gailhoustet in projects for other communes in the Parisian red belt, such as Saint-Denis and Aubervilliers. Regarding the terraces she designed for *La Maladrerie*, a new urban block replacing a *bidonville* in the latter, Gailhoustet considered these spaces not as "complements" but as the foundations of her design. This, she wrote, was because she believed that

> when it comes to a house, a real house, a family house, an individual house, the garden is not a complement. It is almost always what determined the inhabitant's choice: a private domain, the distance from the neighbour, a play area for the children, for drying clothes, for a vegetable garden or for *bricolage*.[43]

This arrangement of flats evoked an idea of the home which to a certain point met the popular and working-class aspiration to own a house with a garden of one's own.[44] Through a finer reading of complexity, such as that characteristic of the Parisian periphery, they pursued a balance between collective and personal space, aiming to dialectically overcome the distance between urbanity and rurality.

"Not tearing down is a strategy"

As Renaudie and Gailhoustet's first designs for Ivry-sur-Seine began to see the light of day, the plan to build *grands ensembles* as a response to mass housing began to recede. Since 1965, urbanisation policies had been leaning towards the programme of creating *villes nouvelles* (new towns) in the countryside, such as the town Renaudie was supposed to design for *Le Vaudreuil* (the construction of which was ultimately blocked by a ministerial decision decreed in 1973).[45]

Faced with the deterioration of HLM (*habitation à loyer modéré*) housing stock, which had been built over the previous three decades, demolition began to be viewed by the state as an increasingly attractive solution to the buildings' technical obsolescence and the social problems with which they were associated. This decision was in keeping with the times; since at least 1972, with the failure of the Pruitt-Igoe complex in Saint-Louis, Missouri, demolition had been considered a legitimate alternative to rehabilitation, even for buildings only two decades old. In France, the renovation of *grands ensembles* included partial demolitions as early as 1978, but the intention had been voiced since 1975.

Throughout the 1970s, the demographics in these quarters changed significantly. As less underprivileged sectors of the working class reached some level of solvency, financially encouraged by the state itself, they sought to exchange these *grands ensembles* for other types of housing, notably single-family pavilions with their own plot of land.[46] As disinvestment in their maintenance grew, the image and reputation of social housing estates deteriorated. As the Société Française d'Histoire Urbaine observes, "the triptych: large housing estates/immigrants/poverty then took root in public opinion without the precise historical contours being known",[47] and this vacancy was used to legitimate demolition. This view marked the perspective of political leaders and their urban policies in the following decades, culminating in 2002 with the Ministry of Social Cohesion's plan to demolish 20,000 dwellings in just five years, an approach that was to be signed into law the following year and which remained in tension with the difficulty that some sectors of the population were having when it came to finding decent housing.[48]

In 2004, commissioned by the Directorate of Architecture and Heritage of the Ministry of Culture and Communication, Frédéric Druot, Anne Lacaton and Jean-Phillipe Vassal conducted a study on the impact of the demolition and reconstruction of new dwellings, namely in the form of single-family houses.[49] From a divergent perspective, which anticipated reflections that would later be developed by sociologists, they concluded that the policy of demolition was a mistake and that "its transformation would allow needs to be addressed more economically, more effectively and more qualitatively".[50] As a design strategy, this represented "recreating the impact of postwar reconstruction, which had initiated the move from insalubrious to salubrious housing, and of instigating the pleasure of living in it".[51] From a radical and pragmatic perspective, their research-turned-manifesto declares that

> the architecture of each suburban block or high-rise [ought to] attain maximum levels of comfort and quality, equal to those seen in the luxury buildings of more elegant neighbourhoods[,] and must guarantee the durability of the buildings in a definitive manner,[52]

as opposed to their demolishment.

To do so, the intervention should make the most of their intrinsic qualities to build more space than would be possible if part of the budget were dedicated to demolitions. The construction of this extra space can be understood in the sense of meeting a common goal which had historically characterised the aspirations of working-class housing: more space, more air and light and securing a piece of land of one's own.

On this issue, Druot, Lacaton and Vassal's research aimed to address the tensions between models of individual and collective housing, concluding that what had fuelled the working class's preference for the former was largely a sense of freedom. This feeling, although ideologically instrumentalised at different times throughout history, was based on proper material reasons. For Jean-Phillipe Vassal,

> "this idea of freedom refers to the fact that there might be a little garden, namely an adaptable space, even if it's not used for anything"; therefore, "when one posits the dwelling, [one] reckon[s] it's necessary to offer the same amount of empty space as spaces with attributed uses".[53]

In fact, for Druot, Lacaton and Vassal, "the discourse on single-family housing [was] not so different from that on communal housing", given the current state of affairs. The dichotomy is irrelevant on the abstract dimension, for "on the one social level, a single-family house is no more than a worse built flat, but positioned in the centre of a small garden".[54] As Frédéric Druot puts it, both are

> already the extremes of the absolute materialisation of a single abstraction. On the one hand, the perfect putting into practice, in a vertical equation, of congestion; on the other, the perfect putting into practice of congestion in a horizontal equation.[55]

To a certain extent, the material conditions that define the qualities of a house in the collective imagination are transposable to the architecture of the *grands ensembles*. In Druot, Lacaton and Vassal's proposals, this is accomplished via the addition of winter gardens to the original building, the character of which is intended to be as polyvalent as a *workshop* or an individual garden. This is one of the assumptions that their theoretical research sought to demonstrate, namely through the collages that illustrate the proposals. These were mostly composed of fragments of mid-century Case Study Houses.[56]

A prototype for the interventions envisioned in *Plus+*, their theoretical research, can be found in the first house designed by Lacaton and Vassal in 1993: la *Maison Latapie*. Designed for a working-class family who previously lived in an apartment in HLM collective housing, the house is, according to Hubert Tonka, a "pavilion of a new type . . . offering for the first time a fabulous art of inhabitation and revolutionary economic conditions".[57] Half a "machine for living in" (to use Le Corbusier's expression, which was dear to the modern movement) and half a (winter) garden of freedom, this single-family house was a laboratory in which ideas about dwelling were unfurled. This exercise provided answers to key issues in collective housing that have since been tested in the refurbishment of *Tour Bois-le-Prêtre*[58] in Paris, demonstrating, as Renaudie and Gailhoustet had previously attempted to show, that density and quality of space are not mutually exclusive and that every dwelling can potentially share the spatial qualities of a villa.

Conclusion

When one reflects upon the *banlieues* of Paris beyond the preconceived notions one may have inherited, in particular those that have historically sheltered the working class, one recognises their multiple and fragmented character. What they have in common is above all their peripheral condition – that is, they are places that both unite and separate the city from what is beneath it, and precisely because of this they have the potential to unfold it. Peripheries are meeting places between distinct physical and social geographies – places which, in a simultaneously centripetal and centrifugal movement, reconstruct themselves in a specific condition. Historically, this movement has been animated by the development of the capitalist city, in a spatial dialectic which operationalises the landscape to extend its urban condition to the rest of the territory. In this process, a rural world whose echoes continue to reverberate was emptied of its rituals to build in its place a city that even today does not reach everyone in the same way. Between the darkness of industry, the red of politics and the green that grew on the fringes of the metropolis, the landscape of these peripheries still bears the marks of a spatial history of the working class. Between success and failure, utopia and successive disenchantments, architecture and urbanism were sometimes imposed and sometimes conquered through politics. In any case, both were mobilised to participate in an effort to reorganise the meanings of this landscape. Today, it is up to us to understand the limits of what has been (and what may still be) accomplished with these disciplinary instruments: to learn from our mistakes, to gather the spoils and to continue the work left unfinished.

Through their non-linear processes of expansion, contemporary cities open up vacant spaces between voracious leaps of development, *terrains vagues* whose value lies precisely in what they are, which is to say, in their potential to become something else. In an era where urban forms have spread across the globe to the point of unsustainability, it seems clear that new possibilities lie precisely in the in-between spaces generated by urban fragmentation. After all, "our century is no longer the one to extend cities, but to deepen our territories".[59]

Acknowledgements

This work was developed as part of the ongoing PhD thesis *On the Periphery: From Paris to the World; City and Landscape, Subalternity and Subversion*, under the supervision of Joaquim Moreno, Vírgilio Borges Pereira and Sébastien Marot. This research is being undertaken at the Center for Studies in Architecture and Urbanism (CEAU-FAUP) and is supported by national funds through the FCT (Fundação para a Ciência e a Tecnologia), grant no. 2020.08189.BD. The editing of this chapter was supported by funds from the FCT – Fundação para a Ciência e a Tecnologia, under the project UIDP/00183/2020.

Notes

1 Depaule, *Les mots de la stigmatisation urbaine*, 9–12.
2 Faure, "Un faubourg, des banlieues", 11.
3 Ibid., 20.
4 See Farcy, "Banlieues 1891".
5
> Until around 1914, and even well beyond, the image, or rather the value, persists of a suburb that remained a countryside on the outskirts of Paris, but a countryside that no longer had rural or agricultural character, that had no peasants or even inhabitants, but was now essentially populated by trees and pretty places to rest.
> Faure, "Un faubourg, des banlieues", 20–22 (translation mine)

The periphery is not where the city ends but where it unfurls 229

6 Fortier, "L'urbanisme parisien", 5–17.
7 On the techno-scientific, economic and political aspects that drove leaps in the scale and further delocalisation of Parisian industries, and on how norms and legislation concerning this process of industrialisation accelerated the fragmentation of the Parisian landscape, see Guillerme et al., *Dangereux, Insalubres et Incommodes*, 204–252.
8 See Faure, "Spéculation et société", 433–448.
9 Rhein, "Structures de l'emploi", 213–214.
10 Marchand, *Paris: Histoire d'une ville*, 9.
11 See Faure, *Les premiers banlieusards*.
12 Ibid., 7–12; Fourcaut, *Bobigny, banlieue rouge*.
13 Gailhoustet, *Des raciness pour la ville*, 119 (my translation).
14 With the exception of a few patronage and philanthropic initiatives, which ultimately had little effect given the magnitude of the problem. For further information on the subject, see Dumont, *Le logement social à Paris*.
15 I am referring in particular to the work of Émile Pataud and Émile Pouget, both of whom were trade union leaders associated with the *Confédération Générale du Travail*. See Pataud and Pouget, *Comment nous ferons la Révolution*, 148.
16 At the time, the Catholic Church was committed to offering the working class a moral alternative both to the negative consequences of capitalist development and to the labour and socialist movements that were emerging as a result. Concerning the relationship between capital and labour, Pope Leo XIII wrote the encyclical *Rerum Novarum* in 1891.
17 At least since the publication of Friedrich Engels's "The Housing Question" in 1872, the problem of working-class housing was the subject of lively debate among the different political factions. On the development of this debate between right- and left-wing intellectuals and surrounding the issues of houses, housing and land property, cf. Lancry, *Le Terrianisme*.
18 Originally, "working-class gardens" were strongly linked to political movements that were guided by paternalistic and conservative ideologies, such as Terrianism, and were seen as a way of preserving the integrity of the working-class family. As they flourished, however, they garnered the support of other secular political sectors, such as municipal socialism. The collective structure of these gardens played an important role in the organisation and circulation of information in the resistance to the German invasion and against the collaborationist Vichy government, which had found in the workers' gardens an important pillar of its fascist state structure. Cf. Cabedoce, "1940–1952: une période charnière pour les jardins ouvriers".
19 Concerning hygienist principles, promoters of "working-class gardens" such as Abbé Lemire and Dr Gustave Lancry were especially influenced by the ideas of Frédéric Le Play. See Cabedoce and Pierson, *Cent ans d'histoire des jardins ouvriers*.
20 Ibid.
21 Cabedoce, "Jardins ouvriers et banlieue", 250.
22 The last decades of the 19th century and the first decades of the 20th century in France were an important time in the struggle for labour rights, in particular concerning resting time. In 1906, the right to weekly rest was enshrined in law; in 1919, the same happened for the eight-hour working day. Later, in 1936, the left-wing Popular Front government instituted the right to paid vacation.
23 The relationship between "family, home and land" was one of the pillars of social Catholicism and the paternalistic ideologies that were emerging at the time to address the dissolution of traditional ties brought about by industrial capitalism,

230 Rethinking the City

although the aspiration to own one's own house and a piece of land was also rooted in popular culture itself. As Dubost writes,

> we must take into account the weight of cultural traditions specific to each environment. The rural or semi-rural origins of a large proportion of the working classes obviously play a part in their attachment to the garden and their use of it.
>
> Dubost, *Les jardins ordinaires*, 31 (translation mine)

24 See Dumont, *Le logement social à Paris*; and APUR, *Les Habitations à Bon Marché*.
25 For a general overview of the history and policies behind these "*grands ensembles*", see the summary by Jean-Michel Léger at: https://politiquedulogement.com/dictionnaire-du-logement/g/grands-ensembles/.
26 The *Athens Charter* is a book published by Le Corbusier in 1941, based on a 1933 document that built on his previous plans for the Radiant City (Ville Radieuse), which laid out fundamental guidelines for a 20th-century urbanism and a modern Functional City. Although not officially a collective output, the document played a fundamental role in the debates of the International Congresses of Modern Architecture (CIAM) and was an important blueprint for urban planning after World War II.
27 Verret, *L'espace ouvrier*, 45–71.
28 The commune of Ivry-sur-Seine had been managed by the French Communist Party since 1925, except for a brief interruption during World War II. See Belanger, *Ivry Banlieue Rouge*.
29 See Faure, *Les premiers banlieusards*.
30 *Atelier de Montrouge* was a collective architecture agency founded by Gérard Thurnauer, Jean Renaudie, Pierre Riboulet and Jean-Louis Véret in 1958.
31 Scalbert, *A Right to Difference*, 11–51.
32 Ibid., 42.
33 Renaudie, *La ville est une combinatoire*, 12–21.
34 Grossman, "To Give Voice", 109.
35 For an account of his position in his own words, see the documentary "Mon quartier c'est ma vie" (1979), available online at: www.dailymotion.com/video/xw8k9m.
36 Renaudie, *La ville est une combinatoire*, 92.
37 All thought-provoking features associated more with an individual house than a flat, properly speaking. For a visual representation of the project, see https://openverse.org/image/726110bf-9397-4b8b-9f25-9d4532eb4513?q=jean%20renaudie.
38 Scalbert, *A Right to Difference*, 144.
39 At one point, according to Gailhoustet, Renaudie walked around Ivry with the model of the Casanova building, the first in their new masterplan for Ivry to be built, which generated excitement among the inhabitants at the fact that each flat had its own garden. The interview can be watched online at: www.youtube.com/watch?v=ISv6p8dfH2U&t=120s.
40 Renaudie, "The Terrace", 145.
41 Ibid.
42 Ibid., 19.
43 Gailhoustet, *Éloge du logement*, 27.
44 On the relationship between working-class culture and the aspiration to have a pavilion of one's own at the particular historical moment in which these buildings were designed, see Topalov, *Se loger en liberté*.
45 I am referring here in particular to a circular issued by the Minister of Equipment and Housing, Olivier Guichard, on 21 March 1973.

46 Baudin and Genestier, "Faut-il vraiment démolir . . . ?", 214. For further discussion of this demographic transformation, see Chamboredon and Lemaire, "Proximité spatiale, distance sociale", 3–33; Masclet, *La gauche et les cités*; and Topalov, *Se loger en liberté*.
47 Société Française d'Histoire Urbaine, "Faire: l'histoire", 155. See also Berland-Berthon, *La démolition des immeubles*.
48 Baudin and Genestier, "Faut-il vraiment démolir . . . ?", 207.
49 Druot et al., *Plus+*, 209.
50 Lacaton and Vassal, *Lacaton & Vassal*, 152.
51 Druot et al., *Plus+*, 29.
52 Ibid., 31.
53 Ibid., 87.
54 Ibid., 85.
55 Ibid. In Jacques Hondelatte and Épinard Bleu's text included in the same book, we read:

> Strangely, never has "additional" housing looked as much like "communal" housing than today; nor "urban" housing like the "rural" kind; strangely, never has housing been as monotonous a reproduction of the model of middle-class housing than it is today, a more or less reduced reproduction, one more or less adapted to today's socio-economic norms. Strangely, this traditionally precise response to the so-called precise needs of the average ideal family seems to be admitted and assumed as being definitive: the man who works and the woman who stays at home to take care of the three kids of school age.
> Bleu and Hondelatte, "Apartments? – Areas to Make Use of", 35

For an illustration, see https://openverse.org/image/16704c01-d4ea-41a6-8b20-8a1d59c19471?q=lacaton%20vassal
56 See Smith, *Case Study Houses*.
57 Sens and Tonka, *Une maison particulière*, 1.
58 The "Bois-le-Prêtre" tower was originally designed by Raymond Lopez and built between 1959 and 1961 by the *Office Public d'Habitations à Loyer Modéré de la Ville de Paris*. In 2005, a competition was held to refurbish the tower, the winners of which were Druot, Lacaton and Vassal. The principles of their proposal had been previously developed in their theoretical research, published as *Plus+. Les grands ensembles de logements. Territoire d'exception*. This included not only the renovation of façades but also the reorganisation of the existing collective spaces, as well as the redistribution of families among existing dwellings. In addition, the project included negotiations with the relevant authorities to ensure that, following the transformation of the tower, rents would be indexed not to the apartments' (new) size but rather to their type. See Ruby and Ruby, *Druot, Lacaton & Vassal*.
59 Marot, *L'art de la mémoire*, 131.

Bibliography

APUR (Atelier Parisien d'Urbanisme), *Les Habitations à Bon Marché de la Ceinture de Paris: étude historique*, Paris: 2017. www.apur.org/sites/default/files/documents/publication/documents-associes/habitations_bon_marche_ceinture_paris_historique.pdf?token=Mu_3L2OA

Baudin, Gérard and Philippe Genestier, "Faut-il vraiment démolir les grands ensembles?", *Espaces et Sociétés*, 124–125, no. 1–2 (2006): 207–222.

Belanger, Emmanuel, *Ivry Banlieue Rouge*, Cachan: Éditions Lavoisier, 2017.

Berland-Berthon, Agnès, *La démolition des immeubles de logements sociaux: Histoire urbaine d'une non-politique publique*, Paris: Cerema, 2009.

Bleu, Épinard and Jacques Hondelatte, "Apartments? – Areas to Make Use of", in *Plus +. Les grands ensembles de logements: territoire d'excepción*, edited by Frédéric Druot, Anne Lacaton and Jean-Philippe Vassal, 33–37, Barcelona: Gustavo Gilli, 2007.

Cabedoce, Béatrice, "Jardins ouvriers et banlieue: le bonheur au jardin", in *Les premiers banlieusards*, edited by Alain Faure, 249–281, Grâne: Éditions Creaphis, 1991.

Cabedoce, Béatrice, "1940–1952: une période charnière pour les jardins ouvriers", *In Situ* 37 (2018), [online]. https://doi.org/10.4000/insitu.18752.

Cabedoce, Béatrice and Philippe Pierson, *Cent ans d'histoire des jardins ouvriers – 1989–1996*, Grâne: Éditions Créaphis, 1996.

Chamboredon, Jean-Claude and Madeleine Lemaire, "Proximité spatiale et distance sociale. Les grands ensembles et leur peuplement", *Revue Française de Sociologie* 11, no. 1 (1970): 3–33.

Depaule, Jean-Charles, ed., *Les mots de la stigmatisation urbaine*, Paris: Éditions de la Maison des Sciences de l'Homme/Éditions UNESCO, 2017.

Druot, Frédéric, "Not Tearing Down is a Strategy", *Architecture d'Aujourd'hui* 374 (2009): 66–74.

Druot, Frédéric, Anne Lacaton and Jean-Philippe Vassal, *Plus +. Les grands ensembles de logements: territoire d'excepción*, Barcelona: Gustavo Gilli, 2007.

Dubost, Françoise, *Les jardins ordinaires*, Paris: Éditions L'Harmattan, 1997.

Dumont, Marie-Jeanne, *Le logement social à Paris 1859-1930. Les Habitations à Bon Marché*, Brussels: Pierre Mardaga, 1991.

Engels, Friedrich, *Para a Questão da Habitação*, translated by João Pedro Gomes, Lisboa: Avante!, 1983.

Farcy, Jean-Claude, "Banlieues 1891: Les enseignements d'un recensement exemplaire", in *Les premiers banlieusards. Aux origines des banlieues de Paris*, edited by Alain Faure, 15–70, Paris: Éditions Créaphis, 1991.

Faure, Alain, *Les premiers banlieusards. Aux origines des banlieues de Paris*, Grâne: Éditions Créaphis, 1991.

Faure, Alain, "Spéculation et Société: les grands travaux à Paris au XIXe siècle", *Histoire, Économie et Société*, 23rd year, no. 3 (2004): 433–448.

Faure, Alain, "Un faubourg, des banlieues, ou la déclinaison du rejet", in *Les mots de la stigmatisation urbaine*, edited by Jean-Charles Depaule, 9–39, Paris: Éditions de la Maison des Sciences de l'Homme/Éditions UNESCO, 2017.

Flamand, Jean-Paul, *Loger le peuple. Essai sur l'histoire du logement social*, Paris: Éditions La Découverte & Syros, 2001.

Fortier, Bruno, "L'urbanisme parisien à la fin de l'ancien régime", *Espaces et Sociétés*, no. 13/14 (1974): 5–17.

Fourcaut, Anne, *Bobigny, banlieue rouge*, Paris: Les Éditions Ouvrières/Presses de la Fondation Nationale des Sciences Politiques, 1986.

Gailhoustet, Renée, *Éloge du logement*, Bobigny: SODEDAT/Massimo Ripossati, 1993.

Gailhoustet, Renée, *Des racines pour la ville*, Paris: Les Éditions de l'Épure, 1998.

Grossman, Vanessa, "'To Give Voice to What Has Heretofore Been Silent'. The 'Third Zone' and the Crisis of Representation in Ivry-sur-Seine's City Center Urban Renewal, 1962–1986", in *Architecture and Democracy 1965–1989: Urban Renewal, Populism and the Welfare State*, edited by Dirk van dn Heuvel, Monteiro de Jesus and Sun Ah Wang, 105–112, Rotterdam: Jaap Bakema Study Centre, 2019.

Guillerme, André, Gérard Jigaudon and Anne-Cécile Lefort, *Dangereux, Insalubres et Incommodes: paysages industriels en banlieue parisienne XIXe-XXe siècles*, Seyssel: Éditions Champ Vallon, 2004.

Harvey, David, *Paris, Capital of Modernity* (ebook edition), New York/London: Routledge, 2005.
Lacaton, Anne and Jean-Philippe Vassal, *Lacaton & Vassal*, Paris: HYX/Cité de l'Architecture & du Patrimoine, 2009.
Lancry, Gustave, *Le Terrianisme: la propriété insaisissable et assurée à tous*, Dunkirk: A. Delville – Imprimeur-éditeur, 1899.
Marchand, Bernard, *Paris: Histoire d'une ville XIX-XXe siècle*, Paris: Éditions du Seuil, 1969.
Marot, Sébastien, *L'art de la mémoire, le territoire et l'architecture*, Paris: Éditions de La Villette, 2010.
Masclet, Olivier, *La gauche et les cités: enquête sur un rendez-vous manqué*, Paris: La Dispute/SNÉDIT, 2003.
Meyer, Esther da Costa, *Dividing Paris: Urban Renewal and Social Inequality, 1852–1870*, Princeton: University Press, 2022.
Pataud, Émile and Émile Pouget, *Comment nous ferons la Révolution*, Paris: Librairie Illustrée Jules Tallandier, 1909.
Pinson, Daniel, "Les grands ensembles comme paysage", *Cahiers de la Méditerranée* 60, no. 1 (2000): 157–178. https://doi.org/10.3406/camed.2000.1279
Renaudie, Jean, "The Terrace", in *A Right to Difference. The Architecture of Jean Renaudie*, edited by Irénée Scalbert, 145, London: AA publications, 2004.
Renaudie, Jean, *La ville est une combinatoire*, Ivry-sur-Seine: Movitcity édition, 2014.
Rhein, Catherine, "Structures de l'emploi et marchés du travail dans l'agglomération Parisienne au cours de l'entre-deux-guerres", in *Villes Ouvrières 1900–1950*, edited by Susanna Magri and Christian Topalov, 201–217, Paris: Éditions de l'Harmattan, 2004.
Rossi, Aldo, "La città e la periferia", in *Scritti scelti sull'architettura e la città*, edited by Rosaldo Bonicalzi, 158–174, Milan: Cooperativa libraria universitaria del politecnico, 1975.
Ruby, Ilka and Andreas Ruby, ed., *Druot, Lacaton & Vassal. Tour Bois le Prêtre*, Berlin: Ruby Press, 2012.
Scalbert, Irénée, *A Right to Difference. The Architecture of Jean Renaudie*, London: AA Publications, 2004.
Sens, Jeanne-Marie and Hubert Tonka, *Une maison particulière à Floirac (Gironde) de Anne Lacaton & Jean-Phillipe Vassal architectes*, Paris: Sens & Tonka, 1994.
Simmel, Georg, "The Metropolis and Mental Life", in *The Blackwell City Reader*, edited by Gary Bridge and Sophie Watson, 11–19, Oxford/Malden: Wiley-Blackwell, 2002.
Smith, Elizabeth, *Case Study Houses: The Complete CSH Program, 1945–1966*, Cologne: Taschen, 2002.
Société Française d'Histoire Urbaine, "Une Histoire à faire: l'histoire de la démolition des logements sociaux en France à la fin des Trente Glorieuses", *Histoire Urbaine* 2, no. 34 (2012): 153–156.
Topalov, Christian, *Se loger en liberté: Propositions pour une politique démocratique et sociale de l'habitat*, Paris: Editions Sociales, 1978.
Verret, Michel, *L'espace ouvrier*. Paris: Éditions de L'Harmattan, 1979.
Williams, Raymond, "Culture is Ordinary", in *Raymond Williams on Culture and Society: Essential Writings*, edited by Jim McGuican, 1–18, London: SAGE, 2014.

15 On some fragments of *Trás-os-Montes*, a film by António Reis and Margarida Cordeiro

Maria Filomena Molder

Theme

In the two films by António Reis and Margarida Cordeiro that I know best – *Jaime* (1973) and *Trás-os-Montes* (1976) –, we witness the constant experience of not being susceptible to reconfiguration. In the first case, the life of Jaime Fernandes, which always eludes him.[1] In the second, the atmosphere of that place Reis refers back to, Trás-os-Montes,[2] whose "intolerable pain" was not imprinted in the photographs he took a few years before the shooting, which is why all of them lie, as he wrote: "I see, once again, the photographs I took in Trás-os-Montes. Almost all of them lie. No intolerable pain has remained in them. No hope. No root".[3]

That man, those villages, those mountains, those animals, that cold, those voices, resist reconfiguration, but they may be more docile towards figuration, that is, by allowing always and once again that resistance to be sensed. It is this that I will devote myself to.

I dedicate these words – in so far as they are mine – to José Bogalheiro.[4]

First clarification: which fragments are those? Those that show the intolerable pain that António Reis claims was not imprinted in the photographs he took in Trás-os-Montes. For example, the pain of the accidents in the mine, the pain of goodbyes that are forever[5] (for those who depart to Lisbon or Argentina), the almost forgotten pain one sees in the eyes of women. Those which bear witness to what will never again return. Those which originate in the recitation of excerpts from Kafka's "The Great Wall of China" in *mirandês*,[6] in three separate moments.

Second clarification: Without any pretention of substitution or as a proposal of a new one, I have ruined, mortified, following the Benjaminian sense,[7] the original montage. My operation is not artistic, filmic, it has to do with the selection (in fact, many different selections) of scenes, which I call fragments, that created their own conceptual logic. As with every montage this one has an inherent intelligibility and is an expression of something that enables it to be a montage. It is a montage inspired by the Benjaminian and Goethean manner,[8] which is at the same time "a method and an artistic and

DOI: 10.4324/9781003452928-19

conceptual principle that feeds on both chance and elective affinities",[9] and thus waives deductive and inductive operations, since the montage speaks for itself, it is *index sui*.

Third clarification: I am writing an essay whose method might be called a "close reading" but in a rather wild fashion, without taking the procedure as an *attitré* hermeneutical technique. A procedure that is reinforced by the fact that most of the words coming out of my mouth were not borne in it, but in the mouth of António Reis and of Margarida Cordeiro, and also in the mouths of the characters in the film.

The whole film is a formidable almost sumptuous collection of fragments that fit together like/through the movement of a boomerang (a concept used by António Reis himself). It was entirely acted by the inhabitants of the villages close to the cities of Bragança and Miranda do Douro, in total 43 villages.

Now I'm going to describe the selected fragments in the sequence-montage of mine:[10]

Development

1st Fragment

1:33:56/1:36:38

We are almost at the end of the film (which lasts 111 minutes). We hear the voice of a young woman, with that slow rhythm, typical of speech from that region, in which the mouth seems pregnant with voice: words roll between the tongue, the teeth, the roof of the mouth, wet with saliva:

> In Trás-os-Montes, Bragança district, there is a small village called Constantim. It's very far from the big city. It is surrounded by the fields and the shade of ancient oaks. The looms rattle cheerfully. The ox-carts'wheels squeak through the narrow streets. Girls [as rapazas] go to the fountain for water and the younger kids gather dry sticks. The inhabitants of Constantim are poor. Alive, they are the folk of the village of Constantim. Dead, they are the dust of the village of Constantim.[11]

This is a lyrical and epic self-description of inhabiting Constantim, a very small and poor village, worlds away from the big city. The words recited by a sweet, precise, and nostalgic voice of a young woman compose a powerful and dense landscape, an act of *dichten*, as Wittgenstein would say:[12] full of sounds and senses, living movements and rhythms, pointing out to the spatial abyss between the land and the big city, and to the longing affinity between the dead ones (the dust) and the living ones (the folk).

2nd Fragment

00:2:35/4:37

The film begins, *in media res*: stunning, surprising. This is the film's opening scene, where the interplay erupts – which reigns thought-out the film – between image and sound with their slidings, contrasts, suspensions, disarticulations (also in the case of the music). Right in the first few minutes (the second ones in my sequence), that is clear in an almost Dionysian manner: while the film camera shows us the mountains and their ranges, we hear sounds that do not seem articulate: shouts, gargles, tongues clicking teeth and palate, whistling, and sometimes the semblance of a word forming. António Reis and Margarida Cordeiro made the sound synchronously, they organized blocks "as if it was possible to have a symphonic sound. They are units, which, in fact, will sometimes have repercussions further along".[13] This is what happens in these minutes of deep sound immersion: a ripple is created that is communicated throughout the entire film.

The secret is revealed immediately afterwards, when the little shepherd is seen by us. However, even before this, anticipating it, we hear the clanging of sheep bells, and the camera moves, scrutinizing the stones, stopping next to one of them engraved with human shapes, reminiscent of the prehistoric engravings of Foz Côa.[14] This vision of the humanized stone already belongs to the look of the little shepherd, from whose mouth a splendid smile radiates across his entire face, which spreads across the entire landscape.

3rd Fragment (a Diptych)

A) 00:4:57/7:09

(In the film, this bloc follows immediately from the one just discussed). We see another little boy climbing the exterior granite staircase that leads to a room. You can already hear the mother's voice telling an enchanting story, *Branca-Flor*, the Devil's daughter with whom a prince falls in love. They both decide to run away. The boy comes in and looks, and so do we, at the scene before him in which his sister helps his mother put his little brother to bed. The mother's voice never stops, and they, brother and sister, listen to her spellbound, the girl sitting next to her brother eating a pomegranate. The mother lights the fire, prepares supper, and continues: in the stable, says Branca-Flor to the prince, there are two horses, of the wind and of thought. In order that the prince wouldn't make a mistake she tells him that he needs to prepare the horse of thought. But the prince, in a rush to escape, harnesses the horse of the wind. Deceived by his daughter's spells, the Devil doesn't immediately notice the escape. But as soon as he does notice it, he pursues them on the horse of thought. After several adventures, in which the prince forgets Branca-Flor, she is kidnapped and imprisoned in the Tower of Babylon. Then the prince remembers her and goes in search of the cursed Tower: "whoever goes there does not return".

At this moment, the mother turns to the camera and suspends the narration, silencing her voice. The camera focuses on her eyes, her face resting on one of her hands, a black scarf on her head, she doesn't look at the camera, she doesn't look at us, her gaze goes so far away that it sinks, the face of a suffocating beauty, also distant.

B) 1:21:33/1:23:59

According to António Reis, the peasants' reaction to the film was generally favourable, but there were aspects of it that were incomprehensible (perhaps unacceptable) to them as is particularly the cases with the sequence in which both directors requested that the peasants should gather and eat snow,

> When the peasants saw the film, they recognized things they loved and that belonged to them, even if sometimes our imagination [his imagination and that of Margarida Cordeiro] or our freedom of expression disoriented them. For example, the snow scene. They never ate snow, as is seen in the film, but they suffer because of the snow, the beauty of the snow, the snow that burns. Thus, as there are peoples who eat dust or straw, I had them eat snow.[15]

The snow-covered landscape, the intense cold, are brothers of the sovereign silence that reigns from the moment the mother, accompanied by one of her children, collects the snow into a large bowl until the moment when, as in a sacrificial ceremony, she serves the children and her husband the white delicacy. When we see them take the snow to their mouths, we shudder. They shudder too. It's not just one's hands that are burned by the cold, one's mouth will also feel that burning sensation.

These two cases can make us ask if we are before a documentary or a fictional film. Deep down this is an inopportune, irrelevant question, asked by the interviewers from *Cahiers du Cinéma*, Serge Daney and Jean-Pierre Oudart, and also by me. But it is worth listening to the answer of António Reis: "Both", he says, going on to explain that "in a village an event becomes part of a fiction". If we stay still "we only see golden dust, the animals at the fountain, etc.". But if we walk from house to house, cross a river, enter a door, "then things become so complex that one can no longer speak only of fiction or of documentary".[16]

4th Fragment

00:57:46/00:58:00

First, we see children playing, girls and boys – the colours are stunning[17] –, the girls dance, holding hands in rings, rings within rings, the boys (in smaller numbers) play with spinning tops (during the film, it is usually only boys that are seen playing; one of the times, the girl, the sister of one of them – those who their mother tell the story of *Branca-Flor* – asks them if she can join them, and the answer comes back immediately: No!). On the other hand, women are more present than men, most of them wearing black, since their men are already dead or are far, far away.

Then a man comes, the son of a miner. He doesn't look like a peasant.[18] He makes conversation with two women working (making soap) one of them has a brother who is a miner, he's very ill.

00:58:00/1:00:00

This is followed by a long voice-over lament about the life of the miners: peasants who start by finding bread for their mouths and end up with lungs full of silicosis. There are afternoons when horror and fear take their toll, when a gallery collapses on the small miners dressed in the clothes of men: "it seemed as if everything was frozen, only the machines keep going. The machines were never switched during the chaos".[19] While his voice sounds, we see intriguing images of a man and a young boy walking among the abandoned buildings of the mines and detailed inspections of their interior, ruins to be deciphered, traces of intolerable pain and of death.

1:03:58/1:04:50

The terrible "tragic" thing is that everyone knew, while the funerals went on (for several days), that the disasters would repeat themselves and that once again, the intolerable pain would have its ration: every day they would compose and perform a play, always already rehearsed. Then the lament changes direction and addresses the land where those miners were born, this land that he can no longer recognize, a no man's land inhabited only by absent names that once lived there:

> But I don't know my land today . . . alas! My land used to be a place where a lot of people lived. But today, mine is a village of absentees. They have their name, their empty spot: "Mr. So-and-so used to live here".[20]

Important observation by António Reis about the lament of the miner's son:

> The voice over acts as a counterpoint to the life of the miners . . . There is always an intersection, a dialectic of sound and image, which interests me much more than all the *raccords*, ellipses and other rules of the handbooks of cinema.[21]

As we have already seen and will see again, this dialectic is a repercussion of the boomerang effect.

5th Fragment (a Triptych)

A) 1:05.59/1:09

B) 1:13:53/1:16:46

This fifth fragment originates from the recitation of excerpts from Kafka's "The Great Wall of China" in *mirandês*, in three separate moments: in two of them, we see two men, one with a grave and serious countenance, and the other with a beautifully severe and luminous face; we hear someone speaking, perhaps one of them. In the second moment facing them a landscape of women, men (among them, we recognize miners with their helmets) young people and children who glide away before our gaze and disappear: the camera surrounds them with tenacity and affection.

"We translated the text by Kafka to the subdialect and, all of a sudden, the text became very guttural, very expressive, filled with an extraordinary force".[22] To a contemporary city ear (from Lisbon), the Mirandese with which the characters express themselves sounds like an archaic language, the high tone that obeys the demands of clarity and conciseness incomparable with the language used by those who watch the film and listen to them. The musicality is serious, rough, the rhyme slow, majestic. The voice sounds, we do not see who makes the sound (which is an essential constructive gesture of *Trás-os-Montes*).

In any case, it is necessary to go further than the reference to the origin of the text recited, "The Great Wall of China". In fact, it is an amalgam in the alchemical sense, a kind of *cadavre exquis*. In other words, António Reis and Margarida Cordeiro tore out pieces of Kafka's story and put these pieces together, so that the inhabitants of the Trás-os-Montes villages, so distant from the capital ("Peking" is always replaced by "the capital") can be recognized. From these excerpts, the filmmakers highlight all the disturbing aspects of time in the vertiginous replacement of the present by the past and the coincidence of the past with the present, the upheaval of whatever the present is, although you don't hear the parable of the dying Emperor and his messenger, whose movement never reaches its conclusion, so the message will never be communicated, even though its effects are felt.

On the other hand, if the first-person narration was kept intact, which includes descriptions, doubts, and various reflections about the construction of the great wall in instalments, any reference to the wall and its method of construction is avoided. What incites and inspires António Reis and Margarida Cordeiro has to do with the immeasurable distance between the villages and the capital, which reaches its climax in the precise and humorous statement: "To the villages the capital is still more unknown than the next world itself!"[23] An abysmal distance that soon unfolds conceptually into two aspects, one that introduces the condition of possibility in the act of the city itself, unimaginable:

> Can a town really exist, where, as far as the eye can see, one house touches another in an area larger than the fields seen from the top of our hills and where among those houses, men press in multitudes?[24]

The other praises the immutable nature of the village administration, a kind of silent sabotage of the constant changes in which the city invests and the satisfaction that the village's inhabitants feel with this:

> The way we're ruled here saw no changes. The high-ranking officers always come from the capital city. At least the middle-tier ones do. And the lower ranks, those are the ones from here. Nothing changed. And we're pleased with that.[25]

What will have to be tempered, and in what way, with what is said about the laws (already in the second moment): that they are made by people who are completely unaware of these distant villages and their inhabitants. This is felt as a real torture, which expands into all kinds of harm. And suddenly a rebellious and redemptive thought appears in the mouth of the speaker, reducing to spectres all efforts at domination through laws written in secret and even where mortified. Kafka does not remain incognito:

> We're told that laws exist, and always have, as a secret entrust only to the powerful and nobleman. Only to the big ones and only for their profit. But that is not and cannot be anything else but old. Those laws we patiently search for, which we do not know, which we guess at, they are nothing but figments of the imagination. Maybe, in truth they don't even exist.[26]

Regarding this sequence, the words of António Reis come to my aid again, clarifying the opposition between written, abstract laws and the flexible laws of custom, shared and altered according to the occasion and the rhythm of life, "by historical becoming": "One day, a shepherd takes the sheep grazing, the other day, it's a different shepherd. There is a sort of primitive communism in those regions".[27] And it is precisely because they are not made forever that unwritten laws tend to be dilapidated and repressed by written laws, which will end up swallowing them.

C) 1:36:11/1:36:34

In the third moment, we witness the exit of a multitude of people in the middle of the night carrying lights, perhaps coming from a cave, all wearing a heavy boiled wool cape similar to the one worn by the former men. It is like a nocturne community, a demand for community.

Here, the particular form of revolutionary disposition typical of these villages is inscribed, the refusal to separate daily life from the poetic imagination, both fed by the dust of the dead (evoking the voice of the young woman who represents the village of Constantim), a refusal underlined with insight by António Reis who turns it into a progressive and revolutionary element, although unknown as such, of village life:

> In these Portuguese villages, what one realizes is that it is wrong to separate the ancient culture, the civilizations that came afterwards and today's daily life. It is precisely there, in that refusal to separate, that I find a progressive and revolutionary element.[28]

6th Fragment

1:25:20/1:27:32

Another lamenting voice is heard, now it is the blacksmith's lament, in which his love for his craft is manifested, and the pain of realizing better than anyone that his craft is dying, which is linked to his acute perception that the village is dying: "When the blacksmith laments people leaving the village, that refers precisely to the mutilated children and to the dead of the colonial wars".[29] The colonial wars lasted from 1961 until the revolution of 25 April 1974, and its effects were still being felt during the filming. We do not quite realize that, but we are able to guess it, for example, due to the notable absence of young men in the villages, which symbolically erupts through the very long nocturnal scream of the locomotive, which will be heard almost at the end of the film and which will be appearing in the last fragment.

7th Fragment (a Diptych)

A) 1:33:49

"My daughter leaves tomorrow she's going to become a maid", says a woman to her neighbour.

B) 1:39:59/1:40:54

Another woman looks tenderly at her sleeping children for a long time.

The first moment of this diptych portrays the abandonment, uncertainty, and concern felt about the fate of the children, in this case, a daughter who leaves to become a maid in a house in Lisbon, news announced in the first moment. The second woman's gaze reflects her precise awareness of the abandonment of the land, of the bloodletting.

Last Fragment (a Triptych)

A) 1:42.05/1:44:16

The whistling, the hiss of the train, a very long and mournful cry in the night. The film is almost over. And this cry is the background of the night from which the boomerang is launched, giving rise to repeated variations of its paradoxical back-and-forth movement.[30]

B) 00:51:16/00:51: 46

The magical herd, not a sound is heard, only the flow of light and movement, the golden dust floating.

C) 00:51:47/00:52:16

We see a woman, wearing black, the usual feminine attire, running and running accompanied by a little boy, they go on running and running through the fields. And at the end, they stop far in the distance and hug each other. Why do they run through the fields, what urgency pushes them, why do they stop in the open, why do they hug each other? We will have to wait for the boomerang effect that the train's whistle produces – someone has left, someone is waiting, someone despairs – affecting, in the manner of Bresson's "effects precede causes", our understanding of *Trás-os-Montes*: "Let the cause follow the effect, not accompany it or precede it".[31]

Between the unsettling whistle of the train and the rush to decipher the woman and the little boy, the vision of the magical herd is like an exorcism of pain, a vision of a sacred marriage between hope and roots.

Recapitulation and Finale

No city is present in this film, but the central nervous system of the modern cities – the offspring of the post-industrial revolutions and the radical transformation of mores – resends its signals: those regarding the written unknown law that no one may share or even know; those regarding the abandonment of villages, where the labour market and industry are sovereign, to the mines, to emigration (the men), to serve, "to go and become a maid" (the young women). The expression "to become a maid" has the potency of generating a grammatical torrent.

António Reis then continues his analysis and goes beyond what one sees in the film, that is, the off-screen, so to speak, makes his surprising entrance, when he talks about the indocility of those people in relation to the return of their children who have since emigrated. "Those who go to Lisbon, to Europe, to the degraded neighbourhoods, to the factories, etc."[32] no longer build their houses according to tradition: "And from there rises the disagreement that old people feel regarding their own children. They are well aware that they possess richness and that they are the victims of genocide".[33] Spurred on by these disasters, they might even decide to "cut off all supplies of food to Lisbon". Which is a form of provocation that goes beyond resistance, demanding "the importance and validity of their ways of doing and thinking to be recognized".[34]

The sense of loss is overwhelming, the sense of all that cannot exist but in that place, where everything escapes the laws imposed by the mandate of the city. No, it is neither a longing for the past, nor conservatism, nor anti-progressivism, even if such concepts could be taken seriously. It is something other, which I cannot yet express unless to bear witness to what will never again return, similarly to when Nietzsche speaks, in *Human, All Too Human* (I) §248, of the unfulfilled impetus to be Greek again: "we have burnt our boats".[35] It's terrible to think that the land which António Reis and Margarida Cordeiro have known does not exist anymore.

However, it is not permitted to conclude in this way. To my aid come sequences that do not appear in the fragments selected by me and that are part of some of the most decisive filmic gestures in *Trás-os-Montes*. Those sequences in which popular poetic imagination takes the lead (e.g., in the 3rd Fragment, but here it is embedded in everyday life: the mother telling the story of Branca-Flor). By standing out, this poetic takes on a life of its own, as is the case with the wonderful journey of the two little boys, decked out in medieval clothes, through distant lands and above all through distant times, to the point where two elderly men, who they meet at the end of the journey, prepare to confront them, and they are surprised, in a state of disbelief and fright, when they realize that they are the descendants of the little boys. Yes, the young boys realize that they are in danger, that the journey could enclose them forever in its magic and therefore, they run at full speed home, where they will once again be younger than the old. Here is the boomerang effect in action again: their journey endures in all those who have just seen *Trás-os-Montes*, as an expression of that kind of eternal return that Benjamin authorizes us to apply: not allowing pain to close in on those who suffered, accept that once experienced, joy can be experienced again.[36] Yes, those children have not yet emigrated, they have not yet become miners, they have not yet entered the spiral of despair: "This is why we treated those children with such intensity. . . . They . . . are still a bit like angels".[37]

At the beginning I thought about the reconfiguration operation finding resistance in the construction of *Trás-os-Montes* itself, suggesting that, in contrast, figuration is welcome and gives shape to that resistance. That, I think, might intersect with António Reis's idea that what is at stake in the lives of the inhabitants of these villages is resistance: "Look how a peasant, in the midst of the hardness of his life, faces snow, fire, heat, etc. With what resistance". Hence the peasant appears to him as what might give rise to the future: "And one feels that, sometimes, they are closer to the future than city people".[38]

However, I still have not clarified what I mean by figuration. To my aid comes the paleontologist André Leroi-Gourhan, who uses the concept of figuration in the context of his unparalleled presentation of what human imaginative force is, always codified emotionally, in the second volume of *Le geste et la parole* (titled "La mémoire et les rythmes"). Although neither ignoring nor putting aside the modern opposition between abstraction and figuration, a use of figuration outside this traditional opposition is observable, elevating it to a method of restoring life, which only art, in its various expressions, is capable of carrying out, going so far as to speak of a "figurative abstraction". It is evident that this restitution, always multiple, cannot, therefore, be anything but fragmentary, renewing itself without ceasing, dispensing with any theoretical gesture of definitive unification.[39]

If the lack of aptitude for reconfiguration is primarily the viewer's own, it immediately becomes embedded, whether one likes it or not, in the construction of the film itself, not as a lack of aptitude, but as a decision that exempts the film from it. *Trás-os-Montes* is made up of blocks, views, or sequences that adjust to each other, or rather, slide past each other, through the boomerang effect, which is a kind of shuttle that weaves and, at the same time, breaks free of the hand of the weaver and follows its own laws, creating magnetic fields between the blocks, which never cease to become others, in different configurations.

Why bring this up in a book on cities? The city is the dragon, the tireless chewer, with its ferocious jaws. *Trás-os-Montes* is a guide to disappearance and, at the same time, a sea chart for the rediscovering of desires, gestures, and sounds that await only a look to be awakened. It is crucial to highlight, alongside the operative concept of boomerang, the experimental concepts of threatened lyricism and of film undergoing a metamorphosis:

> [T]here is in fact a tension in the film. That tension is lyricism. [it] is always a threatened world. I believe the film is always undergoing a metamorphosis. The so-called "final" part must act as a boomerang: it is necessary that the viewers be compensated by the lyrical space and time of the first part to endure what comes next.[40]

Unlike the photographs he took before filming, here, in the film, we see roots and hope enter a dancing constellation with pain. The roots are the support of the community which, without hope, is an empty shell. "In our film, we never speak of the communities of villages, but their existence must be felt. They dance, walk together in the dark".[41] The peasants dance and walk together. In other words, community seems to have stopped being a concept to come and unfolds in real movements of reciprocal belonging: walking together and, even more so, dancing together, where the frenzy of bodies and their desires provide the condiments for any form of hope. Pain, however, is still its pitch-black background, "in the dark".

(Translation by Robert Vinten).

Notes

1 Jaime Fernandes was born in 1899 in the village of Barco in Beira Baixa, a shepherd and a peasant, was committed at the age of 30 to a psychiatric hospital in Lisbon, where he died when he was 69. From when he was 60/65 and the year of his death, he drew and painted what he himself qualified as "obscure photographs", that is, portraits (animals and human beings) which are not clear, and he also wrote hundreds of pages of delirious, visionary texts which were expressive of his whole life. That Jaime's life always eludes him is an expression used by António Reis himself in an interview given to João César Monteiro, quoted in Molder, "Causas que seguem os efeitos", 22.
2 Trás-os-Montes is the name of a province in the extreme northeast of Portugal, characterized as being very mountainous with a harsh climate. It is one of the historic provinces of Portugal with the largest number of emigrants and one of those that most suffers from depopulation.
3 Moutinho and Lobo, *António Reis e Margarida Cordeiro. A Poesia do Cinema*, 38.
4 Due of his 2022 lecture called "until the shadows become long" on the shadows in the film *Trás-os-Montes* and on António Reis's way of filming). See Bogalheiro, *"até as sombras se alongarem"*.
5 Here, it is impossible not to evoke the angels the children wave to in Benjamin, *The Arcades Project*, 813 [<G°, 25> 1]:

> The senseless, desperate, cutting wave from the departing train. Waving has gone astray in the railroad station. On the other hand, the wave to strangers passing by on a moving train. This above all with children, who are waving to angels when they wave to the noiseless, unknown, never returning people. (Of course, they are also saluting the passing train.)

6 *Mirandês* is the name given to the Asturleonese language in the Portuguese territory (Miranda do Douro). At the time that António Reis and Margarida Cordeiro made this film (around 1976), it was considered a dialect divided into sub-dialects.
7 "Criticism means the mortification of the works . . . not then – as the romantics have it – awakening of the consciousness in living works, but the settlement of knowledge in dead ones", awakening "the beauty of works". Benjamin, *The Origin of German Tragic Drama*, 182. Of course, the application of this methodological precept needs to be done in homeopathic doses, since the dead works to which Benjamin refers are the German *Trauerspiele* that no one dares to perform anymore and almost no one reads – clumsy and extravagant, forgotten. The role of the critic in relation to them is redemptive. This is no longer my case nor that of *Trás-os-Montes*, a living work. But I also put aside the romantic gesture of awakening their consciousness in living works, that is, criticism as the works' self-awareness and, therefore, a point above themselves.
8
> This work has to develop to the highest degree the art of citing without quotation marks. Its theory is intimately related to that of montage.
> Benjamin, *The Arcades Project*, 458 [N1,10].

> Formula: construction out of facts. Construction with the complete elimination of theory. What only Goethe in his morphological writings has attempted.
> Ibid., 864 [<O., 73>].

This means that the facts are already the theory, not to be confused with the lazy belief that the facts do not need a critical gaze:

> The ultimate goal would be: to grasp that everything in the realm of fact is already theory. The blue of the sky shows us the basic law of chromatics. Let us not seek for something behind the phenomena – they themselves are the theory.
> Goethe, *Maxime*, 488, 432 (for the English translation, cf. Goethe, *The Essential Goethe*, 1002)

9 See my essay on the work of the Portuguese photographer Daniel Blaufuks, "Lorem Ipsum" in Molder, *Daniel Blaufuks*, 13–14.
10 I had initially intended to insert an image corresponding to each of the fragments. However, as I rewatched and rewatched the film and immersed myself in describing the fragments, I decided that no images would be welcome, not only because the film has splendid colour and the images would have to be reproduced in black and white but also, and above all, because cinema lives on the sensation of movement and time encapsulated in it, ready to burst forth again and again, and this sensation would remain entirely in parentheses. Therefore, I rely on the words that these sensations provoked and demanded, inviting the reader to watch the film.
11 *Trás-os-Montes Script*, 20–21. Translation modified.
12 See Wittgenstein, *Vermischte Bemerkungen*, 28 [MS 146 25v: 1933–1934]: "Philosophie dürfte man eigentlich nur *dichten*". Philosophy should be only as a poetic gesture (my translation).
13 Daney and Oudart, "*Trás-os-Montes* – Entretien", 40 [2nd column].
14 Foz Côa, the largest open air sanctuary of prehistoric engravings, belongs to the Beira Alta region, which borders Trás-os-Montes "As an immense open-air gallery, the Côa Valley features more than a thousand outcrops with rock art, identified in over 80 different sites, predominantly from the Upper Paleolithic, some 30,000 years ago" (Information provided by the website of the Foz Côa Museum https://arte-coa.pt/en/).
15 Daney and Oudart, "*Trás-os-Montes* – Entretien", 41 [1st column].
16 Ibid., 39 [1st and 2nd columns]. Reis's intuition, that walking from one side to the other in a village, repeating gestures and visits, is the source of the original construction of the film, obliging us to suspend the opposition between documentary and fiction, is in great affinity with the idea of Jean-Marie Straub that

> it is always a question of walking everywhere in the place where you're going to film, looking for its water reservoir – the film in question is *Too Early/Too Late* – and then transforming it into an irrigation system (a Brechtian concept).

See my essay on Straub/Huillet oeuvre, Molder, "Man-Enfolding Earth", 248–249. Straub's idea is developed in Marhöfer, "A Thousand Cliffs".

17

> The people there used to dress in dark clothes: grey, brown . . . without fail. The women who got married automatically dressed in dark brown. The children didn't, they had a lot of freedom in terms of bows, bibs, and caps, mothers even made bright colours for the children. . . . a punctuation of colour is like a note in a symphony . . . For example, the beautiful colours that were seen in a village (the parsley green or the red of the heart of Jesus) of the banners of the processions in its dark granite streets.
>
> Interview with António Reis in Mendes,
> *Sobre a "Escola Portuguesa"*, 20

18 Here is the director's description of this man, his voice, and the task he imposed on himself, witness to despair and emptiness:

> The voice over that you hear, a bit violent, a bit oppressed, is the voice of a character seen only briefly in the film. It is the son of a miner. . . . His father spent fifty years working in the mine. The voice of that man is traumatized. He speaks of the old community of miners that used to be peasants.
>
> Daney and Oudart, "*Trás-os-Montes* – Entretien",
> 40 [1st column]

19 *Trás-os-Montes Script*, 11.
20 Ibid., 13.

21 Daney and Oudart, "*Trás-os-Montes* – Entretien", 40 [1st column].
22 Ibid.
23 *Trás-os-Montes Script*, 14. Translation modified. "for the people in our village Peking itself is far stranger than the next world", Kafka, "The Great Wall of China", 68.
24 *Trás-os-Montes Script*, 14. Translation modified. "Can there really be a village where the houses stand by side, covering more fields than can be seen from the top of our hill, and can crowds of people be packed between these houses day and night?", Kafka, "The Great Wall of China", 68.
25 *Trás-os-Montes Script*, 15.
26 Ibid., 16–17.
27 Daney and Oudart, "*Trás-os-Montes* – Entretien", 40 [1st and 2nd columns].
28 Ibid., 39 [2nd column].
29 Ibid., 40 [1st column].
30 Serge Daney thinks that the theme of the film *Trás-os-Montes* is "distancing" [*l'éloignement*] in a "double sense, of being far away (exile) and the act of moving away itself (out of sight, then forgotten)". But it is also an operation within the film, at every moment it sends us back to "another side" [*ailleurs*] and also, finally, the subject of the film itself:

> The astonishing last scene of the film in which the train goes through the night, followed, we could say, by force by the camera, which does not always distinguish it well from the obscurity and which never ceases to rediscover it (fort/da), whether in the form of smoke (for the eyes) or in the form of whistles (for the ears).
> Daney, "Loin des lois", 43–44

31 Bresson, *Notes on the Cinematograph*, 92. In an associated footnote, Bresson narrates an extraordinary story, which is the touchstone for that inversion:

> The other day I was walking through the gardens by Notre-Dame and saw approaching a man whose eyes caught something behind me, which I could not see: at once they lit up. If, at the same time as I saw the man, I had perceived the young woman and the child towards whom he now began running, that happy face of his would not have struck me so; indeed, I might not have noticed it.
> For a development of this enigma, see my essay on *Jaime* (1973)
> "Causas que seguem os efeitos", 47–49.

32 Daney and Oudart, "*Trás-os-Montes* – Entretien", 39 [2nd column].
33 Ibid., 39 [2nd column].
34 Ibid., 38 [2nd column] and 40 [1st column].
35 Nietzsche, *Human, All Too Human (1)*, 169.
36 See Benjamin, *The Arcades Project*, 471 [N8, 1].
37 Daney and Oudart, "*Trás-os-Montes* – Entretien", 40 [1st column].
38 Ibid., 40 [2nd column].
39

> Whether one is talking about a sacrificial rite, a political address, or a play, the relationship between the individual performing the representation and the matter being represented is less important than the values that the performer and the audience hold in common, for these values make it possible to graft an aesthetic apparatus attuned to the appropriate emotions upon an operating sequence of a religious or social nature. It is this emotional language, some of whose values have a very general biological origin but whose code of symbols is highly specific, that really constitutes figurative art.
> Leroi-Gourhan, *Gesture and Speech*, 364

40 Daney and Oudart, "*Trás-os-Montes* – Entretien", 40 [1st column].
41 Ibid., 40 [2nd column].

Bibliography

Benjamin, Walter, *The Origin of German Tragic Drama*, translated by John Osborn, London: Verso, 1998.

Benjamin, Walter, *The Arcades Project*, translated by Howard Eiland and Kevin McLaughlin, Cambridge, MA/London, UK: Harvard University Press, 1999.

Bogalheiro, José, *"até as sombras se alongarem"*, Presentation given at the Conference *Há Ouro em Todo o Lado* [There is Gold Everywhere] – 5th April 2022, School of Arts – Catholic University of Porto. www.youtube.com/watch?v=uFanDOteBxg&t=248s

Bresson, Robert, *Notes on the Cinematograph*, translated by Jonathan Griffin, New York: New York Review of Books, 2016.

Daney, Serge, "Loin des lois", *Cahiers du Cinéma*, no. 276 (May 1977): 43–44.

Daney, Serge and Jean-Pierre Oudart, "*Trás-os-Montes* – Entretien avec António Reis", *Cahiers du Cinéma*, no. 276 (May 1977): 37–41.

Goethe, Johann Wolfgang von, *Werke in 14 Bänden, Vol. XII: Schriften zur Kunst, Schriften zur Literatur, Maxime und Reflexionen*, München: Hamburger Ausgabe, DTV, 1981.

Goethe, Johann Wolfgang von, "Selections from *Maxims and Reflections*", in *The Essential Goethe*, edited by Matthew Bell, 998–1007, Princeton: Princeton University Press, 2016.

Kafka, Franz, "The Great Wall of China", in *The Great Wall of China and Other Short Works*, edited by Malcolm Pasley, 58–70, London: Penguin Books, 1973.

Leroi-Gourhan, André, *Le geste et la parole. 2 La mémoire et les rythmes*, Paris: Albin Michel, 1965.

Leroi-Gourhan, André, *Gesture and Speech*, translated by Anna Bostock Berger, introduction by Randall White and Adam Lehner, Cambridge MA: MIT Press, 1993.

Marhöfer, Elke, "A Thousand Cliffs", in *Tell It to the Stones. Encounters with the Work of Danièle Huillet and Jean-Marie Straub*, edited by Annett Busch and Tobias Hering, 365–390, London: Sternberg Press, 2021.

Mendes, João Maria, ed., *Sobre a "Escola Portuguesa" de Cinema*, Amadora: Escola de Teatro e de Cinema, 2017.

Molder, Maria Filomena, "Causas que seguem os efeitos ou ameixas doiradas com orvalho", in *Descasco as Imagens e Entrego-as na Boca – Lições António Reis*, edited by José Bogalheiro and Manuel Guerra, 13–65, Lisboa: Documenta, 2020.

Molder, Maria Filomena, *Daniel Blaufuks. PH 08*, Lisboa: IN-CM, 2022.

Molder, Maria Filomena. "Man-Enfolding Earth. Oh Earth, My Cradle!", in *Jean-Marie Straub. Danièle Huillet*, 247–263, Porto: Fundação de Serralves, 2023.

Moutinho, Anabela and Maria da Graça Lobo, ed., *António Reis e Margarida Cordeiro. A Poesia do Cinema*, Faro: Cine-Clube de Faro, 1997.

Nietzsche, Friedrich, *Human, All Too Human (1)*, translated by Gary Handwerk, afterword by Gary Handwerk, Stanford, CA: Stanford University Press, 1995.

Trás-os-Montes Script, LiveSubtitling: Filmprojektion Mondt, Viennale, Vienna International Film Festival, translated by Subs Hamburg, Kristin Gerdes and Matthew Way, Lisboa: Cinemateca Portuguesa, 2012.

Wittgenstein, Ludwig, *Vermischte Bemerkungen/Culture and Value* (2nd revised edition), edited by G. H. von Wright in collaboration with Heikki Nyman, revised edition of text by Alois Pichler, translated by Peter Winch, London: Blackwell, 1998.

Index

abandonment 9, 33–34, 69, 187; abandonment of villages 241–242
Abreu, Inês 47
absence 8, 17, 40, 46, 51, 62, 79, 171, 177, 187, 199, 205, 208, 214, 214n1, 215n14, 241
absentmindedness 72, 75n35
action 18, 46, 66–67, 71–73, 93–94, 100–101, 106, 109, 120–121, 128n30, 128n31, 143, 155, 169, 172, 179n16, 185, 243; collective action 120
Adorno, Theodor Wiesengrund 189–190, 192
Aeneas 5, 84
aestheticisation 6–7, 47, 138
affective tonality 141–142
Agamben, Giorgio 216n17
Alberti, Leon Battista 19, 21
Albrecht, Glenn 140
Alexander, Christopher 174, 180n60
Alexandria 102
alienation 46, 67–69, 106–107, 172, 190
allegory 4, 16–17, 19, 23, 39, 51
alterity 2, 121, 127n9, 194
de Almeida, Fialho 45
Alÿs, Francis 72
Amanhã não há arte (Carla Filipe) 65
amateur films 201; amateur filmmaking 199, 201, 215n15
ambient sensitivity 7, 145, 145n4; ambiental sensitivity 136–137, 142–145
antagonism 119, 124
Anthropocene 138, 141
anti-progressivism 243
de Araújo, Norberto 49

architecture 7–9, 81–82, 90–93, 219, 223–224, 226–228; Modern Movement in 20, 172; vernacular architecture 168–169
archive 8, 41, 199–201, 203, 205–217; home movie archive 200, 205, 207–208, 213–214; Lisbon Municipal Archive 200
Arendt, Hannah 4, 60, 65–69, 71, 73–75, 80–81, 127n16, 128n30
Aristotle 80, 82, 169
Armstrong, Justin 40
art of dwelling 8, 178
Assunto, Rosario 3, 19–21
Athens 35, 96n19, 187
atlas 9, 210–211, 213–214
atmosphere 6, 40, 42, 45–46, 53, 141–142, 167, 176, 192, 206, 234
attention 7, 72, 75n35, 135–137, 140–141, 160–161
Augé, Marc 40
Aureli, Pier Vittorio 94, 96n27
Auster, Paul 4, 32–33
autonomy 68, 117–119, 154, 174, 180n53, 201, 211

Bacon, Francis 20
Ballard, J. G. 39
banlieue 219–221, 223, 227
Batista, Joaquim Renato 45
Baudelaire, Charles 72, 74n18, 102–104, 188
Beijing 102
Belluschi, Pietro 168
Benjamin, Walter 2–3, 8–9, 10n4, 16, 18, 21–24, 27, 32, 35, 38–40, 42, 44, 46, 50–51, 60, 68–69, 72, 75n35, 89, 105, 109–110, 112, 135, 185–186, 188–189, 192, 194–195, 234, 243, 245n7

Berlin 19, 23, 35, 101–103, 105, 110, 139, 154, 158, 200
Biel, Karl Emil 44
biopolitics 5, 80
blasé 7, 32, 68, 155; *Blasiertheit* 155, 158
blind spots 200, 203
Bloch, Ernst 42
body 7, 40–41, 46, 64–65, 67, 72–73, 81, 89, 92, 121–122, 128n35, 141, 142–144, 154, 159–160, 170, 174, 177, 186, 194, 203, 205, 212
Corpo-mente I (Vísceras) (Carla Filipe) 61, 64
Bogalheiro, José 234
boomerang effect 235, 238, 242–244
border 21, 161–162
Borgmann, Albert 175
Borinski, Karl 18
bourgeoisie 5, 45, 101, 107, 110
Bragança 235
Branca-Flor 236–237, 243
Bresson, Robert 242, 247n31
bridge 4, 7, 43–48, 105, 161–162
Bruno, Giuliana 199–200, 214n1, 214n3
Buck-Morss, Susan 42, 44
built environment 7, 39–40, 167–172, 174–178
Butler, Judith 123

Cabedoce, Béatrice 222
cadavre exquis 239
Cahiers du Cinéma 237
Callimachus 86
camera 9, 200, 204, 215n14, 216n17, 236–237, 239; camera movements 8, 205, 215n16; cameraman 202
capitalism 2, 40, 67, 69, 100–102, 104, 112–113, 128n26, 201, 220, 222, 229n23; aesthetic capitalism 138; anti-capitalism 124
Carvalho, Luísa 49
catastrophe 3–4, 168, 196n7
certainty 100, 112–113, 170
Chourmo (Jean-Claude Izzo) 188
cinema 8, 199–203, 214–216, 238; cinematic image 199, 203, 214n5, 215n14; cinematic practice 201; cinematic vision 199
citizen 5, 7–8, 35–36, 65–67, 80, 93, 111, 155, 224; citizenship 3, 95n8, 125

city: of Amphion and Orpheus 3, 20; ideal 19, 20, 119; as a locus of experience 5, 79–80, 93–94, 95n3; medieval 19, 20, 172; of memory 23; modern 5, 9, 19, 20, 32–33, 65, 70, 101, 104, 112, 152; monad- 20; Neoplatonic 19; Platonic 21; as a project 94; of Prometheus 3, 18, 20; Renaissance- 19; schizoid 3, 26
cityscape 192–193
civitas 17, 66
class 6, 33, 42, 67, 105, 107, 112, 121, 123, 127n12, 160; class consciousness 107, 112; working class 124, 206, 220–222, 224–229
Climacus, Johannes (Kierkegaard) 106, 111–112; Anti-Climacus 109–111
climate change 7, 140–141
collection: home movies 201, 203, 205–206, 208–209; of fragments 235
commodity 104, 107, 109, 138, 171; commodification 67, 138, 168, 174
common: common good 118–119, 125, 169, 171, 178; common world 4, 60, 65–66, 68, 73
communism 104; primitive communism 240
community 8, 49, 52, 56n82, 62, 64–70, 73, 74n2, 80, 106, 117, 120, 122–123, 128n40, 129n44, 155–156, 167–171, 174–178, 241, 244
Conceição, Nélio 211
confabulation 190, 192, 196
Constantim 235, 241
contextual knowledge 178
Copenhagen 5, 101–103, 110–112
Le Corbusier 227, 230n26
countryside 9–10, 102, 220, 225, 228n5
Crenshaw, Kimberlé 123
crisis: of culture 157; ecological 2, 7; economic 43–44; financial 4, 46; socio-environmental 140
crowd 32, 68, 73, 111, 114n44; crowd person 5, 108, 109, 111
culture: tragedy of (Simmel) 153–154

Dakar 186–187
Dante 24
death 27, 31, 154, 187, 189, 191–202, 196, 197n22, 202–203, 238; dead 34, 119, 126, 154, 235, 238, 241; Madame Death 27

Index

Debord, Guy 9, 114n29, 212–213
decay 15, 17–18, 47, 177
Deleuze, Gilles 10n4, 29
democracy 2, 109, 117–119, 123, 125–126, 127n9
Derrida, Jacques 93–94, 97n35, 214n3, 217
Descartes, René 68, 112, 179n37
design: of the built environment 170, 175, 177–178; urban design 173–174, 215n15
destruction 1, 16–18, 21–24, 47, 70, 105, 168, 189
dialectical image (Benjamin) 4, 18, 186
dichten 235
diCorcia, Philip-Lorca 72–73
differences: group differences 119; ontological differences 122
digital 7, 48, 50, 55n54, 138–139, 174, 200; digitalisation of the urban world 139
Diogenes the Cynic 70
disappearance 9, 105, 109, 244
disaster 40, 145, 238, 243
distraction 72, 75n35, 135, 140, 195
distribution of the sensible (Rancière) 3, 6, 136–137, 144
documentary and fiction 237, 246n16
Dom Pedro V 41
domus 5, 81, 92
door 7, 161–162, 185–187, 191, 195, 237
doubt 100, 112–113, 239
drift 8–9, 110, 187, 212–213
Druot, Frédéric 9, 219, 226–227, 231n58
Dubai 50
Dublin 102
Dubrulle, Roland 223
dust 235, 237, 241–242
dwelling 7–8, 67, 105, 109, 125, 167–178, 227, 231n58

ecology 2, 6–7, 119, 136–138, 140–145, 212, 219
elements: material and atmospheric 136, 141–143
emancipation 5–6, 44, 113, 120
Emery, Jay 40
emotional maps 211–212
environment: living 135–141; urban 48, 100, 102–103, 110, 135, 139–142
Ereignis 36

Erfahrung 135
Erlebnis 135
erotic 118
eternal return 243
eudaimonia 82
exclusion 5–6, 67, 85–87, 90, 117, 126
experience: locus of (*see* city); object of 79, 93; subjects of 79

fado 45–46, 53, 54n41
Fairbairn, Roland 4, 29–31
faith 108, 111–112
Família (Carla Filipe) 62
Fanon, Frantz 194
fashion 27, 152, 159–160
Ferreira, Reinaldo 45
Ficino, Marsilio 19
figuration 234, 243–244; figurative abstraction 244
Filarete 19
Filipe, Carla 4, 60–61, 63–65, 73
film 9, 27, 105, 199–203, 206–208, 211–214, 235–237, 239, 241–242, 244; film history 214n1
Firebrace, William 191
flâneur 5, 32–33, 72, 101–105, 109–110, 112
folk 235
Fonseca, Graça 48
Fontismo 41–42, 44, 49
Foucault, Michel 10n4, 80, 128n31
foundation 23, 79–80, 83–84, 90, 92, 95n11, 96n15
Foz Côa 236
fragment 1, 17, 43, 152, 235–237, 239, 241–243
fragmentation 1–4, 6–8, 10n4, 35, 38, 41, 44, 53, 54n25, 61, 67–68, 109, 113, 118, 135–137, 162, 168, 178, 204, 211, 214, 223, 228, 229n7
freedom: vs. unfreedom 90, 92–93
Freud, Sigmund 26, 31
Friedlichkeit 16
functionalist urbanism 20

Gailhoustet, Renée 9, 219, 223–225, 227, 230n39
garden 168, 176, 206–207, 216n19; working-class 221–222, 224–227, 229n18

Garlic, Mint and Sweet Basil: Essays on Marseilles, Mediterranean Cuisine, and Noir Fiction (Jean-Claude Izzo) 197n28
Gehl, Jan 8
generic city (Koolhaas) 167, 174, 177, 178n2
gentrification 52, 138
Germania anno zero (Roberto Rossellini) 19
Gestalt 151
globalisation 2, 6, 117, 122, 125
Goethe, Johann Wolfgang von 9, 10n4, 234
Gordillo, Gaston 47, 51
grands ensembles 223, 225, 227, 230n25, 231n58
Great Wall of China (Kafka) 234, 239
Guattari, Félix 216
Guernica 17
Guntrip, Harry 4, 29, 31–32

habitat 171, 176
Harvey, David 5, 83, 87, 112
Haussmann, Baron 9, 220
Havana 102
Heads (Philip-Lorca diCorcia) 72
Hegel, Georg Wilhelm Friedrich 26–27, 29, 51, 100–101, 105, 110, 112, 151
Heidegger, Martin 16, 24n10, 36, 70, 75n27, 115n71
Heraclitus 35, 87
HLM (habitation à loyer modéré) 225, 227
home 8, 10, 35, 46, 68–69, 104–105, 140, 156, 159, 169, 175, 178, 186, 188, 190, 193, 220, 222, 225, 229n23, 243; home movies 8, 199–203, 205–208, 213–214, 215n5, 215n14, 215n15, 216n27
homeless 33
Hong Kong (Philip-Lorca diCorcia) 72
hope 23, 40, 42, 51, 174, 187, 234, 242, 244
Horace 86
Horkheimer, Max 189–190
hospitality 5, 82–83, 88, 93–94, 96n28, 144, 159
house 5, 7, 18, 22–23, 45, 49, 92–93, 156–157, 159–161, 168–169, 187, 193, 214n3, 222, 225–227, 229n17, 230n37, 237, 240–242

housing: collective housing 223, 226–227; problem of 221; working class 221, 226, 229n17
Hub Criativo do Beato 48, 50
human flourishing 168–170, 177

identity politics 6, 118, 121–123, 125
Illich, Ivan 171
image and sound: interplay between 236, 238
In My Own Language I Am Independente (Carla Filipe) 60, 64
incommensurability (Laclau) 120
indifference 32–33, 71
individual: individual practice 100, 105, 108–111; single individual 5, 101, 106, 110–111, 113
individualism 71, 73, 106, 113, 155, 160
Industrial Revolution 9, 105, 108, 220
industrialisation 40–42, 67, 154, 229n7; de-industrialisation 43
inequality 6, 117, 119
informal settlements 42
inhabitation 81, 83, 88, 92–94, 96n28, 206, 216n17, 227
interior 7, 64, 68–69, 74n13, 154, 156, 158, 204, 224, 238; interiority 160–161
interruption 195, 206; of action in Brechtian theatre 185; city as a site of 194; dialectics at a standstill 186; Messianic 115n71
intersectionality 123
intimacy: ambivalences of intimacy 68; modern discovery of (Arendt) 4, 60, 66; tyrannies of (Sennett) 70
Invisible Cities (Calvino) 190
Iquitos 39
isolation 6, 34, 67, 69, 159, 170
Ivry-sur-Seine 223, 225, 230n28
Izzo, Jean-Claude 8, 185, 188–195

Jacobs, Jane 34
Jaime (Reis e Cordeiro) 234, 245n1
journey 41, 112, 174, 188, 243
judgement 28, 30, 73, 74n13, 80, 82–83, 90, 92, 94–95, 158, 170, 174

Kafka, Franz 4, 28–29, 189, 234, 239–240
Kant, Immanuel 16, 71, 74n13, 150–151

katastrophikón 17, 24n10
Kierkegaard, Søren 5–6, 100–113
Klein, Melanie 29, 31
kosmische Tragik 15

labyrinth 32, 109, 188, 192
Lacan, Jacques 31
Lacaton, Anne 9, 219, 226–227, 231n58
Laclau, Ernesto 120–121, 123
Laing, Olivia 4, 34
Laing, R. D. 4, 27–28, 34
lament 238, 241
land 8, 38, 42, 44, 47, 55n46, 79, 141, 186, 193–194, 216n19, 221–222, 225–226, 229n17, 229n23, 235, 238, 241, 243
landscape 4, 8, 26, 41–43, 136, 142, 152, 186, 208, 216n19, 220–223, 228, 229n7, 235–237, 239
Lavinium 5, 79, 83–84
law 21, 28, 87, 156–157, 170, 226, 240, 242–244
Le Vaudreuil 223, 225
Lefebvre, Henri 5, 108, 114n29, 171, 176, 190, 196n21
Leibniz, Gottfried Wilhelm 20
Leopardi, Giacomo 27
Leroi-Gourhan, André 244
levelling 109
life: good 17, 81–83, 90; housing of 81, 92; locus of 81; mere life (Benjamin) 89–90, 97n32
Lisbon 4, 8, 26, 29, 35, 38, 42–43, 45–46, 48–51, 102, 200, 203, 205–208, 212, 234, 239, 241–243, 245n1
locus: of experience (*see* city); of judgement 82; locus of life 81
London 5, 43, 101–104, 110, 112, 158, 174
loneliness 34, 67, 71, 74n15, 105
longing 8, 177, 188, 235, 243
Loraux, Nicole 34–35
Los Angeles (Philip-Lorca diCorcia) 72
loss: sense of 243
Lourenço, Eduardo 44, 51
Lukács, Georg 16, 106–107
lyricism 244

machinic turn of sensitivity (Stiegler) 140
map 9, 195, 199–200, 203, 205–206, 208, 210–214

mapping 210, 214
Mariupol 17
Marseilles 8, 185–188, 190–196
Marvila and Beato Riverfront (MBR) 38
Marx, Karl 5–6, 39, 67, 100–102, 104–107, 109, 112–113, 121, 124
masses 67, 73, 102, 105–107, 109–110, 135, 157–158, 221
de Matos, Melo 45
medium 18, 135, 141–144
de Melo, António Maria Fontes Pereira 41
memory: childhood 23–24; involuntary memory (Proust) 23; mix-up 192
Merleau-Ponty, Merleau 118
metamorphosis 244
metropolis 1, 4–7, 9, 20, 33, 102, 105, 135, 153–155, 219, 221, 228
Miami 50
Michelet, Jules 42
migration 123, 194; centripetal and centrifugal 9, 220, 227; emigration 9, 242; rural exodus 9, 220
mines: miners 238–239, 243
Miranda do Douro 235
mirandês 234, 239, 245n6
modernism 103–104
modernity 2, 4, 34, 40, 42, 44, 66, 68, 72, 95n12, 100, 104–105, 110, 113, 118, 125, 136–137, 153, 157
Moedas, Carlos 49
money 103, 154, 157
Monsanto 208
montage 8–9, 39, 41, 202–203, 208, 210–211, 215n6, 215n11, 215n14, 234–235
Moscow 102, 196n13, 200
Mouffe, Chantal 123, 127n12, 129n44
myth of origin 5, 80, 84, 89

Naples 199–200
natality (Arendt) 66
Naturgeschichte 17
New York 3, 26–27, 33–36, 103, 105, 200
New York (Philip-Lorca diCorcia) 72
New York Trilogy (Auster) 32
Nietzsche, Friedrich 10n4, 28, 107, 243
nomos 87–88, 92
non-human 7, 145
non-places (Augé) 40

normative 38, 46, 86, 120, 122, 170, 174
Notari, Elvira 199, 200

object relations theory 29, 31
Odysseus 8, 188–190, 194–195
oikophilia (Scruton) 169

pain 31, 35, 40, 196, 234, 238, 241–244
Pais, Miguel Carlos Correia 44, 46
pandemic 2–3, 26, 32, 35–36, 145
Paris 2, 5, 9, 32–33, 35, 51, 72, 101–103, 110, 158, 188, 219–221, 223–225, 227
Pasolini, Pier Paolo 202–203
peasant 224, 237–238, 243–244, 245n1
Penelope 186–187
performance 35–36, 71, 127n9, 204; performative 73, 143, 178, 204–205
periphery 9, 105, 160, 219–221, 225
Pessoa, Fernando 4, 10n4, 29, 102
phantasmagoria 42–43, 47, 104
phantom 4, 40, 46, 48, 50, 108
philia 8, 169, 171, 173–178
photography 44, 72, 210, 216n17
Piano, Renzo 49
Pienza 19
place: of life 80–83, 87, 90; loss of 173
Plato 21, 87
plurality 18–19, 22, 60, 62, 65–67, 71, 73, 75n29, 87
Polanyi, Michael 169, 173
poetic imagination 241, 243
polis 1, 20–21, 65–67, 70, 80, 125
political: ecology 6, 137, 140–141, 144–145; legitimation 126; life (Arendt) 66; subjects 123
politics: aesthetics and politics 6, 19, 73
porosity 7, 35, 144
Porto 43, 60, 216n22
post-industrial 43, 47–48, 52, 54n41, 137, 140, 242
power: differentials of 5, 80–81, 83, 87, 93, 95n4; as *dynamis* or *potentia* 66
Prague 29
praxis: collective praxis 100, 105–108
precariousness 136, 140, 145, 221–222
present: archaeology of the present 65; *Jetztzeit* 15; the ruin of the present, the present as *ruina* 15
private: and public 3, 65–66, 70, 93, 119, 154; private realm 66–67, 74n15

professionalisation of architecture and urban planning 171
progress 3–4, 41–43, 46, 50, 118, 168, 170, 220
proletariat 100–101, 105, 107, 112, 221
psychogeography 26, 212, 214
public: public realm 66–70, 128n30; public space 65, 93, 118, 120–122, 125, 127n9, 139, 167, 172, 174–177, 216n18

Queirós, Pedro 47

radical democracy 123
recognition 6, 117, 119–121, 125, 160, 186
reconfiguration 1–9, 10n4, 13, 35, 60–61, 65, 83, 113, 136–137, 139, 144, 151, 178, 234, 243–244
redistribution 121, 125
refugees 5, 82–84, 125, 127n21
reification 107, 192
Reis, António 9, 234–243
relativism 152, 163n9
Renaudie, Jean 9, 219, 223–225, 227, 230n39
resistance 71–72, 90, 121, 123, 128n31, 153, 204, 229n18, 234, 243
resonance 137, 144, 145
revolution 5, 6, 9, 16, 42, 46, 65, 67, 101–102, 104–109, 112, 136, 139, 206, 216n18, 220, 222, 227, 241–242
right to the city (Lefebvre) 5, 83, 92, 120
Rodrigues, Daniela 47
Rome 5, 26, 35, 79, 83–84, 88–89, 95n11, 96n14, 97n39
roots 242, 244
Rosenzweig, Franz 16
Rossi, Aldo 22–23, 95n2
Roth, Joseph 194
Rousseau, Jean-Jacques 68–70
rubble 17–19, 22–23, 47–48, 51, 53
ruins 2–4, 15–23, 41, 47, 49, 51, 53, 56n76, 56n83, 152, 176–177, 199–200, 214n1, 238

sabotage 240
Saint Petersburg 102, 106
Sartre, Jean-Paul 30, 105
saudade 43–44, 46, 53
Scalbert, Irénée 223

Index   255

Schuch, Nina 223
Scruton, Roger 169
Sebald, W. G. 18–19, 24
self: duality of 71; self-absorption 4, 65, 69, 72–73; self-consciousness 27; self-identity 23, 89; self-memory 22; self-starvation 31; self study 4, 26
Seneca 82, 89, 96n31
Sennett, Richard 4, 60, 69–71
sensibility 7, 154–155, 158
sensitivity 7, 135–140, 142–145
sensorium 136–137, 140, 144
Shakespeare, William 28, 101
shepherd 236, 240, 245n1
Simmel, Georg 4, 7, 10n4, 15–16, 18, 32, 60, 68, 71, 135, 150–155, 157–162
Simondon, Gilbert 140
Simoni, Paolo 216n27
situationist 212
slave 5, 80, 82–83, 89–90, 92–94, 96n17, 96n31, 97n32, 97n33, 97n34, 158, 188
Smithson, Robert 4
snow 141, 237, 243
Solà-Morales. Ignasi 203–204
solastalgia 140
Solea (Jean-Claude Izzo) 188, 197n22
solitude 70–71, 75n18, 156
space: heterotopic 120, 125; of appearance (Arendt) 60, 65–67, 73, 121, 127n15; urban 2, 7, 9, 34, 38, 40, 138, 204, 212
spectral: entrenchment 40; ethnography 4, 38, 40, 53, 56; fragmentation 53; materiality 38; spectrality 46
speech 66–67, 121, 128n30, 235
spleen 188
Springsteen, Bruce 23
stasis 35
Stiegler, Bernard 140
Stimmung 16, 144
Stoler, Anne 47
street 6, 19, 23, 32–34, 49, 51, 53, 61, 65, 71–73, 101–105, 110, 112, 121, 143, 160, 167, 175–176, 190, 199–200, 207, 212, 216n18, 235
suburb 203–204, 208, 219, 221–222, 226
A Sun for the Dying (Jean-Claude Izzo) 188

tacit knowledge 7, 140, 170, 172
take: long take 202
taste 7, 156–158; of Marseilles 192–194

Tavani, Elena 73
technology 8, 21, 41–44, 48–49, 119, 139, 170, 174–177, 180n53, 201
terraces 221, 224
terrain vague (Solà-Morales) 203–204
territorialisation 92; territorialization 87, 90, 92
terroir 190, 193–194, 196
Total Chaos (Jean-Claude Izzo) 188
Trás-os-Montes 234–235, 239
Trás-os-Montes (Reis and Cordeiro) 9, 234, 239, 242–244
Trauerspiel 3, 17–18, 21, 23, 245n7
Trotsky, Leon 106–107

unfreedom *see* freedom
universalism 124, 129n44
urban: design 173–174, 215n15; environment 100, 102–103, 110, 135, 139–142; forms 170, 172, 175, 177, 228; fragmentation 54n25, 228; landscape 26, 105, 139; peripheries 219–222; planning 7, 168, 170–173, 175, 177–178, 230n26; regeneration 46; renewal 223–224; trauma 39–40, 53n9
urbanisation 3, 6, 9, 38–39, 53, 55n46, 67, 171, 221, 225
urbanity 100, 118, 221, 225
Urbino 19
urbs 5, 91–92
utopia 42, 125, 228

value 3, 8, 16, 18, 69, 124, 129n48, 137, 139, 142, 154, 157–158, 170, 172
Vassal, Jean-Philippe 9, 219, 226–227, 233
Venice 191
village 102, 154, 186, 221, 234–235, 237–244, 245n1, 246n16
vita beata (Seneca) 82
Vitruvius 85–86

waiting 186–187, 191, 242
walking 72, 95n3, 246n16
wall 5, 21, 30, 49, 53, 66, 68, 83–90, 92, 96n19, 102, 188, 220, 234, 239
war 2–3, 5, 16–24, 34–36, 40, 101, 139, 171, 223–224, 230n26, 241
Warburg, Aby 9, 85, 96n16, 210
weather 141–142
Wilson, Japhy 39

Winnicott, Donald 4, 33–34
withdrawal 4, 54n31, 60, 62, 65, 69–73, 75n29
Wittgenstein, Ludwig 10n4, 235

Young, Iris Marion 95n4, 119, 128n40

Zenith, Richard 29
Zimmerman, Patricia 201

Printed in the United States
by Baker & Taylor Publisher Services